Damian
Williams

speakout

Advanced
Teacher's Resource Book

TEACHER'S RESOURCE BOOK CONTENTS

STUDENTS' BOOK CONTENTS

LISTENING/DVD	SPEAKING	WRITING
	talk about names	write a personal profile; learn to plan your writing
listen to a radio programme about a personality test	talk about ways to improve your language learning; discuss the results of a personality test	
listen to a discussion about portraits of famous people	speculate about people based on their portraits; learn to use vague language	
Francesco's Venice: watch an extract from a programme about Venice	describe a treasured possession	write a description of an object
	talk about words of wisdom	
listen to people talking about their experiences of a living library	discuss controversial statements	write a discursive essay; learn to use linking devices
listen to people discussing whether we can trust the news we read; learn to express doubt	debate how to deal with untrustworthy employees	
The Making of Me: Vanessa-Mae: watch an extract from a documentary about a famous violinist	plan and take part in a panel discussion	write a summary of an opinion
	talk about special holiday memories	write a description of a place for a guidebook; learn to add detail
listen to people describing the space where they work	discuss work spaces; describe your ideal space to work/study	
listen to a proposal for a scheme to improve a city	plan and present a proposal to improve your local area; learn to suggest modifications	
An African Journey: watch an extract from a travel programme about Africa	talk about your country; develop a documentary proposal	write a proposal for a documentary about your country
listen to and read film synopses	talk about issues related to crime and punishment	
listen to people talking about someone they admire	discuss social issues and solutions	write a problem-solution essay; learn to use parallelism
listen to people discussing what they would do if they witnessed a crime; learn to add emphasis	talk about how to deal with different moral dilemmas	
Blackadder: watch an extract from a comedy set during the First World War	present the arguments for the defence and the prosecution in a court case	write a summary of a court case
listen to a radio programme about when and how you should reveal a secret	talk about secrets	write a narrative; learn to use time phrases
	debunk a myth	
listen to a conversation about WikiLeaks	discuss questions related to freedom of information; learn to manage a conversation	
North and South: watch an extract from a drama set in 19th century England	describe seven secrets about yourself	write personal facts people don't know about you

COMMUNICATION BANK PAGE 158   AUDIO SCRIPTS PAGE 164

LISTENING/DVD	SPEAKING	WRITING
	evaluate possible inventions of the future	
listen to a radio programme about English around the world	discuss different trends in language learning	write a report based on statistics; learn to describe trends
listen to people describing how trends started; learn to summarise your views	talk about the causes and effects of recent changes in your country	
BBC **History of Now: The Story of The Noughties:** watch an extract from a documentary about the first decade of the 21st century	talk about a decade you remember	write a review of a decade
	plan your escape from an island	
listen to people describing what they do to relax	talk about activities which help you escape your routine	write a promotional leaflet; learn to use subheadings
listen to people discussing whether children are over-protected	discuss personal choice and the role of the state; learn to convince someone	
BBC **Little Dorrit:** watch an extract from a drama based on a Charles Dickens novel	develop a plot and tell a story	write a story
	choose objects to represent you in a 'Museum of Me'	
listen to a radio programme about smells that evoke memories	talk about memories from a particular stage of your life	write a personal story for a magazine; learn to improve descriptive writing
listen to people brainstorming ideas	discuss ways to save time; learn to solicit more information	
BBC **Wonders of the Universe:** watch an extract from a documentary about the history of the universe	talk about a turning point in your life	write a description of a major decision
	choose sculptures to suit different clients' needs	
listen to people talking about where they get their ideas	ask and answer creative questions	write a review of an exhibition; learn to use a range of vocabulary
listen to people ranting and raving	rant or rave about a given topic; learn to use comment adverbials	
BBC **The Culture Show: Tate Modern is 10!:** watch an extract from a programme about an art gallery	recommend a cultural place for a visitor	write a recommendation for a travel forum
	plan your dream adventure holiday	
listen to an author reading from his memoir *Teacher Man*	talk about the consequences of sudden success; talk about dreams and ambitions	write a 'for and against' essay; learn to describe pros and cons
listen to an expert talking about the stages of a negotiation; learn to stall for time	negotiate a plan for a film festival	
BBC **Wildest Dreams:** watch an extract from a reality show about wildlife film-makers	talk about the skills and experience you have for your dream job	write an application for your dream job

COMMUNICATION BANK PAGE 158   AUDIO SCRIPTS PAGE 164

Before we started writing *Speakout*, we did a lot of research to find out more about the issues that teachers and students face and how these can be addressed in a textbook for the 21st century. The issues that came up again and again were motivation, authentic content and the need for structured speaking and listening strategies.

As English teachers, we know how motivating it can be to bring the real world into the classroom by using authentic materials. We also know how time consuming and difficult it can be to find authentic content that is truly engaging, at the right level and appropriate for our students. With access to the entire archive of the BBC, we have selected some stunning video content to motivate and engage students. We have also created tasks that will encourage interaction with the materials while providing the right amount of scaffolding.

We realise that the real world is not just made up of actors, presenters and comedians, and 'real' English does not just consist of people reading from scripts. This is why *Speakout* brings real people into the classroom. The Video podcasts show people giving their opinions about the topics in the book and illustrate some of the strategies that will help our students become more effective communicators.

Speakout maximises opportunities for students to speak and systematically asks them to notice and employ strategies that will give them the confidence to communicate fluently and the competence to listen actively. While the main focus is on speaking and listening, we have also developed a systematic approach to reading and writing. For us, these skills are absolutely essential for language learners in the digital age.

To sum up, we have tried to write a course that teachers will really enjoy using; a course that is authentic but manageable, systematic but not repetitive – a course that not only brings the real world into the classroom, but also sends our students into the real world with the confidence to truly 'speak out'!

From left to right: Frances Eales, JJ Wilson, Antonia Clare and Steve Oakes

OVERVIEW OF THE COMPONENTS

STUDENTS' BOOK

- Between 90 and 120 hours of teaching material
- Language Bank with reference material and extra practice
- Vocabulary bank to expand vocabulary
- Audioscripts of the class audio

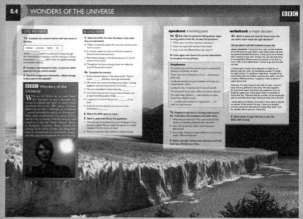

CLASS AUDIO CDs

- Audio material for use in class
- Test audio for the Mid-course and End of Course Tests

DVD & ACTIVE BOOK

- DVD content
- Digital Students' Book
- Audio, video and Video podcasts

WORKBOOK

- Grammar and vocabulary
- Functional language
- Speaking and listening strategies
- Reading, writing and listening
- Regular review and self-study tests

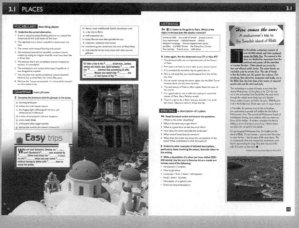

AUDIO CD

- Audio material including listening, pronunciation and functional practice

MYSPEAKOUTLAB

- Interactive Workbook with hints and tips
- Unit tests and Progress Tests
- Mid-course and End of Course Tests
- Video podcasts with interactive worksheets

TEACHER'S RESOURCE BOOK

- Teaching notes
- Integrated key and audioscript
- Five photocopiable activities for every unit
- Mid-course and End of Course Test

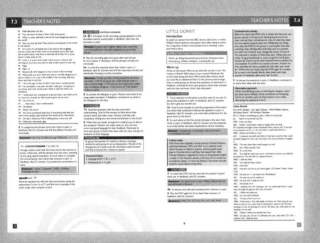

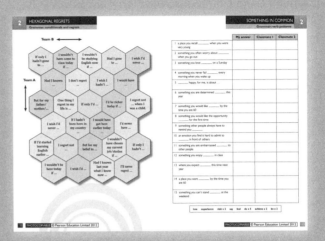

SPEAKOUT ACTIVE TEACH

- Integrated audio and video content
- Video podcasts
- Test master containing all course tests
- Answer reveal feature
- Grammar and vocabulary review games
- A host of useful tools
- Large extra resources section

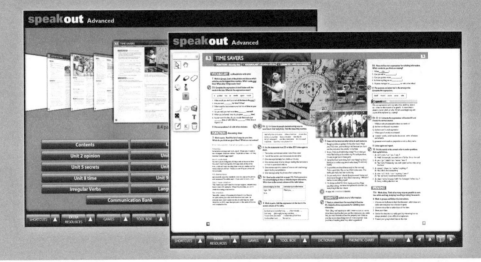

SPEAKOUT WEBSITE

- Information about the course
- Sample materials from the course
- Teaching tips
- Placement test
- A range of useful resources
- Video podcasts

A UNIT OF THE STUDENTS' BOOK

UNIT OVERVIEW

Every unit of Speakout starts with an Overview, which lists the topics covered. This is followed by two main input lessons which cover grammar, vocabulary and the four skills. Lesson three covers functional language and focuses on important speaking and listening strategies. Lesson four is built around a clip from a BBC programme and consolidates language and skills work. Each unit culminates with a Lookback page, which provides communicative practice of the key language.

INPUT LESSON 1

Lesson one introduces the topic of the unit and presents the key language needed to understand and talk about it. The lesson combines grammar and vocabulary with a focus on skills work.

> The target language and the CEF objectives are listed to clearly show the objectives of the lesson.

> Clear grammar presentations are followed by written and oral practice as well as pronunciation work.

> Each input lesson has either a focus on listening or a focus on reading.

> Every grammar section includes a reference to the Language bank with explanations and further practice.

INPUT LESSON 2

Lesson two continues to focus on grammar and vocabulary while extending and expanding the topic area. By the end of the second lesson students will have worked on all four skill areas.

Grammar and vocabulary sections often include a listening element to reinforce the new language.

All lessons include a focus on speaking where the emphasis is on communication and fluency building.

Regular Speakout Tips help students to develop their study skills both inside and outside the classroom.

PRACTICE

6A Underline the correct alternatives.
1 A: Are you coming to the party?
  B: Yes, I think *do/so/not*.
2 A: Did you just delete the file?
  B: I hope *not/such/do*.
3 A: Do you want to try this perfume?
  B: No, but I'll try that *some/much/one*.
4 A: Do you think we'll have enough time to discuss this later?
  B: We'll have *so/a little/one* time.
  A: Are you going away on holiday this year?
  B: No, Ann Marie doesn't have enough money and *more/her/so do I*.
6 A: Are you sure you've got enough copies for everyone?
  B: Yes, I've got *none/one/lots*.

B ▶ 8.3 Cross out any words which could be left out of the conversations in Exercise 6A. Listen and check your answers.

7 Work in pairs. Student A: turn to page 161. Student B: turn to page 162. Take turns to read out your sentences and choose the correct responses.

VOCABULARY memories

8A Complete the sentences. Choose the correct word in brackets and put it in the appropriate place.
1 This place lots of memories for us. (gets/holds)
2 When I hear those old songs it back a lot of memories. (brings /takes)
3 It's one of my memories. (oldest/earliest)
4 I have very memories of my time at primary school. (vague/slim)
5 I only have a very recollection of what my grandparents' house looked like. (light/hazy)
6 It was a long time ago, but I remember it. (strongly/vividly)
7 I remember her dress. It was blue with a red belt. (distinctly/heavily)
8 Every time I go there, the memories come back. (flooding/running)

B Which words from Exercise 8A can you use to talk about memories which are not very strong? Which words can you use to talk about memories which are very strong or clear?

➤ page 155 **VOCABULARYBANK**

SPEAKING

9A Read about the website and choose a stage of your life to talk about.

talking**memories**.com

Do you have vivid memories of your childhood or is it just a hazy blur? At talkingmemories.com you can record your memories of particular stages or events in your life, adding photos and videos. It allows you to preserve meaningful memories of your life, record important milestones and share memories of special events with friends, family and future generations.

B Prepare to talk about memories from that stage of your life. Make notes using the prompts below.

the area where you lived/went to school
your earliest memory
people you spent time with
what you wanted to be when you grew up
Childhood (0–16)
games you played

mealtimes in your house (smells/noises/food)
special memories (holidays/birthdays/celebrations, etc.)
where you lived
music
first experiences of work or university
Young adult (16+)
things that were important to you
people or events that shaped your life

C Work in groups and take turns. Talk about the special memories you have. Do others in the group have similar memories from that time?

WRITING a personal story

10A Read the personal story on page 97. Answer the questions.
1 Why was the fig tree so important?
2 What happened to the house?

B Read the advice for writing a story for a magazine. Does the writer of *The Fig Tree* follow the advice?
1 Remember your audience (who is going to read this?) and use a range of structures and vocabulary.
2 Use an informal, chatty style. It makes your article sound more personal, so the reader can identify with you.
3 Capture the reader's attention with an anecdote, something surprising or a strong image.
4 'Close the circle': the ending could echo the beginning or refer to the wording in the task.

LEARN TO improve descriptive writing

11 Read guidelines a)–d) for descriptive writing and follow instructions 1–4 below.
a) Include precise language. Use specific adjectives and nouns and strong action verbs (verbs that carry a specific meaning) to give life to the picture you are painting in the reader's mind.
   The lion ate (weak) the antelope.
   The ravenous (specific) lion devoured (strong) the antelope.
b) Include all the senses. Remember to describe sounds (using onomatopoeia – where the sound of the word imitates the meaning being described), smells, tastes and textures.
   The car screeched to a halt.
   The murmuring of innumerable bees.
c) Make use of contrasts. Describe how someone's mood changed from good to bad, or describe a location at different times of year.
d) Use figurative language (metaphor, simile, personification) and imagery can help to engage a reader.
   The stars danced playfully in the sky.
   (personification – giving human qualities to something which is not human)
   Her home was a prison.
   (metaphor – when you say one thing is another thing)
   She felt as free as a bird.
   (simile – when you say one thing is like another thing)
1 Find examples of specific adjectives and strong action verbs in the story of *The Fig Tree*.
2 Find an example of onomatopoeia. Where does the writer describe a texture?
3 How does the writer use contrast in this story?
4 Find an example of personification of an object and an example of metaphor.

speakout TIP

It's important that you communicate to your reader exactly what you mean in the clearest possible way. Using strong verbs and adjectives helps you to paint accurate pictures of what you mean in the reader's mind. How do the verbs change the meaning of the following sentences? 'I love you,' he said. / 'I love you,' he screamed. / 'I love you,' he whispered. / 'I love you,' he mumbled. Keep a list of strong verbs.

12 Read the instructions and write a personal story.
1 Work alone. Think about any particular people, objects or places which hold special memories for you. Can you remember particular sights, sounds, smells or textures associated with them?
2 Make some notes about the memory, including personal details (how you felt, why it was special, etc.).
3 Write your story (220–250 words). Add a title.
4 Check your writing. Try to improve the description by using more precise language.

THE **FIG TREE**

I remember we used to visit my grandmother's house at weekends. It was a huge house with gardens leading down to a field, and it seemed almost like a palace to me. At the bottom of the field was an orchard, planted with apples, and twenty-one walnut trees. In the middle of the field stood an ancient fig tree. It was here, in the tree, that my cousins and I would sit and play for hours on end. I can remember the smell of the green leaves, the sticky sap that would leak from the leaves and the figs as they ripened. We each had our own special branch and we would climb up and then sit looking out over the countryside. I can almost feel the warmth of the sun on our faces and the feeling of safety and security as we hid among the branches. In that tree, we would sit and chatter about life, feast on the sweet, crunchy apples, hold meetings, tell jokes, read books, make plans, have fig fights and discuss what we wanted to be when we grew up. The fig tree knew all our secrets.

When I was twelve, my grandmother moved into a small flat and we stopped going to the house. But a few years ago, I was in the area, so I drove back there to see if it was how I had remembered it. The house was almost unrecognisable. It had been turned into a doctor's surgery, with signposts all around and cars parked all over the drive. The gardens had been redesigned, and there were pathways to walk along and benches to sit on and enjoy the views. Gone was my grandmother's wild flower garden. But behind the house, in the middle of the field, just as if time had never passed, stood the fig tree, full of lush green leaves, and juicy figs. Its branches hung heavily towards the ground, almost beckoning me to climb up. Just standing in the field brought all the memories of my grandmother and our life there flooding back to me. And touching the smooth bark on the trunk, it was all I could do to resist sprinting to the end of the field to pick an apple or two and then back to the fig tree to enjoy the rest of the warm afternoon.

Lexical sets are introduced in context. Practice of new words often includes pronunciation work.

Lexical sets are often expanded in the Vocabulary bank at the back of the Students' Book.

Every pair of input lessons includes at least one writing section with focus on a variety of different genres.

FUNCTIONAL LESSON

The third lesson in each unit focuses on a particular function, situation or transaction as well as introducing important speaking and listening strategies.

The target language and the CEF objectives are listed to clearly show the objectives of the lesson.

Students learn a lexical set which is relevant to the function or situation.

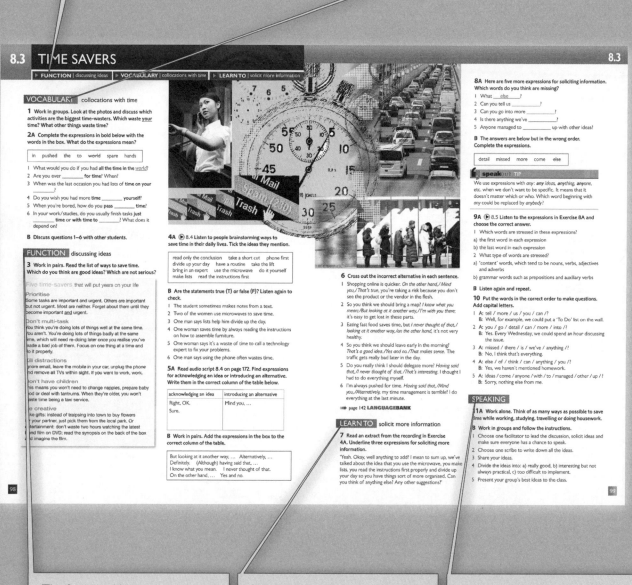

The functional language is learnt in context, often by listening to the language in use.

Students learn important speaking and listening strategies which can be transferred to many situations.

The lesson ends with a speaking activity which gives students the chance to practise the new language.

DVD LESSON

The fourth lesson in each unit is based around an extract from a real BBC programme.
This acts as a springboard into freer communicative speaking and writing activities.

A preview section gets students thinking about the topic of the extract and introduces key language.

A series of different tasks helps students to understand and enjoy the programme.

The Speakout task builds on the topic of the extract and provides extended speaking practice.

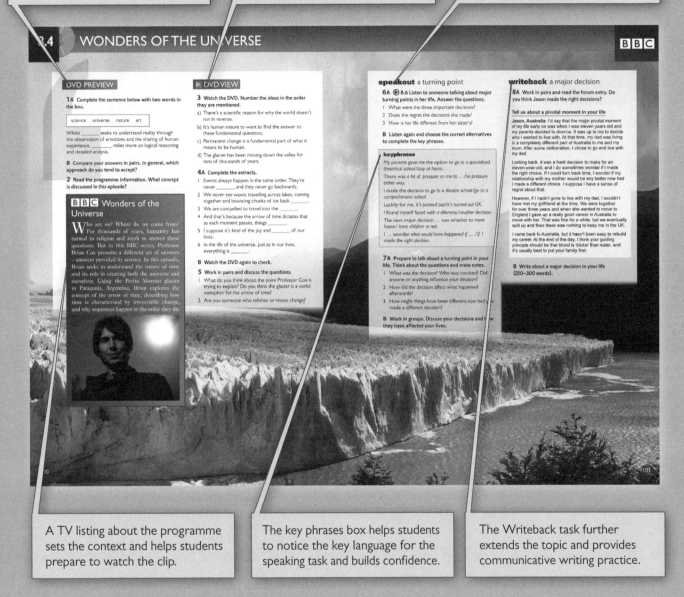

A TV listing about the programme sets the context and helps students prepare to watch the clip.

The key phrases box helps students to notice the key language for the speaking task and builds confidence.

The Writeback task further extends the topic and provides communicative writing practice.

LOOKBACK PAGE

Each unit ends with a Lookback page, which provides further practice and review of the key language covered in the unit. The review exercises are a mixture of communicative activities and games. Further practice and review exercises can be found in the Workbook. The Lookback page also introduces the Video podcast, which features a range of real people talking about one of the topics in the unit.

DESCRIPTION OF THE OTHER COMPONENTS

WORKBOOK

The Workbook contains a wide variety of practice and review exercises and covers all of the language areas studied in the unit. It also contains regular review sections as well as self-study tests to help students consolidate what they have learnt.

> A variety of language practice activities consolidate the areas covered in the Students' Book.

> The Workbook contains regular listening practice using the accompanying audio CD.

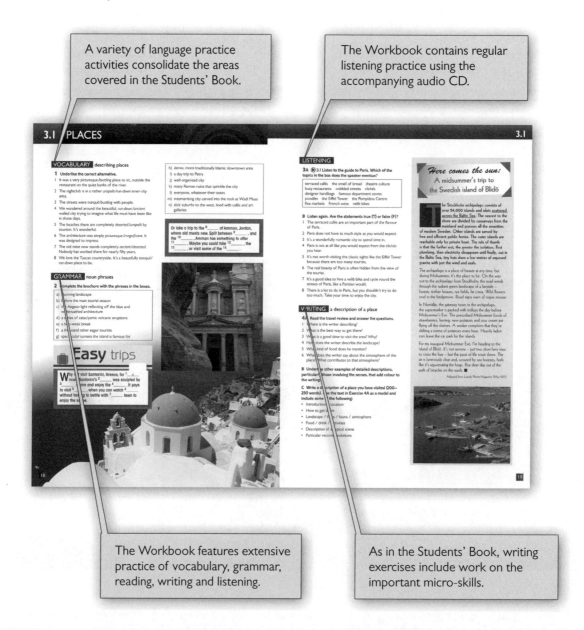

> The Workbook features extensive practice of vocabulary, grammar, reading, writing and listening.

> As in the Students' Book, writing exercises include work on the important micro-skills.

MYSPEAKOUTLAB

MySpeakoutLab provides a fully blended and personalised learning environment that benefits both teachers and students. It offers:

- an interactive Workbook with hints, tips and automatic grade book.

- professionally written Unit Tests, Progress Tests, Mid-course and End of Course tests that can be assigned at the touch of a button.

- interactive Video podcast worksheets with an integrated video player so students can watch while they do the exercises.

ACTIVETEACH

Speakout ActiveTeach contains everything you need to make the course come alive in your classroom.
It includes integrated whiteboard software which enables you to add notes and embed files.
It is also possible to save all of your work with the relevant page from the Students' Book.

An answer reveal function lets you show the answers to an exercise at the touch of a button.

All audio and video content is fully integrated and includes subtitles as well as printable scripts.

Shortcuts to the relevant pages of the Language bank and the Vocabulary bank make navigation easy.

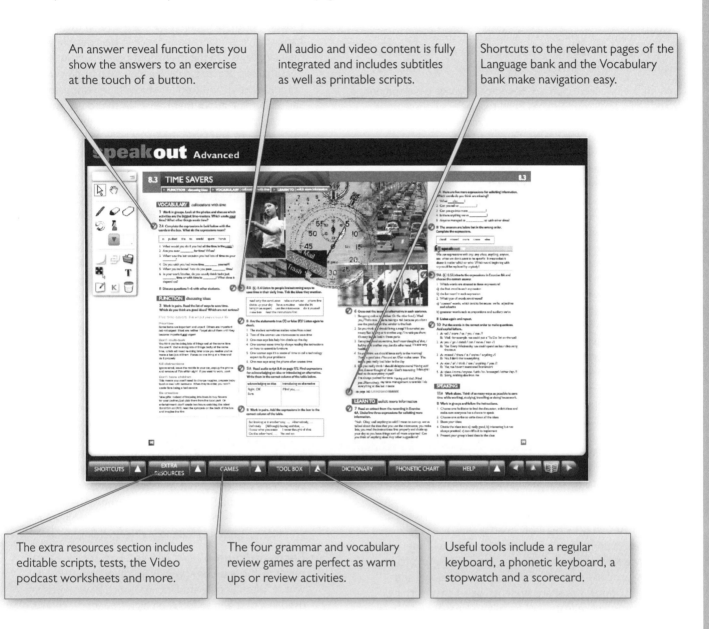

The extra resources section includes editable scripts, tests, the Video podcast worksheets and more.

The four grammar and vocabulary review games are perfect as warm ups or review activities.

Useful tools include a regular keyboard, a phonetic keyboard, a stopwatch and a scorecard.

WEBSITE

The Speakout website will offer information about the course as well as a bank of useful resources including:
- introductory videos by the authors of the course.
- sample materials.
- teaching tips.
- placement test.
- CEF mapping documents.
- Video podcasts for all published levels

TEACHING APPROACHES

speakout is designed to satisfy both students and teachers on a number of different levels. It offers engaging topics with authentic BBC material to really bring them to life. At the same time it offers a robust and comprehensive focus on grammar, vocabulary, functions and pronunciation. As the name of the course might suggest, speaking activities are prominent, but that is not at the expense of the other core skills, which are developed systematically throughout.

With this balanced approach to topics, language development and skills work, our aim has been to create a course book full of 'lessons that really work' in practice. Below we will briefly explain our approach in each of these areas.

TOPICS AND CONTENT

In *Speakout* we have tried to choose topics that are relevant to students' lives. Where a topic area is covered in other ELT courses we have endeavoured to find a fresh angle on it. It is clear to us that authenticity is important to learners, and many texts come from the BBC's rich resources (audio, visual and print) as well as other real-world sources. At lower levels, we have sometimes adapted materials by adjusting the language to make it more manageable for students while trying to keep the tone as authentic as possible. We have also attempted to match the authentic feel of a text with an authentic interaction. Every unit contains a variety of rich and authentic input material including BBC Video podcasts (filmed on location in London, England) and DVD material, featuring some of the best the BBC has to offer.

GRAMMAR

Knowing how to recognise and use grammatical structures is central to our ability to communicate with each other. Although at first students can often get by with words and phrases, they increasingly need grammar to make themselves understood. Students also need to understand sentence formation when reading and listening and to be able to produce accurate grammar in professional and exam situations. We share students' belief that learning grammar is a core feature of learning a language and believe that a guided discovery approach, where students are challenged to notice new forms works best. At the same time learning is scaffolded so that students are supported at all times in a systematic way. Clear grammar presentations are followed by written and oral practice. There is also the chance to notice and practise pronunciation where appropriate.

In *Speakout* you will find:

- **Grammar in context** – We want to be sure that the grammar focus is clear and memorable for students. Grammar is almost always taken from the listening or reading texts, so that learners can see the language in action, and understand how and when it is used.
- **Noticing** – We involve students in the discovery of language patterns by asking them to identify aspects of meaning and form, and complete rules or tables.

- **Clear language reference** – As well as a summary of rules within the unit, there is also a Language bank which serves as a clear learning reference for the future.
- **Focus on use** – We ensure that there is plenty of practice, both form and meaning-based, in the Language bank to give students confidence in manipulating the new language. On the main input page we include personalised practice, which is designed to be genuinely communicative and to offer students the opportunity to say something about themselves or the topic. There is also regular recycling of new language in the Lookback review pages, and again the focus here is on moving learners towards communicative use of the language.

VOCABULARY

Developing a wide range of vocabulary is key to increasing communicative effectiveness; developing a knowledge of high-frequency collocations and fixed and semi-fixed phrases is key to increasing spoken fluency. An extensive understanding of words and phrases helps learners become more confident when reading and listening, and developing a range of vocabulary is important for effective writing. Equally vital is learner-training, equipping students with the skills to record, memorise and recall vocabulary for use.

In *Speakout* this is reflected in:

- **A prominent focus on vocabulary** – We include vocabulary in almost all lessons whether in a lexical set linked to a particular topic, as preparation for a speaking activity or to aid comprehension of a DVD clip or a listening or reading text. Where we want students to use the language actively, we encourage them to use the vocabulary to talk about their own lives or opinions. At lower levels, the Photo bank also extends the vocabulary taught in the lessons, using memorable photographs and graphics to support students' understanding.
- **Focus on 'chunks'** – As well as lexical sets, we also regularly focus on how words fit together with other words, often getting students to notice how words are used in a text and to focus on high-frequency 'chunks' such as verb-noun collocations or whole phrases.
- **Focus on vocabulary systems** – We give regular attention to word-building skills, a valuable tool in expanding vocabulary. At higher levels, the Vocabulary plus sections deal with systems such as affixation, multi-word verbs and compound words in greater depth.
- **Recycling and learner training** – Practice exercises ensure that vocabulary is encountered on a number of occasions: within the lessons, on the Lookback page, in subsequent lessons and in the Photo bank/Vocabulary bank at the back of the book. One of the main focuses of the Speakout tips – which look at all areas of language learning – is to highlight vocabulary learning strategies, aiming to build good study skills that will enable students to gain and retain new language.

FUNCTIONAL LANGUAGE

One thing that both teachers and learners appreciate is the need to manage communication in a wide variety of encounters, and to know what's appropriate to say in given situations. These can be transactional exchanges, where the main focus is on getting something done (buying something in a shop or phoning to make an enquiry), or interactional exchanges, where the main focus is on socialising with others (talking about the weekend, or responding appropriately to good news). As one learner commented to us, 'Grammar rules aren't enough – I need to know what to say.' Although it is possible to categorise 'functions' under 'lexical phrases', we believe it is useful for learners to focus on functional phrases separately from vocabulary or grammar.

The third lesson in every unit of *Speakout* looks at one such situation, and focuses on the functional language needed. Learners hear or see the language used in context and then practise it in mini-situations, in both a written and a spoken context. Each of these lessons also includes a Learn to section, which highlights and practises a useful strategy for dealing with both transactional and interactional exchanges, for example asking for clarification, showing interest, etc. Learners will find themselves not just more confident users of the language, but also more active listeners.

SPEAKING

The dynamism of most lessons depends on the success of the speaking tasks, whether the task is a short oral practice of new language, a discussion comparing information or opinions, a personal response to a reading text or a presentation where a student might speak uninterrupted for a minute or more. Students develop fluency when they are motivated to speak. For this to happen, engaging topics and tasks are essential, as is the sequencing of stages and task design. For longer tasks, students often need to prepare their ideas and language in a structured way. This all-important rehearsal time leads to more motivation and confidence as well as greater accuracy, fluency and complexity. Also, where appropriate, students need to hear a model before they speak, in order to have a realistic goal.

There are several strands to speaking in *Speakout*:

- **Communicative practice** – After introducing any new language (vocabulary, grammar or function) there are many opportunities in *Speakout* for students to use it in a variety of activities which focus on communication as well as accuracy. These include personalised exchanges, dialogues, flow-charts and role-plays.

- **Focus on fluency** – In every unit of *Speakout* we include opportunities for students to respond spontaneously. They might be asked to respond to a series of questions, to a DVD, a Video podcast or a text, or to take part in conversations, discussions and role-plays. These activities involve a variety of interactional formations such as pairs and groups.

- **Speaking strategies and sub-skills** – In the third lesson of each unit, students are encouraged to notice in a systematic way features which will help them improve their speaking. These include, for example, ways to manage a phone conversation, the use of mirror questions to ask for clarification, sentence starters to introduce an opinion and intonation to correct mistakes.

- **Extended speaking tasks** – In the *Speakout* DVD lesson, as well as in other speaking tasks throughout the course, students are encouraged to attempt more adventurous and extended use of language in tasks such as problem solving, developing a project or telling a story. These tasks go beyond discussion; they include rehearsal time, useful language and a concrete outcome.

LISTENING

For most users of English (or any language, for that matter), listening is the most frequently used skill. A learner who can speak well but not understand at least as well is unlikely to be a competent communicator or user of the language. We feel that listening can be developed effectively through well-structured materials. As with speaking, the choice of interesting topics and texts works hand in hand with carefully considered sequencing and task design. At the same time, listening texts can act as a springboard to stimulate discussion in class.

There are several strands to listening in *Speakout*:

- **Focus on authentic recordings** – In *Speakout*, we believe that it is motivating for all levels of learner to try to access and cope with authentic material. Each unit includes a DVD extract from a BBC documentary, drama or light entertainment programme as well as a podcast filmed on location with real people giving their opinions. At the higher levels you will also find unscripted audio texts and BBC radio extracts. All are invaluable in the way they expose learners to real language in use as well as different varieties of English. Where recordings, particularly at lower levels, are scripted, they aim to reflect the patterns of natural speech.

- **Focus on sub-skills and strategies** – Tasks across the recordings in each unit are designed with a number of sub-skills and strategies in mind. These include: listening for global meaning and more detail; scanning for specific information; becoming sensitised to possible misunderstandings; and noticing nuances of intonation and expression. We also help learners to listen actively by using strategies such as asking for repetition and paraphrasing.

- **As a context for new language** – We see listening as a key mode of input and *Speakout* includes many listening texts which contain target grammar, vocabulary or functions in their natural contexts. Learners are encouraged to notice this new language and how and where it occurs, often by using the audio scripts as a resource.

- **As a model for speaking** – In the third and fourth lessons of each unit the recordings serve as models for speaking tasks. These models reveal the ways in which speakers use specific language to structure their discourse, for example with regard to turn-taking, hesitating and checking for understanding. These recordings also serve as a goal for the learners' speaking.

TEACHING APPROACHES

READING

Reading is a priority for many students, whether it's for study, work or pleasure, and can be practised alone, anywhere and at any time. Learners who read regularly tend to have a richer, more varied vocabulary, and are often better writers, which in turn supports their oral communication skills. Nowadays, the internet has given students access to an extraordinary range of English language reading material, and the availability of English language newspapers, books and magazines is greater than ever before. The language learner who develops skill and confidence in reading in the classroom will be more motivated to read outside the classroom. Within the classroom reading texts can also introduce stimulating topics and act as springboards for class discussion.

There are several strands to reading in *Speakout*:

* **Focus on authentic texts** – As with *Speakout* listening materials, there is an emphasis on authenticity, and this is reflected in a number of ways. Many of the reading texts in *Speakout* are sourced from the BBC. Where texts have been adapted or graded, there is an attempt to maintain authenticity by remaining faithful to the text type in terms of content and style. We have chosen up-to-date, relevant texts to stimulate interest and motivate learners to read. The texts represent a variety of genres that correspond to the text types that learners will probably encounter in their everyday lives.

* **Focus on sub-skills and strategies** – In *Speakout* we strive to maintain authenticity in the way the readers interact with a text. We always give students a reason to read, and provide tasks which bring about or simulate authentic reading, including real-life tasks such as summarising, extracting specific information, reacting to an opinion or following an anecdote. We also focus on strategies for decoding texts, such as guessing the meaning of unknown vocabulary, understanding pronoun referencing and following discourse markers.

* **Noticing new language** – Noticing language in use is a key step towards the development of a rich vocabulary and greater all-round proficiency in a language, and this is most easily achieved through reading. In *Speakout*, reading texts often serve as valuable contexts for introducing grammar and vocabulary as well as discourse features.

* **As a model for writing** – In the writing sections, as well as the Writeback sections of the DVD spreads, the readings serve as models for students to refer to when they are writing, in terms of overall organisation as well as style and language content.

WRITING

In recent years the growth of email and the internet has led to a shift in the nature of the writing our students need to do. Email has also led to an increased informality in written English. However, many students need to develop their formal writing for professional and exam-taking purposes. It is therefore important to focus on a range of genres, from formal text types such as essays, letters and reports to informal genres such as blog entries and personal messages.

There are four strands to writing in *Speakout*:

* **Focus on genres** – In every unit at the four higher levels there is a section that focuses on a genre of writing, emails for example. We provide a model to show the conventions of the genre and, where appropriate, we highlight fixed phrases associated with it. We usually then ask the students to produce their own piece of writing. While there is always a written product, we also focus on the process of writing, including the relevant stages such as brainstorming, planning, and checking. At Starter and Elementary, we focus on more basic writing skills, including basic written sentence patterns, linking, punctuation and text organisation, in some cases linking this focus to a specific genre.

* **Focus on sub-skills and strategies** – While dealing with the genres, we include a section which focuses on a sub-skill or strategy that is generally applicable to all writing. Sub-skills include paragraphing, organising content and using linking words and pronouns, while strategies include activities like writing a first draft quickly, keeping your reader in mind and self-editing. We present the sub-skill by asking the students to notice the feature. We then provide an opportunity for the students to practise it.

* **Writeback** – At the end of every unit, following the DVD and final speaking task, we include a Writeback task. The idea is for students to develop fluency in their writing. While we always provide a model, the task is not tied to any particular grammatical structure. Instead the emphasis is on using writing to generate ideas and personal responses.

* **Writing as a classroom activity** – We believe that writing can be very usefully employed as an aid to speaking and as a reflective technique for responding to texts – akin to the practice of writing notes in the margins of books. It also provides a change of pace and focus in lessons. Activities such as short dictations, note-taking, brainstorming on paper and group story writing are all included in *Speakout*.

PRONUNCIATION

In recent years, attitudes towards pronunciation in many English language classrooms have moved towards a focus on intelligibility: if students' spoken language is understandable, then the pronunciation is good enough. We are aware, however, that many learners and teachers place great importance on developing pronunciation that is more than 'good enough', and that systematic attention to pronunciation in a lesson, however brief, can have a significant impact on developing learners' speech.

In *Speakout*, we have taken a practical, integrated approach to developing students' pronunciation, highlighting features that often cause problems in conjunction with a given area of grammar, particular vocabulary items and functional language. Where relevant to the level, a grammatical or functional language focus is followed by a focus on a feature of pronunciation, for example, the weak forms of auxiliary verbs or connected speech in certain functional exponents. Students are given the opportunity to listen to models of the pronunciation, notice the key feature and then practise it.

TEACHING ADVANCED LEARNERS

Advanced classes can be extremely rewarding for the teacher. The students are able to express their opinions in greater depth than at other levels, conduct extended discussions and debates, and deal with a wide variety of authentic input. Besides this, advanced students tend to be highly motivated and able to use effective learning strategies – both of which explain how they became advanced students in the first place.

At the same time, an advanced class provides a real challenge, particularly for the less experienced teacher. The students have probably studied the most important grammatical structures several times, and they may have discussed certain topics repeatedly, e.g. work, holidays, hobbies. Furthermore, because they are already so competent in the language, it can be difficult for them to see progress. Teachers of advanced classes need to be flexible and prepared to adopt a slightly different approach. At this level, traditional teacher-centred presentations of new language may be less appropriate than low-key 'noticing' activities, as advanced students can often see patterns and work out rules for themselves.

There is also the question of level. Advanced students can be anything from post-First Certificate to Proficiency level, or they may have spent extended periods in an English-speaking environment and simply wish to brush up on their English. This variety, as with all mixed-ability classes, presents a challenge in itself. In addition, many students in advanced classes possess what can be termed 'false fluency' – that is, they speak extremely fluently about a very narrow range of topics and with a number of fossilised errors. The challenge here is to broaden the students' range, have them develop linguistic self-awareness, and take them out of their comfort zone.

Another key to teaching advanced classes is getting students to interact with the language outside the classroom. This might involve cross-curricular projects or internet research or journal-keeping. All students need to extend their contact with the target language beyond the classroom, but at advanced level it is a more achievable goal, as they are better equipped to deal with authentic English and the many opportunities offered to them through internet and Web 2.0 tools.

Here are our top tips for teaching at this level:

- Do a thorough Needs Analysis at the beginning of the course. Find out what tasks your students need to achieve in English, and then tailor your course to include these tasks. Also find out the students' strengths and weaknesses. Usually, advanced students need to focus on refining their output for very specific purposes and audiences. While we may be unable, for reasons of time and preparation, to treat an advanced class as an ESP (English for Special Purposes) class, setting personalised homework and focusing closely on where individuals need to improve will always be beneficial.

- Help students to sustain their motivation by showing them ways to track their progress. The students can use vocabulary notebooks, journals, and language portfolios (CEF) that include essays, other written compositions, language projects, audio recordings, video podcasts, etc. A combination of these enable students to document their linguistic achievements.

- Be a resource for pointing out useful websites, podcasts, books, magazines and other sources of language input. At advanced level, students are able to interact with many authentic materials, e.g. literature, journalism and film clips.

- Work on collocations and chunks. It is usually more beneficial to teach interesting combinations of words the students already know (e.g. idioms) rather than obscure individual words. Generally, advanced students are independent enough to discover for themselves any obscure lexis that they need for their work or studies. What is harder for them to find without the teacher's help are phrases that use common words in new combinations. Help students to focus on the rich nature of natural spoken English with the video podcasts, and use this as a resource for learning new phrases.

- Encourage critical engagement, for example with reading texts. At this level, students are able to perceive nuances of tone and language that allow a deeper appreciation of a speaker's or a writer's intention. For example, they may be able to pick up on nuances such as irony, hyperbole and humour.

- Learn ways to exploit materials to the full. Advanced students tend to need less time to get through material than lower levels. They read more quickly, and have more resources to fall back on when it comes to dealing with new grammar and lexis. Teachers of advanced students need a number of extension activities in their repertoire. These might include text-reconstruction, open-ended questions, simulations, and 'treasure hunts' in which students find words or phrases belonging to specific categories, e.g. phrasal verbs. In addition, it may be beneficial if the teacher views the material as a springboard for explorations of the students' own ideas, rather than an end in itself.

Antonia Clare, Frances Eales, Steve Oakes and JJ Wilson

TEACHER'S NOTES INDEX

1 ORIGINS

OVERVIEW

WHAT'S IN A NAME?

Introduction
Ss revise and practise the continuous aspect in the context of talking about common names and personality types. They also practise writing a personal profile.

SUPPLEMENTARY MATERIALS
Resource bank p137

Warm up: write the questions below on the board and prepare your own answers.

Ex 1A: prepare your own answers to the questions

Ex 4B: bring dictionaries for Ss to use

Warm up
Write the following questions on the board: *Which names are popular in your country at the moment for boys and girls? If you were about to have a baby boy/girl, what names might you give him/her? Why?* Start by telling Ss your own answers to the questions. Ss discuss the questions in pairs. In feedback, nominate Ss to share their answers with the class, and write the names they suggest on the board, asking them to spell them out to you.

SPEAKING
1A The aim of this activity is to introduce the topic of names, and help you assess Ss' language and speaking skills. Begin by writing your name on the board, and share your answers to questions 1–4 with the class. Give Ss two minutes to think about their own answers to the questions alone, and make notes if they want.

B Ss discuss the questions in pairs. In feedback, nominate Ss to share their answers with the class.

Teaching tip
Ss at Advanced level have often spent many years studying English, and will have come across similar activities and language many times. In order to make language learning effective at this level, it's therefore important to 'stretch' Ss in order to make the most of their abilities. When Ss are speaking, encourage them to ask follow-up questions in order to exploit speaking activities. Ask follow-up questions yourself when conducting feedback, and elicit reasons for their answers and opinions. Also, try to make topics appealing by bringing (yours and the Ss') real experience into the discussion where possible.

VOCABULARY names
2A Ss read sentences 1–8 alone, then discuss questions a)–f) in pairs. Monitor and help where necessary. In feedback, elicit Ss' answers and check understanding of the words in bold, giving more examples where necessary.

Answers: a) given name, surname, middle name, married name b) maiden name (if you are a woman), married name (if you get divorced and remarry) c) live up to my name, made a name for myself, clear her name d) named after e) put my name forward f) household name

Watch out!
In the reading text in Ex 3B, *first name* and *forename* are used. These are synonyms of *given name*. Similarly, *last name* is used as a synonym of *surname*.

B Ss discuss how they'd finish the sentences in pairs. In feedback, nominate Ss to share their ideas with the class.

Teaching tip
When Ss ask you for vocabulary, or if new words and phrases arise naturally during an activity, it's important to exploit this as far as possible at this level. This is where real learning takes place, as Ss have a genuine need for the language. Write new words on the board, but also add common collocations, phrases, synonyms and opposites to exploit the new language as far as possible.

Alternative approach
Ss complete sentences alone, and write their sentences in a random order on a blank piece of paper (just the answers without the questions). When they are ready, Ss show their answers to a partner, who guesses which sentences they complete.

READING

3A Ask *What are some common first names in your country or countries?* and write Ss' suggestions on the board. Ss discuss the questions in pairs. In feedback, elicit Ss' answers, and have a brief class discussion.

B Elicit/check the meaning of *CV*. Give Ss one minute to skim the article and complete the sentence. Explain that they will have a chance to read again in more detail afterwards. Stop them after one minute and give them time to compare their answers in pairs, before eliciting their ideas in feedback.

Suggested answer: The main idea of the text is that your name can influence how successful you are.

Teaching tip
When we read in our first language, we unconsciously employ a range of subskills, such as reading for gist, reading for detail, reading for specific information and reading to infer meaning. In our first language, we usually take a 'top-down' approach by starting with general understanding then homing in on the detail. When Ss practise reading, it's important we also encourage this approach by asking them to read quickly for general understanding first. This will help them become more fluent readers.

C Go through the questions with the class and elicit what Ss can remember, but don't give any answers yet. This will give you a chance to assess how much information they picked up from the first reading. Give Ss enough time to read the text again in more detail, before checking their answers in pairs. Tell Ss not to worry about new vocabulary for now, as they will have a chance to work on it in the next exercise. In feedback, elicit Ss' answers.

Answers: 1 Some names carry positive associations and are linked with success, while others carry negative associations. 2 Co-author of eight baby-naming books 3 She thinks they are making a mistake because they should be looking for skills, experience and what the interviewee can do for the business. 4 Celebrity culture and ethnic diversity are making people keen to make more individual choices about names.

4A Ss discuss the questions in pairs. In feedback, nominate Ss to share their opinions with the class.

B If you've brought dictionaries to class, distribute them for Ss to use. Ss find the words and phrases in the text and discuss the meanings in pairs. Encourage them to use the context and co-text (the words surrounding the words being focused on) in the article before referring to the dictionaries. Monitor and help where necessary. In feedback, elicit Ss' answers, and be prepared to clarify further if necessary.

Answers: 1 a woman who is frumpy looks unattractive because she dresses in old-fashioned clothes 2 (informal) be given something (e.g. an object or a responsibility) that you don't want 3 to reach a position of power or a top position (e.g. professionally) 4 settled, decided with little debate 5 when a company calls potential employees for an interview after looking at their CV 6 disapprove of something 7 famous people were the first to give their children strange and unusual first names 8 very strange and unusual

GRAMMAR the continuous aspect

5A Write the following sentences on the board: *I'm thinking about changing my name, I often think about changing my name.* Ask: *Which sentence uses a continuous form? Why does it use it?* (The first sentence, to show that it's an activity in progress during a particular period, though not necessarily at this exact moment.) Focus attention on the first sentence, and elicit the answer. Ss read the other sentences then discuss in pairs why the continuous form is used. In feedback, elicit Ss' ideas, but don't give any answers yet.

B Ss match the uses and sentences alone, then check in pairs. In feedback, elicit Ss' answers.

Answers: a) 5 b) 4 c) 1 d) 2 e) 3 f) 6

Teaching tip
By the time Ss reach Advanced level, they will have met most of the grammar of English previously, though they will have studied structures separately. At this level, it's important to bring everything together, by looking at common features e.g. the continuous aspect. Therefore, when looking at the different uses of the continuous aspect, try to highlight similarities of its function as a whole i.e. that it usually focuses on the action rather than the result and that this is why we don't use state verbs in continuous forms.

▶ LANGUAGEBANK 1.1 p128–129
Stronger classes can read the notes and do the exercises at home. Otherwise, check the notes with Ss, especially the fact that the continuous aspect focuses on the action and its duration, rather than the result. In each exercise, do the first sentence as an example. Ss complete the exercises alone, then check their answers in pairs. Ss can refer to the notes to help them.

Answers: 1 1 isn't working 2 Correct. 3 had been having 4 is weighing 5 Correct. 6 was looking 7 am talking 8 Correct. 9 has been studying 10 am doing
2 1 Why are you crying? 2 How long was he working/ How long had he been working there before they fired him? 3 What have you been doing since you graduated? 4 How long have you been living in Madrid? 5 Who were you talking to when I saw you earlier? 6 What did you want to be when you were a child? 7 Have you been waiting long? 8 Why didn't you finish your degree? 6 and 8 have to use the simple form.

PRACTICE

6 Read the first example with the class. Ss discuss in pairs which verbs would be better in the continuous form and why. Monitor and help where necessary. In feedback, elicit Ss' answers and be prepared to give further clarifications where necessary.

> **Answers:** 2 *have been waiting* It is an unfinished action and emphasises the length of time. 3 Correct. 4 *am trying* It is an action in progress at this time. 5 *had been expecting* It emphasises the length of time. 6 Correct. 7 Correct. 8 *will have been living* It emphasises the length of time. 9 *am/'m working* It refers to something still in progress. 10 *was making* It talks about something that was in progress when I got home.

7 Give Ss three or four minutes to complete the sentences so they are true for them. Monitor and help with ideas, writing any new words and phrases on the board. When they are ready, arrange Ss in small groups to compare their sentences. In feedback, elicit any common answers with the class.

WRITING a personal profile

8A Write on the board: *a personal profile* and elicit where Ss might see one (a blog, a social networking site, an online course, a job application). Focus Ss' attention on the personal profile. Give them two minutes to read it and discuss in pairs where they think it appears. In feedback, elicit Ss' answers.

> **Answer:** This profile will appear in an online class called BLED 514.

B Read the guidelines with the class, and check understanding. Ss read the profile again and in pairs, discuss how far Danny Garcia's profile follows them. In feedback, elicit Ss' answers.

> **Answer:** It follows all of the guidelines.

9 Ss categorise the words and phrases from the box in pairs. Monitor and help with any new vocabulary. In feedback, elicit Ss' ideas.

speakout TIP

Read the **speakout tip** with the class and emphasise the importance of considering your audience when you write. Refer back to the four formats discussed so far (a blog, an online course, a social networking site and a job application) and answer the questions with the class for each type of text.

LEARN TO plan your writing

10A Books closed. Write on the board: *planning your writing*. In pairs Ss brainstorm a list of things they can do when planning to write. In feedback, elicit Ss' ideas and write them on the board. Ask Ss to open their books again and say which of the things in the list they do.

B Give Ss one minute to read the outline and elicit what job it might be.

> **Suggested answers:** nursery school teacher, au pair, babysitter, children's entertainer, summer camp worker

11 Give Ss one minute to read the stages and check understanding. Refer Ss back to the **speakout tip** for stage 1. Encourage Ss to make notes in stage 1, and monitor, helping with ideas where necessary. Give Ss enough time to write their profiles, and monitor and help with vocabulary, writing any new words and phrases on the board. When they are ready, Ss compare their profiles in small groups and discuss any common features. In feedback, nominate Ss from each group to share any common features with the class.

> **Teaching tip**
>
> Many teachers avoid doing writing activities in class, as it's perceived as a 'quiet' activity best done alone. However, doing writing in class allows us to monitor Ss *during* the writing process, and so help them with ideas, planning, structuring, editing, etc., and not just focus on the finished product.

> **Homework ideas**
> * **Ex 11**: write a final draft of your personal profile
> * **Language bank** 1.1 Ex 1–2, p129
> * **Workbook** Ex 1–5, p4–5

WHAT ARE YOU LIKE?

Introduction

Ss revise and practise describing present and past habits in the context of language learning. They also learn and practise personality adjectives and idioms for describing people.

SUPPLEMENTARY MATERIALS

Resource bank p135, p136 and p138

ff write the two headings below on the board.

Warm up

Arrange the class in two large groups (A and B), and write at the top of the board: *Good language learners …, Bad language learners …*

Group A makes a list of things good language learners do (e.g. read books in English), and group B makes a list of things bad language learners do (e.g. always use their first language during class). When they have finished, arrange Ss in pairs (one from each group) to compare their answers. In feedback, elicit Ss' ideas and build a list on the board under the two headings. Before starting Ex 1A, Ss quickly read the questionnaire and tick any of the ideas they have already mentioned.

SPEAKING

1A Focus attention on the questionnaire, and check understanding of the task by eliciting how Ss mark each statement if they strongly agree, agree, disagree or strongly disagree. Ss work alone to read the questionnaire and mark each statement. Monitor and help with any new vocabulary.

B Ss compare their answers in pairs and discuss the questions. In feedback, nominate Ss to share their answers with the class.

GRAMMAR describing habits

2A Write on the board: *Present habits* and *Past habits*. Elicit what expressions Ss already know to describe them, and write them on the board. Focus attention on the table. Ss underline verbs and expressions in the questionnaire from Ex 1 and use them to complete the table. In feedback, elicit Ss' answers and drill the expression chorally and individually.

Answers: 2 I'm always watching videos…/ I'm always looking for opportunities… 4 inclined 5 a tendency 6 rule 7 out of ten 8 I would spend hours studying… 10 I kept making mistakes 13 I tended to

Teaching tip

Drilling is sometimes seen as an activity for Ss at lower levels, who have more difficulties with the sounds of the language. While this is true, drilling new language at higher levels is also important, particularly with English where the pronunciation and spelling are so different. Drilling also helps us to focus on stress and intonation, which are very important in being understood clearly.

B ▶1.1 Ss listen to the recording and write the sentences, then check in pairs. Play the recording a second time if necessary. In feedback, elicit Ss' answers and write the sentences on the board.

Answers: 1 She kept on making mistakes. 2 He'll spend hours studying grammar. 3 They would complain all the time.

C ▶1.2 Before playing the recording, ask Ss to pay attention to the pronunciation, especially the stressed words. Play the recording and elicit Ss' ideas.

Answers: The stress is on a different word in the two versions. In the B sentences the stress is on *kept / will / would* and the effect is to make the speaker sound irritated or annoyed about the habit.

⫸ **LANGUAGEBANK** 1.2 p128–129

Stronger classes can read the notes and do the exercises at home. Otherwise, check the notes with Ss, and check Ss understand that we use *will/would* to describe habits, not states. In each exercise, do the first sentence as an example. Ss complete the exercises alone, then check their answers in pairs. Ss can refer to the notes to help them.

Answers: 1 1 On Sunday mornings, I'll/I will get up early and go for a run along the river before anyone else is awake. 2 I'll/will sometimes wait for hours before the bus arrives. 3 My mother-in-law will always bake a cake for us when we visit. 4 He will keep bothering me for my telephone number, but I don't want to give it to him. 5 The children won't stop fighting. It's driving me crazy. 6 She will spend the first half an hour chatting before she even starts work. 7 My parents would take us on camping holidays in the rain. We hated it. 8 My grandfather wouldn't shout, or tell you off. He was a very gentle man.
2 1 The drug has a tendency to cause headaches if used for prolonged periods. 2 He is inclined to buy paintings which cost far too much money. 3 We're prone to arguing about politics at the dinner table. 4 I keep wondering whether or not I've been given the job. 5 She is always making a fuss about the way I dress. 6 They kept cheating at cards, so I decided not to play with them. 7 As a rule, I don't use a lot of herbs and spices in my cooking. 8 My father would always bring me back a present from his travels.

PRACTICE

3A Read the first example with the class. Ss work alone to complete the sentences then check in pairs. In feedback, elicit Ss' answers.

Answers: 2 My mother is prone to worrying about everything. 3 He keeps failing his driving test. 4 I'm not inclined to be very laid-back. 5 I'm always looking for new things to learn. 6 As a rule, I try not to work at the weekend. 7 Nine times out of ten I'll be right about my first impressions. 8 As a child I would spend hours reading.

B Give the Ss one or two examples about yourself first to demonstrate. Ss work alone to choose two or three of the sentences and change them with true information, then compare in pairs. In feedback, nominate Ss from each pair to share their ideas with the class.

Alternative approach

Ss choose four sentences, and change them so that two are true and two are false for them. In pairs, they read out their sentences and answer follow-up questions for their partner to decide which are true and which are false.

VOCABULARY personality

4A Write on the board: *Adjectives of personality*, elicit one or two from the class and write them on the board (e.g. *kind*, *rude*, *intelligent*, etc.). Arrange Ss in pairs and give them a few minutes to brainstorm and write down as many adjectives as possible. In feedback, elicit Ss' answers, check understanding and write them on the board.

B Focus attention on the words in the box, and check/explain any new vocabulary. In pairs, Ss give examples of what each person does. In feedback, nominate Ss to share their ideas with the class.

C Ss work alone to match the sentences to the words in the box from Ex 4B, then check in pairs. In feedback, elicit Ss' answers.

Answers: 1 perceptive 2 prejudiced 3 apathetic 4 obstinate 5 rebellious 6 solitary 7 neurotic 8 open-minded

D Ss work in pairs to write their sentences. Monitor and help with vocabulary, writing any new words and phrases on the board. When they've finished, arrange Ss in small groups to compare their sentences. In feedback, nominate Ss from each group to share their ideas with the class.

Suggested answers: Thoughtful: takes other people's feelings into consideration; Obsessive: thinks about one thing too much; Inspirational: does things which encourage other people to have ideas; Over-ambitious: tries to do too much; Conscientious: works hard; Insensitive: doesn't notice or think about other people's feelings; Mature: behaves in a sensible, adult way; Inquisitive: is curious to know more

➡ VOCABULARYBANK p148 PERSONALITY

1A Ss match the opposites alone, then check in pairs. In feedback, elicit Ss' answers and be prepared to provide further explanations/examples where necessary.

B Ss match the adjectives to the statements alone, then check in pairs. In feedback, elicit Ss' answers.

C In pairs, Ss describe people they know and/or famous people who match the adjectives. Make sure they don't describe other Ss in the class, though.

Stronger classes can do the exercises at home.

Answers: 1A considerate/selfish, circumspect/impetuous, conservative/liberal, temperamental/easygoing, gregarious/introverted
B 1 selfish 2 temperamental 3 conservative 4 introverted 5 easygoing 6 circumspect 7 liberal 8 impetuous 9 considerate 10 gregarious

LISTENING

5A Introduce the listening by asking Ss if anyone has heard of the Myers-Briggs Test Indicator before. Ss read the radio information alone then answer the questions in pairs. In feedback, elicit Ss' answers.

Answers: 1 It is a test of your personality. 2 Anybody can use it, but it is widely used by companies for their workers.

B ▶1.3 Focus attention on the questions and elicit Ss' predictions. Ss listen to the recording and answer the questions, then check in pairs. In feedback, elicit Ss' answers.

Answers: 1 the people we work with 2 all kinds of people, often office workers 3 The interviewer asks questions about Mariella's lifestyle, how she does her shopping, whether she can put together flat-pack furniture, what she does at the end of the day, how she would react in certain situations.

Teaching tip

When we listen in our first language, we often (consciously or unconsciously) make predictions about what we are going to hear, depending on the context and what we expect to hear. We then process new information by 'attaching' it to what we know already. Therefore it's important to give Ss opportunities to predict before they listen. Not only will this help them absorb new information, but it will also clarify what they are listening for.

6A Ss discuss the meaning in pairs. In feedback, elicit Ss' ideas and check understanding. Be prepared to give further explanations and examples where necessary.

Answers: 1 people who make statements that are too general and do not consider all the facts 2 people who argue about small, unimportant details 3 people who worry excessively about plans 4 people who leave doing their work until the last minute before it needs to be finished. 5 to regain your energy/strength 6 furniture that you can buy in warehouses which you unpack and assemble yourself at home.

B Give Ss five minutes to see how many of the questions they can answer from memory, then play the recording again for them to check. In feedback, elicit Ss' answers.

Answers: 1b) 2c) 3b) 4c)

C Ss answer the questions alone, then compare their answers in pairs. Monitor and help with vocabulary, writing any new words and phrases on the board. In feedback, nominate Ss to share their ideas with the class.

Unit 1 Recording 3

M = Mariella J = John

M: For any of you who work surrounded by other people, you'll know that one of the biggest stressors in the world of work is not the work itself, but the people we work with. There are the people who need to be noisy, while you're trying to be quiet, the ones who 'shh' you when you tell them a really good story, there are the sweeping generalisers, and the detail-obsessed nit-pickers, the obsessive planners, and the last-minute deadline junkies. You, of course, are perfect. These days there are tests for just about everything, and personality is no exception. If you've ever been intrigued to define your type, or sat down and completed a questionnaire at work, then it's likely you'll have come across the Myers-Briggs Type Indicator, known to its fans as the MBTI. Myers-Briggs is the world's most widely used personality questionnaire. From Beijing to Boston to Bournemouth, office workers, college students, and people who are simply curious to find out more about themselves, answer a series of questions to determine which of sixteen different personality types they fall into.

Preferences are split into four sections, so prepare yourself for the psychological bit. The first category determines whether you are an extrovert or an introvert. The second tells you whether you prefer to sense or intuit information. The third deals with decision-making, thinking or feeling. And the fourth, our approach to actions, judging and perceiving. Ultimately, you end up with a four-letter acronym like ENFP, or ISFJ, which describes your personality type.

27

J: How do you prefer to, if you like, recharge your batteries at the end of the working day?

M: Well, most of the time, I prefer to go home and be quiet and read, or slow down …, put the children to bed and so on,

J: Typically when we ask people this sort of question. Typically, introverts are more likely to talk about spending quiet time, time on their own, reading, etc. Extroverts are more likely to talk about spending time with people. I don't know if you ever had the opportunity to put together any flat-pack furniture, or anything like that, how did you go about doing it?

M: Well, you know, I'd lose the screws, and then the directions would be underneath the box, and then I'd lose another part of it, and it would take quite a long time, and be quite an infuriating process.

J: OK. Typically when we ask that question, people with a preference for sensing will like to follow the instructions. People who have a preference for intuition, it's not that they disregard instructions, but they are a little bit more of a guide. If you imagine that perhaps a friend of yours gives you a call, and says, 'I've just been burgled,' what would you, what would your reaction be, what would you do?

M: Do you know, it's so difficult, because I think it depends on the person, you know …

J: In some ways … matter .. to me it's a matter of what you do first, because both people with a preference for thinking, (and both people with a preference for feeling?) … will do both things. They'll do the practical things, 'Have you called the police?', 'Is the person still there?' 'Have you, you know, called the insurance?', etc., etc. And they'll then go on to 'And how are you?'

M: Well, in that instance I would definitely fall into the thinking category, I think.

J: How do you go about doing the food shopping?

M: I..ah I, I'm in love with internet food ordering, um so I do that, and then all the things that I've forgotten, because I don't do it with any great system, I spend the rest of the week running out and picking up.

J: Typically, people with a preference for judging will be quite organised about those sorts of things. People with a preference for perceiving may also make lists, but those lists have a more aspirational quality

M: Random feel, shall we say?

J: Yeah, they have things that they might buy, or they might not buy. If they see something more interesting when they get to the supermarket, then they'll get that instead.

M: At the end of my conversation with John, I got my personality type, which I'll illuminate you on later.

SPEAKING

7A Focus attention on the scales, and demonstrate how to complete them e.g. if a student answers b) or c) for question 1 in Ex 6B, they mark the first scale near *Introvert*. Ss work alone to mark their other scales, then check their profiles with the information on p158.

B Ask Ss to stand up, mingle and compare their profiles. In feedback, nominate Ss to tell the class who they are most similar to, and if they agree with their profiles.

VOCABULARY *PLUS* idioms for describing people

8A Ss work alone to work out the meanings of the idioms. Encourage them to use the information in the sentences, and tell them not to worry if they don't understand them fully at this stage. When they are ready, Ss compare their ideas in pairs. In feedback, elicit Ss' answers, and be prepared to give further explanations and examples where necessary.

Answers: 1 Yes-man: someone who always agrees with and obeys his/her employer, leader, wife etc. 2 whiz kid: a young person who is very skilled or successful at something 3 busybody: someone who is too interested in other people's private activities 4 chatterbox: someone (especially a child) who talks too much 5 pain in the neck: someone or something which is very annoying 6 dark horse: a person who doesn't tell others very much about himself/herself, but has surprising qualities or abilities. 7 old hand: someone who has a lot of experience at something 8 set in her ways: unlikely to change her habits or opinions 9 black sheep: someone who is regarded by other members of his/her family group as not fitting in or an embarrassment. 10 life and soul of the party: someone who enjoys social occasions and is fun to be with

B Ss match the idioms to the situations in pairs. In feedback, elicit Ss' answers.

Answers: 1 He/She is very set in his/her ways. 2 He's an old hand. 3 He's/She's a chatterbox 4 She's a dark horse. 5 It's a pain in the neck. 6 He's a whiz kid. 7 He's a busybody. 8 She's the life and soul of the party.

speakout TIP

Read the **speakout tip** with the class and ask Ss if they use any of these methods already. Explain that there is no 'correct' way to learn idioms, and that it's a case of Ss experimenting and finding out which way works best for them.

C Arrange Ss in small groups. Ss use the idioms to describe people they know in their lives, or famous people. Make sure Ss avoid describing other people in the class though. In feedback, nominate Ss from each group to share their ideas with the class.

VOCABULARYBANK p148 IDIOMS

2A Write on the board: *apple, cannon, potato, blanket, cheese* and *cookie*. Ask if anyone knows any idioms for describing people which use these words. Ss work alone to identify the idioms, then check in pairs. Don't give any answers at this stage.

B Ss match the idioms to the pictures, then check in pairs. In feedback, elicit Ss' answers.
Stronger classes can do the exercises at home.

Answers: 1 e) 2 c) 3 b) 4 a) 5 f) 6 d)

Homework ideas
• Vocabulary bank p148
• Language bank 1.2 Ex 1–2, p129
• Workbook Ex 1–5, p6–7

THIS IS ME …

Introduction
Ss learn and practise phrases for speculating and how to use vague language.

SUPPLEMENTARY MATERIALS

Resource bank p139

Warm up: Bring or download a range of modern/old portraits (preferably less well-known) to the class, one for each group of three Ss. Write the prompts below on the board.

Warm up
Write the following prompts on the board: *Name, From, Age, Profession, Background, Hopes for the future.* Arrange Ss in groups of three and distribute a portrait to each group. Ss invent a life story for the person in the portrait, using the prompts on the board to help. Monitor and help with ideas and vocabulary, writing any new words and phrases on the board. When Ss have finished, collect the portraits and display them so the whole class can see them. Groups take it in turns to read out their life stories, while other Ss guess which portrait they are describing.

VOCABULARY images

1A Focus attention on the portraits and ask if Ss can identify who the people are. Don't give any answers yet. Ss read what the sitters said and match the paragraphs to the portraits, then check in pairs. In feedback, elicit Ss' answers.

Answers: Alan Bennett C Germaine Greer A Kazuo Ishiguro B

B Read the example with the class. Ss work in pairs to discuss the meanings of the words in bold from the texts. Encourage Ss to use the context and co-text to help. In feedback, elicit Ss' answers, and be prepared to give further explanations and examples where necessary.

Answers:
caricatured: drawn or described in a way that is only partly true and which exaggerates certain features for humorous effect
flicker: a feeling or expression that is visible for a very short time
posed: sat or stood in a particular position in order to be painted
flattering: makes you look as attractive as it possibly can

FUNCTION speculating

2A Focus attention on the portraits and elicit what Ss can see. Ss discuss the questions in pairs. Monitor and help with vocabulary where necessary. In feedback, elicit Ss' answers and write them on the board.

B ▶ 1.4 Ss listen to the recording and make notes under the subheadings, then check in pairs. In feedback, elicit Ss' answers and compare against their original ideas on the board.

Answers:

	character/appearance	job
A	intelligent, relaxed, confident, rebellious	teacher, academia, writer, TV presenter/ broadcaster
B	intellectual, studious, glasses = intelligent, not British, comfortably dressed, kind, guarded	writer, academia
C	no pretensions, not posh, not intellectual, dressed formally, creative	artist, novelist, playwright

C Ss work in pairs to answer the questions from memory. Monitor and help where necessary, but don't give any answers yet.

D Ss listen again and check their answers. In feedback, elicit Ss' answers.

Answers: 1 A 2 C 3 A 4 B 5 B 6 C

3 Focus attention on the expressions used for speculating, and explain that we can use these expressions when we're making guesses about something. Ss find examples of the expressions being used in the audio script on p164–165, then check in pairs. In feedback, elicit Ss' answers and drill the expressions chorally and individually.

Unit 1 Recording 4
Portrait A
W1=Woman 1 M1 = Man 1 M2=Man 2
Portrait A
W1: I think this woman looks very intelligent.
M1: Mmm – she's got, she's got an in … a kind of intensity to her her face, hasn't she?
M2: She looks a bit puzzled to me.
W1: I think she looks thoughtful.
M1: Yeah, pensive.
M2: Yes, maybe.
M1: But the way she's sitting … it's unusual isn't it …
W1: It's very unusual … she's …
M2: It seems like she's trying to say something – do you know what I mean?
M1: Oh, by the way she's …
W1: Yes.
M2: Trying to make a statement by … 'this is the sort of person I am. That I …
M1: Mmm
W1: It …
M2: … am relaxed … and … confident with … myself,' I suppose.
M1: Yeah, she gives the impression of being very at ease with herself – doesn't she?
M2: Yeah.
W1: I think she's … the …it …it looks to me as if she's listening …
M1: Mmm
W1: … to someone else talking …
M1: Yes.
W1: … that we can't see.
M1: Yeah … off … off frame … yeah.

W1: I wonder what she … does for a living …

M1: Mmm … possibly …

W1: D'you think she's a teacher?

M1: I was gonna say … academia, I wonder if she's a …

M2: But something that's not … within the system, if you know what I mean … some … she looks … there's something rebellious about …

W1: Yes … she could be a writer.

M2: The way she's … just the way she's holding herself there, it's just very confident, and very 'I'm gonna do it my way'.

M1: Yeah yeah. I I …

W1: Do you think she works ah … on television … something like that?

M2: Hmm

M1: Possibly … she could be a presenter, or a broadcaster?

W1: Yes.

M2: That kind of stuff.

M1: Umm … I wouldn't wanna get into an argument with her though.

W1: No.

Portrait B

M2: This guy looks kind of I'd say intellectual. You've got all the books behind him, he looks quite, umm studious – wouldn't you say?

M1: Mmm

W1: Yes … he he looks very thoughtful.

M1: But don't you think that it's the glasses that are making us think that? Put a pair of glasses on someone and they suddenly look intelligent.

M2: Hmm, maybe.

W1: I'd …

M2: But it's also …

W1: …hazard a guess that he was a writer.

M2: It's a –yeah, something like that. It's also the hand on the chair that I'm I'm …

M1: It's quite posed isn't it?

M2: Yes.

W1: He … he doesn't look British I don't think.

M2: Ahh!

M1: Yes!

M2: Interesting.

M1: Yeah. I'd say he looks mm … maybe Eastern European?

W1: He could be American.

M2: Hard to say isn't it?

M1: Ahh, yeah

W1: Do you think that's his room?

M2: I wonder if it's his study – yes.

M1: Like a study or a library? Again, it makes me think maybe he's in academia.

W1: Yes, it could be … university.

M1: But again he's dressed … he's dressed quite comfortable … comfortably, isn't he?

M2: Yeah.

W1: Very casually.

M1: It's not formal, is it?

M2: So you'd think that might suggest it's his home or something.

M1: How … how d'you think he comes across though, personality wise?

M2: Um

W1: I think he looks kind.

M2: Hmm, I think there's something guarded there. I think there's …

M1: He knows something. There's something knowing in his eyes … as if he's got a secret.

M2: Yes and not necessarily going to tell us.

Portrait C

M1: Now this chap looks like he's in a world of his own … like his thoughts have just drifted off somewhere far away.

W1: Yes. I can't make out where this is.

M1: Difficult, isn't it?

M2: It looks quite set up, doesn't it?

M1: Yeah.

W1: Yes it does.

M2: They look like props in front of him.

M1: Theatre … the colours in the background remind me of theatres – the colour of theatre seats.

W1: Yes – there is a mug, there's … is this a plug?

M1: Oh yes.

M2: I wondered that, with the … look … with the wire there …

W1: I can see … and a bag.

M2: And that looks like a paper bag with his lunch in or something.

M1: Brown paper bag … so maybe he's trying to tell us that he's … he's got no pretensions. He he's not a … he's not posh. He's he's brought his lunch in a …

M2: Yes.

M1: … in a grocers' bag.

W1: I think it looks …

M2: I don't get the plug if it is a plug. I don't understand that.

W1: …quite funny.

M1: Yeah – incongruous.

W1: It's quite amusing.

M1: Yeah – as if he's trying to make a point about how ridiculous or absurd er his life is or life in general is.

W1: Yes.

M1: What d'you reckon his job might be?

W1: I don't know.

M2: When you said you thought somebody with glasses looked intellectual – do you think he's intellectual?

M1: No, this time not.

M2: What is it then, what …

W1: He could be an artist.

M1: Mmmhmm

W1: Possibly.

M2: 'Cos he's dressed very, sort of formally.

M1: Yes.

M2: But there's something otherworldly about the … where he's sitting, if you know what I mean.

M1: Mmm

W1: Yes.

M2: It's all that red behind him.

M1: Like he's bridging different worlds.

M2: Exactly.

M1: So he he could be a creative; he could be a novelist or a playwright, or something like that. Somebody who fuses fiction and reality.

> ⏵ **LANGUAGEBANK** 1.3 p128–129
>
> *Stronger classes* could read the notes and do the exercise at home. Otherwise, drill the phrases from the chart, checking Ss are using natural intonation. Ss work alone to complete the conversations, then check their answers in pairs. In feedback, elicit Ss' answers. Ss practise the conversations in pairs.
>
> **Answers:** 1 looks 2 hazard 3 sure 4 guess 5 wonder 6 say, seems 7 give

4 Ss work alone to rewrite the sentences, then check in pairs. In feedback, elicit Ss' answers.

Answers: 1 It seems to me that she's a bit lonely.
2 He gives the impression of being angry. 3 I reckon she's probably an actress. 4 If I had to make a guess, I'd say she was happy with her life. 5 I'm pretty sure he's not telling us everything. 6 I'd hazard a guess that she's an only child.

LEARN TO use vague language

5 Ss read the language in the chart, then discuss the questions in pairs. In feedback, elicit Ss' answers.

Answers: Vague language sounds casual. Also see speakout tip.

speakout TIP

Read the **speakout tip** with the class and explain that using vague language, hedges and fillers is a useful strategy to give yourself time to think when speaking. Ss read the audio script on p164 (Unit 1, Recording 4) and find examples of these, then check in pairs.

6A Ss work alone to correct the mistakes in the sentences, then check in pairs. In feedback, elicit Ss' answers.

Answers: 1 a couple of 2 at about 8-ish 3 stuffs 4 got a plenty of 5 sort of 6 forty or so

B ▶1.5 Focus attention on the descriptions of linking and elision, and be prepared to give further explanations/examples if necessary. Ss work alone to listen and mark the sentences from Ex 6A as in the examples, then check in pairs. Play the recording a second time if necessary. In feedback, elicit Ss' answers and drill the sentences chorally and individually.

Answers: 2 Why don't we meet at about eight-ish?
3 I left a lot of stuff at the hotel, but I can pick it up later.
4 Don't worry. We've got plenty of time.
5 We've sort of finished the accounts.
6 There'll be about forty or so people attending.

Watch out!

Elision occurs when a sound disappears in rapid, natural speech. This makes it easier to say, and avoids having to put certain consonant sounds together to maintain a regular rhythm and speed.

/t/ and /d/ are the two sounds which are most commonly elided in English, when they have a consonant sound before and after e.g. *Why don't we* becomes /waɪdəʊnwiː/, and *an old man* becomes /ənəʊlmæn/. Raising Ss' awareness of this can help them both speak more fluently and distinguish words more easily when listening.

The /t/ and /d/ sounds are also elided (or glottalised) when they are preceded by a vowel and followed by a consonant which means that instead of pronouncing the sound, we briefly close the vocal chords and then open them again, e.g. *about forty* which becomes /əbaʊfɔːtɪ/

Note that as well as the linking indicated in the phrases above, the /j/ sound is also used to link some of the phrases. In *be about*, this is an intrusive /j/ sound, as it isn't written. In *plenty of* and *forty or so*, it's a linking sound as it's written.

C Ss mark the examples alone then check in pairs. Encourage them to practise saying the phrases if they're not sure. Monitor and model where necessary.

Answers: 1 It looks as if he's got a lot of work to do.
2 She looks about fifty or so. 3 It's a bit dark, isn't it?
4 I've got a couple of things to ask.

D ▶1.6 Ss listen and check their answers. Elicit the correct answers, then play the recording once more for Ss to repeat the phrases.

SPEAKING

7A Ss turn to p158 and describe and discuss the portraits in pairs. Monitor and note any common errors or examples of good language, and encourage Ss to use the language from the unit. In feedback, nominate Ss to share their ideas with the class.

Optional extra activity
Ss search the internet to find a portrait they really like using, for example, a Google image search, or a photo-sharing website such as www.flickr.com. When they have found one they like, Ss show it to each other in small groups, and discuss why they like it.
Encourage Ss to find ways of describing what kind of portrait it is – formal, relaxed, spontaneous, posed, etc

B Write the following questions on the board: *Where would you be? What would you wear? What pose would you choose? What mood would you be in? Would there be any other objects in the portrait? Would you be on your own? Would it be formal or informal?* Give Ss one or two minutes to think about where they would want to be if they were having their portrait painted and what style they would like the picture to be. Ss can make notes if they want to. When they are ready, Ss discuss their ideas in pairs. In feedback, nominate Ss to share their ideas with the class. Correct any common class errors that you heard, and drill any examples of good language you heard.

Teaching tip
When Ss are doing fluency work, it's important not to interrupt them to correct errors, to ensure they can maintain their 'flow'. Therefore, while Ss are speaking, monitor unobtrusively and make note on common errors (and good examples of language use). During feedback, write any common errors on the board and correct them as 'class errors', being careful not to highlight who made the errors. Also, explain and drill any good examples of language use you heard.

Homework ideas
• Ex 7B: draw/write about your portrait.
• Language bank 1.3 Ex 1, p129
• Workbook Ex 1–4, p8

FRANCESCO'S VENICE

Introduction

Ss watch an extract from the BBC documentary *Francesco's Venice*, in which a historian describes the history of Venice. Ss learn and practise how to talk about a possession, and write a description of an object.

SUPPLEMENTARY MATERIALS

Warm up: Write the questions below on the board.

Warm up

Write the following questions on the board: *What do you know about your family history? Has your family always lived in the place where you live now? Who is your oldest living relative?* Arrange Ss in small groups to discuss the questions. In feedback, nominate Ss from each group to share their answers with the class.

▷ DVD PREVIEW

1 Arrange Ss in small groups. Focus attention on the photo and elicit what city it is. Ss discuss the questions in groups. Monitor and help with vocabulary, writing any new words and phrases on the board. In feedback, nominate Ss from each group to share their ideas with the class.

Culture notes

Venice is a city in Northern Italy, which is famous for its rich culture, history, and architecture. It has a population of around 272,000 and is popular with tourists from around the world. It is unique in its geography in that it is composed of 117 small islands, and the main form of transport is by river, with the maritime part of Venice having no roads or cars. The most famous form of transport is the gondola, though this is now mostly used by tourists and for ceremonies. Venice was a very powerful city during the Middle Ages and Renaissance period, and is the birthplace of the composer Antonio Vivaldi.

Optional extra activity

Do a 'Venice Quiz' with the class, before sharing the information in the culture notes. Arrange Ss in groups of three, elicit a team name from each group and write it on the board. Ask each group to appoint a 'secretary' who will write their answers down. Read out the following statements, and ask each group to write *true* or *false* for each one (but not to call the answers out):

1. Venice has lots of rivers. (*False* – it has lots of salt water canals)

2. Over 2 million tourists visit Venice every year. (*True*)

3. No other city in the world has more canals than Venice. (*False* – Birmingham, England's 2nd largest city, has more miles of canals)

4. Most Venetian residents use gondolas every day to go to work. (*False* – nowadays these are mostly only used by tourists and for ceremonial occasions).

5. Venice has no internal roads for cars. (*True*)

6. Leonardo da Vinci was born in Venice. (*False* – he was born in Florence)

When Ss have written their answers, award points for each correct answer and write a tally on the board. The group with the most points wins.

2 Give Ss two minutes to read the programme information then discuss the question in pairs. In feedback, elicit Ss' answers.

Answer: Francesco is a good person to host the programme because he is a historian and writer and his family has lived in Venice for centuries.

3 Ss work alone to complete the sentences, then check in pairs. With *weaker classes*, elicit/check the meaning of the words in the box first. In feedback, elicit Ss' answers, and be prepared to give further explanations and examples where necessary.

Answers: 1 rotting (becoming destroyed by age)
2 bequeathed (left to someone after your death)
3 warehouse 4 showroom 5 modest 6 storeys

▷ DVD VIEW

4 Go through the sentences with the class and check any new vocabulary. Play the DVD. Ss watch and put the events in the correct order, then check their answers in pairs. In feedback, elicit Ss' answers.

Answers: 1 b) 2 c) 3 d) 4 a)

5A Ss answer the questions in pairs from memory. Monitor and help where necessary, but don't give any answers yet.

B Play the DVD again for Ss to check their answers. In feedback, elicit Ss' answers.

Answers: 1 Because the house is now rotting and in terrible condition. 2 In the 13th century. 3 It was bequeathed to another family. 4 They did business there. They used their house as a warehouse, a showroom, a place to make money and a landing stage.

6 Ss discuss the questions in pairs. Monitor and help with vocabulary, writing any new words and phrases on the board. In feedback, nominate Ss to share their ideas with the class.

Francesco's Venice

FdM=Francesco da Mosto

FdM: It was around this time my family became successful merchants and decided to build a grand house. It is the oldest palazzo to survive on the Grand Canal. Now it is rotting and one of the saddest sights of the city. It breaks my heart. This palace is called Ca' da Mosto. It was built by my family in the thirteenth century and my ancestors lived here nearly four hundred years until 1603, when it was bequeathed to another family. I've driven past it a thousand times, but I've never been inside.
If I have to be sincere, I'm a little shy to come inside this place – because I have always seen this house from outside; the mask that normally the public sees. It's difficult to enter a world where you have never been before, a place you know all the people of your family lived over many centuries. It's quite a strange sensation, something that gives you a feeling of all the history on your shoulders, the thing of who you are in this moment of your life.
My family didn't just live in this house, they did business here. They used their house as a warehouse, a show room, a place to make money and a landing stage, because the most profitable goods were from overseas, so a successful merchant had to be a sailor too.

speakout a possession

7A ▶1.7 Read through the points with the class and check they know what to listen for. Ss listen and take notes, then check in pairs. In feedback, elicit Ss' answers.

> **Answers:** The object is a very old carpet.
> Background: Her great-grandfather took it from Calcutta to South Africa. The speaker inherited it from her grandmother.
> Physical description: brightly coloured, red, white, green and gold with patterns like leaves, frayed.
> Value: it's important because of the story of the great-grandfather taking it from Calcutta to South Africa. Also because she inherited it and will pass it on to her children.
> Memories: Childhood memory of it hanging on her grandmother's wall.

Unit 1 Recording 7

W=Woman

W: My treasured possession is a very old carpet that has been in my family for four generations.
My great grandfather was a salesman. He sold carpets in Calcutta. During the nineteen-fifties he went bankrupt and went to South Africa to find his fortune. Legend has it that he took nothing but the clothes he was wearing and this carpet. I'm not sure this is true, but that's the story. Anyway, he made his fortune in South Africa and the carpet remained in the family. When he died, my grandmother inherited it and instead of putting it on the floor of her house in Durban, she hung it on the wall. Even as a young child I remember it. It's brightly coloured, reds, white, green and gold, with these beautiful patterns that look like leaves, and I just remember it hanging on the wall of the dining room and always wondering why a carpet was on the wall. Anyway, eventually it was bequeathed to me and, um, it's now on my wall. It's a little bit old and frayed now. I suppose I should repair it. Some of the weaving is falling apart, but it still looks OK. When I die, my children will have it, and then their children, so it will always be in the family.

B Focus attention on the **Key phrases**. Ss listen and tick the phrases they hear, then check in pairs. In feedback, elicit Ss' answers and drill the **Key phrases** chorally and individually.

> **Answers:** (It) has been in my family for four generations. ✓
> My grandmother inherited it. ✓
> It was bequeathed to me. ✓
> I should repair it. ✓

8A Give Ss five minutes to choose a possession of their own or think of a place that their family has special associations with and make notes on the points from Ex 7A. Monitor and help with vocabulary, writing any new words and phrases on the board.

B When Ss are ready, arrange them in small groups. Ss describe their objects to each other. Encourage Ss to ask follow-up questions to find out more information. In feedback, nominate Ss from each group to share what they found out with the class.

> **Alternative approach**
> Ss describe their objects to each other, as in Ex 8B, but don't say what the object is. Other Ss listen and guess what the object is.

writeback a description of an object

9A Elicit/check: *gramophone* (an old-fashioned record player), *a scratchy recording* (one that has been played so many times it has got damaged), *handed down* (passed on from generation to generation) and *an heirloom* (valuable object that has been owned by a family for many years). Ss read the description then answer the question in pairs. In feedback, elicit Ss' answers.

> **Answer:** It is associated with childhood memories and memories of the writer's grandfather.

B Make sure Ss choose a different object or place to the one they spoke about in Ex 8B. However, they can use the points in Ex 8A to help them plan their ideas. Refer Ss back to the ideas for planning on p10, and encourage them to plan their ideas carefully before beginning writing. Ss write their descriptions alone. Monitor and help with vocabulary, writing any new words and phrases on the board. When they have finished, Ss show their descriptions to each other.

> **Alternative approach**
> When Ss have finished, collect their descriptions and pin them up on the wall. Ss walk round and read the descriptions. In feedback, elicit which descriptions Ss liked best, and why.

> **Homework ideas**
> • Ex 8B: write about the possession you described.
> • Ex 9B: write a final draft of your description.

LOOKBACK

Introduction

Ss revise and practise the language of Unit 1. The notes below provide ideas for exploiting the exercises and activities but your approach will depend on your aim, e.g. as a diagnostic or progress test or as revision and fluency practice. For example, if done as a test then it would not be appropriate to monitor or help them.

NAMES

1   After explaining the activity, elicit the first answer as an example in order to check Ss understand what to do. Ss underline the correct alternatives alone then check their answers in pairs. In feedback, elicit Ss' answers. Listen carefully to Ss' pronunciation of the phrases and if necessary, drill them chorally and individually.

> **Answers:** 1 clear 2 after 3 maiden 4 herself 5 household 6 nickname

> **Optional extra activity**
> Do a backwards dictation. Arrange Ss in small teams, elicit a name for each team and write them on the board. Dictate the phrases, starting with the last letter of each one and working backwards. The first team to guess the word or phrase gets a point. The team with the most points at the end wins.

THE CONTINUOUS ASPECT

2A   Explain that Ss need to add a verb to each sentence, using a continuous form in one and a simple form in the other (e.g. past simple and past continuous). With *weaker classes* elicit the first answer as an example. Ss complete the sentences alone then check in pairs. In feedback, elicit Ss' answers.

> **Answers:** 1 a) is coming b) comes 2a) have had b) have been having 3a) was being b) was 4a) don't get b) isn't getting 5a) had worked b) had been working

B   Read the example with the class, and elicit the reason for 1b). Ss discuss why we use each form in pairs. Monitor and help where necessary. In feedback, elicit Ss' answers and be prepared to provide further explanations and examples where necessary.

> **Optional extra activity**
> To provide extra practice of the continuous aspect, write the following verb forms on the board: *is coming/comes, have been having/have had, was being/was, don't/doesn't get/isn't/aren't getting, had worked/had been working.* Ss work alone to write five true sentences about themselves, using one of the verb forms from each option. Monitor and help with ideas where necessary. When they have finished, Ss compare their sentences in pairs.

DESCRIBING HABITS

3A   After explaining the activity, elicit the first answer as an example in order to check Ss understand what to do. Ss correct the sentences alone then check their answers in pairs. In feedback, elicit Ss' answers.

> **Answers:** 1 I'm prone **to** leaving things until the last minute, and then I always have to rush. 2 I don't tend **to need** as much sleep as I used to. 3 I keep forget**ting** people's birthdays. 4 My parents were always very strict, and they wouldn't **let me out** late at night. 5 I'm more **inclined** to phone people than to send them a text. 6 I'm always tidy**ing** my house. I can't stand it when it's in a mess.

> **Alternative approach**
> Do this exercise as a race. Arrange Ss in pairs, and ask them to work together to find the mistakes as quickly as possible. The first pair to finish wins.

B   Read the example with the class. Give Ss five minutes to choose three or four sentences and change them about their partners. Monitor and check they are forming correct sentences. When they are ready, Ss read out their sentences for their partners to confirm or correct. In feedback, nominate Ss to tell the class something new they learnt about their partner.

PERSONALITY

4A   Check that Ss understand the first letter(s) of the missing words is given. Ss complete the sentences alone then check in pairs. In feedback, elicit Ss' answers. Listen carefully to Ss' pronunciation of the words (especially *mature, obstinate and conscientious*), and if necessary drill them chorally and individually.

> **Answers:** 1 mature 2 perceptive 3 obstinate 4 conscientious 5 open-minded 6 inquisitive

B   Read the example with the class. Ss work in pairs to describe occasions and guess the word. *Early finishers* can choose more words and repeat. In feedback, nominate Ss to share their occasions with the class.

SPECULATING

5A   Ss match the sentence halves alone then check in pairs. In feedback, elicit Ss' answers. As a follow-up, Ss can test each other in pairs by covering the first half of the sentences, then reading out the second halves in order to try and remember the phrases.

> **Answers:** 1 c) 2 f) 3 g) 4 d) 5 b) 6 h) 7 a) 8 e)

B   Give Ss some of your examples to demonstrate the activity (e.g. *I reckon my country will win the world cup. I'd hazard a guess that my boss won't give me a pay rise,* etc.). Ss write their sentences alone then check in pairs. In feedback, nominate Ss to share their ideas with the class.

OVERVIEW

WORDS OF WISDOM

Introduction

Ss revise and practise conditionals and regrets in the context of advice and learning. They also learn and practise metaphors related to careers and learning.

SUPPLEMENTARY MATERIALS

Resource bank p141 and p142

Warm up: write the words below on the board.

Warm up

Write the following on the board: *Teacher, family member, celebrity, doctor, author, other.* Ask Ss to choose one of these who has taught them an important lesson in life, and give them five minutes to think about what it was, when they heard it, and how it helped them. Monitor and help with vocabulary, writing any new words and phrases on the board. When they are ready, arrange Ss in small groups to share their ideas. In feedback, nominate Ss from each group to share their ideas with the class.

READING

1 Ss discuss which pieces of advice they agree/disagree with and why. Encourage them to expand on their reasons, giving examples where appropriate. In feedback, nominate Ss to share their opinions with the class, and find out how many Ss agree/disagree with each statement.

2A Elicit/check: *have the privilege of doing something* (something you are very lucky to do), *break a record, trust your instincts* and *the real estate* (property, especially in US English) *business*.

Ss read the article and match the speakers with the advice alone, then check in pairs. In feedback, elicit Ss' answers.

Answers: 1 e) 2 c) 3 f) 4 a) 5 i) 6 h) 7 d)

B Ss discuss the questions in small groups. Monitor and help with vocabulary, writing any new words and phrases on the board. In feedback, nominate Ss from each group to share their ideas with the class.

VOCABULARY learning

3A Focus attention on the introduction of the article and read the definition with the class. Elicit the answers as an example. Ss work alone to find the other expressions then check in pairs. In feedback, elicit Ss' answers and be prepared to give further explanations and examples where necessary.

Answers: 1 learning the ropes 2 came under attack
3 trusted my instincts 4 take advantage of opportunities
5 never (ever) give up 6 had a profound affect on
7 believe in yourself 8 on a steep learning curve

B Give Ss a few minutes to choose four questions and think about their answers. When they are ready, arrange Ss in small groups, and ask them to share their answers. Monitor and encourage Ss to ask follow-up questions. In feedback, nominate Ss from each group to share their ideas with the class.

Alternative approach

Arrange Ss into A/B pairs, and explain the activity. Ss discuss the questions as in Ex 3B, but each time you clap your hands, student B moves clockwise to the next student A. Repeat until Ss are back in their original places, then give student Bs 2 mins to tell student As everything they can remember from their discussions.

GRAMMAR conditionals and regrets

4A Write on the board: *I didn't study, so I failed the exam.* and elicit a conditional sentence and phrase for describing a regret (e.g. *If I'd studied, I would have passed. I regret not studying.*). Ss work alone to underline four conditional sentences and three phrases to describe regrets in paragraphs 2, 6 and 7, then check in pairs. In feedback, elicit Ss' answers.

> **Answers:** <u>Conditionals:</u> Had I been more confident, I wouldn't have listened. I could have done more interesting things if I'd trusted my instincts. If I'd known that statistic when I was learning the ropes, I'd be selling insurance today. But for our trust in each other, we would never have become so successful. <u>Regrets:</u> I regret wasting my twenties. If only I'd known then what I know now. I wish we hadn't listened.

B Ss answer the questions alone then check in pairs. In feedback, elicit Ss' answers.

> **Answers:** 1 *Had I* + past participle, *But for* + clause
> 2 More formal 3 Past perfect

C Ss answer the question alone then check in pairs. In feedback, elicit Ss' answers and be prepared to offer more explanations and examples where necessary.

> **Answer:** Mixed conditional: If I'd known that statistic when I was learning the ropes, I'd be selling insurance today.

⟹ **LANGUAGEBANK** 2.1 p130–131

Stronger classes can read the notes and do the exercises at home. Otherwise, check the notes with Ss, especially the use of *But for*. In each exercise, do the first sentence as an example. Ss complete the exercises alone, then check their answers in pairs. Ss can refer to the notes to help them.

> **Answers:** 1 1 had listened, wouldn't be 2 becoming, had spent 3 would have found, had called 4 had taken over, would have caused 5 told, would be staying 6 arriving, would have died 7 had known, wouldn't have cooked 8 not pulled, would have won
> 2 1 If we hadn't gambled on red, we would have won.
> 2 They wouldn't have asked him to the party if he wasn't/weren't famous. 3 The boys regret borrowing your car. 4 Had she known you were a vegetarian, she wouldn't have bought fish. 5 If only I hadn't forgotten my keys, we wouldn't be locked out! 6 If I hadn't dropped out of university, I wouldn't be working in a boring, low-paid job. 7 Ahmed wishes he had spoken to you before you left. 8 But for his injury, we would have won.

Watch out!

After *I wish I …* and *If only I …*, or in 2nd conditional sentences we can use *were* or *was* (e.g. *I wish I were rich*, or *I wish I was rich*) *He would love this if he was/were here.* *Were* is recommended and more acceptable, but *was* is increasingly used in spoken English, and sounds more informal.

PRACTICE

5A Elicit/check: *a stonecutter, to chip stone,* and *a magic spirit.* Write on the board: *How many times did the spirit transform the man?* and give Ss one minute to read the text quickly, ignoring the gaps, and answer the question (answer: 6). Ss work alone to complete the gaps in the story, then check in pairs. In feedback, elicit Ss' answers.

> **Answers:** 1 been 2 wish 3 Had 4 have 5 But 6 only
> 7 would 8 regret

Teaching tip

Gapped texts such as in Ex 5A are very common in many international exams. It's a good idea for Ss to read the text quickly (ignoring the gaps) first, as this helps them familiarise themselves with the context. This in turn will help them generate ideas when completing the gaps.

B Elicit/check what the moral of a story is (a piece of advice that the story is used to illustrate). Ss complete the moral in pairs. In feedback, elicit Ss' ideas. There is no 'correct' answer here, so accept all suggestions.

C ▶ 2.1 Elicit the first answer as an example. Ss discuss which sentences can use contractions in pairs. Play the recording for Ss to check their answers, then check answers with the class. Play the recording again for Ss to repeat the sentences, and make sure they are pronouncing the contractions correctly.

> **Answers:** 3 Had I known this, <u>I'd</u> have asked to become a cloud. 4 If <u>I'd</u> been stronger, I <u>could've</u> stopped the wind. 5 But for my weakness, I <u>would've</u> blown that mountain down. 6 If only <u>I'd</u> been transformed into a mountain, <u>I'd</u> be the strongest of all. 7 If only <u>I'd</u> known this I <u>would've</u> remained a stonecutter.

Optional extra activity

Take 8 blank sheets of paper (or fewer if you have a small class), and at the top of each one, write one of the following sentence starters:

If my teacher hadn't arrived today …

I wouldn't have got out of bed this morning if …

But for my friend's recent actions, …

If I married a monkey …

I wouldn't be here now if …

I'd eat my shoes if …

I could have become an astronaut if …

Had I not started learning English when I did, …

Stick the pieces of paper to the walls around the classroom. Ss walk round the class and add their own endings to each sentence on the pieces of paper. When they have finished, arrange Ss in small groups and allocate one or more of the sheets to them (depending on numbers in your class). Ss work in groups to correct any errors in the sentences, and choose their favourite sentence for each one. In feedback, nominate a student from each group to share their answers.

As a follow-up, collect the pieces of paper and correct any errors on the board with the class.

SPEAKING

6A Ss complete the sentences alone. Monitor and help with vocabulary, writing any new words and phrases on the board, and check they are forming conditionals and regrets correctly.

B Arrange Ss in small groups. Ss share their sentences, elaborating as much as possible. Monitor and note any common errors and good uses of language for later feedback. In feedback, nominate Ss from each group to share any interesting information with the class, and give Ss feedback on their language.

VOCABULARY *PLUS* metaphors

7A Ss read the metaphor and choose the correct meaning in pairs. In feedback, elicit the answer, and ask if Ss have a similar metaphor in their own language(s).

Answer: a)

B Ss discuss the questions in pairs. In feedback, nominate Ss to share their ideas with the class, and have a brief class discussion.

Answers: 2 Metaphors add colour to descriptions and help us to visualise a subject. 3 They help to communicate an idea because they allow us to compare one thing to another.

speakout TIP

Read the **speakout tip** with the class and explain that recording metaphors by topic helps them remember them and also makes it easier to retrieve them when they want to use them. Explain that they are now going to learn some metaphors, and they should record them in their notebook by topic, as suggested. After Ex 9B, elicit any similar idioms in the Ss' language(s).

8 Focus attention on the picture and elicit which two 'themes' are illustrated (work/business and journeys). Ss underline the phrases and match them to their meanings alone then check in pairs. In feedback, elicit Ss' answers.

Answers: 1 go downhill 2 at a crossroads 3 you'll go far 4 reach the peak

9A Divide the class into two halves: As and Bs. As underline the metaphors and match to their meanings on p22, and Bs do the same on p159, then check with other Ss in the same group. When they are ready, go to each group and check Ss' answers.

Answers: p22: 1 regurgitate 2 hard to swallow 3 half-baked (idea) 4 food for thought
p159: 1 put aside some time 2 wasting precious time 3 can't afford to spend time 4 living on borrowed time

B Rearrange Ss in pairs, so that each pair has a student A and a student B (if you have an odd number of Ss, have one group of three). Ss take it in turns to read out their texts twice, while their partner listens for metaphors. Ss peer-teach their four metaphors to their partners. Monitor and help where necessary. In feedback, check Ss understand the metaphors and be prepared to provide further explanations and examples where necessary.

Alternative approach

When Ss read out their texts for their partners, they can do this as 'human audio players'. Elicit/check the basic 'controls' (*play, pause, rewind, forward*). While their partner, is listening they use the 'controls' (eg calling out 'Rewind!' 'Stop!' 'Play!' 'Pause!') in order to get further clarification or help to identify the metaphors. This helps them feel in control and listen at their own pace.

10 Read the example with the class. Ss replace the underlined phrases alone then check in pairs. In feedback, elicit Ss' answers.

Answers: 2 hard to swallow 3 put aside some time 4 half-baked 5 go downhill 6 living on borrowed time 7 the peak 8 food for thought

11A Give Ss enough time to think of and write their ideas alone. Monitor and help with vocabulary, writing any new words and phrases on the board.

B Arrange Ss in small groups. Ss take it in turns to explain their ideas to the group. Monitor and encourage Ss to ask follow-up questions. In feedback, nominate Ss from each group to share their ideas with the class.

➡ VOCABULARYBANK p149 METAPHORS

1 Write on the board: *Intelligence as light, Theories as buildings* and *Business as war*, and elicit any metaphors Ss know under these topics. Ss match the idioms to their meanings alone then check in pairs. In feedback, elicit Ss' answers.
Stronger classes can do the exercises at home.

Answers: 1 a flash of inspiration = a clever idea that comes suddenly 2 shone = was especially good at something 3 bright = intelligent 4 dim = not very intelligent 5 constructed = developed 6 support = help prove 7 falls down = fails 8 foundations = basis 9 a killing = a big profit 10 launched an aggressive campaign = began an intense series of actions 11 targeting = aimed at 12 join forces = merge together

Homework ideas
- Language bank 2.1 Ex 1–2, p131
- Vocabulary bank p149 Ex 1
- Workbook Ex 1–6, p9–10

CHANGING YOUR MIND

Introduction

Ss revise and practise verb patterns in the context of living libraries. They also practise writing a discursive essay.

SUPPLEMENTARY MATERIALS

Resource bank p140 and p143

Warm up: write the words below on the board.

Warm up

Write the following words on the board: *university students, homeless people, foreign tourists, the elderly* and *teenagers*. Ss discuss which common stereotypes of these groups exist in their country or countries in pairs, and how far they agree with them. In feedback, elicit ideas and have a brief discussion.

LISTENING

1A Elicit/check: *preconceptions* and *stigmas*. Write the following question on the board: *Do you think living libraries are a good idea? Why/why not?* Ss read the text then discuss the question in pairs before feedback with the class.

B ▶ **2.2** Read the questions with the class and check understanding. Ss listen and answer the questions alone then check in pairs. In feedback, elicit Ss' answers.

Answers: 1 A 2 S 3 S 4 A 5 A 6 S

2 Give Ss three or four minutes to try to answer the questions from memory. Play the recording for Ss to check their answers, then check in pairs. In feedback, elicit Ss' answers.

Answers: 1 'lazy', 'politically apathetic', 'do useless degrees' 'wastes tax payers' money' 'can't cook' and 'spends all his money on beer' 2 Nervous that he wouldn't be able to deal with the accusations. 3 He expected him to make accusations against him. 4 They talked about life as a student in the 1960s and compared it with student life today. 5 That she was fiercely independent. 6 She is hoping to tackle the stigma often associated with being blind (that it makes you helpless) 7 She leads a fairly normal life, doing most things for herself, but she is unable to drive.
8 She feels that she is able to 'see' people for who they really are, on the inside, rather than just how they want to present themselves, by their appearance. She is less likely to judge people for how they look. She is able to 'see with her heart' rather than her eyes.

Unit 2 Recording 2

A = Alex S = Saba

The book – Alex

A: Now, you might think of a library as a dusty old place full of books that nobody uses any more. After all, when we need to research something, we tend to do it on the net nowadays. But in a 'living library' the books are real people. People who can share a significant personal experience, or a particular perspective on life. I volunteered to be a book at a living library event in Sheffield. The event was organised by the university and was meant to tackle prejudices. Arriving in a bit of a hurry, I looked through the catalogue of available books to sign myself in, as 'a student'. Against each 'book' are a few of the typical prejudices and preconceptions people might associate with your 'title'. Next to 'student' were written things like 'lazy', 'politically apathetic', 'do useless degrees'.

And also 'wastes tax payers' money' 'can't cook' and 'spends all his money on beer'. Thinking back to the previous night, I wasn't sure how I was going to tackle any of these accusations. Sitting in the waiting room was rather surreal, with 'books' asking each other 'Who are you?' and already I was beginning to have second thoughts. When the public started coming in, it was like sitting on a shelf, waiting and hoping that someone would choose you, and hoping that you would be able to find something to say when they did. Luckily, I didn't have to wait long. An older man, grey hair and a suit, came to collect me. As we walked over to our designated corner, I planned my responses to the rail of expected accusations. In fact, as we talked over coffee, we compared experiences – student life in the 1960s, with the riots and protests, wild music, and the ambitions they had of changing the world. And student life now. Interestingly, we found that we shared a lot of the same ideologies, that many things haven't really changed. I think the directness of the experience was eye-opening really. The candid discussion forces people to keep an open mind about things, and that has to be good.

The reader – Saba

S: If, like me, you're the kind of person that is curious about other types of people that you don't know personally, then I think you'd enjoy the 'living book' experience. I went to a three-hour session in Norwich, and was surprised at how much I learned. It gives you a chance to really talk to people, who may be from a different religion, or culture – people who you don't normally get to talk to in your everyday life. I met all kinds of people, some wonderful people. One of them was Karrie, a blind woman. Karrie is visually impaired, having lost her sight due to illness when she was a child. The first thing that struck me about Karrie is that she's fiercely independent. She doesn't like other people doing things for her, so you can imagine that can be a bit difficult. Her mission was to tackle the stigma that people attach to blind people, that they are helpless. She wants to challenge the stereotype that just because a person can't see, they can't do anything for themselves. Karrie lives a perfectly normal life, gets dressed by herself, goes to work, goes out socially – and does all the things that the rest of us do. Well, she can't drive, but that was really one of her few limitations. She told me about successful blind people around the world who have had a great impact on society – people who have been successfully employed, er taken advanced degrees, published books, written music, and participated in athletic and even Olympic events. These are the people that have been Karrie's inspiration. She also talked about how many blind people use their other senses, which happen to be quite developed. So, Karrie feels that she is quite a good judge of character, because she is able to 'see' people for who they really are, on the inside, rather than just how they want to present themselves, or how you may judge them because of the clothes they're wearing, or the scar they may have. As she put it, she is able to 'see with her heart' rather than her eyes. My conversation with Karrie gave me a whole new perspective. It taught me not to be narrow-minded about disability, and I thank her for that.

VOCABULARY opinions

3A Ss underline the correct alternatives alone then check in pairs. In feedback, elicit Ss' answers and be prepared to provide further explanations and examples where necessary.

Answers: 1 preconceptions 2 challenge the stereotypes 3 have second thoughts 4 keep an open mind 5 narrow-minded 6 eye-opening 7 perspective 8 convincing

B Read the first example with the class. Ss respond to the situations alone, then check in pairs.

Answers: 2 It was an eye-opening experience. It has given me a whole new perspective. 3 I had some preconceptions about what he was going to be like. 4 I don't find the arguments for nuclear power very convincing. 5 Losing my job gave me a whole new perspective on what life is like without work.

C Ss discuss the questions in pairs. Monitor and help where necessary. In feedback, nominate Ss from each pair to share their ideas with the class.

⟹ VOCABULARYBANK p149 OPINIONS

2A Ss choose the correct alternatives alone then check in pairs. In feedback, elicit Ss' answers, and be prepared to provide further explanations/examples where necessary.

B Ss complete the sentences alone then check in pairs. In feedback, elicit Ss' answers.
Stronger classes can do the exercises at home.

Answers: 2A 1 general 2 keep 3 personal 4 opinionated 5 difference 6 divided 7 matter 8 entitled
B 1 personal 2 opinionated 3 difference 4 divided 5 matter 6 entitled 7 keep 8 general

GRAMMAR verb patterns

4A The aim of this exercise is to give you (and Ss) a chance to test how much they know about verb patterns. Feedback to this exercise should give you an idea of how much detail you need to go into, and whether you need to do the **Language bank** exercises in class, or whether Ss can do them at home. Ss underline the correct alternatives alone then check in pairs.

Answers: 1 to say 2 to ask, being, feeling 3 to offer, to challenge 4 talking, being 5 to be 6 sleeping, to deal

B Read the example with the class and check Ss understand what to do. Ss find examples of the verbs alone then check in pairs. In feedback, elicit Ss' answers.

Answers: 2 scared to say 3 wanted to offer 4 admit feeling 5 freedom to ask; arguments for being 6 wanted to offer 7 enjoyed talking 8 Sleeping outside 9 advised me to be

C Read the example with the class and check Ss understand what to do. Ss find examples of the verbs alone then check in pairs. In feedback, elicit Ss' answers, and check which situation can be used with both structures.

Answers: 2 infinitive with *to* 3 infinitive with *to* 4 verb+ *-ing* 5 freedom to ask = infinitive with *to*; arguments for being = verb+ *-ing* 6 infinitive with *to* 7 verb+ *-ing* 8 verb+ *-ing* 9 infinitive with *to*

Watch out!

Like can be followed by the infinitive or verb + *-ing*, however there is a subtle difference in meaning between the two. *Like* + verb + *-ing* describes a true feeling e.g. *I don't like getting up early*. *Like* + infinitive means there is a reason for the preference e.g. *On a Monday morning, I like to get up early to plan my work for the week.*

D Ss match the examples with the rules alone then check in pairs. In feedback, elicit Ss' answers and be prepared to give further explanations and examples where necessary.

Answers: 1 rule b) 2 rule c) 3 rule a)

⟹ LANGUAGEBANK 2.2 p130–131

Stronger classes can read the notes and do the exercises at home. Otherwise, check the notes with Ss, especially the use of the passive/perfect infinitive and *-ing* form. In each exercise, do the first sentence as an example. Ss complete the exercises alone, then check their answers in pairs. Ss can refer to the notes to help them.

Answers: 1 1 making 2 to underestimate 3 to impress 4 walking 5 to have formed 6 to say 7 judging 8 to do 9 to give
2 1 Correct. 2 I don't know why you waste all your time sitting in front of the computer. 3 Cooder was encouraged to play the guitar by his father. 4 They hoped to meet up with some of the stars after the show. 5 They were rumoured to have got married in secret. 6 I gave up the idea of going into politics when I was in my 30s. 7 We were tempted to ask if we could stay the night, but we thought it might seem rude. 8 Correct.

PRACTICE

5A Ss complete the sentences alone then check in pairs. In feedback, elicit Ss' answers.

Answers: 1 to feel 2 Meeting, having 3 to ask 4 to imagine 5 leaving 6 to marry 7 to have lost 8 being

Alternative approach

Arrange Ss in small groups. Give Ss 3–4 mins to discuss their answers to Ex 5A, but don't let them write their answers yet. When they are ready, call out a number to the class, and the first team to call out the correct answer for that sentence wins a point. At the end, the group with the most points wins. Give Ss 3–4 mins to complete Ex 5A alone, writing their answers. In feedback, elicit Ss' answers.

B Give Ss two or three minutes to think of ideas and write them down alone. Monitor and help with vocabulary, writing any new words and phrases on the board.

C When they are ready, Ss discuss their ideas in pairs. In feedback, nominate Ss to share their ideas with the class.

SPEAKING

6A Give Ss a few minutes to read the statements and mark how strongly they agree/disagree with each one.

B Arrange Ss in small groups. Ss first decide which two statements they want to discuss, then share their opinions. They then modify the sentence (not their opinions), until everyone in the group agrees. Monitor and note any common errors, examples of good language for later feedback. *Early finishers* can discuss/modify more of the statements.

C Nominate Ss from each group to share their modified sentences with the rest of the class, and allow a class discussion to develop. Encourage all Ss to contribute by asking for their opinions. At the end, give feedback on their language.

WRITING a discursive essay

7A Focus attention on the photo and elicit what Ss can see. Write two headings on the board: *Reasons for homelessness. Ways to reduce the problem.* Ss discuss the questions in pairs. Elicit Ss' ideas and write them under the headings.

B Ss read the essay, and check if any of their ideas are mentioned. In feedback, elicit the ideas in the article, and tick any of the ones on the board that are mentioned.

8 Ss read the guidelines and compare the essay alone then check in pairs. In feedback, elicit Ss' answers by going through the guidelines and checking how far the essay meets them.

Answers: It follows the advice: 1 It has an introductory paragraph. 2 It uses paragraphs to explain the for and against arguments. 3 It includes linkers. 4 It has a concluding paragraph which includes the writer's opinion

LEARN TO use linking devices

9A Ss complete the table alone then check in pairs. In feedback, elicit Ss' answers and be prepared to further explain the meaning/use of each linker where necessary.

Answers: 1 Additionally, in addition to this, furthermore, Likewise 2 however, On the other hand, nevertheless 3 Consequently, so, for this reason … 4 In fact, In conclusion

speakout TIP

Read the **speakout tip** with the class, and explain that using correct punctuation in discursive texts is important in order to have a good effect on the reader. Ss find examples of the linkers in the different positions, then compare in pairs.

B Check Ss understand that two of the alternatives are correct, and one is incorrect. Ss delete the incorrect alternative alone then check in pairs. In feedback, discuss why the incorrect alternative can't be used.

Answers: 1 in conclusion, However 2 On the contrary 3 hence 4 thus 5 To conclude 6 In addition to this, obviously

10A Arrange Ss in small groups. Remind Ss of the discussions they had in Ex 6A. Ss choose one of the statements and discuss how far they agree/disagree with it in their groups. Encourage Ss to takes notes of any interesting arguments/reasons that come up and explain that they will be able to use these later. In feedback, nominate Ss from each group to share their ideas with the class.

B Remind Ss of the advice for planning your writing from Unit 1.1 Ex 10A. Ss plan their essays, making notes of arguments they can make and reasons for them. Monitor and help where necessary.

C Ss write their essays alone. Monitor and help with vocabulary, writing any new words and phrases on the board. Check Ss are using a range of appropriate linkers. When they have finished, Ss swap essays with a partner and discuss how well they follow the guidelines in Ex 8.

Homework ideas
• Ex 10C: write a final draft of your discursive essay.
• write a discursive essay based on one of the other topics in Exercise 6A.
• Language bank 2.2 Ex 1–2, p131
• Workbook Ex 1–6, p11–12

WHO DO YOU TRUST?

Introduction

Ss learn and practise phrases for introducing their opinions and how to express doubt.

SUPPLEMENTARY MATERIALS

Resource bank p144

Warm up: write the letters of the alphabet on the board.

Warm up

On the board, write the letters of the alphabet in order, with space next to each letter to add a word. Arrange Ss in small groups. Ss try to think of a job that begins with each letter of the alphabet and write it down. Stop them after five minutes and elicit their answers, writing the jobs on the board. The group with the most jobs wins.

SPEAKING

1A Arrange Ss in small groups. With *multilingual classes*, try to include a mix of nationalities in each group. Focus attention on the photos and elicit which jobs Ss think they show. Write any new vocabulary on the board. Ss discuss the questions. In feedback, nominate Ss from each group to share their ideas with the class.

B Elicit/check: *trustworthy*, *clergy* (the official leaders of religious activities in organised religions) and *in good faith* (intending to be honest and not deceive anyone). Ss read the article, then discuss if the same is true in their country or countries in pairs. In feedback, ask Ss to share their ideas with the class. With *monolingual classes*, ask if other Ss agree, and with *multilingual classes*, compare ideas from different countries.

VOCABULARY idioms of opinion

2A Ss underline the idioms in the article alone then check in pairs, and discuss what they mean. In feedback, elicit Ss' answers.

Answers: Dr David Bailey says, 'I've got a real vested interest'. To have a vested interest means you are not neutral because you have personal reasons for wanting things to be a particular way. Professor Justin Lewis says, 'We don't have an axe to grind', which means the opposite.

B Ss underline the idioms and choose the correct meanings alone then check in pairs. In feedback, elicit Ss' answers and be prepared to provide further explanations and examples where necessary.

Answers: 1 play devil's advocate – b) 2 speak my mind – b) 3 sitting on the fence – a) 4 beat about the bush – b)

Optional extra activity

Ss choose two of the idioms from Ex 2B, and think of and write a situation (true or false) from their lives when they did the action described in the idiom. Monitor and help with vocabulary, writing any new words and phrases on the board. When they are ready, arrange Ss in pairs. Ss read out their situations to their partner for them to try and guess the idiom.

C Answer the question with the class.

Answer: All of these can be used to introduce opinions or knowledge.

FUNCTION introducing opinions

3A ▶ 2.3 Ss listen to the debate and answer the question in pairs. Tell Ss not to worry if they don't understand everything, just to listen for the main points. In feedback, elicit Ss' answers.

Answers: Issue: whether we can trust the news we read these days. Conclusion: that most journalists are honest but a few of them give all journalists a bad name.

B Give Ss a couple of minutes to read the statements and check what they can remember. Play the recording again for Ss to listen and tick which ideas are mentioned, then check in pairs. In feedback, elicit Ss' answers.

Answers: 1, 3, 4, 5, 6, 7, 8

Teaching tip

At this level, it's important to train Ss to get as much information as they can from listening to an extract once. This mirrors real life, where Ss may not get a second chance to listen. By allowing them to compare their answers in pairs before feedback, they may be able to combine answers. This means they'll be more confident in feedback and may not need to listen again.

4A Ss complete the expressions from memory then check in pairs. In feedback, elicit Ss' ideas but don't give any answers yet.

B Ss find the expressions in the audio script 2.3 on p166 and check their answers. In feedback, elicit Ss' answers and drill the expressions chorally and individually.

Answers: 1 opinion 2 frankly 3 to 4 gather 5 concerned 6 ask

Teaching tip

Some researchers make an important distinction between *acquisition* and *learning*. The first is where Ss 'pick up' language, often unconsciously, and the second is where Ss consciously study new language. By providing Ss with authentic texts, and asking them to 'pick out' language, we are combining the two processes, and making language learning more memorable.

Unit 2 Recording 3

M1= Man 1 W1=Woman 1 M2 = Man 2 W2 = Woman 2

M1: As far as I'm concerned, we cannot trust the news we read these days.

W1: Mmm

M2: Why not?

M1: Because journalists have an axe to grind.

M2: What? That's debatable.

M1: I think it's very rare to get a truly impartial journalist. I don't think it's within human nature to be impartial. You side on one side or the other.

M2: Why why would a journalist want to be partial? Why would a journalist not want to be impartial? Surely that's the job of a journalist.

W2: Oooh, I don't know about that.

M1: It it is … why?

W2: No I I'm agreeing with you. I'm just saying I think there are some journalists who cannot be trusted. They have an agenda … they, they aren't there to tell the truth, they're there to sell newspapers … or they have an axe to grind.

M1: Yeah, it's a job, they're being paid and er effectively they're the mouthpiece for whoever is paying them.

M2: But isn't the job of a journalist to be, to be rigorous. I mean if somebody comes up with a piece of nonsense, or just whatever er you know a piece of received information that they're spouting, isn't the job of a journalist to get to the bottom of that and say: what do you really mean by that, have you got proof of it, who, you know, what are your sources? That's their job, surely?

W1: Exactly, you know they're going in there asking where's the evidence for what you're saying? They're not just going to say, you know – oh you tell me every sheep in Wales is blue and they're not going to go ooh right I'll just write down every sheep in Wales is blue. They're going to say right, well show me photographs, take me and show me these sheep.

M1: But but the bigger issue here if you ask me is that they're there to sell newspapers and newspaper owners have political agendas.

W2: Quite frankly, it's a business as well isn't it?

M1: It's a political business.

M2: From what I can gather about the nature of … of the dispassionate idea of being a journalist, what a journalist is after is the truth. If that journalist then goes to work for a particular paper that's got a particular angle … a particular axe to grind then, certainly that journalist may err towards one side of the political spectrum or the other. But only a bit, I would say. I would say they are still after truth at its heart.

W1: Exactly. Surely any journalist worth his or her salt is going to make the case for both sides? Anybody just arguing one side in a totally biased way is not going to be taken seriously.

M1: Why? Why are there so many libel trials then if we can trust everything journalists write?

W2: And from what I can gather, people and journalists included don't even know that they're biased and they'll write, you know, something trying to be impartial and they, they won't realise that actually they have a slant on it, you can't help it.

W1: I find that highly unlikely. I mean, they're not stupid people, are they?

M1: Some of them are, for some newspapers, the way they write, incredibly stupid.

W2: But surely the people being libelled are just people who didn't like what was said about them?

M2: Could we … do you think we could agree that the basic honesty of journalists is probably not to be questioned but that there are a few bad apples in the cart?

W2: Yeah.

M2: And that there are journalists who give other, you know, who are bad journalists, who are partisan and who are arguing a particular political slant who give other journalists a bad name.

M1: Well, I'd say that there are a few bad carts rather than a few bad apples!

⟹ LANGUAGEBANK 2.3 p130–131

Stronger classes could read the notes and do the exercise at home. Otherwise, drill the phrases from the chart, checking Ss are using natural intonation. Ss work alone to match the sentence halves, then check their answers in pairs. In feedback, elicit Ss' answers.

Answers: 1 a) 2 c) 3 i) 4 h) 5 f) 6 g) 7 b) 8 d) 9 e)

5A Ss chooser the correct alternative alone then check in pairs. In feedback, elicit Ss' answers.

Answers: 1 In 2 gather 3 concerned 4 knowledge 5 ask 6 honest

B Ss discuss their opinions in pairs. Encourage them to give reasons for their opinions. In feedback, nominate Ss to share their opinions with the class and have a brief discussion.

LEARN TO express doubt

6A ▶ 2.4 Elicit what Ss say when they doubt someone's opinion. Focus attention on the phrases. Ss listen and tick the phrases they hear, then check in pairs. In feedback, elicit Ss' answers and drill the phrases chorally and individually.

Answers: phrases 1, 3 and 4 are used.

Unit 2 Recording 4

Extract 1
A: Journalists have an axe to grind.
B: What? That's debatable.

Extract 2
A: Why would a journalist not want to be partial?
B: Oooh… I don't know about that.

Extract 3
A: Journalists don't even know that they're biased.
B: I find that highly unlikely.

B Read the question with the class and elicit Ss' answers.

Answer: 1

C ▶ 2.5 Ss listen to the recording, paying attention to the intonation on the modifiers. Play the recording again for Ss to listen and repeat.

Unit 2 Recording 5

1 I really don't know about that.
2 I'm really not sure about that.
3 That's highly debatable.
4 I find that highly unlikely.

SPEAKING

7A Give Ss five minutes to read the cases and make notes. Monitor and help with ideas and vocabulary, writing any new words and phrases on the board.

B Arrange Ss in groups of 3. Ss debate the issues in each case. Encourage them to use the phrases for introducing opinions and expressing doubt, and monitor and note any common errors and examples of good language for later feedback. In feedback, nominate Ss from each group to share their ideas with the class, and give Ss feedback on their language.

Alternative approach
Arrange the Ss in two large groups. While making notes for Ex 7A, one half of the class should adopt a 'strict' approach, while the other should adopt a 'lenient' approach. Each group should think of measures to take and reasons for their respective measures. When they are ready, arrange Ss in pairs with one student from each group to discuss which measures they would take, and try to agree on the best course of action.

C Ss turn to p159 and compare their ideas with what the bosses did, then discuss if they agree in their groups. In feedback, elicit Ss' ideas.

Homework ideas
• Ex 7B: write about your advice for each situation.
• Language bank 2.3 Ex 1, p131
• Workbook Ex 1–4, p13

THE MAKING OF ME

Introduction

Ss watch an extract from the BBC documentary *The Making of Me*, in which a famous violinist talks about her ability. Ss learn and practise how to take part in a panel discussion, and write a summary.

SUPPLEMENTARY MATERIALS

Warm up: Bring or download pictures of Beethoven and Picasso.

Warm up

Bring or download pictures of Beethoven and Picasso to show Ss and write their names on the board. Arrange Ss in small teams. Elicit a name for each team, and write it on the board. Each group appoints a 'secretary', who will write their answers on a separate piece of paper. Read out the statements. Ss listen, confer and write *B* for Beethoven or *P* for Picasso for each one.

1 He became deaf in later life. (B)

2 His father was very strict. (B)

3 His full name consisted of 23 words. (P)

4 He dedicated one of his works to Napoleon. (B)

5 His first word was 'pencil'. (P)

6 He only drank coffee made with exactly 60 beans per cup. (B)

7 He married twice and had four children. (P)

8 When he was born, the midwife thought he was stillborn. (P)

When they are ready, teams exchange their answers with other teams to mark. Go through the answers, and award points. The team with the most points wins.

▶ DVD PREVIEW

1A Arrange Ss in small groups to discuss the meanings of the words in bold. In feedback, elicit Ss' answers and check understanding. Be prepared to provide further explanations and examples where necessary.

Answers: innate talent: a special ability that you were born with; put their success down to: attribute their success to; lifelong passion: something you have been dedicated to all your life; academically/artistically gifted: particularly good at academic studies / art; inherit: derive genetically from your parents / ancestors; traits: distinguishing qualities or characteristics; to shape: help determine

B Ss discuss the questions in the same groups as in Ex 1A. In feedback, nominate Ss from each group to share their ideas with the class.

Culture notes

Vanessa-Mae Vanakorn Nicholson was born in Singapore to a Chinese mother and Thai father, but moved to England when she was four when her mother married Graham Nicholson. She is an internationally successful violinist who has produced over 12 albums and describes her music as 'violin techno-acoustic fusion'. In April 2006 she was named as the wealthiest young entertainer under 30 in the UK. She also plans to compete as a downhill skier in the 2014 Winter Olympics, representing Thailand.

2 Elicit/check: *the Rich List* and *a turbulent* relationship. Give Ss 2 mins to read the programme information then discuss the question in pairs. In feedback, elicit Ss' answers.

Answers: 1 She is a talented musician / violinist. 2 Her mother was very influential. 3 She would like to understand whether her musical success is due to a talent she was born with, or is the result of her upbringing and own work.

▶ DVD VIEW

3 Read the questions with the class and check Ss know what to listen for. Ss watch the DVD and answer the questions, then check their answers in pairs. In feedback, elicit Ss' answers.

Answers: 1 It was a turbulent relationship because she understood that her mother's love was conditional on her being good at playing the violin. Her mother groomed her to be a violinist. 2 She feels that she was born with a special ability, but that her practice and dedication helped her to develop her talent, so in the end, the ratio was about 50:50. Initially, she had thought that her innate talent accounted for more than 50% (75%) of her ability. 3 No, Vanessa doesn't seem very happy because she feels that she missed out on having a 'normal childhood'.

4A Ss complete the extracts in pairs from memory. Monitor and help where necessary, but don't give any answers yet.

B Play the DVD again for Ss to check their answers. In feedback, elicit Ss' answers.

Answers: 1 30 million pounds 2 history, memory, beauty 3 conditional 4 mind, psychologists 5 parent 6 tears

5 Ss discuss the questions in pairs. Monitor and help with vocabulary, writing any new words and phrases on the board. In feedback, nominate Ss to share their ideas with the class.

The Making of Me: Vanessa-Mae

C=commentary V=Vanessa-Mae P=Psychologist

C: With a fortune in excess of thirty million pounds, Vanessa-Mae is one of Britain's most successful young musicians.

V: This beautiful instrument has given me so much history and memory and beauty in my life. It has basically dictated my life.

C: From her early years as a musical prodigy to the glamour of money and celebrity, Vanessa's entire life has been shaped by music. But for fifteen years someone else helped to forge her career: Pamela, Vanessa's mother.

V: I was always made to appreciate that the love my mother had for me was conditional. She said to me, you know 'I will always love you cos you're my daughter, but you're only special to me because you play the violin. And if you play the violin well then you're special to me.'

C: Now Vanessa wants to know whether her musical success was down to her or her mother.

V: I need to work out whether I was born to play the violin or if I was talked into playing the violin. Was it nature or nurture that played a bigger part? … That's really my brain?

C: To help Vanessa find the answer, science will test her body and her mind.

V: Whoa!

C: She'll be observed by psychologists.

P: She seems quite aggressive at this point. I think she realises she's running out of time.

C: And be pushed to the limit.

C: Vanessa ends her journey by answering the question that started it: how much did Pamela contribute to her musical life?

V: The key thing for me on this was finding out that emotionally I may have become the person I became because of, you know, the parent in my life. I mean I was groomed to be a violinist. It wasn't a normal childhood and to be cut off from so many different things, means that I didn't get to know who I was or make any choices until I was pretty old.

At the start of my journey, I thought that what set me apart from say another violinist with the same amount of training was nature, so that's why I thought seventy-five percent nature, twenty-five percent nurture.

But now I think there's nothing to be ashamed of that it was my blood, my sweat and my tears that brought me here today, even though there was a huge part my mother played in that, it's still the experiences I went through.

So I'm gonna shift towards fifty percent nurture now, and fifty percent nature.

speakout a panel discussion

6A ▶ 2.6 Read through the questions with the class and check they know what to listen for. Ss listen and answer the questions, then check in pairs. In feedback, elicit Ss' answers.

> **Answers:** The speaker presents the 'nurture' side of the argument, suggesting that people do not inherit their abilities but that they develop them through experience.
> She uses the example that a child born with a natural ability for music will not develop into a good pianist unless he or she practises the piano.

B Focus attention on the **Key phrases**. Ss listen and tick the phrases they hear, then check in pairs. In feedback, elicit Ss' answers and drill the **Key phrases** chorally and individually.

> **Answers:** I'd like to begin by stating that, As I see it …, I think it's ridiculous to suggest …, I absolutely reject the idea that …, So, to conclude I would have to argue that, Does anyone have a question …? / Are there any other questions?, That's a good question, because …

C Ss categorise the phrases alone, then check in pairs. In feedback, elicit Ss' answers and drill the phrases chorally and individually.

> **Answers:**
> Introduce the argument: I'd like to begin by stating that
> Justify their opinion: As I see it … /What I think is… I would say it depends on…, What you need to consider is …, I think it's ridiculous to suggest …, I absolutely reject the idea that …
> Conclude: So, to conclude I would have to argue that …
> Invite questions: Does anyone have a question …? / Are there any other questions?
> Respond to questions: That's a good question, because …

Unit 2 Recording 6

S=Speaker C=Chairperson Q=Questioner

S: OK, I'm going to talk about the influence of nature versus nurture. And I'd like to begin by stating that, as I see it, by far the strongest influence has to be 'nurture'. The reason I think this is that I believe the way we're brought up will have a much stronger influence on how we behave than anything that's in our genes. I mean, some people will argue that our abilities are determined pretty much exclusively by our genes, so if your father was a great scientist with a natural ability for mathematics, then there's a pretty good chance that you might inherit that same ability. Personally, I think it's ridiculous to suggest this. I think that when a parent has a particular strength, or interest, or achieves something wonderful in a particular field, then the chances are that when they have children, they

will try to instil in the children the same kind of interest, they will pass on their knowledge, their passion for the subject, they are quite likely to engage the child in activities related to that field, perhaps for quite a lot of the child's time. And it's as a result of this that the child may also develop strengths or abilities in the same field. I absolutely reject the idea that nature endows us with these inborn abilities. I mean, you can be born with the best natural musical ability in the universe, but if you don't practise the piano, then nothing will come of it. On the other hand, I think you can teach people to do just about anything, so long as you dedicate time and give the child the right kind of encouragement, or put them in the right situation. So, to conclude I would have to argue that 'nurture' plays a much stronger role in the development of who you are, and the talents that you develop than 'nature' does.

C: OK. Thank you. And now, let's open the discussion up and take questions from the floor. Does anyone have a question for one of the speakers?

Q: Yes, I'd like to ask a question to the last speaker. I think it is quite obvious if you look around you, that people often very much resemble their parents in terms of their physical appearance, and even their characters. Why then, do you not think that it is equally possible that a child will inherit its parents' ability, or intelligence?

S: That's a good question, because yes, we can see that we do inherit physical characteristics from our parents. However, the point I'm trying to make is that we cannot rely on something we are assumed to be born with. For me, the influence of nurture is far stronger. I believe that everyone has the same potential, they just need to be given the right conditions to nurture and develop that potential. Thank you for the question.

C: Thank you. Are there any other questions?

7A Arrange Ss in small groups. Read the statement with the class, and elicit an example of a point 'for' and 'against' e.g. *For: they would learn basic skills such as reading and writing more quickly, Against: Children need time to develop through play before they start school.* Ss work together to create their lists. Monitor and help with vocabulary, writing any new words and phrases on the board.

B Ss choose whether their group will argue 'for' or 'against'. Check you have a balance of groups for each side. While Ss are preparing, monitor and encourage them to use the **Key phrases** from Ex 6B.

C When they are ready, Ss present their arguments to the class. Act as chairperson and encourage Ss to ask questions. In feedback, elicit which group argued their case most clearly.

writeback a summary

8A Ss read the post then summarise the key points in pairs. In feedback, elicit Ss' answers.

> **Suggested answer:** The writer suggests that teaching a young child to play a musical instrument will offer them huge benefits in their later life, perhaps helping them to develop other skills, such as reasoning and problem-solving, but certainly enabling them to broaden their understanding and appreciation of the world.

B Ss write their summaries alone. Monitor and help with vocabulary, writing any new words and phrases on the board. When they have finished, Ss show their descriptions to each other, and suggest places where they can use more **Key phrases** from Ex 6B.

> **Homework ideas**
> • Ex 8B: write a final draft of your summary.

LOOKBACK

Introduction

Ss revise and practise the language of Unit 2. The notes below provide ideas for exploiting the exercises and activities but your approach will depend on your aim, e.g. as a diagnostic or progress test or as revision and fluency practice. For example, if done as a test then it would not be appropriate to monitor or help them.

LEARNING

1 After explaining the activity, elicit the first answer with the class as an example in order to check Ss understand what to do. Ss find and correct the mistakes alone then check in pairs. Monitor and help where necessary. In feedback, elicit Ss' answers.

> **Answers:** 1 I've only been working here for two weeks so I'm still learning the **ropes**. 2 You are so talented, you should believe in yourself. 3 Correct. 4 I decided to **take** advantage of the opportunity. 5 David didn't need to think because he trusted his instincts (no *on* needed after *trust*). 6 correct 7 Correct. 8 It's a difficult course and Frank's on a steep learning **curve**.

> **Optional extra activity**
> Arrange Ss in teams. Elicit a name for each team and write it on the board. Dictate the last word in each of the phrases by spelling it backwards e.g. *S-E-P-O-R* (for learn the ropes). As soon as Ss think they know the phrase, they call it out. The first team to call out the correct phrase gets a point. The team with the most points at the end wins.

CONDITIONALS AND REGRETS

2A Divide the class into 3 groups and assign one of the situations to each group. Ss write as many sentences as they can in ten minutes. Monitor carefully and check Ss are forming the sentences correctly, and help with ideas where necessary.

B Rearrange Ss into groups of three, with one student who wrote about each situation in each group. Ss read out their sentences to each other. In feedback, nominate Ss from each group to share their ideas with the class.

OPINIONS

3A Read through the topics with the class and check understanding. Give Ss three or four minutes to think about what they want to say and make notes if they want. Monitor and help with vocabulary, writing any new words and phrases on the board.

B Arrange Ss in pairs and give them five minutes to talk about as many of the topics as possible. In feedback, nominate Ss to share their ideas with the class.

> **Optional extra activity**
> Write the following topics on the board: *a story involving prejudice; a politician with a narrow-minded view; a story which was eye-opening; a story which makes a convincing argument.* If you have access to the internet, Ss search news websites (e.g. www.bbc.co.uk/news) to find news stories under the topics above. When they have found one for each topic, arrange Ss in groups of four to discuss and share the stories. If you don't have access to the internet, Ss can think of recent news stories from their country or countries.

VERB PATTERNS

4A Ss complete the sentences alone. With *weaker classes* give one or two examples first to demonstrate. Monitor and help where necessary, and check Ss are using the correct verb patterns.

B Ss compare their ideas in pairs. Monitor and encourage them to ask follow-up questions to find out more information. In feedback, nominate Ss to share their ideas with the class.

> **Alternative approach**
> Ss only read out their sentence endings to their partner. Their partner listens and guesses which sentence they are finishing.

INTRODUCING OPINIONS

5A After explaining the activity, elicit the first answer as an example, in order to check Ss understand what to do. Ss complete the conversations alone then in pairs. In feedback, elicit Ss' answers.

> **Answers:** 1 Quite frankly, 2 According to, I'm concerned 3 To my knowledge, If you 4 can gather, reality is

B Ss choose three topics and write sentences for each. Explain that they don't need to be their own opinions, but should be opinions that are likely to be controversial and spark debate. Monitor and help where necessary. When Ss are ready, arrange them in small groups to discuss the opinions they wrote.

> **Homework ideas**
> • **Workbook** Review and check 1, p14–16
> • **Workbook** Test 1, p17

OVERVIEW

LONELY PLANET

Introduction

Ss learn and practise noun phrases in the context of describing a place. They also practise writing a guidebook entry.

SUPPLEMENTARY MATERIALS

Resource bank p147

Warm up: Bring/download photos of landscapes and city areas.

Ex 1a (alternative approach): write the words from Ex 1A on cards.

Ex 8A: find a video of fado music on youtube.com to introduce the topic.

Warm up

Arrange Ss in groups of three and distribute a photo to each group. Ss work together to write three adjectives to describe the photo on the back of the photo. When they have finished, ask one student from each group to move to another group, taking the photo with them. In the new group, Ss work together to add two more adjectives to the list on the back of the photo. When they have finished, a different student takes the photo to another group, where they add another two adjectives to the list. When they have finished, nominate Ss from each group to show the class the photo and share the adjectives. Help with new vocabulary, providing further explanations and examples where necessary, and writing any new words and phrases on the board.

VOCABULARY landscapes

1A Ss work alone to match the words and synonyms, then check in pairs. In feedback, elicit Ss' answers and be prepared to provide further explanations and examples where necessary. Drill the words chorally and individually, paying particular attention to where each word is stressed.

Answers: 2 tranquil 3 magnificent 4 ancient 5 unspoilt 6 bustling 7 picturesque 8 deserted

Alternative approach
Write the words from Ex 1A on cards. Distribute one card to each student. Ss stand up and arrange themselves in groups with other 'synonyms'.

B Ss complete the sentences alone then check in pairs. In feedback, elicit Ss' answers.

Answers: 1 bustling 2 magnificent 3 ancient 4 unspoilt

C Focus attention on the photos. Elicit what things Ss can see and write any new vocabulary on the board. Ss use the adjectives from Ex 1A to describe the photos in pairs. In feedback, nominate Ss to share their ideas with the class.

READING

2A Elicit Ss' ideas as to where the places in the photos are, but don't give them any answers yet. Ss read the introduction to find out who took them.

Answers: Readers of the BBC *Lonely Planet Magazine*.

B Give Ss 2 mins to read the texts quickly and match the photos with the stories. Tell them not to worry about new vocabulary yet, as they'll have a chance to read the texts more carefully afterwards. In feedback, elicit Ss' answers. Ss discuss which photo/story they like best and why in pairs. In feedback, nominate Ss to share their ideas with the class, and find out if anyone has visited these places.

Answers: 1 A 2 C 3 B

C Ss read the article again and answers the questions alone then check in pairs. In feedback, elicit Ss' answers.

Answers: 1 in a long-tail boat 2 the driver took them on a detour, the boys showed off their diving 3 the Malecón is a long sea road with lots of dilapidated old buildings in front of it. *Habaneros* get together there at the weekends and relax and enjoy themselves 4 waves crashing against the sea wall, the sunset and the car 5 They are built in caves. 6 He felt humbled knowing that his hotel room once housed a family of ten and their livestock

Optional extra activity
While Ss are reading the text more carefully in Ex 3, write the following sentences on the board:

1 Our driver **took us on a** ____ to Thailand's longest wooden bridge.

2 As he **cut the** ____ , we idled up to the bridge for a closer look.

3 The boys **seized the** ____ to showcase some of their diving.

4 One after the other (they) **plunged into the** ____ .

5 There was **a warm** ____ **blowing** and a strong sea swell.

6 For me this photo captures **the** ____ of Havana.

7 The jumbled stack of cave houses seemed/appeared to ____ **down a ravine**.

After you've elicited Ss' answers to the questions in Ex 3, Ss close their books and try to complete the sentences from memory in pairs. When they've finished, Ss open their books and check their answers with the texts. In feedback, elicit Ss' answers and be prepared to provide further explanations/examples where necessary.

Answers: 1 detour 2 engine 3 moment 4 water 5 breeze 6 essence 7 tumble

SPEAKING

3A Give Ss five minutes to think of a 'snapshot' moment and make notes. Monitor and help with vocabulary, writing any new words and phrases on the board.

B Arrange Ss in groups. Ss compare their 'snapshot' moments. In feedback, nominate Ss from each group to share their ideas with the class.

GRAMMAR noun phrases

4 Ss read the rules and working alone, complete the examples, then check in pairs. Monitor and help where necessary. In feedback, elicit Ss' answers, and be prepared to give further explanations and examples where necessary.

Answers: 1 film set 2 five-mile-long, six-lane sea road 3 uniquely photogenic city 4 longest wooden bridge 5 for a closer look 6 approaching in the distance

⟶ **LANGUAGEBANK** 3.1 p132–133
Stronger classes can read the notes and do the exercises at home. Otherwise, check the notes with Ss, especially the order of words in longer noun phrases and when to use hyphenation. In each exercise, do the first sentence as an example. Ss complete the exercises alone, then check their answers in pairs. Ss can refer to the notes to help them.

Answers: 1 1 I like small cups of freshly-ground, strong, black coffee. 2 He bought the pretty little house by the river. 3 She made two delicious, dark chocolate cakes with strawberries and fresh cream on top. 4 He smokes those hugely expensive, enormous Cuban cigars, which Juan gives him. 5 They carried the massive pile of ridiculously heavy bags all the way up seven flights of stairs. 6 It was an incredibly smelly, hairy but rather friendly guard dog.
2 1 I went to the shoe shop advertised on television. 2 He was an old man walking with a stick. 3 We ate the absolutely delicious, home-made cakes, sitting in the sunshine. 4 They rented a nice house with a swimming pool near the airport. 5 We went to a big pizza restaurant on the outskirts of town, run by two Italian brothers called Gino and Rino.

PRACTICE

5 Ss put the words in the correct order alone, then check in pairs. In feedback, elicit Ss' answers.

Answers: 1 A slice of delicious, home-made cake with cherries on top. 2 A brand new, bright red, heavy-duty mountain bike with fifteen gears. 3 It's a small, Greek restaurant, which serves some of the best fresh seafood in the area. 4 A very expensive, black, cashmere jumper with extra-long sleeves. 5 A traditional, Tuscan bean soup with freshly-baked bread. 6 A fascinating, ancient, Medieval castle on top of a very steep hill.

Alternative approach
Books closed. Arrange Ss in small teams, and ask each team to appoint a 'secretary'. Read out the groups of words, or give out the words on slips of paper and Ss listen and form the sentences in their groups, with the secretary writing them down. When they are ready, Ss call you over to check. The first team to write the sentence correctly wins a point. The team with the most points at the end wins.

6A Ss describe the parts of speech in pairs. Monitor and help where necessary, referring Ss back to the rules in Ex 4. In feedback, elicit Ss' answers.

Answers: 2 delicious –adjective, hand-made – compound adjective; extraordinarily good – adverb + adjective combination; strong, black, espresso – adjectives 3 With a sprinkle of cinnamon on top – prepositional phrase; tiny cups of – adjective + noun 4 old – adjective, pastry shop – compound noun; in central Lisbon – prepositional phrase

B Ss work alone to add extra information to the sentences. Monitor, check Ss' word order carefully, and help with ideas where necessary. When they are ready, Ss compare their sentences in pairs. In feedback, nominate Ss to share their answers with the class.

Sample answer: 1 The fat, grumpy old man lives in a run-down house at the end of the road, with rubbish piled outside and stray cats with their many kittens running around everywhere.

C Focus attention on the topics, and give Ss three or four minutes to think of ideas they can use for each situation. Tell them not to worry about writing noun phrases yet. Monitor and help with vocabulary, writing any new words and phrases on the board. When they are ready, Ss use their ideas to write three complex noun phrases to describe the topics. Monitor and check Ss are forming the noun phrases correctly.

D Arrange Ss in small groups. Ss compare their sentences. Monitor and encourage Ss to ask follow-up questions to find out more information. In feedback, nominate Ss from each group to share their ideas with the class.

Teaching tip
At this level, Ss may use English on a day-to-day basis, but in a limited way (e.g. at work). By focusing on adding more detail in exercises in class, we can provide them with an opportunity to stretch what they can do with the language.

WRITING a description of a place

Optional extra activity
Find a video of fado music on the internet e.g. on Youtube.com. Books closed. Write on the board: *What type of music is this? Is it happy or sad? How does it make you feel? Where does this music come from?* Ss watch/listen, then discuss the questions in pairs. In feedback, nominate Ss to share their ideas with the class.

7A Introduce the text by asking: *Has anyone ever been to Lisbon? What do you know about the city?* and elicit what Ss know about the headings in the book. Elicit/check: *quaint, backstreets* (unusual and attractive little streets), *a hilltop district, scattered* (spread over a wide area) and *window-shopping* (looking in shop windows without buying anything). Ss work alone to read the guidebook entry and make notes under the headings, then check in pairs. In feedback, elicit Ss' answers.

Answers: <u>Location</u>: south western coast of Portugal, overlooking the river Tejo
<u>History</u>: old quarters of the city, the poet Pessoa, 1930s-era cafés
<u>Nearby sights</u>: Sintra, beaches, fishing villages
<u>Architecture</u>: Gothic and Moorish, monasteries, cathedrals and a castle, narrow streets
<u>Things to see/do</u>: visit museums and cathedrals, walk through the narrow backstreets, eat at a small patio restaurant, listening to Fado, sit in a 1930s café, go to bars/restaurants in Bairro Alto, or to nightclubs in the docks or in old mansions, go shopping in Chiado, go to a neighbourhood festival, watch the sunset from the castle
<u>Food and drink</u>: fresh pastry and espresso coffee, fresh bread and wine

B Ss discuss the questions in pairs. Monitor and help where necessary. In feedback, elicit Ss' answers.

Answers: 1 Present tenses for giving information and facts about a place. Makes the description more immediate. 2 Fairly informal, and friendly (words like *stroll, revellers partying until dawn, scattered*) – also contractions like *you'd, they've*. 3 The writer likes the place very much. We can see this from the positive language he/she uses to describe it.

LEARN TO add detail

8A In pairs Ss compare the sentences in this exercise with the sentences in the guidebook entry. In feedback, elicit Ss' answers.

Answers: The writer has added a wider range of vocabulary and details such as colours, shapes, sounds and feelings.

speakout TIP
Read the **speakout tip** with the class, and elicit the different ways you can add colour to a piece of writing based on what Ss have read in Unit 3.1. Ss work alone to underline places in the text where the author adds colour then compare in pairs. In feedback, elicit Ss' ideas.

B Read the first sentence with the class and elicit which sense is referred to and how it is referred to. Ss underline the phrases in the rest of the text alone then check in pairs. In feedback, elicit Ss' answers.

Answers: hear the voices of the market sellers (sound), sweet smell of fruit (smell), ripened in the hot sun (touch), aroma of strong, fresh coffee and petrol fumes (smell), small, three-wheeled motorised vans (sight/sound), farmers, or 'contadini' (sight), mountains of different coloured fruits and vegetables (sight), firm red peppers, purple beans, tomatoes of all shapes and sizes (sight/touch), liveliness in the air (sound), old ladies haggle over the price of the cherries (sight/sound), wave their arms in rebuke at the younger workers (sight/sound).

9A Ss choose a place and make notes for their guidebook entries alone, using the headings in ex 8A to help with ideas. Monitor and help with vocabulary, writing any new words/phrases on the board, and encourage Ss to think about how they can add colour and refer to the senses, as in Ex 7A and 8B.

B Ss write their guidebook entries alone. Monitor and help where necessary. When they have finished, Ss compare their entries in small groups, and choose which place they would most like to visit. In feedback, nominate Ss from each group to share their choices with the class, and explain why.

Homework ideas
- **Ex 9B:** write a final draft of your guidebook entry.
- Choose a place you would like to visit, and research it on the internet, using the headings in Ex 7A. Present your information to the class next lesson
- Language bank 3.1 Ex 1–2, p133
- Workbook Ex 1–4, p18–19

YOUR SPACE

Introduction
Ss revise and practise relative clauses in the context of personal spaces. They also revise/practise prefixes.

SUPPLEMENTARY MATERIALS
Resource bank p145, p146 and p148

Ex 8A: prepare notes on your own ideal space for work/study to introduce the activity.

Warm up
Do a visualisation activity. Ask Ss to relax, close their eyes, and take a few deep breathes, then read out the following to them: *I want you to imagine you are 15 years old, lying on your bed, and it's the first day of the summer holiday. It's late in the morning and you are waking up slowly. There's no need to rush, as it's the first day of the summer holidays. Looking up, you can see the sun shining through the closed curtains. You take a long, slow look around the room, imagining what adventures await you over the long summer holidays.* Ask the Ss to open their eyes, and describe their room in as much detail as possible to their partner. Monitor and help with vocabulary, writing any new words and phrases on the board. In feedback, nominate Ss to share their ideas with the class.

SPEAKING

1A Arrange Ss in small groups, and focus attention on the photos. Ss discuss the questions in groups. In feedback, nominate Ss from each group to share their ideas with the class.

B Ss match the quotations to the photos alone then check in pairs, then check their answers on p162.

Answers: 1 C 2 B 3 A

C Give Ss a few minutes to think about the place they work/study and make notes on its good and bad points. Monitor and help with vocabulary, writing any new words and phrases on the board. When they are ready, Ss discuss the question in the same groups as in Ex 1A. In feedback, nominate Ss to share their ideas with the class.

VOCABULARY adjectives

2A Ss read the descriptions and write where they are from alone then check in pairs. In feedback, elicit Ss' answers and ask how they know.

Answers: 1 Advertisement. It contains notes rather than full sentences, adjectives that focus on positive aspects, a contact number. 2 Fiction. Danziger is a fictional character. The extract describes part of a story and contains thoughts and actions as well as descriptions. 3 Ratings website. The writer is giving an opinion of the room. 4 Advertisement. It says how many people can sleep there and quotes a price. Use of positive adjectives. 5 Fiction. This contains dialogue and describes a scene. 6 Ratings website. It gives an opinion of the room and says how much the writer paid.

B Ss underline the adjectives alone, then compare in pairs. Ss categorise the adjectives into positive and negative and add more to each category. In feedback, elicit Ss' answers and any new adjectives they came up with, writing them on the board.

Answers: 1 Beautiful – positive; roomy (large with a lot of space inside it) – positive; spacious – positive; generous – positive; shady (protected from the sun or producing shade) – positive 2 gloomy (dark, especially in a way that makes you feel sad) – negative; airless (without much fresh air) – negative 3 comfortable – positive; gaudy (too bright and cheap-looking) – negative; chilly (cold enough to make you feel uncomfortable) – negative 4 airy (with plenty of fresh air because it is large or has a lot of windows) – positive; huge (very big) – positive; sunny – light and sun-filled – positive; peaceful (quiet and relaxing) – positive 5 dreary (dull and making you feel sad or bored)- negative 6 poky (too small and not very pleasant or comfortable) - negative other adjectives: messy, draughty, tidy, untidy, grubby, shabby, grand, well-proportioned, cosy, stark, dingy, minimalist, rustic

speakout TIP
Read the speakout tip with the class, and explain that adjectives which end in –y are very common in English. Elicit any others that Ss know. Elicit what the root word would be for the examples given (dirt, noise, smell). Ss look back at the adjectives in Ex 2A and decide which have a root word.

3A Elicit the first answer as an example. Ss underline the odd one out alone then check in pairs.

B 3.1 Play the recording for Ss to check their answers, then check answers with the class. Play the recording again for Ss to listen and repeat.

Answers: 1 city (the others have long vowel sounds) 2 body (the others have long vowel sounds) 3 footie (the others have long vowel sounds) 4 hockey (the others have long vowel sounds) 5 ready (the others have long vowel sounds) 6 airy (the others have short vowel sounds)

➡ VOCABULARYBANK p150 ADJECTIVES

1A Focus attention on the photos and elicit what Ss can see in each one. Ss match the sentences with the photos alone then check in pairs. In feedback, elicit Ss' answers.

B Ask Ss to underline the adjectives in Ex 1A, and discuss in pairs what they mean. Elicit Ss' ideas, but don't give any answers yet. Ss match the meanings with the adjectives alone then check in pairs. In feedback, elicit Ss answers. *Stronger classes* can do the exercises at home.

Answers: 1A 1 B 2 C 3 A 4 D
B a) vast b) awe-inspiring c) scenic d) sprawling e) quaint f) ramshackle g) secluded h) overpopulated

LISTENING

4A 3.2 Ss listen and work alone to make notes on the places being described and their good and bad points, then check in pairs. In feedback, elicit Ss' answers.

Answers: 1 a huge open plan call centre; good: within walking distance of home; bad: feels poky because everyone is crammed together even though it's a big area, very noisy because everyone is talking at once, gets quite chaotic 2 a conservatory at home; good: lots of light and space, nice to be at home and near amenities, she can meet her neighbours in her breaks, near the kitchen for mealtimes, she has a view of the garden; bad: gets cold in winter

B Ss work alone to decide who uses the phrases then check in pairs. Play the recording again for Ss to check their answers. In feedback, check understanding of the phrases, and be prepared to provide further explanations/examples where necessary.

> **Answers:** Speaker 1: open plan, all crammed up, somewhere nice to hang out, it gets quite chaotic
> Speaker 2: one drawback, a stone's throw away, a little haven of tranquillity

C In pairs Ss describe where they live using the phrases. Encourage Ss to ask follow up questions to find out more information. In feedback, nominate Ss to share their ideas with the class.

Unit 3 Recording 2

M = Man W = Woman

Conversation 1

M: I work in a call centre which is a..

W: Mmm hmm

M: … huge open plan, um well, there's tables everywhere people at little sort of boxed areas where they have to just make call after call.

W: Oh right …

M: Um, it's weird because it's a huge airy space, the actual the big room but everything feels quite poky because it's, you're all crammed up next to each other.

W: Oh dear.

M: All making your separate calls and it's very noisy, you just hear chat all the …

W: mmm

M: … time..you'd love to be able to get away, and have a little bit of quiet, a bit of peace and quiet and somewhere nice to hang out but this isn't it!

W: No …

M: Um basically everybody's talking and depending on, it varies, depending on what what we're trying to sell and if it is a hard sell …

W: Right.

M: If it's something we're trying to sell as many units of as possible then it gets quite chaotic there but yeah, the one benefit of it is it's within walking distance of home so at least I can get home quickly..

W: Yes.

Conversation 2

W: I'm very lucky because I work at home on a very very big dining table in the conservatory so it's very light, very airy, roomy.

M: Right …

W: There is one drawback and that is it's very cold, very chilly in the winter.

M: Oh.

W: I have a fire on but because there's so much glass it's very cold.

M: mmm

W: But it's lovely being at home, it's a stone's throw away from all the shops … it's near my neighbours … when I have a coffee break I can meet a neighbour, have a cup of coffee, catch up on all the local chit-chat.

M: Aha

W: … and then go back to work and at lunchtime, I'm right next to my kitchen, my fridge, make myself a lovely meal, go back to work – no time spent travelling.

M: Mmm … sounds good.

W: … which is wonderful, and it's a very lovely place to work, a little haven of tranquillity … because it looks out on to my garden with all the birds …

GRAMMAR relative clauses

5 Ss read the blog comments alone then discuss if they agree/disagree in pairs. In feedback, elicit Ss' ideas.

6A Draw a simple illustration of a house on the board, and underneath write: *This a house. I live there.* Ask Ss to combine the two sentences into one in order to describe the picture (i.e. *This is the house where I live.*) and elicit that this is a relative clause. Ss answer the questions alone then check in pairs. In feedback, elicit Ss' answers and be prepared to provide further explanations and examples where necessary.

> **Answers:** 1 *who do creative work* is a defining relative clause. 2 *none of whom were bad people* is a non-defining relative clause.
> Defining relative clauses give essential information about a noun. Non-defining relative clauses give extra information about a noun.

B Ss underline the relative clauses in the other sentences.

> **Answers:** 1 Most people who do creative work 2 none of whom were bad people 3 anywhere I feel comfortable, warm and relaxed 4 at which point I decided to work from home 5 on which I sit every day 6 whose major characteristic is brightness

C Ss work alone to match the descriptions a)–f) with the relative clauses from Ex 5, then check in pairs. In feedback, elicit Ss' answers.

> **Answers:** a) 5 b) 4 c) 6 d) 2 e) 3 f) 1

D Ss discuss the questions in pairs. In feedback, elicit Ss' answers and be prepared to provide further explanations and examples if necessary.

> **Answers:** 1 It is possible to use *that* instead of *who*, *where*, *when*, etc. in defining relative clauses. 2 These are non-defining relative clauses. Non-defining relative clauses always use a comma before them. 3 *Where* has been omitted from sentence 3. This is possible because we can omit the relative pronoun if it is the object of the verb.

> ⟫ **LANGUAGEBANK** 3.2 p132–133
>
> *Stronger classes* can read the notes and do the exercises at home. Otherwise, check the notes with Ss, especially the use of commas and when we can omit the relative pronoun. In each exercise, do the first sentence as an example. Ss complete the exercises alone, then check their answers in pairs. Ss can refer to the notes to help them.
>
> > **Answers:** 1 2 of 3 where 4 whose 5 about 6 whose 7 where 8 which 9 time 10 on 11 whom
> > 2 1 There were lots of children there, all of whom sang really well. 2 The fire alarm went off, at which point the lesson ended. 3 That's the woman whose house we stayed in. 4 The person from whom I learned the most is Clare. 5 You may get a scholarship, in which case you won't need to pay. 6 There are two photocopiers in the office, both of which are out of order.

PRACTICE

7 Focus on the exercise and check Ss understand that two options are correct and one is wrong. Ss cross out the incorrect options alone then check in pairs. In feedback, elicit Ss' answers.

Answers: 1 a) 2 c) 3 a) 4 b) 5 b) 6 c) 7 b) 8 b)

SPEAKING

8A Introduce the activity by describing your own ideal space for work/study, using the headings, and encourage Ss to ask you follow-up questions to find out more information. Ss make notes on their own ideal spaces alone. Monitor and help with vocabulary, writing any new words and phrases on the board.

B Arrange Ss in small groups. Ss describe their ideal spaces to each other. Monitor and note any common errors and examples of good language for later feedback. Nominate Ss from each group to share their favourite ideas with the class, and give Ss feedback on their language.

VOCABULARY *PLUS* prefixes

9 Give Ss two minutes to read the text quickly and answer the question in pairs. In feedback, elicit Ss' answers.

Answer: The hotel is famous because many celebrities have lived in it, such as Madonna, Arthur C Clarke and Jack Kerouac.

10A Focus attention on the table. Ss read the text again and working alone, underline the examples of prefixes, then check in pairs. In feedback, elicit Ss answers.

B Ss work alone to complete the table with the meanings, then check in pairs. In feedback, elicit Ss' answers.

Answers:

Prefix	Meaning	Example words
de ir im non un	negatives/ opposites/ reverse	Degenerate Irreplaceable Immortalised Non-conformity unfortunately
under over	size or degree	Understatement overexposed
mal mis	wrong or bad	maladministration misbehaviour
pre post	time (before or after)	Pre-dates Post-war
pro anti	attitude/opinion (for or against)	proactive anti-establishment

C Read the example with the class. Ss answer the question in pairs. In feedback, elicit Ss' answers.

Answers: We use:
un-, im-, ir-, de- with adjectives and adverbs
non-: nouns, adjectives
under- and over-: nouns, adjectives, verbs
mal- and mis-: verbs, abstract nouns, adjectives
pre- and post-: adjectives
pro- and anti-: nouns and adjectives

D Arrange Ss in small groups. Ss work together to add their own examples to the third column of the table in Ex 10A. Monitor and help where necessary. In feedback, elicit Ss' answers and write them on the board.

11 Ss correct the statements alone then check in pairs. In feedback, elicit Ss' answers.

Answers: 1 False. When we add a prefix to the root word, the spelling of the root word **doesn't usually change**. 2 False. We **can** add more than one prefix at a time to root words e.g. *uninhabitable*. 3 True. 4 False. There are **no** rules that tell us which prefixes we can add to each root word.

12A Ss complete the words alone then check in pairs. In feedback, elicit Ss' answers.

Answers: 1 unknown, underexposed 2 non-descript, underrated 3 unattractive, overrated 4 uninhabitable, mismanaged 5 irreplaceable, impossible

B Give Ss five minutes to think of examples alone. When they are ready, arrange Ss in small groups to compare their answers. In feedback, nominate Ss from each group to share their ideas with the class.

➡ VOCABULARYBANK p150 PREFIXES

2A Ss work alone to underline the two prefixes in each sentence then check in pairs. In feedback, elicit Ss' answers and check understanding of the words.

B Focus attention on the table. Ss complete the second column alone then check in pairs. In feedback, elicit Ss' answers.

C Read the example with the class. Ss match the words to the definitions alone then check in pairs. In feedback, elicit Ss' answers.

D Arrange Ss in small groups. Ss add further examples to the third column. In feedback, elicit Ss' examples and write them on the board.
Stronger classes can do the exercises at home.

Answers: 2A 1 <u>super</u>model, <u>mini</u>skirts 2 <u>sub</u>-zero, <u>co</u>-operate 3 <u>bi</u>lingual, <u>inter</u>acting 4 <u>semi</u>-retired, <u>out</u>lasted
B (in order from top to bottom) two, joint, between/among, small, bigger/greater than something else, half, below, more/more powerful/larger
C 2 superhero 3 outgrow 4 sub-plot 5 international 6 semicircle 7 co-founders 8 minibar

---

Homework ideas
- Ex 8A: Write a description of your ideal space for work/study
- Language bank 3.2 Ex 1–2, p133
- Vocabulary bank p150 Ex 1 – 2
- Workbook Ex 1–4, p20–21

WELCOME TO PERFECT CITY

Introduction

Ss learn and practise phrases and ways to structure a proposal and how to suggest modifications.

SUPPLEMENTARY MATERIALS

Resource bank p149

Ex 4A (Optional Extra activity): Write the phrases on slips of paper

Ex 7A: make notes on an area you know well.

Warm up

Arrange Ss in small teams. Elicit a name for each team, and write it on the board. Each group appoints a 'secretary', who will write their answers on a separate piece of paper. Read out the following questions, and give Ss time to confer and write their answers:

1 Which city was Samuel Johnson describing when he said that when a man is tired of it, he is tired of life?
2 Which city was founded over 2,000 years ago on seven hills?
3 Which city has a famous statue of Christ overlooking a bay?
4 Which city is famous for its opera house and large harbour?
5 Which city has a large square with St. Basil's Cathedral and the GUM department store?
6 In which city would you find gondolas?
7 In which city would you find a huge square and a section called 'The Forbidden City'?
8 What is the capital city of Australia?.

When they are ready, teams exchange their answers with other teams to mark. Go through the answers, and award points. The team with the most points wins.

Answers: 1 London 2 Rome 3 Rio de Janeiro 4 Sydney 5 Moscow 6 Venice 7 Beijing 8 Canberra

VOCABULARY city life

1A Arrange Ss in small groups. Focus attention on the photos and elicit what Ss can see. Ss discuss the questions in groups. In feedback, nominate Ss from each group to share their ideas with the class.

B Elicit/check: *loitering* (standing around somewhere for no clear reason), *catch on* (become popular, of an idea), *pickpockets* (people who steal from your pockets) and *clutter* (a lot of things, not stored in a tidy way). Ss read the text alone then compare the information in the texts with their ideas from Ex 1A in the same groups. In feedback, elicit if any of Ss' ideas were mentioned in the texts and which solutions Ss found most surprising.

2A Ss complete the sentences alone then check in pairs. In feedback, elicit Ss' answers and be prepared to give further explanations/examples where necessary.

Answers: 1 amenities 2 infrastructure 3 abandonment, regeneration 4 congestion, tolls

Optional extra activity

Ss work alone to decide which of the sentences are true about the city where they are from, and change any that aren't to make them true. Monitor and help with vocabulary, writing any new words and phrases on the board. When they are ready, arrange Ss in small groups to compare and discuss their ideas.

B Ss answer the questions in pairs. In feedback, elicit Ss' answers.

Answers: congestion comes from congest, abandonment comes from abandon, regeneration comes from generate

Watch out!

With words that end in the suffix *–tion*, the stress is always on the syllable immediately before. This can be a useful rule to teach Ss to help them pronounce new words.

FUNCTION making a proposal

3A 3.3 Elicit/check: *to be piloted* (tested on people to find out if it will be successful). Ss listen then answer the questions in pairs. In feedback, elicit Ss' answers.

Answers: The idea is to introduce 'cycle hubs' in the city centre. The speaker proposes getting everyone together to discuss the advantages and disadvantages.

B Ss complete the notes alone, then check in pairs. Play the recording again for Ss to check their answers. In feedback, elicit Ss' answers and write them on the board.

Answers: 1 five 2 bicycle 3 centre 4 safer 5 cheap

4A Focus attention on the headings and elicit the first answer as an example. Ss match the phrases to the headings alone then check in pairs. In feedback, elicit Ss' answers and drill the phrases chorally and individually.

Answers: 1 f) 2 a) 3 g) 4 e) 5 b) 6 c) 7 d)

Alternative approach

Divide the board into seven sections, and at the top of each one, write one of the functions from Ex 4A (i.e. *Introducing your proposal, Stating the purpose,* etc.). Write all of the phrases from Ex 4A on separate slips of paper, and distribute to the Ss. Ss decide which category each phrase belongs to, then come up and stick their slip of paper in the relevant section. This type of activity can appeal to kinaesthetic learners, and help change the pace after the listening in Ex 3B. In feedback, check answers with the class and drill the phrases. Ss then complete Ex 4A alone.

B Ss turn to the audio script on p167 and find which six expressions are used then check in pairs. In feedback, elicit Ss' answers.

Answers: Just to give you a bit of background information, …, The aim of the project is to …, What we plan to do is …, This solution will help us to …, So, basically, what we're proposing is to …, Does anyone have any questions?

Unit 3 Recording 3

M=Man

M: Just to give you a bit of background information, Harrogate council has announced the creation of cycle hubs er, as part of its cycling strategy for the next 5 years. Now, the aim of this project is to set up cycle hubs. What are hubs? Hubs are areas where innovative ideas for cycling can be piloted and where resources can be targeted to increase er cycling. So what we plan to do is to introduce these new hubs in the centre of Harrogate located in areas with a high concentration of cyclists. Er, this solution will help us er, to create a more safe environment for the cyclist. Cycling is an incredibly efficient mode of transport. It's fast, it's environmentally friendly, and it's cheap – with of course the added bonus of keeping you fit. So basically, what we're proposing to do is to get everybody around the table to discuss the merits and demerits of whether or not the idea of a cycling hub in the centre of Harrogate is a good or a bad idea basically. So um, does anyone have any questions?

▶ **LANGUAGEBANK** 3.3 p132–133

Stronger classes could read the notes and do the exercise at home. Otherwise, drill the phrases from the chart, checking Ss are using natural intonation. Ss work alone to choose the correct alternatives, then check their answers in pairs. In feedback, elicit Ss' answers.

Answers: 1 background information 2 with 3 of 4 aim 5 what 6 up with 7 feasible 8 solution 9 instance 10 long-term 11 what 12 sum up

5 Elicit the first answer as an example. Check Ss understand that not all the sentences have extra words. With *weaker classes*, tell Ss there are seven extra words. Ss cross out the extra words alone then check in pairs. In feedback, elicit Ss' answers.

Answers: 1 up 2 Correct. 3 goals 4 Correct. 5 but 6 Correct. 7 too 8 Correct. 9 of 10 Correct. 11 is 12 the

LEARN TO suggest modifications

6 Introduce the exercise by eliciting ways to suggest modifications or changes to a proposal e.g. *I'd like to suggest a change, What about combining our ideas?*. Write Ss' ideas on the board. Focus attention on the phrases in the book and see if any of their ideas are mentioned. Ss discuss the questions in pairs. In feedback, elicit Ss' answers.

Answers: 1 a) I'd like to propose a compromise. d) How about if we combine our ideas? 2 e) Is there any way we can reduce the costs? f) Is there any leeway regarding the schedule? 3 b) Let's try to come up with a solution. 4 c) Let's look at it another way.

SPEAKING

7A Arrange Ss in small groups. Introduce the activity by describing an area you know and answering the questions. Encourage Ss to ask you follow-up questions in order to find out more information.

B Ss plan their proposal in groups. Make sure Ss assign a role to each group member and that everyone has a chance to speak. Monitor and help with vocabulary, writing any new words and phrases on the board.

C Ss take it in turns to present their proposals to the class. While they are giving their presentations, make notes on any common errors and examples of good language for later feedback. When all the groups have presented, ask each student to vote for the best proposal (but don't let them vote for their own), in order to decide which group gets the grant. Go through any common errors with the class and give praise for good language used.

Teaching tip

When Ss give a presentation to the class, it's important to give the other Ss a task for listening, to ensure they pay attention. For example, choosing their favourite one and why, or thinking of two questions to ask.

Homework ideas
- Ex 7B: write up your proposal.
- Language bank 3.3 Ex 1, p133
- Workbook Ex 1–3, p22

AN AFRICAN JOURNEY

Introduction

Ss watch an extract from the BBC documentary *An African Journey*, in which Jonathan Dimbleby visits Mali. Ss learn and practise how to talk about their country, and write a proposal.

SUPPLEMENTARY MATERIALS

Warm up: Bring or download a map of Africa.

Warm up

Bring a map of Africa to class. Show it to Ss and elicit what Ss know about this continent. Arrange Ss in small teams. Elicit a name for each team, and write it on the board. Each group appoints a 'secretary', who will write their answers on a separate piece of paper. Read out the following questions, and give Ss time to confer and write their answers:

1 What percentage of the world's land area is covered by Africa: 40% or 20%? (20%) 2 Which river are the Victoria Falls on, the Zambezi or the Nile? (Zambezi) 3 What is the name of the world's largest desert, found in North Africa? (The Sahara) 4 In which country is Mt. Kilimanjaro: Tanzania or Kenya? (Tanzania) 5 Are tigers found in Africa? (No) 6 What is the capital of Zimbabwe: Lusaka or Harare? (Harare) 7 Which country is famous for its gold and diamonds: Egypt or South Africa? (South Africa) 8 Which is the most populous country in Africa: Nigeria or Morocco? (Nigeria)

When they are ready, teams exchange their answers with other teams to mark. Go through the answers, and award points. The team with the most points wins.

DVD PREVIEW

1 Ss discuss the questions in pairs. In feedback, nominate Ss to share their ideas with the class.

Culture notes

The Republic of Mali is a landlocked country in West Africa. The capital city is Bamako. Mali became independent from France in 1960, and the official language is still French. Most of the country is made up of The Sahara Desert, receiving little rainfall and suffering frequent droughts. It is one of the poorest countries in the world, though GDP has been steadily increasing since Mali joined the World Trade Organisation (WTO) in 1995. Agriculture is the key industry and cotton is the country's largest crop export.

2 Give Ss 2 mins to read the programme information then discuss the question in pairs. In feedback, elicit Ss' answers.

▷ DVD VIEW

3 Read the questions with the class and check Ss know what to listen for. Ss watch the DVD and answer the questions, then check their answers in pairs. In feedback, elicit Ss' answers.

Answers: 1 It's the fastest-growing city in Africa. 2 The business sells mopeds. 3 It is successful because the economy is growing and they are selling affordable mopeds, which can be quickly assembled. 4 Cheaper technology means that it is more accessible to people in Bamako. The cheaper mopeds mean, for example, that people can get to work on time, or students can get to university.

4A Ss complete the extracts in pairs from memory. Monitor and help where necessary, but don't give any answers yet.

B Play the DVD again for Ss to check their answers. Make sure Ss understand that the speakers don't always use the exact words in the sentences. In feedback, elicit Ss' answers.

Answers: 1 vitality 2 Mali 3 moped 4 400,000 5 five 6 45 / 46

5 Ss discuss the questions in pairs. Monitor and help with vocabulary, writing any new words/phrases on the board. In feedback, nominate Ss to share their ideas with the class.

An African Journey

JD=Jonathan Dimbleby M=Mamadou

JD: I'm on a journey which will take me seven thousand miles across nine countries through the ferment that is Africa. I've been coming here for almost four decades, but this is quite different from anything I've done before. This series is not about failure or despair, but vitality and hope. It's about nations in flux, about individuals who are changing the face of this continent. West Africa's largest nation is the Republic of Mali.

I'm starting my journey in one of the very poorest countries in Africa: Mali. And I'm taking a lift into the capital, Bamako, which is the fastest growing city on the continent. And I'm using the fastest growing means of transport here, the moped, in a city which seems to be consumed by a kind of moped mania.

Africa is a restless continent; more than a billion people, fifty-three nations with diverse languages, cultures and histories, but with a common urge to make a future for themselves and for their families.

My driver's name is Serpent, which is of course French for snake, and I hope he's got it because of his reputation for weaving his way through the traffic. 'Ça va, Serpent?' Because if so and we make it, he's taking me to see the family business in the moped market in Bamako. 'On va!'

Sales have risen sharply in the last five years. There are now more than four hundred thousand mopeds in a city of two million people. The sales hub is the Dabanani market, where Serpent works with his brother Mamadou. The business is flourishing, in a country where the economy has grown on average by five percent a year for over a decade.

JD: Apparently it takes only forty-five minutes to put these together. They come in these flat-packs here, unload the flat-pack and you've got a moped, a motorcycle.

M: We'll assemble it right now, as the customer is waiting for his moped. Take it out and assemble it quickly.

JD: It's really making a difference to life in Bamako and, and, and in Mali as well.

M: Since mopeds were introduced, everybody gets to work on time, students aren't late. You can't imagine how important mopeds are.

JD: You say the bikes come overwhelmingly from China. Why China? What's the reason for that?

M: We used to have Japanese and French bikes. They cost £2000 each. That is not affordable for a Malian or any African. It is too expensive.

JD: The Chinese have captured the market. Their Power Ks, at around four hundred and fifty pounds a piece, cost a third of any foreign rival. And because public transport is far from cheap, the moped will soon pay for itself.

JD: Finished, and it was forty-five minutes, well forty-six minutes.

speakout your country

6A ▶ 3.4 Write on the board: *Canada* and *Argentina*, and elicit what Ss know about these countries. Ss work alone to listen and make notes. Don't elicit any answers yet.

B Ss compare their answers using the questions. If necessary, play the recording again for Ss to check their answers. In feedback, elicit Ss' answers.

Answers: <u>Canada</u>: 1 incredible diversity / huge
2 highs: one of the highest standards of living in the world / long life expectancy / one of the wealthiest countries
Lows: bad winter weather / cold temperatures
3 geographically massive / second largest country in the world after Russia, Documentary: huge range of fresh water / great lakes and rivers, three coasts, incredible diversity of wildlife, climate and landscape (temperate rain forests, deserts, arctic prairies, volcanoes, mountains, forests) / longest coastline in the world.
6 The USA and Canada both have a history of indigenous people and they share the longest border in the world.
The speaker doesn't answer questions 4 or 5.
<u>Argentina</u>: 1 people's characteristics and values
2 highs: values, value of family and friends. Great sense of solidarity and care for friends, resourcefulness and laid back quality of people dealing with problems.
2 Lows: a lot of strikes and struggles and uncertainty.
3 Documentary – day in someone's life showing what's going on in the country.
5 Family get together on Sundays to catch up on the week, Celebrate Friends' Day. Very different from other parts of Latin America, e.g. Brazil. Brazilians are upbeat while Argentinians have a melencholy temperament and yearning for the old way of life.
The speaker doesn't answer the first part of question 3 (geographical), or question 4

C Ss complete the phrases alone, then check in pairs. When they are ready, Ss check their answers with the audio script on p167. In feedback, elicit Ss' answers and drill the **Key phrases** chorally and individually.

Answers: Canada has one of the highest standards of living in the world., On the downside, I suppose, … you have to deal with bad winter weather., I would describe Canada as geographically massive., We're very lucky in Canada to have a huge range of fresh water, great lakes, rivers everywhere., Undoubtedly one of the best things about Argentina is the values., People are very warm, very caring and we've got a great sense of solidarity., Argentinians, we've got a sense of longing for the old world.

Unit 3 Recording 4

W1=Woman 1 W2=Woman 2

W1: Er Canada has one of the highest standards of living in the world and, you know, long life expectancy. Um and it's one of the world's wealthiest nations so it's really quite a nice – nice place to live. Um and on the downside I suppose there's um – in a lot of areas you have to deal with bad winter weather so um not – not in all places but in a lot of places we get a lot of snow and um really cold temperatures in the winter um and that can be quite difficult to deal with, although you do get used to it.
I would describe Canada as er geographically massive. Um I think it's kind of difficult to explain how – just how big the country is. It's the second largest country in the world apart from Russia, or next to Russia, um and yeah, so it's just really, really, really big and very, very diverse.
Every province is different um and, you know, to visit Canada you really have to go far and go for a long time to – to really appreciate the – the vastness of the country. Um what um if I was making a documentary I'd probably focus on things like, you know, we're very, very lucky in Canada to have a huge range of fresh water, um great lakes, rivers everywhere, literally.
Um we have three coasts: the Pacific coast, the Atlantic and the Arctic, and we actually have the longest coastline in the

world. So you get incredible um diversity, um everything from wildlife to bird life um and also diversity in climate so, you know, we have temperate rain forests and we have deserts, we have um arctic er prairies, we have volcanoes, mountains, um you know, almost half of Canada is covered in forests. Er some similarities um between the United States and Canada um that I can think of is that um we both have a strong history and a long standing history of aboriginal peoples um and we share the longest border in the world.

W2: Well undoubtedly one of the best things about Argentina is um the values, um people and – and their values, how they view life and they – we tend to attribute quite a lot of um – um sort of value to our – our family, we care a lot about our families and – and our gatherings and we kind of gather on Sundays and we have a big barbecue and everybody comes and we all talk about our weeks and what we've been up to and it's a good chance to catch up.
Um we also care a great deal about our friends, um we celebrate Friend's Day, which is a big celebration and we have a lot of fun and we give each other cards and thank each other for our friendship. Um so I think that's kind of the best thing about Argentina, people are very warm, very caring and there's a – we've got a great sense of solidarity. Um I guess if you – a lot of people think that Latin America is just Latin America and that all the countries are the same and, you know, like Brazil and Argentina are the same thing but we're very different um with our – we – we've got like I – I guess if you could put it in – into words, Brazilians are very upbeat and very happy and Argentinians we're – we've got a sense of longing for – for the old world and this er melancholic view of the – of the world and so we – the outlooks are very different and hence the culture is – is very different. An interesting way of seeing Argentina would be um if you were to film a documentary it would be through following one person like through a day or through a couple of days because then you start getting a sense for all the things that um go on in the country and like, you know, for instance when I used to teach it – it was like I used to start my day not knowing what my day would about because there's always a strike, there's always a picket line, there's always all these difficulties you have to overcome through – throughout a day and – but at the same time you can see how resourceful people are when dealing with difficulties and how er relaxed and – and laid back they are about them, in a way. So it's – it's an interesting way of living. Um it's as constant struggle but at the same time keeping your smile.

7A Ss discuss the questions in pairs. With *multilingual classes*, arrange Ss so they discuss different countries.

B Give Ss two minutes to read the instructions and check understanding. Ss work alone to make notes on a documentary for their country. Monitor and help with vocabulary, writing any new words and phrases on the board.

C When they are ready, Ss take turns to present their ideas to the class. Encourage Ss to ask questions to find out more information. When they have finished, hold a class vote to choose the best ideas.

writeback a proposal

8A Ss read the proposal then discuss the questions in pairs. In feedback, elicit Ss' answers.

B Ss write their proposals alone. Monitor and help with vocabulary, writing any new words/phrases on the board. When they have finished, Ss show their descriptions to each other, and suggest places where they can use more **Key phrases** from Ex 6C.

> **Homework ideas**
> • **Ex 8B**: write a final draft of your proposal.

LOOKBACK

Introduction

Ss revise and practise the language of Unit 3. The notes below provide ideas for exploiting the exercises and activities but your approach will depend on your aim, e.g. as a diagnostic or progress test or as revision and fluency practice. For example, if done as a test then it would not be appropriate to monitor or help them.

LANDSCAPES

1A After explaining the activity, elicit the first answer as an example, in order to check Ss understand what to do. Ss match the sentence halves alone then check in pairs. In feedback, elicit Ss' answers.

Answers: 1 d) 2 c) 3 f) 4 a) 5 e) 6 b)

B Demonstrate the activity by choosing three adjectives and using them to describe places you know to the class. Ss describe places they know in pairs. Encourage Ss to ask their partner follow-up questions to find out more information. In feedback, nominate Ss to share their ideas with the class.

Alternative approach
Ss describe places as in Ex 1B without saying the adjective. Their partner listens to the description and guesses the adjective. Demonstrate with the following example: *My bedroom is very quiet and I find it very easy to relax there – too easy sometimes! (tranquil).*

NOUN PHRASES

2A Focus attention on the box and check understanding of the words. After explaining the activity, elicit the first answer as an example, in order to check Ss understand what to do. Ss work alone to add detail to the sentences then check in pairs. Monitor and check they are forming noun phrases using the correct word order. In feedback, elicit Ss' answers.

Sample sentences: 1 I drink cups of steaming hot Japanese green tea to keep me awake. 2 They bought the old farmhouse on top of the hill. 3 I bought a brand-new top-of-the-range laptop computer with all the latest graphic technology. 4 She went for a five-mile-long cross-country run in the rain.

B Read the example with the class, and elicit ways in which Ss can continue it. Ss take turns to extend the sentences by adding information in pairs. Monitor and help where necessary. In feedback, nominate Ss to share their best sentences with the class.

ADJECTIVES

3A After explaining the activity, elicit the first answer as an example, in order to check Ss understand what to do. Ss complete the descriptive adjectives alone then check in pairs. In feedback, elicit Ss' answers.

Answers: 1 gloomy, poky 2 roomy, airy 3 gaudy, chilly

B Ss discuss the questions in pairs. In feedback, nominate Ss to share their opinions with the class.

Optional extra activity
Ss think of a place they know well, and work alone to write a description of it, using at least four adjectives from Ex 3A and Unit 3.2. Monitor and help with vocabulary, writing any new words and phrases on the board. When they are ready, arrange Ss in small groups. Ss take it in turns to read out their descriptions for other Ss in the group to try and guess which place they are describing. In feedback, nominate Ss from each group to share their descriptions with the class.

RELATIVE CLAUSES

4A Ss underline the correct alternatives alone then check in pairs. In feedback, elicit Ss' answers.

Answers: 1 from which 2 in which I live alone 3 to which you can never answer 'yes'? 4 at which point

Alternative approach
Arrange Ss in small groups. Give Ss 3–4 mins to discuss their answers to Ex 4A, but don't let them write their answers yet. When they are ready, call out a number to the class, and the first team to call out the correct answer for that sentence wins a point. At the end, the group with the most points wins. Give Ss 3–4 mins to complete Ex 4A alone, writing their answers. In feedback, elicit Ss' answers.

B Ss try to solve the riddles in pairs. Note that the answers are in 4C. Decide if you want to ask students to cover the answers or if it's better not to draw attention to them. In feedback, elicit Ss' guesses but don't give any answers yet.

C Ss match the answers to the riddles alone then check in pairs. In feedback, elicit Ss' answers and ask if they know any other riddles.

Answers: 1 lead in a pencil 2 a chick in an egg 3 Are you asleep? 5 a hole

MAKING A PROPOSAL

5 Ss complete the proposal in pairs. In feedback, elicit Ss' answers.

Answers: 1 to, (you) a bit of 2 The, of our/my/the, is to 3 The (main), of the, is to 4 What we, to do 5 we're going to, with 6 The/This, is, because 7 this, will, us (to) 8 In the, this would 9 The, include 10 So, what we're, to 11 Does, have any

OVERVIEW

This video podcast extends discussion of the unit topic to social issues. Ss can view people discussing the law and what legal or social issues concern them. Use this video podcast at the start or end of Unit 4.

CONVICTION

Introduction
Ss learn and practise the introductory *it* in the context of crime. They also learn and practise lexical chunks.

SUPPLEMENTARY MATERIALS
Resource bank p151 and p152
Warm up: write the headings below on the board.

Warm up
Write the following headings on the board: *Financial crimes, Violent crimes, Political crimes, Driving crimes*. Arrange Ss in small groups, and give them five minutes to list as many types of crime under each heading as possible. In feedback, elicit Ss' answers and write them on the board, adding your own ideas.

READING

1A Focus attention on the film poster on p45 and the headline of the article on p44 and check understanding of the phrases in the box. Ss discuss their predictions in pairs. In feedback, nominate Ss to share their ideas with the class, but don't give any answers yet.

B Elicit/check: *commit suicide* (kill yourself), *a college degree* (both the course or study and the qualification), *split up* (end a marriage or other romantic relationship) and *perpetrator* (someone who does something harmful or illegal). Give Ss a few minutes to read the text quickly and check their predictions. In feedback, elicit which of the Ss' predictions were correct.

2 Ss read the text again and answer the questions alone, then check in pairs. In feedback, elicit Ss' answers.

Answers: 1 Because he had an alibi. 2 No, she never doubted his innocence. 3 Kenny asked her to. He had tried to commit suicide, and they had no more money for lawyers. 4 Her devotion to the case put her personal life under strain, and she later divorced. 5 A piece of bloodied curtain the perpetrator had wiped his hands on. 6 She asked some of the other law students to say that they were doing a project on the Waters case.

3 Ss discuss the question in pairs. Encourage them to give reasons for their answer. In feedback, nominate Ss to share their opinions with the class.

VOCABULARY crime collocations

4 Elicit the first answer as an example. Ss form collocations and complete the sentences alone then check in pairs. Monitor and help where necessary. In feedback, elicit Ss' answers, and be prepared to provide further explanations and examples where necessary.

Answers: 1 protest their innocence 2 fresh evidence 3 under arrest 4 early release 5 perfect alibi 6 brought to justice 7 make an appeal 8 previous convictions

Alternative approach

Write the exercise numbers from Ex 4 in a column on the board. In feedback, give each pair a board pen, and ask one student from each pair to come to the board, without the answers. Their partner then calls the answers out to the student at the board, who writes them in the right place. To provide more of a challenge, play some music loudly so that each student has to listen/pronounce the words clearly. When they've finished, correct any errors on the board.

Teaching tip

With lower levels, it's important where possible to elicit words and phrases rather than meanings. However, at higher levels Ss already have a wealth of language they can draw on to make intelligent guesses about new language. It's important to give them opportunities to use this when presenting new language, and also provides more challenge for them at this level.

⫸ VOCABULARYBANK p151 CRIME COLLOCATIONS

1A Elicit the first answer as an example. Ss complete the sentences alone then check in pairs. In feedback, elicit Ss' answers.

B Ss match the phrases and their meanings alone then check in pairs. In feedback, elicit Ss' answers.
Stronger classes can do the exercises at home.

Answers: 1A 1 on 2 on 3 into 4 for 5 with 6 into 7 in 8 with 9 to 10 at
B a) 3 – comes into force b) 1 – put on probation
c) 9 – posed a serious threat to (the public) d) 4 – was given points on his licence e) 2 – went on the rampage
f) 5 – help the police with their inquiries g) 8 – charged with assault h) 7 – held in custody i) 10 – fired tear-gas at (the protesters) j) 6 – An investigation is being held into the causes (of the accident)

SPEAKING

5A Arrange Ss in small groups and give them one minute to read the topics and choose one they want to discuss. Ss discuss their topic in groups. Monitor and make notes on any common errors and examples of good language for later feedback.

B Nominate Ss from each group to share their ideas with the class and have a brief class discussion. Give Ss feedback on their language.

Optional extra activity

Write on the board: *Prison doesn't work as a deterrent* and divide the group into two groups. One group makes a list of reasons in favour of the statement, and the other makes a list of reasons against it. Monitor and help with vocabulary, writing any new words and phrases on the board. When they are ready, arrange Ss in pairs, with one member of the previous groups in each pair. Ss debate the sentence, using the reasons they came up with before. In feedback, elicit Ss' ideas and have a brief discussion.

GRAMMAR introductory *it*

6A Ss read the text then discuss what *it* refers to in pairs. In feedback, elicit Ss' answers.

Answer: *It* refers to the era being described.

Watch out!

English doesn't have as many inflections as most other languages. For this reason, the order of words in sentences is very important in English. We use introductory *it*, to ensure we have a subject, verb and object in the right order.

B The aim of this exercise is to test how much Ss already know about this area. This should give you an idea of how much detail you need to go into when clarifying and whether you need to do the **Language bank** exercises in class. Ss complete the sentences alone then check in pairs. In feedback, elicit Ss' answers.

Answers: 1 I could hardly believe **it** when the policeman told me what had happened. 2 **It** has been reported that a number of people in the area were affected. 3 **It**'s no use! I've looked everywhere for my wallet but I can't find **it** anywhere. 4 We would appreciate **it** if you didn't tell anyone about this. 5 **It**'s surprising how quickly I was able to master the skill. 6 **It**'s no wonder you couldn't find your bag. You left **it** in the café. 7 A: 'How much further is **it**?' B: '**It**'s not far now.' 8 **It**'s a pity that you won't be able to make **it** to the lunch. 9 **It** was a warm day for the time of year. 10 **It** appears that someone has made a mistake.

7 Give Ss two or three minutes to read the rules and ask any questions they have. Ss find further examples from Ex 6A and B alone, then check in pairs. In feedback, elicit Ss' answers, and check understanding of the rules, especially the word order in each of the uses of *it*.

Answers: a) It was the best of times, It was the age of foolishness, etc, It was a warm day …, How much further is it?, It's not far now b) It's no use …, It's surprising …, It's no wonder …, It's a pity c) It appears that someone … d) It has been reported … e) I could hardly believe it when …; I can't find it anywhere; We would appreciate it if …; You left it in the café. f) you won't be able to make it.

⫸ LANGUAGEBANK 4.1 p134–135

Stronger classes can read the notes and do the exercises at home. Otherwise, check the notes with Ss, especially the order of words in sentences with introductory *it*. In each exercise, do the first sentence as an example. Ss complete the exercises alone, then check their answers in pairs. Ss can refer to the notes to help them.

Answers: 1 1 I can't stand **it** when all **it** does is rain for days on end. 2 I'd appreciate **it** if you could give me a little more notice next time. 3 **It**'s no use just standing there. You'd better get on with **it**. 4 I find **it** hard to believe that the summer is here already. 5 **It** appears that the police have video footage of the incident. 6 **It**'s pointless arguing with her when she's in that kind of state. 7 I'll leave **it** to the others to decide what time we should meet. 8 I've always made **it** clear that my family has to take priority over my work.
2 1 It's pointless crying about the situation now. 2 It's essential to be trustworthy in this profession. 3 It seems (that) he has misplaced his keys. 4 We owe it to them to be hospitable to them as they were welcoming to us. 5 It's no wonder she wasn't very enthusiastic when she had heard the talk before. 6 I find it easy to keep abreast of the latest news online.

PRACTICE

8A Ss complete the sentences alone then check in pairs. In feedback, elicit Ss' answers.

> **Answers: 1** It's difficult to believe he would have left all the money here. **2** It's no wonder you were scared. That car nearly hit you. **3** It's not my fault we didn't finish on time. We started late. **4** I can't help it if I keep making mistakes. Nobody's perfect. **5** It's important that we clear up any misunderstandings **6** It was a shame that we didn't see the beginning. **7** It appears to have been a mistake. **8** It's funny how things always turn out OK in the end.

B Give Ss five minutes to complete the sentences alone. Monitor and help with vocabulary, writing any new words and phrases on the board.

C Read the example with the class. Model the exercise by completing one of the sentences and encourage Ss to ask follow up questions to find out more information. Ss compare their sentences in pairs. In feedback, nominate Ss from each pair to share their ideas with the class.

VOCABULARY *PLUS* lexical chunks

9A Read the examples with the class. Give Ss three or four minutes to brainstorm collocates with *justice* in pairs and write them down. In feedback, elicit Ss' answers and write them on the board.

B Ss work alone to read sentences 1–6 and add any more phrases with *justice* to their list, then check in pairs. In feedback, elicit Ss' answers and add them to the list on the board.

C Ss answer the question alone then check in pairs. In feedback, elicit Ss' ideas.

> **Answer:** Because they're lexical chunks. See **speakout tip**.

D Ss match the phrases alone then check in pairs. In feedback, elicit Ss' answers.

> **Answers: 1** a kind of **2** It's up to **3** take the law into your own hands **4** It's imperative that **5** in the vicinity

speakout TIP

Read the **speakout tip** with the class and explain that the underlined phrases in Ex 9B are lexical chunks. Explain that it's very useful to learn lexis as chunks of language, as they are easier to retrieve from memory when speaking and therefore help fluency. This is in fact what native speakers do. An example of a lexical chunk which acts as an adverbial is 'as soon as possible'.

10A Elicit/check *unjustly accused* (unfairly, for something they haven't done), *vehemently protest* (very strongly), *witness* (someone who sees a crime), *brutal murder* (very violent) and *on the run* (trying to escape from the law). Focus attention on the film posters and synopses. Ss read the synopses alone then discuss the questions in pairs. In feedback, elicit Ss' answers.

> **Answer:** Both films involve someone being convicted of a crime they didn't commit.

B ▶ 4.1 Ss listen to the first synopsis and pay attention to how the language is chunked. In feedback, answer any questions Ss have.

Unit 4 Recording 1

The film ¦ is based on ¦ the true story ¦ of Manny Balestrero ¦, an honest, hardworking musician ¦ who is unjustly accused ¦ of armed robbery ¦ when he goes to an insurance firm ¦ to borrow some money ¦, and employees mistake him ¦ for ¦ the armed robber ¦ who had robbed them ¦ the year before ¦. In classic Hitchcock form ¦, Balestrero vehemently protests his innocence ¦ but unfortunately ¦ he acts guiltily ¦, leading ¦ a host of policemen ¦ and witnesses ¦ to identify him ¦ as the thief ¦. The trial goes badly for Manny ¦, but things are even worse for his wife ¦, Rose, ¦ who struggles to cope with the strain of his ordeal.

C Ss mark the chunks in the second synopsis alone then compare in pairs. Encourage Ss to try reading them aloud to help. Explain that answers may vary according to the speaker.

D ▶ 4.2 Ss listen and compare their answers to the recording. Play the recording again for Ss to listen and shadow read the synopsis.

Unit 4 Recording 2

Dr Richard Kimble, ¦ a well-known Chicago surgeon, ¦ returns home one night¦ to find that his wife ¦ has been viciously murdered ¦ in their own home. ¦ When police find Kimble ¦ at the scene of the crime, ¦ he is arrested, ¦ and later charged and convicted ¦ of his wife's brutal murder. ¦ However, ¦ on the way to the prison, ¦ a failed escape attempt ¦ by other prisoners ¦ gives Kimble ¦ his chance of freedom. ¦ While on the run ¦ from US Marshall Samuel Gerard, ¦ Kimble's only hope of proving his innocence ¦ and clearing his name ¦ is to find out for himself ¦ who was responsible for his wife's death, ¦ and to lead the team of detectives ¦ on his trail to the real perpetrator.

> ### Homework ideas
> - **Ex 10D**: transcribe a movie trailer from youtube.com, mark the chunks and practise shadow reading it.
> - **Language bank** 4.1 Ex 1–2, p135
> - **Workbook** Ex 1–6, p23–24

SOCIAL JUSTICE

Introduction

Ss revise and practise the perfect aspect in the context of social issues. They also practise writing a problem-solution essay.

SUPPLEMENTARY MATERIALS

Resource bank p150 and p153

Warm up: write the topics below on the board.

Ex 7A: bring dictionaries to class for Ss to use.

Warm up

Write on the board: *climate change, HIV/AIDS* and *destruction of the natural environment*. Ss work alone to put these three issues in order of importance and think of reasons for their choices. When they are ready, arrange Ss in groups of three to compare their ideas and try to agree on an order. In feedback, nominate Ss from each group to share their ideas with the class and have a brief discussion.

LISTENING

1 Arrange Ss in pairs, and focus attention on the photos. Elicit who the people are (*Al Gore, Annie Lennox* and *Sting*). Ss discuss the questions in groups. In feedback, nominate Ss from each group to share what they know with the class, but don't give any answers yet.

Culture notes

Al Gore served during the 1990s as 45th Vice President of the US, and ran for president in the 2000 US presidential elections, when he lost out to George W. Bush. Since then he has become very active in campaigning against climate change, and in 2006 released *An Inconvenient Truth*, a feature-length presentation on the effects of climate change and the action needing to be taken. In 2007, he won the Nobel Peace Prize.

Annie Lennox is a Scottish musician who found fame in the 1980s with Dave Stewart in Eurythmics, before embarking on a solo career in the 1990s. She has, for many years, been a political and social activist, championing a range of causes. She is best known for her work raising money and awareness for HIV charities in Africa.

Sting is a British rock musician and actor who found fame in the 1970s/early 1980s with The Police, before becoming a successful solo artist. He has been an activist for many causes since the early 1990s and is perhaps best known for his work with Amnesty International and in founding the Rainforest Foundation Fund, working closely with Amazon Indians to help conserve the rainforest.

2A ▶ 4.3 Elicit/check: *cut straight through to the heart* (appeal directly to the emotions), *huge swathes* (an enormous amount), *a role model, plaudits* (praise) and *embark on a campaign*. Ss listen and take notes alone, then check in pairs. Monitor and help where necessary.

B Ss answer the questions from memory. When they are ready, play the recording again for Ss to check their answers. In feedback, elicit Ss' answers, and feed in any further information from the culture notes that wasn't mentioned in the recording.

Answers: 1 She became involved in an HIV campaign started by Nelson Mandela. 2 The fact that she's dedicated time to other people, even though she's very successful herself. 3 Because he was serving under Bill Clinton as Vice President (and Bill Clinton had a very high profile in the news). 4 He admired him for his integrity. 5 Her father wrote a book on how to write a hit song, and Sting read it. 6 Start her own campaign to save the rainforests.

Unit 4 Recording 3

M1 = Man 1 M2 = Man 2 W = Woman

Speaker 1

M1: I really admire Annie Lennox, the singer. Not - not just a singer um I don't know what you'd call her. I suppose a humanitarian, in a way, because of the work she does, er raising awareness of the impact of HIV and AIDs on women and children in particular, especially in South Africa. Um in 2009 she won the Woman of Peace award, for that work and er and it all started when um she went to take part in a concert for er a campaign, an HIV campaign that Nelson Mandela had organised er in South Africa.

And from then on - I think she's raised over two million dollars now um to help with treatment, testing, HIV education and prevention programmes. And um, you know, like from a personal point of view, er I've got nearly all of her albums and there are certain of her songs that just take me back to very particular times in my life, like sad times and happy times, and so, you know, she kind of cuts straight through to the heart. But I particularly admire the fact that she's dedicated time to helping other people. I mean when you find great success like that and you actually have the time and resources to enjoy your wealth and success and money er and you take out huge swathe of - swathes of time um to help other people around the world and be of service to others, I think that's very admirable and er and a role model for us all.

Speaker 2

M2: Al Gore was vice president of the USA um in the nineties and at the turn of the century um and I think it's fair to say that he didn't get um that much attention because he was serving under Bill Clinton at the time, who was um generally taking the headlines and the plaudits. Um but he sort of became better known when he tried to become president himself.

Um but anyway, soon after that he sort of dedicated himself um, well at least more in the public consciousness, um he became known as a kind of environmental activist. He - he helped um he helped with a documentary called *An Inconvenient Truth*, which was based on his own book.

Um and it had a huge effect on raising awareness of global warming and environmental issues. A lot of these things are - are spoken about now and it seems um it's much more commonly in the news but at that stage really it was … it was not a very common subject and it made a massive difference and I really admired him for that.

I actually got to meet him at um Notre Dame University in - in America and I found him really … there was something … there's a real integrity about the man that I really admired. The only thing I wonder about is of course he's always flying around here and there, um, giving these talks, and you sort of wonder how much fuel he's burning in doing that. But I think um he's offset that by - by his message and um the number of people he's managed to help create an awareness for.

Speaker 3

W: I'm going to talk about Sting because he's first of all gorgeous, also a fantastic singer, amazing songwriter, wonderful actor and, of course, really respected humanitarian. But personally for me um I've always been interested in him because I know that my dad years ago wrote a book on how to write a hit song, cos he had a few hits as a songwriter, and apparently um Sting er read the book and started - and embarked on his amazing career.

So that um, for me, was what sparked my interest and er he started, as far as I know, in the 1980s after um he was a teacher, that was his background, so obviously he's a really clever man and knowledgeable as well, um and that was when I was growing up in the 1980s, so I remember him touring and singing in concerts for Amnesty International.

And some of his songs um also deal with social justice, um like Driven to Tears, which I think was around the same time, um which was about world hunger. Um he also co-founded the Rainforest Foundation to help save rainforests in South America and to protect the indigenous tribes living there, which affected me um so much that I decided I'll embark on a campaign myself to help stop the destruction of rainforests.

GRAMMAR the perfect aspect

3A Ss complete the sentences alone, then check in pairs. In feedback, elicit Ss' answers.

> **Answers:** 2 Al Gore 3 Sting 4 Annie Lennox 5 Al Gore 6 Sting 7 Al Gore

B With *weaker classes*, quickly review the form of the perfect aspect with sentence 4, by eliciting which verb forms we use (a form of auxiliary *have* and the *past participle*). Ss match the forms and examples alone, then check in pairs. In feedback, elicit Ss' answers and review how we form the perfect aspect across the different tenses.

> **Answers:** present perfect continuous 1, past perfect 3, past perfect continuous 6, future perfect 7, future perfect continuous 5, perfect infinitive 2

4 Ss answer the questions alone, then check in pairs. In feedback, elicit Ss' answers.

> **Answers:** 1 1, 2 and 4; 2 3 and 6; 3 5 and 7; 4 1, 5 and 6

Teaching tip

The perfect aspect is notoriously difficult for Ss, since it doesn't exist in the same way in many languages. At this level, Ss will have met all the forms of the perfect aspect, so it's important at this stage to bring it all together, by generalising i.e. referring to the fact that in all cases it links two time periods together.

▶ LANGUAGEBANK 4.2 p134–135

Stronger classes can read the notes and do the exercises at home. Otherwise, check the notes with Ss, especially the different uses of simple and continuous forms. In each exercise, do the first sentence as an example. Ss complete the exercises alone, then check their answers in pairs. Ss can refer to the notes to help them.

> **Answers:** 1 1 has been providing 2 had been living 3 will have been 4 have closed 5 appeared to have abandoned 6 will have been running 2 1 Yes. The workers have been marching since 8.00 this morning. 2 They had been talking throughout the whole lesson. 3 Yes. This time next year she will have been working here for forty years. 4 Yes. It's 8.00. They will have arrived by now. 5 He seems to have forgotten how to play! 6 That's right. She had only been working there for two months when the company closed.

PRACTICE

5 Read the example with the class. Ss discuss the sentences in pairs. Monitor and help where necessary. In feedback, elicit Ss' answers.

> **Answers:** 2 no difference 3 no difference 4 In *a*, we know the listener studied with Professor Robson. This question asks if the listener also studied with Robson at a time before this more recent time. In *b*, the speaker asks if the listener has ever studied with Professor Robson. He/She knows that the other person is studying with him now, and is asking if this is the first time. 5 In *a*, the task is finished. In *b*, the task is not finished. The emphasis is on the activity in progress.

6A Ss correct the mistakes alone then check in pairs. Check Ss understand there are only three mistakes. In feedback, elicit Ss' answers.

> **Answers:** 1. 1 What do you hope **to have** achieved by the time you're eighty? 3 By 2030, how long will you **have** been working? 5 How long have you **known** your best friend?

B Ss discuss the questions in pairs. Monitor and help with vocabulary, writing any new words and phrases on the board. In feedback, nominate Ss to share their answers with the class.

VOCABULARY social issues

7A If you've brought dictionaries to class, distribute them for Ss to use. Arrange Ss in two large groups. Ss discuss the meanings and write example sentences in their groups. Monitor and help where necessary, and check understanding of the expressions.

B Arrange the Ss in pairs, with one student from each group in Ex 7A in each pair (you may need to have a group of three). Ss teach each other the expressions, using their example sentences. Monitor and help where necessary. In feedback, check understanding of the expressions, and be prepared to give further explanations and examples where necessary.

> **Answers:**
> human rights: the basic rights that everyone has to say what they think, vote, be treated fairly, etc.
> child labour: the regular and sustained employment of children (it is illegal in many countries)
> economic development: the process of improving the financial situation of a place (often a country)
> intellectual property: the product of an intellectual activity (e.g. in artistic or commercial fields) that nobody else can legally copy
> capital punishment: the practice of killing someone who has committed a serious crime
> religious freedom: the ability to practise any religion that you choose, without being arrested or otherwise persecuted
> environmental awareness: understanding of problems related to the land, water and air on Earth
> illegal immigration: when people cross international borders in a way that breaks the immigration laws of the destination country
> civil liberties: the right of all citizens to be free to do what they want while respecting the rights of other people
> free trade: a situation in which the goods coming into or going out of a country are not controlled or taxed
> freedom of speech: the ability to say what you wish without being censored
> gun control: laws that limit the ways in which guns can be sold, owned and used

C Ss brainstorm other words and expressions in pairs. In feedback, elicit Ss' ideas and write them on the board. Drill any new expressions chorally and individually.

8A Focus attention on the example and drill the expression. Ss work alone to match the expressions from Ex 7A to the stress patterns, then check in pairs. Encourage Ss to say the expressions aloud.

B ▶ 4.4 Ss listen and check their answers. Pause the recording after each expression and give Ss time to practise saying them while tapping their fingers, then play again to allow Ss to repeat at full speed.

> **Answers:** 2 human rights 3 free trade 4 freedom of speech 5 religious freedom 6 illegal immigration 7 intellectual property 8 gun control 9 environmental awareness 10 capital punishment 11 economic development 12 child labour

> **Optional extra activity**
> In pairs, Ss play 'expression tennis'. Each student starts by reading out the first word from an expression (e.g. *human*) and their partner continues by completing the expression and saying the first word of another (e.g. *rights*, *free*). Ss try to keep a 'rally' going for as long possible without pausing.

speakout TIP

Read the **speakout tip** with the class and demonstrate/ explain the different methods mentioned. Ask Ss which of the methods they use and elicit any other methods they use.

> ➡ **VOCABULARYBANK** p151 SOCIAL ISSUES
>
> **2A** Focus attention on the pictures and elicit what Ss can see in each one. Elicit the first answer as an example. Ss match the issues and pictures alone then check in pairs. In feedback, elicit Ss' answers.
>
> **B** Ss complete the sentences alone then check in pairs. In feedback, elicit Ss' answers, and be prepared to provide further explanations/examples where necessary.
>
> > **Answers:** 2A 1 H 2 D 3 C 4 E 5 A 6 F 7 G 8 B
> > B a poverty b gender inequality c antisocial behavior d white-collar crime e censorship f illiteracy g organised crime h ageism

SPEAKING

9A Give Ss three or four minutes to read the questions and think about their answers alone. When they are ready, arrange Ss in small groups to discuss the questions. In *multilingual classes*, try to include a range of nationalities in each group. Monitor and make notes on any common errors and good language use for later feedback.

B Rearrange Ss into new groups. Ss compare their ideas. In feedback, nominate Ss from each group to share their ideas with the class. Give Ss feedback on their language.

> **Teaching tip**
> Rearranging Ss into new groups to repeat tasks, such as in Ex 9B, can be a useful way of providing extra fluency practice, and also goes some way towards helping Ss meet new language '6 times', as mentioned in the Speakout tip above.

WRITING a problem-solution essay

10A Introduce the topic by eliciting Ss' experiences with essays, when and why they write (or have written) them. Elicit what a problem-solution essay is and come up with a definition with the class e.g. an essay which poses a problem, then discusses various solutions before concluding with the best solution. Focus attention on the items in the box and check understanding. Ss discuss the question in pairs. In feedback, elicit Ss' answers.

> **Answers:** reference to research, facts and figures, a description of a problem, rhetorical questions, a plan of action, a conclusion

B Elicit/check: *bite the bullet* (take action to deal with a difficult situation), *a round number* (a whole number, often one ending in zero), *a complete ban* (something that is not allowed at all according to an official order) and *a shot in the dark* (an attempt to guess something without having the facts). Ss read the essay and answer the questions alone, then check in pairs. In feedback, elicit Ss' answers.

> **Answers:** 1 It deals with gun control. 3 It contains facts and figures, a description of a problem, rhetorical questions, a plan of action, a conclusion

11 Ss work in pairs to tick the expressions used then check in pairs. In feedback, elicit Ss' answers.

> **Answers:** This illustrates one of today's most important issues…:One of the causes (of …) is …; This has resulted in …; One possible solution …; There are a number of (other) options. These include … ; In conclusion, …

LEARN TO use parallelism

12A Ss read the examples and discuss the meaning of 'parrallelism'. Check understanding before Ss find a third in the text alone, then check in pairs. In feedback, elicit Ss' answers and check which form is being used in each case (past participle as part of a present perfect passive construction).

> **Answer:** The problem is that these solutions have already been proposed, passed into law and denounced as failures.

B Ss discuss the question in pairs. In feedback, elicit Ss' answers, and ask if it's common in their language(s) too.

> **Answer:** 4

C Ss complete the sentences alone then check in pairs. In feedback, elicit Ss' answers.

> **Answers:** 1 b) 2 c)

13 Arrange Ss in groups and give them two minutes to choose a topic. Ss follow stages 1–5. Monitor and help with ideas and vocabulary, writing any new words and phrases on the board. When they are ready, Ss write their essays alone. When they've finished, Ss exchange essays with Ss from other groups and read their essay. In feedback, nominate Ss to share what they liked about other Ss' essays.

> **Homework ideas**
> • Ex 13: write a final draft of your essay.
> • Language bank 4.2 Ex 1–2, p135
> • Workbook Ex 1–5, p25–26

DO THE RIGHT THING

Introduction

Ss learn and practise phrases for discussing hypothetical preferences and how to add emphasis.

SUPPLEMENTARY MATERIALS

Resource bank p154

Warm up: write the questions below on the board.

Ex 1D: make notes on a dilemma/difficult decision you've faced.

Warm up

Write the following questions on the board:

Have you ever witnessed a crime? What happened?
What would you do if you saw someone being robbed in the street?
Would you do anything if you knew someone hadn't declared a major source of income on their tax form?
Have you ever committed a 'small' crime e.g. driving too fast, kept something you've found, etc.?

Ss discuss the questions in pairs. In feedback, elicit Ss' ideas (as long as they are willing to share them).

VOCABULARY decisions

1A Give Ss two or three minutes to read the text alone and check understanding. Arrange Ss in small groups to discuss the question. In feedback, nominate Ss from each group to share their ideas with the class and have a brief class discussion.

B Ss find and underline the expressions alone, then check in pairs. In feedback, elicit Ss' answers and drill the expressions chorally and individually.

Answers: 1 faced with a dilemma 2 thinking it through 3 take all these things into consideration 4 weighed up the pros and cons

C Read the example with the class. Ss discuss the question in small groups. In feedback, nominate Ss from each group to share their ideas with the class.

Alternative approach

Write the following sentences on the board: *how to best help learners remember new vocabulary; whether they should put money into a company which they know has a poor ethical record; whether to allow their child to go on holiday with his/her friends; whether to experiment on animals; whether to participate in a war which they know is morally wrong; how to help someone they know is addicted to drugs.* Ss work alone to match the decisions/dilemmas to the professions in Ex 4C and think of another one for each. Monitor and help where necessary. When they are ready, arrange Ss in small groups to compare their ideas. In feedback, nominate Ss from each group to share their ideas with the class.

2A Introduce the activity by describing a difficult decision/dilemma you've faced, using some of the expressions in Ex 1A and B if possible. Give Ss five minutes to plan their ideas. Monitor and help with vocabulary, writing any new words and phrases on the board.

B Ss share their experiences in pairs. In feedback, nominate Ss to share their experiences with the class.

FUNCTION expressing hypothetical preferences

3 Elicit/check: *bash* (hit), *flimsy* (not strong, made of light material), and *hammer-wielding* (carrying a hammer). Ss read the article and answer the questions alone then check in pairs. In feedback, elicit Ss' answers.

Answer: 1 Ann Timson had to decide whether to stop the burglars or not.

4A ▶ 4.5 Ss listen to the recording and answer the question alone, then check in pairs. In feedback, elicit Ss' answers.

Answer: The speakers wouldn't do what Ann Timson did.

B Ss discuss the meanings in pairs. When they are ready, play the recording again for Ss to listen and check. In feedback, elicit Ss' answers and be prepared to provide further explanations and examples where necessary.

Answers: a have-a-go-hero: someone who gets involved when a crime occurs and tries to stop the criminal(s)
When push comes to shove: when faced with the reality rather than the story.
jumped on the bandwagon: did or supported what everyone else was because it's fashionable or might bring you personal gain
I take my hat off to her: I respect her for what she did
I'd probably leg it: it's likely that I'd run away
I'd do my bit: I'd do what's expected of me

5A Ss complete the expressions alone then check in pairs. Don't elicit any answers yet.

B Ss find the expressions in the audio script 4.5 on p168 and check their answers. In feedback, elicit the missing words, which expressions are used in the audio script and how they are used.

Answers: 1 up 2 choice 3 found 4 far 5 would 6 doubt
Only expression 1 is used in the audio script

Unit 4 Recording 5

M=Man W=Woman

M: So did you see that thing on the news about that er seventy year old grandmother who um who stopped the jewel thieves?

W: Oh the – the one yeah, who knocked one of them off their bike, off their motorbike

M: Yeah.

W: That was amazing.

M: Wasn't it extraordinary? And they were robbing this jewel store and smashing the windows

W: Yeah yeah yeah, and she just came up and

M: And nobody was doing anything about it.

W: Completely hit them straight over the head with her massive great handbag.

M: With her shopping bag.

W: Shopping bag or something.

M: Full of, I don't know, beans or something…

W: Cans of beans, yeah.

M: But I mean would you do that in that situation?

W: Oh I – I – if it was up to me I think I would probably be too cowardly and I'd end up just calling the police, I'm afraid to say.

M: I know, it's interesting, isn't it? I mean, you know, if – if I ever found myself in that situation I would like to think that I would be, you know, a have-a-go-hero as well but come, you know, push come to shove, whether or not you actually do it or not is another question, isn't it?

W: Yeah, yeah, I mean.

M: I mean the fact is that it's dangerous. … how many - were there six of them she took on?

M: Something like that, yeah.

W: That really is …

M: And she knocked one of them off their scooter and then – and it was only then that all the other passersby came and, you know, landed on him yeah.

W: Oh yeah, jumped on the bandwagon, yes.

M: But she'd done – done the whole thing.

W: No you have to - I completely take my – my hat off – hat off to her for that be — because that is truly heroic to just charge in there, but no way would I do that. I just can't see my – er yes I – I own up to cowardice. I would be ringing someone.

M: Well a friend of mine said that he thought it was absolutely, you know, completely stupid, totally wrong thing to do. I said no, I thought that if more people, you know, were like that you'd have a better society.

W: Yeah. I completely agree. The thing is, as you said before, I don't know, I think it has to be one of those instantaneous reactions. You either don't think about the consequences and you - you pile in and you - you do what you can, or it's, I mean as soon as you hesitate I think you're lost really.

M: Yeah.

W: And er

M: I think to be absolutely honest, if it was up to me, in the same situation, I'd probably leg it.

W: Really? Yes, well I – I think I'd probably do my bit by calling the police.

⟫ LANGUAGEBANK 4.3 p134–135

Stronger classes could read the notes and do the exercise at home. Otherwise, drill the phrases from the chart, checking Ss are using natural intonation. Ss work alone to match the sentence halves, then check their answers in pairs. In feedback, elicit Ss' answers.

Answers: 1d) 2 e) 3 b) 4 h) 5 c) 6 j) 7 f) 8 a) 9 i) 10 g)

---

6 With *weaker classes*, elicit the first answer as an example. Ss rewrite the sentences alone then check in pairs. In feedback, elicit Ss' answers and drill the expressions chorally and individually.

Answers: 1 Far better/It's far better to weigh up the pros and cons than decide now. 2 If it was/were up to you, which of the two candidates would you choose? 3 Without a shadow of a doubt, we can come up with some better ideas than these. 4 Given the choice, would you ban all web advertising? 5 I would ask my boss for advice if I (ever) found myself in this situation. 6 Instead of acting rashly, I'd sooner put important decisions on hold. 7 My preference would be to buy a house now rather than wait until the economy gets better. 8 She'd just as soon quit her job as do something unethical.

Optional extra activity

Ss work alone to read the sentences from Ex 6 again and decide which are true/could apply to them, and in what ways. When they are ready, arrange Ss in groups to compare their ideas. In feedback, nominate Ss to share their ideas with the class.

LEARN TO add emphasis

7A Elicit the first answer as an example. Ss categorise the expressions alone then check in pairs. In feedback, elicit Ss' answers.

Answers: 1 a) 2 d) 3 e) 4 b) 5 c)

B ▶ 4.6 Ss listen to the recording, paying attention to the intonation. Play the recording again for Ss to listen and repeat.

speakout TIP

Ss work alone to choose two of the expressions in Ex 7A and translate them into their own language. Read the **speakout tip** with the class, then nominate Ss to share their sentences from their own language(s) with the class, demonstrating how they add emphasis.

SPEAKING

8A Ss read the dilemmas and make notes alone. Monitor and help with ideas where necessary.

B Arrange Ss in small groups to discuss their ideas. Monitor and make notes on any common errors and examples of good language for later feedback. In feedback, nominate Ss from each group to share their ideas with the class and give Ss feedback on their language.

Homework ideas

• Write about a difficult decision/dilemma from Ex 2A.

• Language bank 4.3 Ex 1, p135

• Workbook Ex 1–4, p27

BLACKADDER

Introduction

Ss watch an extract from the BBC comedy *Blackadder*, in which a soldier goes on trial. Ss learn and practise how to talk about a possession, and write a description of an object.

SUPPLEMENTARY MATERIALS

Warm up: Write the questions below on the board.

Warm up

Write the following questions on the board:
What do you know about The First World War?
Do you have compulsory military service in your country?
Do you think this is a good thing?
For what things might a soldier be 'court-marshalled'?

Ss discuss the questions in pairs. In feedback, elicit Ss' answers and have a brief class discussion.

▶ DVD PREVIEW

1A Arrange Ss in pairs to explain the words taken from Unit 4. In feedback, elicit Ss' answers and check understanding.

Answers: the evidence: information given in court that proves that someone is guilty or not guilty
a courtroom: a place where cases of law are judged
sentence: a punishment that a judge gives to someone who is guilty of a crime
trial: a legal process in which a judge and jury examine information to decide if someone is guilty of a crime

B Ss match the words and definitions alone then check in pairs. In feedback, elicit Ss' answers and be prepared to provide further explanations/examples where necessary.

Answers: 1 the deceased 2 a witness 3 the defendant
4 the case (for the prosecution/the defence)

2 Give Ss 2 mins to read the programme information then answer the question in pairs. In feedback, elicit Ss' answers.

Answer: Captain Blackadder is on trial because he shot General Melchett's pigeon.

Culture notes

The BBC comedy *Blackadder* was first screened in 1983. It is a historical comedy, with four series set in different periods of history. It was written by Richard Curtis, Rowan Atkinson and Ben Elton, and stars a number of well-known British comedians: Rowan Atkinson (who later became internationally famous as Mr. Bean), Stephen Fry, Hugh Laurie and Tony Robinson. In 2000 the fourth series, *Blackadder Goes Forth* (where the clip in this unit is taken from) was ranked 16 in the '100 Greatest British Television Programmes' list created by the British Film Institute.

▶ DVD VIEW

3A Go through the sentences with the class and check any new vocabulary. Ss discuss the question in pairs.

B Play the DVD. Ss watch and answer the questions, then check their answers in pairs. In feedback, elicit Ss' answers.

Answers: Captain Blackadder is not given a prison sentence. He is condemned to death.

4A Ss match the people and actions in pairs from memory. Monitor and help where necessary, but don't give any answers yet.

B Play the DVD again for Ss to check their answers. In feedback, elicit Ss' answers.

Answers: General Melchett – 1, 7; Captain Blackadder – 8; George (the defence lawyer) – 3, 5; Captain Darling (the prosecuting lawyer) – 2, 6; Private Baldrick – 4

Optional extra activity

Write the following punishments on the left-hand side of the board: *pay a fine, a prison sentence, a suspended sentence, community service, restorative justice, the death penalty, pay compensation* and *electronic tagging/house arrest*, and elicit/check understanding (Note: *a suspended sentence* is where the convict doesn't go to prison, but is given a warning and monitored, so that if they commit another crime during the period of the sentence, they can be recalled to prison. *Restorative justice* is when the convict has to meet their victim, and listen to them describe how the crime has affected them). Arrange Ss in small groups to discuss which of the punishments exist in their country/ies, and what type of crimes they think should receive these punishments.

5 Ss discuss the questions in pairs. In feedback, nominate Ss to share their ideas with the class.

Blackadder

GM=General Melchett CB=Captain Blackadder
G=George CD=Captain Darling PB=Private Baldrick

GM: Come on then, come on. Get this over in five minutes and we can have a spot of lunch. Right ooh, ah, the court is now in session. General Sir Anthony Cecil Hogmanay Melchett in the chair. The case before us is that of the crown versus Captain Edmund Blackadder, the Flanders pigeon murderer.

CB: I love a fair trial.

GM: Right, let the trial begin. The charge before us is that the Flanders pigeon murderer did deliberately, callously and with beastliness of forethought murder a lovely, innocent pigeon, and disobeyed some orders as well. Is this true?

G: Perfectly true sir I was there.

CB: Thanks, George.

G: Damn, damn.

GM: Right, counsel for the defence, get on with it.

G: Oh right yes, yes right um, yes. I'd like to call my first witness, Captain Darling.

GM: You wish to call the counsel for the prosecution as a defence witness?

G: That's right. Don't worry sir I've got it all under control. You are Captain Darling of the General Staff?

CD: I am.

G: Captain, leaving aside the incident in question, would you think of Captain Blackadder as the sort of man who would usually ignore orders?

CD: Yes, I would.

G: Ah! Um, are you sure? I, I was rather banking on you saying no there.

CD: I'm sure. In fact I have a list of other orders he's disobeyed if it would be useful.

GM: Mmhmm.

CB: George!!

G: Oh yeah right yes. Yes, thank you Captain, no further questions.

CB: Well done George! You really had him on the ropes there.

G: Don't worry old man. I have a last and I think you'll find decisive witness. Call Private Baldrick!

CB: Deny everything, Baldrick.

G: Are you Private Baldrick?

PB: No!

G: Oh um, but you are Captain Blackadder's batman?

PB: No!

G: Come on Baldrick! Be a bit more helpful – it's me.

PB: No, it isn't.

CD: Sir, I must protest.

GM: Quite right, we don't need your kind here Private. Get out! Now George, sum up please.

G: Right yes, er … right. Ah gentlemen, you have heard all the evidence presented before you today, but in the end it is up to the conscience of your hearts to decide. And I firmly believe that like me, you will conclude that Captain Blackadder is in fact totally and utterly guilty!

… Of nothing more than trying to do his duty under difficult circumstances.

GM: Nonsense he's a hound and a rotter and he's gonna be shot. However, before we proceed to the formality of sentencing the deceased, uh I mean the defendant, I think we'd all rather enjoy hearing the case for the prosecution, Captain Darling if you please.

CD: Uh, my case is very simple. I call my first witness, General Sir Anthony Cecil Hogmanay Melchett.

GM: Ah um.

G: Clever, clever.

CD: General, did you own a lovely plump speckly pigeon called Speckled Jim, which you hand-reared from a chick and which was your only childhood friend?

GM: Yes! Yes I did.

CD: And did Captain Blackadder shoot the aforementioned pigeon?

GM: Yes, he did.

CD: Can you see Captain Blackadder anywhere in this courtroom?!

GM: It's him! That's him! That's the man. There!!

CD: No more questions sir.

GM: Splendid, excellent, first class! Out the way, come on. I therefore have absolutely no hesitation in announcing that the sentence of this court is that you Captain Edmund Blackadder be taken from this place and suffer death by shooting tomorrow at dawn.

Do you have anything to say?

CB: Yes, could I have an alarm call please?

speakout a court case

6A Elicit/check: *a will* (a legal document that says who you want your money and property to be given to after you die), *assets* (the things that a company owns, that can be sold to pay debts), *ailing* (ill and not likely to get better). Ss read about the court case and think about what should happen, then compare ideas in pairs. In feedback, elicit Ss' ideas.

B ▶ 4.7 Ss listen and answer the question, then check in pairs. In feedback, elicit Ss' answers.

> **Answers:** The woman cites Nicholas Holdicott's lack of evidence about (1) the father being pressurised to change his will and (2) about the father not being 'of sound mind'.

C Focus attention on the **Key phrases**. Ss listen and tick the phrases they hear, then check in pairs. In feedback, elicit Ss' answers and drill the **Key phrases** chorally and individually.

> **Answers:** All the phrases are used except *it's been claimed* and *an expert witness testifies that …*

Unit 4 Recording 7

M=Man W=Woman

W: This kind of thing seems to be quite common. Families are always being torn apart by money.

M: By arguments about money, it's true. But what do you think should happen in this case?

W: Well, my first point is that it's quite rare to have a will overturned in court so you need really solid evidence.

M: Right …

W: And it seems as if the younger brother …

M: Nicholas.

W: Nicholas. He doesn't have any proof that …

M: Um any proof that the father was pressurised …

W: That the father was pressurised into changing his will.

M: And without proof you have no case.

W: Exactly.

M: But having said that, there's also the issue of whether the father was 'of sound mind'. He was taking a lot of medication apparently so maybe he wasn't thinking straight.

W: Again, the question is can you prove that? It's very difficult to do in retrospect, especially if there's no evidence to suggest he'd lost his mental capabilities.

M: Right.

7A Arrange Ss in pairs, and direct them to the instructions on the relevant pages. Monitor and check understanding.

B When they are ready, Ss argue the case in pairs. In feedback, elicit what each pair decided.

writeback a case summary

8A Ss read the summary then discuss if they agree in pairs. In feedback, elicit Ss' answers.

B Ss write their summaries alone. Monitor and help with vocabulary, writing any new words and phrases on the board. When they have finished, Ss swap summaries with a partner to read.

> **Homework ideas**
> • Ex 8B: write a final draft of your summary.
> • Ex 8B: write a summary of a famous case in the news.

LOOKBACK

Introduction

Ss revise and practise the language of Unit 4. The notes below provide ideas for exploiting the exercises and activities but your approach will depend on your aim, e.g. as a diagnostic or progress test or as revision and fluency practice. For example, if done as a test then it would not be appropriate to monitor or help them.

CRIME COLLOCATIONS

1A After explaining the activity, elicit the first answer as an example, in order to check Ss understand what to do. Ss complete the sentences alone then check in pairs. In feedback, elicit Ss' answers.

> **Answers:** 1 brought 2 release 3 alibi 4 appeal 5 fresh
> 6 convictions

B Read the example with the class. Ss test each other in pairs in the same way. Monitor and help where necessary. In feedback, nominate Ss to share their descriptions for the class to guess their collocation.

> **Optional extra activity**
> Ss choose 3 of the collocations, and invent a crime story, which they write in pairs. Monitor and help with new vocabulary, writing any new words and expressions on the board. When they are ready, they read out their story to other Ss. In feedback, elicit which story Ss liked best.

THE PERFECT ASPECT

2 Introduce the idea of doctor, doctor jokes with the following example: 'Patient: Doctor, doctor, I think I'm losing my memory.' Doctor: 'How long has this been going on?' Patient: 'How long has what been going on?'. Ask if Ss have similar jokes in their country or countries. Ss complete the jokes alone then check in pairs. In feedback, elicit Ss' answers and which jokes they liked best.

> **Answers:** 1 have you been feeling 2 have turned 3 I've
> broken 4 it will have been 5 to have been ignoring

INTRODUCTORY *IT*

3 Read the example with the class. Ss complete the sentences alone, then check in pairs. Monitor and help with vocabulary, writing any new words and phrases on the board. In feedback, nominate Ss to share their ideas with the class.

> **Alternative approach**
> When Ss have written their sentences in Ex 3, arrange them in pairs. Ss take it in turn to read out their sentences at random, without saying the phrase with introductory *it* (they can substitute the phrase by saying 'blank'). Their partner listens and guesses which phrase it completes. In feedback, nominate Ss to share their sentences with the class.

SOCIAL ISSUES

4A Ss complete the definitions alone then check in pairs. In feedback, elicit Ss' answers.

> **Answers:** 1 child labour 2 illegal immigration 3 religious
> freedom 4 human rights 5 economic development
> 6 intellectual property

B Ss complete the definitions in pairs. Monitor and help with vocabulary, writing any new words and phrases on the board. In feedback, nominate Ss to read out their definitions for other Ss to guess which expression they are describing.

> **Optional extra activity**
> Ss work alone to think of example measures/laws from their own country or countries for each of the social issues in Ex 4B. Monitor and help with vocabulary, writing any new words and phrases on the board. When they are ready, Ss compare their ideas in pairs. In feedback, nominate Ss to share their ideas with the class.

HYPOTHETICAL PREFERENCES

5A After explaining the activity, elicit the first answer as an example, in order to check Ss understand what to do. Ss correct the mistakes alone then check in pairs. In feedback, elicit Ss' answers.

> **Answers:** 1 If it was **up to** me I'd have taken the cruise.
> 2 I **would sooner** watch the film than read the book. 3 I'd
> **just as** soon eat local food as dine in a fancy restaurant. 4 If
> I **found myself** in this situation, I'd go to the nearest house
> and beg for help. 5 **Far better** to do that than buy presents
> for everybody! 6 This would be by **far the** best option if
> you want to see places. 7 I'd have done the same **without a**
> shadow of a doubt. 8 **No way** would I do that unless I really
> had to.

> **Homework ideas**
> • **Workbook** Review and check 2, p28–30
> • **Workbook** Test 2, p31

OVERVIEW

5.1   FAMILY SECRETS

GRAMMAR | modal verbs and phrases

VOCABULARY | secrets

HOW TO | talk about obligations

COMMON EUROPEAN FRAMEWORK

COMMON EUROPEAN FRAMEWORK
Ss can use a good range of idiomatic expressions; can write clear, smoothly flowing stories in a style appropriate to the genre adopted.

5.2   TRUTH OR MYTH

GRAMMAR | the passive

VOCABULARY | truth or myth

HOW TO | discuss whether something is true

COMMON EUROPEAN FRAMEWORK
Ss can use language flexibly and effectively; can give clear, detailed descriptions of complex subjects;

5.3   TELL ME NO LIES

FUNCTION | justify a point

VOCABULARY | journalism

LEARN TO | manage a conversation

COMMON EUROPEAN FRAMEWORK
Ss can select a suitable phrase from a readily available range of discourse functions to preface their remarks appropriately in order to get the floor, or to gain time and keep the floor whilst thinking.

5.4   ⊙ BBC DVD

speakout | seven secrets about me

writeback | personal facts

COMMON EUROPEAN FRAMEWORK
Ss can give clear, detailed descriptions of complex subjects; can write clear, detailed, well-structured and developed descriptions in an assured, personal, natural style.

5.5   LOOKBACK

Communicative revision activities

BBC VIDEO PODCAST
Are you good at keeping secrets?

This video podcast extends discussion of the unit topic to keeping secrets. Ss can view people discussing when you should keep a secret and whether they have any secret talents. Use this video podcast at the start or end of Unit 5.

FAMILY SECRETS

Introduction

Ss revise and practise modal verbs and phrases in the context of family secrets. They also practise writing a narrative.

SUPPLEMENTARY MATERIALS

Resource bank p157

Warm up: think of a secret you've told and a secret you've been told, and prepare details to tell Ss.

Warm up

Demonstrate by telling Ss about a secret you've been told in your life (big or small), and give as many details as possible. Give Ss five minutes to think about a secret they've been told. Make it clear that it doesn't need to be a big secret, and should be one that they're happy to talk about. When they are ready, Ss share their information in pairs. Monitor and encourage Ss to ask follow-up questions to find out more information. In feedback, nominate Ss to share their ideas with the class.

LISTENING

1 Arrange the Ss in small groups to discuss the questions. Monitor and help with vocabulary, writing any new words and phrases on the board. In feedback, nominate Ss from each group to share their ideas with the class and have a brief class discussion.

2A Ss read the text alone then discuss the questions in pairs. In feedback, elicit Ss' ideas.

> **Answer:** It means that people are more open, that they are more likely to talk about their experiences, both good and bad.

B ▶ 5.1 Elicit/check: *slap* (hit someone with the flat part of your hand) and *make up* (become friends again after an argument). Ss listen to the recording and answer the questions, then check in pairs. In feedback, elicit Ss' answers.

> **Answers:** 4 secrets: how much her father earned, that a girl was going out with another girl's boyfriend, accidentally telling someone what their Christmas present was, a romance with another man

C Ss answer the questions from memory. Play the recording again for Ss to check their answers. In feedback, elicit Ss' answers.

> **Answers:** 1 His daughter telling people how much money he earned 2 Yes, she was. 3 What her husband had bought her as a Christmas present 4 Yes, she is. 5 Secrets that protect somebody or something in a way that wouldn't damage them when they ultimately find out.

Unit 5 Recording 1

J = Jenni Murray A = Ailish Kavanagh E = Eva Price G = Girl
W1 = Woman 1 W2 = Woman 2

J: Now, if I'd ever told anybody how much my dad earned, he'd have been absolutely furious. I'm not sure that I ever really knew. We were raised in an atmosphere where families kept themselves to themselves and you told nobody your business.

And then it all changed as we became more knowledgeable about the kind of dangerous secrets that might be held behind closed doors, and the damage they could do. We were encouraged as a society to tell these tales and let it all hang out. So, can we still keep a secret?

G: One of my friends told me to keep a secret about how she was going out with this other girl's boyfriend. And I kind of went up to the girl and told her by accident, it just fell out. She got really, really annoyed and it was – oh, it was horrible. It was like I thought she was actually going to slap me. It was so bad. Oh my god. We made up like two hours later but it was just the initial, you know, … I should never have told her secret though. So, it was my fault.

A: Have you ever given away anyone's secret by accident?

W1: Probably, just Christmas presents maybe accidentally telling someone what their Christmas present was. My husband nearly did that yesterday actually. He took an afternoon off work to go and …err … go and get something for my … for Christmas for me. He wouldn't tell me for days where he was going, and almost let it slip where he was … I really wish he had given it away.

A: What's the hardest secret that you've ever had to keep?

W2: I revealed a secret of a of a romance that I had with an older man. That I revealed to my husband because I decided that I had to tell him … er … so that … because I couldn't live with this secret. If I had to live in honesty with my husband, I had to reveal to him this secret and face the consequences. And, as you can see this is the consequence – we've grown closer together as a result of that …

A: So the consequences were quite good then, it seems?

W2: They were. Here he is, still at my side, and I'm at his side. So that was a very big secret that I kept, but I did reveal it.

J: Ailish Kavanagh talking to people in Croydon. So when do you spill the beans and be honest, and when is it better to stay schtum? Well, Christine Northam is a counsellor with Relate. Eva Rice is the author of a novel called *The Lost Art of Keeping a Secret*. Do you really think we have lost the art of keeping a secret?

E: I, I certainly do. I think that nowadays everyone's so encouraged to say everything at all times, and express the way they feel, umm, at the drop of a hat. And I think that the point of my book was to get across the fact that sometimes keeping a secret isn't always a bad thing. It can be something that um … can bring a more positive outcome than always, always telling everyone how you feel.

J: So what kind of secret would you keep?

E: I think well, like the characters in my book, if you're keeping a secret that is, in some way, going to protect somebody from something. Obviously I don't want to give away too much of the plot. But if you're protecting somebody in a way that isn't going to damage them when they do ultimately find out… um…I think that in that case a secret is a very good thing to keep. But nowadays, it's something that is frowned upon, and something that is considered wrong. And you're supposed to tell everyone the way you feel 24 hours a day, and so it's something that you shouldn't do is keep a secret.

VOCABULARY idioms: secrets

3A Ss complete the sentences alone then check in pairs. Monitor and help where necessary, but don't elicit any answers yet.

When Ss are ready, play recording 5.1 again for Ss to check their answers. In feedback, elicit Ss' answers.

Answers: 1 themselves 2 doors 3 let 4 beans 5 stay 6 cat 7 game

B Check Ss understand that some expressions have the same meaning. Ss match the expression to the meanings alone then check in pairs. In feedback, elicit Ss' answers.

Answers: 1 e) 2 b) 3 c) 4 a) 5 d) 6 c) 7 c)

Optional extra activity
Explain that the expressions in Ex 3A are fairly informal. Arrange Ss in pairs and ask them to think of more formal ways to say each expression. In feedback, elicit Ss' answers and write them on the board.

Suggested answers: 1 keep their affairs private 2 confidentially 3, 6 and 7 reveal 4 divulge a secret 5 keep quiet, keep information confidential

➡ **VOCABULARYBANK** p152 IDIOMS: SECRETS

1A Ss match the similar phrases alone then check in pairs. In feedback, elicit Ss' answers, and be prepared to provide further explanations and examples where necessary.

B Focus attention on the pictures and elicit what Ss can see in each one. Elicit the first answer as an example. Ss match the phrases and pictures alone, then check in pairs. In feedback, elicit Ss' answers.

C Ss discuss the question in pairs. In feedback, elicit Ss' answers. *Stronger classes* can do the exercises at home.

Answers: 1A 2 d) 3 b) 4 e) 5 a) B 1 C 2 B 3 E 4 D 5 A C 1, 2, 4, b), e)

SPEAKING

4 Ss discuss the questions in small groups.

Monitor and make notes on any common errors and good language used for later feedback. In feedback, nominate Ss from each group to share their ideas with the class and have a brief class discussion. Give Ss feedback on their language.

GRAMMAR modal verbs and phrases

5A Read the example with the class. Ss match the forms and meanings alone then check in pairs.

Answers: 2 It wasn't possible/I wasn't able 3 I was obliged (strong) 4 it's possible 5 it's expected 6 it isn't a good idea 7 I was obliged (weak) 8 you did it but it was unnecessary

B Ss match the sentences and meanings alone then check in pairs. Monitor and help where necessary. In feedback, elicit Ss' answers and be prepared to provide further explanations and examples where necessary.

Answers: 1 b) 2 a) 3 a) 4 b) 5 a) 6 b)

Watch out!
All English modals have something in common: They express our mood at the time of speaking. You can illustrate this by writing the following two sentences on the board: *She is a doctor* and *She must be a doctor*. Ask: *How many people are involved in each sentence?* In the first sentence, only one person is mentioned (*she*), as it's a fact. In the second sentence, two people are involved, which we can see if we say it in a different way: *From everything I know about her, I think she is a doctor*. Because they express our mood/personal opinion *at the time of speaking*, modals do not have past forms. This can also help explain the difference between *needn't have* (opinion) and *didn't need to* (fact).

C Ss match the sentences alone then check in pairs. In feedback, elicit Ss' answers and be prepared to provide further explanations and examples where necessary.

> **Answers:** 2 forbidden = 7 banned 3 obligatory = 9 compulsory 4 had the courage to = 8 dared to 6 compelled to = 10 forced to

> ⇒ **LANGUAGEBANK** 5.1 p136–137
>
> *Stronger classes* can read the notes and do the exercises at home. Otherwise, check the notes with Ss, especially the difference between *didn't need to* and *needn't have*. In each exercise, do the first sentence as an example. Ss complete the exercises alone, then check their answers in pairs. Ss can refer to the notes to help them.
>
> > **Answers:** 1 1 We weren't allowed to bring our own food to school. 2 I shouldn't have told him that I cheated in the exam. 3 You'd better turn your mobiles off. 4 You have to hand this work in first thing in the morning. 5 I didn't dare tell them the truth.
> > 6 They're not supposed to have their lights on after 10p.m. 2 1 You didn't need to rush. There's another five minutes before the film starts. 2 We'd better to leave plenty of time to get to the airport in case of heavy traffic. 3 You didn't have got to buy a present. That's very kind of you. 4 You shouldn't drive a car if you're tired. 5 We didn't have to stop at all on the way.
> > 6 They were supposed to deliver the furniture today.
> > 7 You ought to try this programme – it's very good.
> > 8 You shouldn't to talk to people like that. It's rude.

6A ▶ 5.2 Read the examples with the class. Ss listen to the recording and notice the elision.

> **Teaching tip**
>
> While we wouldn't (and shouldn't) expect our Ss to sound like native speakers when they speak, working on features of connected speech such as elision can help Ss better understand rapid speech when listening.

B ▶ 5.3 Ss listen and repeat the sentences. Play the recording twice if necessary.

Unit 5 Recording 3

1 Dictionaries are allowed in the exam.
2 It's obligatory for companies to provide details of their industrial processes.
3 She felt compelled to resign because of the scandal.
4 Only a few journalists dared to cover the story.
5 At least she had the courage to tell him what had happened.
6 Cars have been banned from the city centre.

PRACTICE

7 Ss choose the best alternatives alone then check in pairs. In feedback, elicit Ss' answers.

> **Answers:** 1 were never allowed to 2 had to 3 used to 4 should have 5 ought to keep 6 had to hide 7 'd better not 8 was supposed to 9 could have 10 would have

8 Give Ss 5 mins to choose their topics and think about what they're going to say. Monitor and help with vocabulary, writing any new words/phrases on the board. When they are ready, Ss talk about their topics in pairs. In feedback, nominate Ss to share their ideas with the class.

WRITING a narrative

9A Elicit/check: *eager fascination* and *a bit of a dragon*. Ss read the story then discuss the question in pairs. Elicit ideas as a class, then Ss turn to p161 and find the answer.

> **Answer:** love letters

B Ss discuss the questions in pairs. In feedback, elicit Ss' ideas.

10A Ss read the features alone then discuss in pairs which are often found. In feedback, elicit Ss' answers.

> **Answers:** 1, 2, 4, 5, 7, 8 and 9

B Ss read the story and work alone to identify the features used, then check in pairs. In feedback, elicit Ss' answers.

> **Answers:** 1, 2, 4, 5, 7, 8

LEARN TO use time phrases

11A Ss read the extract and underline the time phrase in pairs. Elicit Ss' answers.

> **Answers:** During that time

B Ss work alone to underline the time phrases in paragraphs 4 and 5, then check in pairs. In feedback, elicit Ss' answers and check understanding of the time phrases.

> **Answers:** after a year, subsequently, eventually, From then on, Years later

C With *weaker classes*, check understanding of the phrases in the box before they complete the sentences. Check Ss understand that more than one answer may be possible. Ss complete the sentences alone then check in pairs. In feedback, elicit Ss' answers.

> **Answers:** 1 as soon as/the moment 2 afterwards
> 3 meanwhile/in the meantime 4 instantly/immediately
> 5 subsequently/eventually 6 eventually/subsequently
> 7 ever since 8 from then on/instantly/immediately

D Ss complete the sentences alone then check in pairs. Monitor and help with vocabulary, writing any new words and phrases on the board. In feedback, nominate Ss to share their ideas with the class.

12A Read the stages with the class and check understanding. Monitor and help with ideas and vocabulary, writing any new words and phrases on the board.

speakout TIP

Before reading the **speakout tip**, ask Ss to close their notebooks and take a few moments to relax and take a few deep breaths. Read the **speakout tip** with the class and ask them to think about the questions when they return to their drafts.

B Ss check their drafts. Monitor and help where necessary. When they are ready, Ss write a second draft. When they have finished, Ss show their stories to other Ss. In feedback, nominate Ss to share which stories they liked and why with the class.

> **Homework ideas**
> * Ex 12B: write a final draft of your narrative.
> * Language bank 5.1 Ex 1–2, p137
> * Workbook Ex 1–5, p32–33

TRUTH OR MYTH?

Introduction

Ss revise and practise the passive in the context of truths and myths. They also learn and practise multi-word verbs.

SUPPLEMENTARY MATERIALS

Resource bank p155, p156 and p158

Warm up: Bring a small piece of paper and a larger piece of paper for each pair of Ss.

Ex 8C: bring dictionaries to class for Ss to use.

Warm up

Arrange Ss in pairs and give each pair a large piece of paper and a smaller piece of paper. Elicit how many times Ss think they can fold each piece of paper in half, and ask: *Does anyone think they can fold more than 8 times?* Ss attempt to fold their pieces of paper in half as many times as possible. In feedback, elicit how many folds Ss achieved, and explain that it doesn't matter how large the paper is, it will never fold more than eight times.

READING

1A Introduce the topic by writing the following examples on the board: *Chewing gum takes 7 years to digest* and *Humans have 5 senses*. Ask Ss if they have heard these 'facts' before and whether they think they are true or false (They are both false. Chewing gum is not actually digested by the human body, and passes through the system in the same way as other matter. Balance, acceleration, pain, body and limb position and relative temperature are also human senses.) Ss read the introduction then discuss the question in pairs. In feedback, elicit Ss' ideas.

B Arrange Ss in A/B pairs. Ss read their texts and answer the questions. Monitor and help with vocabulary, writing any new words and phrases on the board.

Answers: Student A: 1 The myths are: 1, that if you drive fast enough you won't get caught by a speed camera, 2, that it's safe to use a hands-free mobile while you're driving 3, that goldfish have short memories and 4, that owls can turn their heads all the way round. 2 Experiments disproved 2 and 3. Science makes 4 impossible. 3 1 is technically possible but you would have to drive extremely fast. 4 is partially true – owls can turn their heads 270 degrees.
Student B: 1 The myths are: 5, that sugar makes children hyperactive, 6, that you get a cold from getting cold, 7, that it damages your computer if you turn it off without shutting it down and 8, that your email is private. 2 Experiments disproved 5, 6, and 7. We know 8 is a myth because Google scans our emails for key words in order to target their advertising. 3 6 is partially true as getting cold does make it more likely that you will catch a virus. In 7, although you won't damage your PC, you could lose data if you turn off when things are running.

C Ss share their answers to the questions in Ex 1B in pairs. Encourage them to describe the myths in their own words. When they have finished, give Ss three or four minutes to read the other texts quickly. In feedback, elicit which ideas the Ss found most surprising.

Teaching tip

At this level, Ss have a lot more language at their disposal when relaying information. 'Jigsaw' reading activities such as in Ex 1 are a good way of providing Ss with an opportunity to do this. Encourage Ss to describe what they read without looking back at the texts. This will ensure they use their own words when describing what they read.

VOCABULARY truth or myth

2A Ss find the expression and answer the questions alone then check in pairs. In feedback, elicit Ss' answers and be prepared to provide further explanations and examples where necessary.

Answers: 1 a fallacy 2 conventional wisdom, a commonly held perception, intuitively true 3 uncover 4 debunk, disprove 5 verify

B Ss add the missing words alone then check in pairs. In feedback, elicit Ss' answers.

Answers: 1 It is a **commonly** held perception that no one can survive a plane crash. 2 **Conventional** wisdom says you shouldn't swim soon after eating. 3 Scientists in Panama recently disproved **the** myth that sloths are lazy. 4 The myth that you lose most of your body heat through your head has been **debunked/disproved**. 5 It seems intuitively **true** that long-distance running is bad for your knees, but recent research suggests otherwise.

C Give Ss two or three minutes to think of examples alone. Monitor and help with ideas and vocabulary, writing any new words and phrases on the board. When they are ready, Ss share their ideas in pairs. In feedback, nominate Ss to share their ideas with the class.

Optional extra activity

Describe some common national stereotypes/ misconceptions about people from your country. Ss work alone to think of and write three national stereotypes/ misconceptions about people from their country/ies. Monitor and help with vocabulary, writing any new words/ phrases on the board. When they are ready, arrange Ss in small groups to share their ideas. In feedback, nominate Ss from each group to share their ideas with the class.

GRAMMAR the passive

3A Ss read the sentences alone then discuss which ones are true in pairs. Monitor Ss and make sure they don't look at the answers below. Don't elicit any answers yet.

B Ss read the sentences and check their answers. In feedback, elicit which ones Ss found most surprising.

C Ss work alone to underline examples of the passive, then check in pairs and discuss why we use the forms. In feedback, elicit Ss' answers.

Answers: 1 cannot be seen, can be made out 2 had the dish named 3 is claimed 4 is processed 5 isn't expected to change

D Ss match the examples and uses alone then check in pairs. In feedback, elicit Ss' answers and be prepared to provide further explanations/examples where necessary.

Answers: a) 4 b) 3 c) 2 d) 1 e) 5

⟹ LANGUAGEBANK 5.2 p136–137

Stronger classes can read the notes and do the exercises at home. Otherwise, check the notes with Ss, especially the different uses of the passive. In each exercise, do the first sentence as an example. Ss complete the exercises alone, then check their answers in pairs. Ss can refer to the notes to help them.

Answers: 1A 1 The case is being investigated by the police. 2 You are allowed to borrow a car for official business. 3 Mike is having his washing machine delivered today. 4 It is claimed (that) the tradition began in the nineteenth century. 5 Wilhelm might have been recognised. 6 She had the players stretch before the game. 7 Our luggage is being checked in right now. 8 The product has only been tested on volunteers.
B Because we want to emphasise the action rather than the doer.
1, 2, 4 and 8 might be formal written English.
2 1 It is said 2 These secrets need to be kept 3 what can be done 4 brainwashing was considered 5 it was discovered 6 certain memories could be erased

PRACTICE

4 With *weaker classes*, elicit the first answer as an example. Ss rewrite the sentences alone then check in pairs. Monitor and check they are forming the passive correctly. In feedback, elicit Ss' answers.

Answers: 1 is believed/thought 2 his wallet stolen. 3 was being fixed 4 should be taken 5 needs to be done 6 have been seen

5 Ss read the text alone, then, in pairs, discuss which phrases are better in the passive. In feedback, elicit Ss' answers.

Answers: 1 has been passed on 2 OK *or* It isn't known 3 it has been attributed 4 OK 5 The fear of the number thirteen is known 6 thirteen is considered 7 OK *or* This superstition can be seen 8 the number thirteen is omitted 9 the house between number 12 and 14 is given the number 12½ 10 the unlucky number four is often omitted

SPEAKING

6A Give Ss enough time to think of a myth and make notes. If Ss are stuck for ideas, they can choose from the examples on p160. Monitor and help with vocabulary, writing any new words and phrases on the board.

B Arrange Ss in small groups to debunk their myths. Monitor and note any common errors and good language for later feedback. In feedback, nominate Ss from each group to share their ideas with the class, and give Ss feedback on their language use.

VOCABULARY *PLUS* multi-word verbs

7A Introduce the topic by telling Ss which of them you do or have done, and answer any questions Ss have. Ss discuss the questions in pairs. Monitor and encourage Ss to ask follow-up questions to find out more information.

B Elicit/check *dire warnings* (extremely serious) and *doom-mongers* (people who spread rumours that terrible things will happen). Ss read the text then discuss the questions in pairs. In feedback, elicit Ss' answers and ideas.

Answer: 1 The message is that technology is not a negative influence and is actually turning children into quick-thinking, multi-tasking, high-achieving citizens of the 21st century'.

8A Books closed. On the board, write: *back, around, away, off, out, down, on, up* and *over* in a column to the right of the board. Elicit what multi-word verbs Ss know which use these particles, and if they can remember any from the text. Write them on the board. Ss work alone to underline the multi-word verbs in the review, then check in pairs. In feedback, elicit Ss' answers and check understanding of the multi-word verbs.

Answers: looked back, stood around, Take away, Switch off, thought it over, boils down, carry on, speeds up, turning them into, find out

B Read the examples with the class. Ss complete the table alone then check in pairs. In feedback, elicit Ss' answers.

Answers: (from top to bottom) (off) remove, cancel or end something; (out) be in the open; (down) decrease or reduce; (away) removal or disposal; (back) return (to the past); (around) with no direction or aim; (over) think or talk about

C If you have brought dictionaries to class, distribute them for Ss to use. Ss write example sentences alone then check in pairs. In feedback, elicit Ss' ideas and check understanding of the multi-word verbs in the table.

speakout TIP

Read the **speakout tip** with the class and discuss the different ways Ss record multi-word verbs.

9 Ss complete the sentences alone then check in pairs. In feedback, elicit Ss' answers.

Answers: 1 down, on 2 over, down 3 off, up 4 around, away 5 out, back

10A Ss choose the correct alternative alone then check in pairs. In feedback, elicit Ss' answers.

Answers: 1 Cast your mind back 2 find out 3 narrow down 4 mull over

B Ss discuss the questions in pairs. In feedback, nominate Ss to share their ideas with the class.

⟹ VOCABULARYBANK p152 MULTI-WORD VERBS

2A Ss complete the sentences alone then check in pairs. In feedback, elicit Ss' answers, and be prepared to provide further explanations/examples where necessary.

B Read the example with the class. Ss rephrase the ideas in pairs. In feedback, nominate Ss to share their ideas with the class.
Stronger classes can do the exercises at home.

Answers: 2A 1 over 2 up 3 on 4 off 5 down 6 away 7 back 8 around

Homework ideas
- Ex 6A: write a wiki entry for the myth you debunked.
- Language bank 5.2 Ex 1–2, p137
- Workbook Ex 1–5, p34–35

TELL ME NO LIES

Introduction

Ss learn and practice justifying a point and how to manage a conversation.

SUPPLEMENTARY MATERIALS

Resource bank p159

Warm up

Read out the following scenario to the class: *You work for a large, multinational company, and have just gained a very big promotion to Chief Financial Officer. You are over the moon, because this means you can now afford to buy a dream house for your family in a nice area, and send your children to an expensive school. However, on the first day of the job, you begin to realise that the company's accounts are not as they should be. On further investigation, you realise the company has been making a loss for the last four years and has run up a huge debt, while lying to the shareholders in order to keep the share price high. What would you do?* Ss discuss the situation in pairs. Monitor and help with vocabulary, writing any new words and phrases on the board. In feedback, elicit Ss' ideas and have a brief class discussion.

VOCABULARY journalism

1A Write: *Wikileaks* on the board, and elicit what Ss know about it. Ss discuss the questions in pairs. Don't elicit any answers yet.

Culture notes

Wikileaks was created in 2006, and is an organisation which aims to publish leaked information from governments and whistleblowers (people who make damaging or sensitive information public from inside organisations). It was founded by a group of people from different countries, and its director is Julian Assange. It has caused huge scandals with the amount of secret information it has made public, and at the time of writing Julian Assange was undergoing an extradition trial to Sweden, where he is wanted for separate charges.

B Ss read the text to check their answers, then compare in pairs. In feedback, elicit Ss' answers.

Answers: 1 Information which was previously kept secret by organisations or governments. 2 Anybody can send the information anonymously. 3 It is increasingly hard for them to keep information secret.

2 Ask Ss to cover the text and try to complete the sentences from memory. When they are ready, Ss read the text again to check. In feedback, elicit Ss' answer and be prepared to provide further explanations and examples where necessary.

Answers: 1 investigative journalism 2 scoop 3 injunction 4 whistle-blowing 5 sensitive 6 source 7 leak 8 truth, out

Optional extra activity

Arrange Ss in pairs. Ss choose two of the words from Ex 2 and include them in a short, fictional news story about a scandal involving leaked information. Monitor and help with ideas and vocabulary, writing any new words and phrases on the board. When they are ready, Ss read out their stories to the class in the style of a television news bulletin.

FUNCTION making a point

3A ▶ 5.4 Give Ss one minute to read the points and check understanding. Ss listen and put them in the order they are mentioned, then check in pairs. In feedback, elicit Ss' answers.

Answers: 1 e) 2 b) 3 d) 4 f) 5 c) 6 a)

B Ss complete the phrases from memory in pairs. When they are ready, play the recording again for Ss to check. In feedback, elicit Ss' answers.

Answers: 1 reason 2 sure, evidence 3 point 4 put 5 account 6 find 7 make

Unit 5 Recording 4

W=woman; M=man MA= Marc

W: What do you think about organisations like WikiLeaks?

M: Well, to be honest, I think they should be stopped. And the reason why I say that is because they are responsible for leaking all kinds of confidential information, some of which is highly sensitive information about people who work in government, or military strategy, and they release this kind of information in a way which is, which is quite honestly … completely reckless. They seem to have no regard for the ethics of what they are doing, and um I think they should be stopped. They've exposed people who they say are informants, and now the lives of those people and their families are now in danger.

W: Hold on a minute. Can you be sure about that? Is there any evidence to prove that?

M: Well, no, probably not, not absolute proof. But that's not the point. The only way to prove it will be if something terrible happens to those people as a result of the information which has been disclosed. The the point is that governments and you know certain organisations simply have to be able to keep some information private. It doesn't make sense for everybody to have access to all the information that they want. Let me put it this way. It's like saying you need to give everybody your bank account details, because we all have the right to know, but you don't. You don't have that right, and it's simply ridiculous to think that you do. If you think about it, it's just irresponsible and it's dangerous.

W: I don't see how you can say that. Don't you think that there are cases when it's quite right for the public to know what's happening? Marc, where do you stand on this?

MA: Well, yes, absolutely. I agree. It's not something I've thought much about before, but in fact, I think that WikiLeaks is one of the best things to happen in the last few years. It has opened up access to information, and it means that big companies and governments will need to be much more careful about how they deal with things in the future, because they can no longer hide behind secrets. And that is how it should be. After all, if you think about it, you can't give people the protection to do whatever they want without fear of being discovered. Whether it's companies using spies to find out what rival companies are planning, or governments holding people illegally, or using illegal practices to get information. I think freedom of information can only be a good thing, and it's like a wake-up call to all those who previously thought that they could get away with wrongdoing by just keeping it quiet. That just doesn't work anymore.

M: But that doesn't take account of the fact that some information, like military information is highly sensitive, and should not be allowed to spread around the internet where simply anybody can get hold of it and use it for whatever purposes they wish.

MA: I think you'll find that actually information has always been leaked. It's just the medium that has changed now, so that with the internet it's a bit easier, but there've always been whistleblowers, and there will continue to be. It's no different. The point I'm trying to make is that if the chances of you being discovered are increased, the likelihood of you being exposed, then it will make you think twice about the actions you're taking, whether you're in government or in a big corporation. I think you'll find that people will be more careful in the future, and in my opinion that can only be a good thing.

C Check understanding of the three functions in the chart. Ss add the phrases from Ex 3B to the table alone, then check in pairs. In feedback, elicit Ss' answers and drill the phrases chorally and individually.

Answers: 1 The reason why I say that is … 2 Let me put it this way. 3 I think you'll find that … 4 The point I'm trying to make is that … 5 Can you be sure about that? 6 But that's not the point. 7 But that doesn't take account of the fact that …

⟱ LANGUAGEBANK 5.3 p136–137

Stronger classes could read the notes and do the exercise at home. Otherwise, drill the phrases from the chart, checking Ss are using natural intonation. Ss work alone to order the words, then check their answers in pairs. In feedback, elicit Ss' answers. Ss practise the conversation in pairs.

Answers: 1 What I'm saying is 2 The facts suggest 3 the point is 4 Do you think that is always the case? 5 After all, 6 There are several reasons why I think 7 if you think about it, 8 I don't see how you can say that 9 let me put it this way 10 the point I'm trying to make is

4 Ss complete the responses alone then check in pairs. In feedback, elicit Ss' answers. Ss practise the conversations in pairs.

Answers: 1 put it this way 2 don't see how you can 3 doesn't take account of the fact 4 I'm basically saying 5 you'll find that

LEARN TO manage a conversation

5A Introduce the topic by telling Ss about any difficulties you've had when trying to discuss an issue in another language, and how they made you feel. Arrange Ss in small groups to discuss the question. In feedback, nominate Ss from each group to share their ideas with the class.

B Focus attention on the functions and check understanding. Ss categorise the phrases alone then check in pairs. In feedback, elicit Ss' answers and drill the phrases chorally and individually.

Answers: 1 Where do you stand on this? 2 Sorry, and another thing … 3 I suppose, if you think about it … 4 Getting back to the point, which is …

Watch out!

When we're speaking, we add voice to the sounds we make by pushing air through our vocal chords. The faster the air travels, the faster the vocal chords vibrate, and so the higher the pitch. Therefore, when we have more to say, the air is still passing through the vocal chords and we produce a rising or steady tone. When we are concluding, the air slows down, as does the vocal chords, and so produce a falling tone. Explaining this to Ss can help Ss sound more natural when they speak.

SPEAKING

6A Give Ss five minutes to write their answers and justifications. Monitor and help with vocabulary, writing any new words and phrases on the board.

B Arrange Ss in small groups to discuss the questions. Monitor and make notes on any common errors and good language for later feedback. In feedback, nominate Ss from each group to report back to the class, and have a brief class discussion. Give Ss feedback on their language.

Alternative approach

Write the phrases from Ex 5B onto pieces of paper or cards, and make one copy for each group. Ss shuffle and deal out the cards equally to the Ss in their group. When they are discussing the questions in Ex 6B, Ss try to insert a phrase from one of their cards into their conversation wherever possible, and then place their card face up in the middle as they use it. Ss should try and use all of their cards during the conversation. You can also keep these cards and use them at other times when discussing ideas, in order to encourage them to use the expressions.

Homework ideas
- Language bank 5.3 Ex 1, p137
- Workbook Ex 1–3, p36
- Write a summary of a famous news story involving a leak of information.

NORTH AND SOUTH

Introduction
Ss watch an extract from the BBC drama *North and South*, in which a brother who is hiding from the law returns home in secret. Ss learn and practise how to talk about themselves, and write a competition entry.

SUPPLEMENTARY MATERIALS
Warm up: Write the questions below on the board.

Warm up
Write the following questions on the board:
What do you know about what your country was like in the nineteenth century?
Would you like to have lived during this time?
If you could choose any period in history to visit, when would you visit?

Arrange Ss in small groups to discuss the questions. In feedback, nominate Ss from each group to share their ideas with the class.

DVD PREVIEW

1 Focus attention on the words in the box and check understanding. Ss read the programme information then discuss which elements they think it contains in pairs. In feedback, nominate Ss to share their ideas with the class.

Answers: The drama involves a family saga and romance.

Culture notes
The BBC drama *North and South*, first screened in 2004, is based on an 1855 novel of the same title by Elizabeth Gaskell. It's about a young woman who moves to the north of England after her father leaves his work with the church, and how their family struggles to adjust to the local customs there. It stars British actors Daniela Denby-Ashe (Margaret) and Richard Armitage (John Thornton).

DVD VIEW

2 Ss watch the DVD then answer the question in pairs. In feedback, elicit Ss' answers.

Answer: John Thornton thought he had seen Margaret with a secret lover. At the end, he learns that the man was her brother.

Optional extra activity
Before Ex 2, Ss watch the DVD with the sound off. As they watch, Ss work alone to make notes to describe how they think the people are feeling, then compare in pairs. Elicit Ss' ideas at this stage and write them on the board. Ss watch the DVD again with the sound on, and compare their original ideas, making any changes they want to.

3A Ss complete the descriptions in pairs from memory. Monitor and help where necessary, but don't give any answers yet.

B Play the DVD again for Ss to check their answers. In feedback, elicit Ss' answers.

Answers: 1 father 2 Frederick 3 funeral 4 John Thornton 5 John Thornton 6 Spain

4 Ss discuss the questions in pairs. In feedback, nominate Ss to share their ideas with the class.

North and South
Mr H=Mr Hale MH=Margaret Hale H=Housekeeper
F=Frederick Hale JT=Mr Thornton HI=Higgins

Mr H: Margaret, are you expecting a letter?
MH: No. Yes. Father I've got something I have to tell you. I've written to Frederick. I know that I shouldn't have.
Mr H: Because of your mother and you think he needs to come quickly?
MH: Please say I did the right thing father. Is the danger to Frederick so very great?
Mr H: Oh yes my dear, I'm afraid it is.
HO: Who'd come visiting at this hour? I'll get the master.
MH: No, I'll go.
F: Is Mr Hale in?
MH: Frederick! Fred … Frederick, oh!
F: Mother?
MH: She's still alive. She's as ill as she could be but she lives.
Mr H: My boy! You've come home.
F: I don't see why I should have to run away before the funeral. I've a good mind to face it out and stand trial.
Mr H: No, you must go Fred.
MH: You must leave tomorrow by the night train.
F: Only a few minutes more. I don't know when I'll see you again. Who was that?
MH: Mr Thornton. Go! Go!
F: God bless you Margaret. Goodbye.
MH: Father is waiting in the sitting room. Mr Thornton …
T: Do you not realise the risk that you take in being so indiscreet? Have you no explanation for your behaviour that night at the station? You must imagine what I must think.
MH: Mr Thornton please, I'm aware of what you must think of me. I know how it must have appeared, being with a stranger so late at night. The man you saw me with, he … the secret is another person's, and I cannot explain it without doing him harm.
Mr H: Is that you John? Come on up.
T: I've not the slightest wish to pry into the gentleman's secrets. I'm only concerned as your father's friend. I hope you realise that any foolish passion for you on my part is entirely over.
HI: I said have you heard aught about Miss Margaret?
JT: Still here?
HI: Just because it's the last shift master doesn't mean we shouldn't finish the job well.
JT: I'm nobody's master anymore Higgins.
HI: Anyway I was asking about Miss Margaret. Have you heard how she's doing?
JT: She's well, she's in London. I'll not see her again.
HI: Thought she might have gone to Spain.
JT: Spain, why would she go there?
HI: Well, to see her brother now he's her only family.
JT: Her brother? She doesn't have a brother.
HI: Him that were over when the mother were dying. Kept it a secret they did.
JT: Why wouldn't Mr Hale tell me that he had a son?
HI: Something to do with the law. He found himself on the wrong side of the navy, in real danger he was.
JT: It was her brother.

speakout seven secrets about me

5A Ss read the extract then answer the questions in pairs. In feedback, elicit Ss' ideas.

> **Answers:** The website wants the reader to write a list of seven personal secrets. The winner will get a book.

B ▶ 5.5 Ss listen and note down the secrets, then check in pairs. In feedback, elicit Ss' answers.

C Focus attention on the **Key phrases**. Ss listen and tick the phrases they hear, then check in pairs. In feedback, elicit Ss' answers and drill the **Key phrases** chorally and individually.

> **Answers:** She uses all of the phrases except: *Something I've never told anyone is that …*

Unit 5 Recording 5

OK, well, to start off with, I have a tattoo on my back. It's a sea horse and I had it done when I was eighteen. Second on my list is my birthday. I was born on Christmas Day. It's a bit of a disadvantage really because no one ever gives you two sets of presents and people tend to forget your birthday because they're so busy celebrating Christmas. Third, it's not what you'd call a big secret but I sing in a local choir. We practise once a week and do occasional concerts. Number four. My favourite film is *The Usual Suspects*. I've seen it about twenty times. Number five. If I didn't work in an office I'd like to be a dancer. I used to dance every day when I was a child and I really loved it. I might have taken it further but as a teenager I had back trouble for a couple of years and had to stop. My next one: a few close friends know this. I like gardening. I have an allotment where I grow vegetables like tomatoes and leeks, and I'm quite good at it. I like to potter around there on Sundays. It's sort of like therapy – very relaxing. And last but not least, at the age of thirty I still don't drive. I'm planning on getting round to it some time, but I've been saying that for years.

6A Give Ss enough time to think of their seven secrets and make notes alone. Monitor and help with vocabulary, writing any new words and phrases on the board.

B Arrange Ss in groups to share their ideas. Write on the board: *When did that happen? How did it make you feel? Why … ? How … ?* and encourage Ss to ask questions to find out more information. In feedback, nominate Ss from each group to share any interesting information with the class.

writeback personal facts

7A Ss read the entry then in pairs, discuss whether they have come to the same conclusions. In feedback, elicit Ss' answers, and answer any questions Ss have about vocabulary in the text.

> **Teaching tip**
> Before Ss start writing, encourage them to look back over the language they have learnt in the unit to see if there's any new lexis/grammar they can include in their texts.

B Ss write their seven personal facts alone. Monitor and encourage Ss to add as much detail as possible.

C When they have finished, Ss swap lists with a partner to read and discuss any unexpected information

> **Alternative approach**
> Ss write their seven personal facts on a separate piece of paper, and don't write their names on it. When they have finished, collect in their work, shuffle, and redistribute to the class. Make sure no-one receives the facts they wrote. Ss read the facts they have and try to guess who wrote them. When they are ready, Ss mingle and check, and find out who wrote the information they have. In feedback, nominate Ss to share any new/interesting information they found out with the class.

> **Homework ideas**
> • Ex 7B: write a final draft of your seven facts.

LOOKBACK

Introduction

Ss revise and practise the language of Unit 5. The notes below provide ideas for exploiting the exercises and activities but your approach will depend on your aim, e.g. as a diagnostic or progress test or as revision and fluency practice. For example, if done as a test then it would not be appropriate to monitor or help them.

IDIOMS: SECRETS

1A Ss underline the correct alternatives alone then check in pairs. In feedback, elicit Ss' answers.

> **Answers:** 1 keeps 2 doors 3 spill 4 schtum 5 slip

B Ss write their conversations in pairs. Monitor and help with ideas and vocabulary where necessary, writing any new words and phrases on the board. When they are ready, Ss perform their conversations for the class.

> **Alternative approach**
> Using a digital camera or mobile phone, Ss create a photo-journal of their conversations. Ss take 6 photos of themselves, acting out the main stages of their conversations, print them out, then underneath each one write key parts of their conversations. When they have finished, pin them up on a display board for other Ss to read.

MODAL VERBS AND PHRASES

2A With *weaker classes*, elicit the first one as an example. Check Ss understand that they should only use between two and four words. Ss complete the sentences alone then check in pairs. In feedback, elicit Ss' answers.

> **Answers:** 1 have gone to bed 2 supposed to finish
> 3 didn't dare/dared not 4 needn't have 5 are banned/
> aren't allowed 6 better not

B Ss complete the sentences alone. Monitor and help with vocabulary, writing any new words and phrases on the board. When they are ready, Ss compare their sentences in pairs. Encourage Ss to ask follow-up questions to find out more information. In feedback, nominate Ss to share their ideas with the class.

> **Optional extra activity**
> Write the following sentences on the board: *I needn't have done my homework. I should have said something sooner. You'd better not tell her. You're not supposed to leave it there. You ought to do it more quickly. He was forced to do it.* Ss choose one of the sentences and work alone to think of and write a short summary of a situation which ends with the sentence. Monitor and help with vocabulary, writing any new words/phrases on the board. When they are ready, arrange Ss in small groups to read out their summary for other Ss in the group to guess the sentence. In feedback, nominate Ss from each group to read out a summary for the class to guess.

TRUTH OR MYTH

3A After explaining the activity, elicit the first answer as an example, in order to check Ss understand what to do. Ss correct the sentences alone then check in pairs. In feedback, elicit Ss' answers.

> **Answers:** 1 conventional 2 debunked 3 verify
> 4 uncovered 5 intuitively 6 perception

B Ss discuss the sentences in pairs. In feedback, nominate Ss to share their ideas with the class.

THE PASSIVE

4A Elicit/check: *to tame (a horse)*. Ss complete the text alone then check in pairs. In feedback, elicit Ss' answers.

> **Answers:** 1 is believed 2 disappeared 3 had been stolen
> 4 came 5 were being 6 was thrown 7 wasn't recruited
> 8 helped 9 have been recognised

B Ss discuss what the moral is in pairs. In feedback, elicit Ss' ideas.

MAKING A POINT

5A After explaining the activity, elicit the first answer as an example, in order to check Ss understand what to do. Ss add the missing words alone then check in pairs. In feedback, elicit Ss' answers.

> **Answers:** Is there any evidence to **prove** that? 2 What **I'm**
> basically saying is we can't afford to waste any more time.
> 3 If **you** think about it, we'd be stupid to let this opportunity
> escape us. 4 I don't **see** how you can argue that economics
> doesn't have an influence on the situation.
> 5 Can we **be** sure about that?

B Ss practise the conversations in pairs, and try to extend them. In feedback, nominate pairs to perform their extended conversation for the class.

OVERVIEW

FUTURE GAZING

Introduction

Ss revise and practise future forms in the context of trends and predictions. They also learn and practise prepositional phrases.

SUPPLEMENTARY MATERIALS

Resource bank p160, p161 and p162

Warm up: write the words below on the board.

Warm up

Write on the board: *Learning English, Medicine, My career, Travel and Transport, Free time* and *Food and Cooking*. Give Ss five minutes to think about one development or invention they would like to see in the next ten years under each topic. Monitor and help with vocabulary, writing any new words and phrases on the board. When they are ready, arrange Ss in small groups to share their ideas. In feedback, nominate Ss from each group to share their ideas with the class.

SPEAKING

1 Introduce the activity by sharing some common predictions you have to make as a teacher (e.g. *how easy Ss will find the language you are going to teach, how long an activity will take,* etc.). Ss discuss what predictions each of the people have to make in small groups. In feedback, nominate Ss from each group to share their ideas with the class, and write any new words and phrases on the board.

Alternative approach

Arrange Ss in four groups, and allocate one of the people in Ex 1A to each group. Give Ss five minutes to brainstorm a list of possible predictions for each person. Monitor and help with vocabulary, writing any new words and phrases on the board. When they are ready, arrange Ss in groups of four, with one member from each of the previous groups to share their ideas. In feedback, nominate Ss from each group to share their ideas with the class.

VOCABULARY   trends and predictions

2A Ss find the expressions alone then check in pairs. Monitor and help where necessary. In feedback, elicit Ss' answers, and be prepared to provide further explanations and examples where necessary.

Answers: 1 e), h) 2 c) 3 a), f) 4 d), g), i) 5 b), j)

B Give Ss 3–4 mins to think about their answers. Monitor and help with vocabulary, writing any new words and phrases on the board. When they are ready, Ss compare their ideas in pairs. In feedback, nominate Ss to share their ideas with the class.

READING

3A Read the definition with the class. Ss discuss the questions in pairs. In feedback, elicit Ss' ideas but don't give any answers yet.

B Elicit/check *business moguls*. Introduce the topic of the text by asking: *Who was Nostradamus? What was he famous for?* (Nostradamus was a 16th Century French pharmacist who claimed to be able to predict the future. Some people believe a lot of his predictions have since come true, though most academic sources maintain that these realisations have largely been the result of misinterpretation or mistranslation). Ss read the text to check their answers then check in pairs. In feedback, elicit Ss' ideas.

Answers: 1 Futurologists work for big companies. 2 They do research, study trends in research and development, go to conferences, read technical magazines, and use common sense. 3 Futurologists have to have revolutionary ideas on a big scale, but big, radical ideas rarely become reality.

Culture notes
On New Year's Eve in 1961, The Beatles were driven to London for an audition with Decca records. The driver got lost and they eventually arrived very late. On 1st January 1962, they auditioned, playing 15 songs in just under one hour. A few weeks after the audition, Decca records rejected The Beatles, saying, 'guitar groups are on the way out' and 'The Beatles have no future in show business'. However, it has been suggested that since they were so tired on the day of the audition, they didn't play so well and this may have just been a polite way of rejecting them.

4A Read the example with the class. Ss write the questions alone then check in pairs. Check Ss understand that more than one answer may be possible. In feedback, elicit Ss' answers.

Suggested answers: 2 What (qualities) do you need to be a futurologist? 3 Where do futurologists go to get ideas? 4 What predictions have not come true?/What are some examples of ideas which have not taken off? 5 What do the next big things/new innovations have to do?

B Ss discuss the questions in pairs. Monitor and help where necessary, and encourage them to use the text to help them answer the questions. In feedback, elicit Ss' answers and be prepared to provide further examples where necessary.

Answers: 1 *Rooting out* ideas means to remove bad ideas. A root is the part of a tree or plant under the ground. If you want to remove a tree or plant permanently, you also need to remove the roots. 2 Things that fly, e.g. aeroplanes 'take off'. But 'take off' also has another meaning: to become extremely fashionable very quickly. 3 A graveyard is a place where dead people are buried. He uses the metaphor to say that some gadgets never become popular and are, therefore, 'dead'. 4 Buzz literally means a vibrating sound, but metaphorically means a 'thrill'. *Give someone a buzz* means to phone someone in colloquial language. In paragraph 5, it has both a literal and metaphorical meaning.

C Arrange Ss in small groups to discuss the questions. Monitor and help where necessary. In feedback, nominate Ss from each group to share their ideas with the class and have a brief class discussion.

GRAMMAR future forms

5 Read the examples with the class and check any new vocabulary. Ss match the sentences and rules alone then check in pairs. In feedback, elicit Ss' answers and be prepared to provide further explanations/examples where necessary.

Answers: 1 b) 2 e) 3 a) 4 d) 5 c)

6 Read the sentence with the class and elicit which form is being used in each case. Ss complete the rules alone then check in pairs. In feedback, elicit Ss' answers and be prepared to provide further explanations/examples where necessary.

Answers: f) an official arrangement or order g) expected to happen or arrive at a particular time h) not certain

7A ▶ 6.1 Ss listen to the recording and underline the sentences they hear, then check in pairs. In feedback, elicit Ss' answers.

Answers: 1 She'll have been running. 2 I'll be seeing him later. 3 I'll be there. 4 We're to be there at 1.00.

B Focus attention on the example and the phonemic transcription. Ss listen to the recording and notice how the grammar words are pronounced. Ss listen again and repeat.

Watch out!
Most grammar words reduce to a shorter vowel sound in connected speech. This is usually /ə/ (as in *We're going to be*) or /ɪ/ (as in *She'll be running*).

⟹ LANGUAGEBANK 6.1 p138–139
Stronger classes can read the notes and do the exercises at home. Otherwise, check the notes with Ss, especially the uses of *be to* and *be due to*. In each exercise, do the first sentence as an example. Ss complete the exercises alone, then check their answers in pairs. Ss can refer to the notes to help them.

Answers: 1 'Yesterday we announced that we are **to** merge with Jonas Inc. We are due **to** do this in May, so today I'm going **to** speak about the company's history and the decision to merge. This time next year the company will have **been** building houses for twenty-five years. By January we will **have** built more than 100,000 homes, and I hope that we'll still be **building** houses in 2050. Although we **will** be discussing the new situation with you individually, we are sure your jobs will **be** secure. Through this merger, we **will** be expanding and so we will be moving into unknown markets. By February, we will **have** sent you a document about the company's plans. For now, I promise there will be opportunities for all.'
2 1 By tomorrow, we will have been married for twenty years. 2 The London–Brussels flight arrives at 2.00/is due to arrive at 2.00. 3 The government is to pass a law prohibiting guns. 4 I'll be seeing John (in the office), so I can speak to him. 5 By July, we'll have been living here for five years. 6 The committee is due to have a meeting with the owners. 7 I imagine Roger will be putting up his Christmas decorations in November. 8 My son will be eighteen years old next March.

PRACTICE

8A Read the example with the class and check understanding. Ss discuss the sentences in pairs. Monitor and help where necessary. In feedback, elicit Ss' answers.

Answers: 2 Both are possible. *Might* is less certain than *will*. 3 Families **will be** racially very mixed. 4 By 2030, scientists **will have found** cures for most illnesses. 5 Both are possible. *Due to* means the decision has already been made by the authorities. *Will* suggests a strong prediction. 6 In fifty years' time most rich people **will live** until they are over 100. 7 Both are possible. There is little difference in meaning. 8 By 2050, it's possible that governments **will have been censoring** the web for years.

B Ss practise saying the sentences, pronouncing the auxiliaries in their shortened forms, as in the *Watch out!* box in Ex 7B. Monitor and check Ss are saying the forms naturally. In feedback, nominate a different student to say each sentence.

C Arrange Ss in small groups to discuss the statements. In feedback, nominate Ss from each group to share their ideas with the class.

SPEAKING

9 Introduce the activity by briefly discussing with the class which inventions you would like to see in the future. Elicit/ check: *black box* (equipment that records what happens on a flight), *soothing sound* (calming) and *contraption* (strange-looking piece of equipment). Ss read the texts alone then discuss the questions in pairs. Monitor and make notes on any common errors and good language for later feedback. In feedback, nominate Ss to share their ideas with the class. Give Ss feedback on their language.

Optional extra activity
Ss invent their own devices in pairs. Arrange Ss in pairs and write the following headings on the board: *Name of device, Who it's for, How it works.* Ss invent their devices in pairs, writing a description under the headings on the board. Monitor and help with ideas and vocabulary, writing any new words and phrases on the board. When they are ready, Ss present their ideas to the class. In feedback, hold a class vote for the best invention.

VOCABULARY *PLUS* prepositional phrases

10A Read the examples with the class, and check Ss understand they need to use one preposition for each paragraph/sentence. Ss complete the paragraphs alone, then check in pairs. In feedback, elicit Ss' answers, but don't go over the meanings of the phrases yet.

Answers: Para 2 **at:** at risk; at present; at least
Para 3 **by:** by far, by nature, by law.
Para 4 **in:** in decline, in danger, in effect,
Para 5 **out of:** out of control, out of sight, out of necessity

B Ss work alone to underline the prepositional phrases in the text, then discuss their meanings in pairs. In feedback, elicit Ss' answers.

speakout TIP

Read the **speakout tip** with the class, and explain that prepositional phrases are very common in English. Ask Ss to choose five of the prepositional phrases from Ex 10A and write an example sentence for each, then compare in pairs. In feedback, nominate Ss to share their sentences with the class.

11A Ss complete the sentences alone then check in pairs. Monitor and help with vocabulary, writing any new words and phrases on the board. In feedback, elicit Ss' answers and nominate Ss to share their ideas with the class.

Answers: 2 in decline 3 out of control 4 out of necessity
5 by far 6 at least 7 by law 8 in danger 9 on average
10 At present

B Write the following headings on the board: *Topic, Consequences, What should be done.* Demonstrate the activity with an example (e.g. *The world population will grow out of control, There won't be enough water, We should develop new ways of producing clean water*). Give Ss five minutes to plan their ideas and makes notes. Monitor and help with ideas, and encourage them to use prepositional phrases where possible.

C When they are ready, arrange Ss in small groups to share their ideas. In feedback, nominate Ss from each group to share their ideas with the class.

➡ VOCABULARYBANK p153 PREPOSITIONAL PHRASES

1A Ss match the phrases alone then check in pairs. In feedback, elicit Ss' answers and be prepared to provide further explanations and examples where necessary.

B Ss write their responses alone then check in pairs and practise their conversations. In feedback, elicit Ss' answers. *Stronger classes* can do the exercises at home.

Answers: 1A 1 b) 2 a) 3 c) 4 b) 5 c) 6 a) 7 b) 8 c)
9 a) 10 c) 11 a) 12 b)

Homework ideas
- Ex 9: Write about your own invention for the future.
- Vocabulary bank p153
- Language bank 6.1 Ex 1–2, p139
- Workbook Ex 1–6, p37–38

A GLOBAL LANGUAGE?

Introduction
Ss learn and practise concession clauses in the context of English as a global language. They also practise writing a report.

SUPPLEMENTARY MATERIALS

Resource bank: p163

Warm up: Prepare the phrases below.

Ex 6 (alternative approach): write the sentences on slips of paper.

Warm up
Teach the class some basic Esperanto. Don't tell the class what language it is at this stage, just tell them you're going to teach them a new language, and teach the following phrases:

Saluton! (Hello!)
Mi nomiĝas /nɒˈmɪdʒæs/ _____ (My name is _____)
Kiel vi nomi ĝas? (What's your name?)
Estas plezuro renkonti vin (It's a pleasure to meet you)
Ĝis la revido! (Goodbye!)

Drill the phrases chorally and individually, and use gestures to illustrate what the phrases mean. After extensive drilling, write the phrases on the board. Ss mingle and have (very) short conversations using the phrases. When they have finished, elicit the meaning of each phrase in English. Elicit what language it is, and ask Ss how useful they think a knowledge of Esperanto is.

VOCABULARY language

1A Books closed. Write on the board: *language* and elicit any phrases Ss know which include language (e.g. *bad language, first language, language death*, etc.). Ss read the questions then discuss the meanings of the words in bold in pairs. In feedback, elicit Ss' answers and be prepared to provide further explanations and examples where necessary.

Answers: 1 lingua franca: a medium of communication used between people who speak different languages; global language: a language used all around the world 2 command of a language: ability to use a language; mind your language: pay attention to the words that you use (for example, in order not to appear rude) 3 language barrier: a breakdown in communication as a result of people not having a common language in which to communicate 4 dead language: a language which is no longer in use, for example Latin or ancient Greek; official language: the language which is used for official (e.g. legal) purposes in a country; everyday language: the language used to communicate on a day-to-day basis

B Ss discuss the questions in pairs. In feedback, nominate Ss to share their ideas with the class.

⟹ VOCABULARYBANK p153 SPEAKING IDIOMS

2A Ss complete the sentences alone then check in pairs. In feedback, elicit Ss' answers and be prepared to provide further explanations and examples where necessary.

B Ss match the situations and idioms alone then check in pairs. In feedback, elicit Ss' answers.
Stronger classes can do the exercises at home.

Answers: 2A 1 word 2 get 3 cross 4 catch 5 good 6 shop 7 run 8 tail 9 least 10 stick
B a) 10 b) 8 c) 4 d) 1 e) 5 f) 7 g) 3 h) 2 i) 9 j) 6

LISTENING

2 Ss read the text then answer the questions in pairs. In feedback, elicit Ss' answers and have a brief class discussion.

Answers: 1 They discuss the evolution of English, and how it might change in the future. 2 1) the fact that far more people speak English as a second language than a first 2) the influence of computers and automatic translators 3 Changes in pronunciation and vocabulary

Culture notes
Fry's English Delight is a BBC radio documentary which looks at various aspects of the English language. It is presented by Stephen Fry, an English actor, screenwriter, author, playwright, journalist, poet, comedian, television presenter, film director and language enthusiast. He is best known as a comedy actor and as the reader for the *Harry Potter* audio books.

Professor David Crystal OBE FLSW FBA is a linguist, academic and author. He is one of the world's leading authorities on the English language, and has been involved with over 120 books on language.

3A ▶ 6.2 Read the topics with the class and check understanding. Ss listen to the recording and tick the topics mentioned, then check their answers in pairs. In feedback, elicit Ss' answers.

B Read the example with the class. Ss discuss what they said about each point in pairs. When they are ready, play the recording again for Ss to check/expand their notes. In feedback, elicit Ss' answers.

Answers:
Culture and identity: different countries have adapted English to express their own culture and identity.
New Englishes: there are now many different types of English, for example Nigerian English, Ghanaian English, Singaporian English, etc..
Local languages/local brand of English: when English is adopted by people, it changes according to how they use it, for example to describe local places and things that are important to them (it becomes their own local brand of English).
English as a mother tongue: there are about 400 million people for whom English is their mother tongue
English as a second or foreign language: there are 2 billion people who speak English as a second or foreign language (five times more than the number of people who speak it as their mother tongue)

4A Ss correct the sentences alone then check in pairs. If necessary, play the recording again for Ss to check their answers. In feedback, elicit Ss' answers.

> **Answers:** 4 English has been adopted by more than **70** countries around the world. 6 Around the world, one **third** of the population speaks English as a second or foreign language.

B Ss discuss the questions in pairs. In feedback, elicit Ss' ideas and have a brief class discussion.

Alternative approach
Arrange the class into two large groups. The Ss in one group work alone to make a list of reasons why English should continue as the global language in the future, then compare their ideas. Ss in the other group work alone to make a list of reasons why their language(s) should become the global language, then compare their ideas in their groups. Monitor and help with ideas/vocabulary, writing any new words and phrases on the board. When they are ready, take it in turns to invite a student from each group to share their reasons with the class. When all Ss have read out their ideas, open the floor to questions and encourage Ss to debate the issue. When they have finished, hold a class vote to decide which language should become/remain the global language.

Unit 6 Recording 2

S = Stephen Fry D = David Crystal

S: Professor David Crystal says that the migratory patterns of our language as it continues to move across the globe, gives us a whole range of Englishes, and that process is becoming ever more intense.

D: So just as once upon a time there was British English and American English, then there came Australian English and South African English, and then Indian English and then Caribbean English. Now, it's down to the level of Nigerian English, Ghanaian English, Singaporian English and so on. And these are the new Englishes of the world. What happens is this: that when a country adopts English as its language, it then immediately adapts it to suit its own circumstances. I mean why have a language? You have to express what you want to say which is your culture, your people, your identity. And when you think of everything that makes up an identity – all the plants and animals that you have, the food and drink, the myths, the legends, the history of your culture, the politics of it, the folk tales, the music, everything has to be talked about in language. And that means your local language, local words to do with the way you are, and different from the way everybody else is. And so the result has been, as English has been taken up by, well over seventy countries in the world as an important medium of their local communication. But they have developed their own local brand of English.

S: How many people spoke the language we are now conversing in say 600 years ago?

D: Ahh, well, certainly we know around about 1500, 1600, there were four million speakers of English in England.

S: And now in the early part of the twenty-first century, how many…?

D: Well, if you distinguish between, sort of first language speakers and foreign language speakers there's about 400 million or so first language speakers, English as a mother tongue – or father tongue, depending on your point of view – around the world, and about five times as many who speak English as a second or a foreign language, so we're talking about two billion people, you know, a third of the world's population really. The

important point to notice is that for every one native speaker of English, there are now four or five non-native speakers of English, so the centre of gravity of the language has shifted with interesting consequences.

GRAMMAR concession clauses

5A Ss underline the correct alternatives alone then check in pairs. In feedback, elicit Ss' answers.

> **Answers:** 1 While 2 Although, Though 3 Difficult though it may be 4 Whichever 5 In spite of 6 Despite 7 Whilst

B Ss discuss the statements in pairs. In feedback, elicit Ss ideas and have a brief class discussion.

C Read the rule with the class and check understanding. With *weaker classes*, elicit the first answer as an example. Ss identify the clauses alone then check in pairs. In feedback, elicit Ss' answers.

> **Answers:** In each case, the concession clause is the clause which is introduced by the phrase in italics. The other clause is the main clause.

D Ss answer the questions alone then check in pairs. In feedback, elicit Ss' answers, and be prepared to provide further explanations and examples where necessary.

> **Answers:** 1 a comma 2 the concession clause 3 Despite, In spite of

> **⟹ LANGUAGEBANK 6.2 p138–139**
>
> *Stronger classes* can read the notes and do the exercises at home. Otherwise, check the notes with Ss, especially the use of *Despite* and *In spite* of. In each exercise, do the first sentence as an example. Ss complete the exercises alone, then check their answers in pairs. Ss can refer to the notes to help them
>
> **Answers:** 1 1 whereas 2 as 3 matter 4 whenever 5 despite 6 spite 7 however 8 although
> 2 1 Despite knowing that it's bad for me, I spend too much time on the Internet. 2 Even though she is nearly ninety-six years old, my grandmother is still fully independent. 3 He's an excellent manager, although he can be a bit scary to work for. 4 Hard as they tried, they couldn't persuade him to give up his work. 5 Whilst I understand how difficult the situation is, I'm afraid I can't help. 6 He's very charming. However, I wouldn't trust him at all.

PRACTICE

6A Read the example with the class, paying attention to the punctuation used. Ss write sentences alone then check in pairs. In feedback, elicit Ss' answers.

> **Answers:** 2 I spend a lot of time studying grammar, though I still make mistakes. 3 Difficult though it may be, I always try to believe what people tell me. 4 However you look at it, technology is changing education. 5 While I agree that English is important, I think students need to learn several languages. 6 Strange as it may seem, I find it hard to remember facts and figures. 7 Despite the fact that I enjoy travelling, I don't get the opportunity very often. 8 Learning a language is difficult, whichever method you choose.

Alternative approach

Write the words in brackets on the board, in random order. Write each sentence half e.g. *I spend a lot of time studying grammar* and *I still make mistakes* on separate strips of paper. Shuffle them, and distribute one slip to each student. Ss mingle and find their partner with the corresponding sentence half. When they've found their partner, they sit down and write the full sentence with a concession clause, using a word from the board. Monitor and check Ss are forming the sentences correctly.

B Give Ss five minutes to choose three linkers and write their sentences. Monitor and help with vocabulary, writing any new words and phrases on the board. When they are ready, Ss discuss their ideas in pairs. In feedback, nominate Ss to share their ideas with the class and find out how many Ss agree.

SPEAKING

7A Arrange Ss in groups of three, and ask them to decide who is A, B and C, and then find the relevant texts. Monitor and help where necessary. When they are ready, Ss describe their texts to the other Ss in their group.

B Ss discuss the pros and cons of each idea in their groups and add any of their own ideas. Monitor and make notes on any common errors and good language for later feedback. In feedback, nominate Ss from each group to share their ideas with the class. Give Ss feedback on their language.

Teaching tip

When Ss are doing speaking activities, it can be useful to play background music quietly. This can make the classroom a more natural environment which is conducive to speaking. When you want Ss to finish, stopping the music can help focus their attention.

WRITING a report

8A Books closed. On the board, write the following questions: *Which were the top three languages used on the internet between 2000 and 2010? Which languages have grown most rapidly in the same period?* Ss discuss the questions in pairs. When they are ready, focus attention on the graphic for Ss to check their answers. Ss discuss the questions in pairs. In feedback, elicit Ss' ideas.

Suggested answers: The graph shows you that Chinese, Arabic and Russian in particular, are likely to be more important in the future as their rate of growth is very high. Possible predictions are: In the future, perhaps English will not be the most dominant language. Chinese, Arabic, Russian and Spanish may become more important than English.

B Ss read the report and answer the questions alone then check in pairs. In feedback, elicit Ss' answers.

Answers: 1 Chinese, because there is a huge increase in demand as the number of Chinese internet users increases. 2 Arabic and Russian are both important to mention because of their huge growth rates.

9 Read the guidelines with the class and check understanding. Ss discuss the questions in pairs. In feedback, elicit Ss' answers.

Answers: Points 1, 2, 3, 5 and 6 are all exemplified. You would expect to find point 4 in the remaining part.

LEARN TO describe trends

10A Ss work alone to delete the alternative which is not possible then check in pairs. In feedback, elicit Ss' answers, and be prepared to provide further explanations of the vocabulary where necessary.

Answers: 1 dropped alarmingly 2 a drop 3 plummeted 4 surge, declined 5 collapsed 6 sharp

Watch out!

Language for describing trends in English often comes from the areas of mountain climbing (e.g. *reach a peak*) and flying (e.g. *soar*). It can be useful to point out the origins of new vocabulary (where known), as it can help make the words or phrases more memorable.

B With *weaker classes*, elicit the first sentence as an example. Ss write the sentences alone then check in pairs. In feedback, elicit Ss' answers.

Answers: 1 There has been an explosion in (the) demand for mobile technology in language learning. 2 The number of people communicating regularly using blogs has increased dramatically. 3 The number of students attending private language schools to study English has plummeted. 4 There has been a sharp increase in the ability of learners to access learning materials on the internet. 5 There has been a gradual decline in the appeal of traditional teaching methods.

11 Ss complete their reports alone. Monitor and help with vocabulary, writing any new words and phrases on the board, and encourage Ss to use the language for describing trends from Ex 10A. When they are ready, Ss swap their texts with another student to compare.

Homework ideas
- Ex 9: write a final draft of your report.
- Language bank 6.2 Ex 1–2, p139
- Workbook Ex 1–5, p39–40

TRENDSETTERS

Introduction

Ss learn and practise phrases for describing cause and effect, and how to summarise their views.

SUPPLEMENTARY MATERIALS

Resource bank p164

Warm up: Bring or download photos of three things (clothes, toys, sports, etc.) that were popular when you were a child.

Warm up

Show Ss photos of three things that were popular when you were a child, and describe them. Encourage Ss to ask you follow-up questions to find out more information. Give Ss five minutes to think of three things that were popular when they were younger and think about how to describe them. Monitor and help with ideas by giving them topics (e.g. toys/games, clothes, technology, sport, etc.). When they are ready, arrange Ss in groups to share their ideas. In feedback, elicit Ss' ideas and find out if there are any common answers.

VOCABULARY fashion

1A Focus attention on the photos and elicit any new vocabulary. Ss discuss the questions in pairs. In feedback, nominate Ss to share their ideas with the class.

B Elicit/check: *stagnated* (stopped growing). Ss read the text and answer the questions alone then check in pairs. In feedback, elicit Ss' ideas.

Answer: Main idea: that the best way to explain a trend is as something that spreads like an epidemic or virus.

2A Ss complete the phrases alone then check in pairs. In feedback, elicit Ss' answers, and be prepared to provide further explanations and examples where necessary.

Answers: 1 off 2 appeal 3 imagination 4 chord 5 thing (can also say *craze*) 6 trend (can also say *fad*) 7 risen 8 mouth

Optional extra activity

Ss test each other on the vocabulary in pairs. One student closes their book, while the other reads out a definition for them to guess the word. When they have finished, Ss swap roles.

B Give Ss two or three minutes to think of their answers. Monitor and help with vocabulary, writing any new words and phrases on the board. When they are ready, Ss compare in pairs. In feedback, nominate Ss to share their ideas with the class.

FUNCTION describing cause and effect

3A ▶ 6.3 Elicit/check: *baggy* (loose-fitting) and *mainstream* (accepted by or involving most people in society). Ss listen and answer the questions then check in pairs. In feedback, elicit Ss' answers.

Answers: 1 wearing trousers below the hip, and showing underwear; reality TV shows 2 in US prisons, because belts weren't allowed; early programmes in the 1970s and 80s 3 through rappers such as Ice T; through programmes such as *Big Brother* and *Pop Idol*

B Focus attention on the expressions in the table and elicit which ones Ss can remembering hearing and what the speakers said.

C Play the recording again for Ss to check their answers. In feedback, elicit Ss' answers.

Answers: 1 it all started; has its roots in; it led to 2 It all started; it originated from; has caused; Because of this; resulted in

Unit 6 Recording 3

Speaker 1

It's a trend that started in the States and spread certainly in Europe. And it's when guys wear their jeans halfway down their hips so you can see their underwear. Apparently it all started in the prison system in the States. What happened was that prisoners aren't allowed to wear belts cos these can be used as a weapon and also they're used in suicides. And the prison uniforms were often too big for the inmates. So you'd have a little guy wearing a huge baggy pair of prison issue trousers and so the prisoners ended up with these trousers halfway down their legs. So the trend has its roots in the prison system but somehow it spread beyond those walls so rappers like Ice T started wearing their trousers like this and it led to widespread adoption of the style. It's known in some parts as a kind of gangster look because obviously it originated in prison, but actually it's pretty mainstream now amongst young people, so basically it's crossed over into the mainstream. And I guess this is how fashions start and spread cos they kind of come from nowhere, out of the blue, and then early adopters, I think they're called, help to make them fashionable and suddenly you've got a trend.

Speaker 2

As a TV producer, I've obviously looked at the trend of reality TV. It all started to take off in the nineties with the emergence of programmes like *Big Brother* and *Pop Idol*. But actually I'd say it originated from earlier programmes, stuff that was done in the seventies and eighties. I think the popularity of these shows has caused a big shift in how programmes are made. Production values are quite low and the emphasis is now on making something cheap and quick. Because of this, TV companies make bigger profits and it's this that resulted in these shows spreading around the world. So what I'm really saying is we'll keep making these programmes now until the, erm, the public tires of them. And it's because of the public's taste for knowing about real people and real lives.

➡ LANGUAGEBANK 6.3 p138–139

Stronger classes could read the notes and do the exercise at home. Otherwise, drill the phrases from the chart, checking Ss are using natural intonation. Ss work alone to choose the correct alternatives, then check their answers in pairs. In feedback, elicit Ss' answers.

Answers: 1 rise 2 back 3 led 4 resulted 5 stem 6 about 7 in 8 attributed

4 With *weaker classes*, elicit the first answer as an example. Ss rewrite the sentences alone then check in pairs. In feedback, elicit Ss' answers.

Answers: 1 Reggae has its roots in Jamaica. 2 The Mohican haircut, in the UK, has its origins in the punk era. 3 Technology has given rise to new types of crime, such as hacking. 4 Some say football can be traced back to China. 5 Global warming has caused/is the cause of many recent environmental disasters. 6 Because of better healthcare and diet, plus fewer babies per family, the population is ageing. 7 The rising number of female world leaders stems from the women's liberation movement. 8 The growth in online publishing has led to new laws. 9 It's thought that chess originated in India over a thousand years ago. 10 Medical procedures for disfigured soldiers resulted in the development of cosmetic surgery. 11 The recent popularity of tattoos can be attributed to celebrities who have them. 12 Globalisation has brought about big changes to the way businesses are run.

LEARN TO summarise your views

5A Focus attention on the expressions and elicit Ss' answers.

Answers: We usually use these expressions at the end of a long 'turn' or the end of a section of speech. Their purpose is to summarise what has been said.

B Ss turn to p170 to find which expressions from Ex 3A the speakers used. In feedback, elicit Ss' answers.

Answers: Basically, …; So what I'm really saying is, …

speakout TIP

Read the **speakout tip** with the class, and explain that summarising and paraphrasing the main points provides useful signposting in a longer turn. Ask if Ss do the same in their language(s).

6A Elicit Ss' suggestions for the first sentence as an example. Ss complete the sentences alone. Monitor and help with vocabulary, writing any new words and phrases on the board.

B Ss compare their ideas in pairs. In feedback, nominate Ss to share their ideas with the class.

C Ss discuss the questions in pairs. In feedback, elicit Ss' answers.

Answers: 4 and 5 are in a formal context.

7A ▶ 6.4 Ss listen to the recording and compare the answers to their own completions. In feedback, elicit any similar endings that Ss came up with.

Unit 6 Recording 4

1 People now expect to download music for free and CD sales are at their lowest ebb. Basically, the music industry has had to completely change its business model.

2 We saw some great presentations at the conference. The hotel was wonderful and we loved the food! So overall, it was really worth it.

3 Bloggers take news from real reporters and write comments. They do hardly any reporting themselves. So what I'm really saying is that without real reporters, there's no news.

4 Sales of the game soared in May, jumped again in July and rose dramatically at the end of the year. To sum up, we've had an incredible year.

5 This report says young people believe in openness. They share details of their private lives online. In conclusion, young people don't value their privacy as much as older generations.

6 We had developed a product, but we had technical problems. Then we ran out of money and a competitor stole the idea. All in all, it was a complete disaster.

B Read the instructions with the class. Ss practise saying the words quickly and decide which sound gets 'swallowed'. In feedback, elicit Ss' ideas, but don't give any answers yet.

C ▶ 6.5 Ss listen and check their answers. In feedback, elicit Ss' answers.

Answers: In each case, the 'a' sound in 'ally' becomes 'swallowed' e.g. basically becomes /ˈbeɪsɪkli/

D Ss practise saying the words in pairs. In feedback, nominate Ss to say the words to the class.

SPEAKING

8A Ss choose a topic and make notes on the causes and effects of changes. Monitor and help with ideas and vocabulary, writing any new words and phrases on the board.

B When they are ready, arrange Ss in small groups to present their ideas to each other. With *multilingual classes*, try to include different nationalities within each group. Monitor and make notes on any common errors and good language for later feedback. In feedback, nominate Ss from each group to share their ideas with the class, and give Ss feedback on their language.

> **Homework ideas**
> • Ex 8B: write about changes in your country during your lifetime.
> • Language bank 6.3 Ex 1, p139
> • Workbook Ex 1–4, p41

HISTORY OF NOW

Introduction
Ss watch an extract from the BBC documentary *History of Now*, which looks at youth culture in the first decade of the 21st Century. Ss learn and practise how to talk about a decade, and write a review of a decade.

SUPPLEMENTARY MATERIALS
Warm up: Write the words below on the board.

Warm up
Write on the board: *The Zeros, The New Millennium, The Singles, The Aughties, The Noughties and The Bush Years.* Explain that these are some names that have been given to the first decade of the 21st Century. Elicit which ones Ss like/dislike. In pairs, Ss think of another name for the first decade of the 21st Century and a name for the current decade in pairs. In feedback, elicit Ss' ideas and write them on the board, then hold a class vote for the best name.

DVD PREVIEW

1 Focus attention on the words in the box, and check understanding. Ss discuss the question in pairs. In feedback, nominate Ss to share their ideas with the class.

Culture notes
Credit crunch is a term that has been coined by the media to describe a reduction in the availability of loans from banks, as a result of the worsening economic situation seen in North America and Europe in the first decade of the 21st Century.

Web 2.0 is a term used to describe how the internet has changed in recent years to facilitate greater sharing of personal information and user-operated design.

A *carbon footprint* describes the total amount of greenhouse gas emissions caused by the activities of one person.

Optional extra activity
Ss work alone to think of and write down 3 more 'buzz words' to describe developments so far this decade. When they are ready, arrange Ss in small groups to share their ideas. In feedback, nominate Ss to share their ideas with the class.

2 Give Ss two minutes to read the programme information then discuss the question in pairs. In feedback, elicit Ss' answers.

Answer: The key trend: 'youth culture' and the way in which this now includes adults who are in their forties and fifties.

Culture notes
The BBC documentary *History of Now: Story of the Noughties* is a three-part documentary film which first aired in 2010. It explores the cultural highlights of the first decade of the 21st Century in Britain, where older people began recapturing their youth. It was hosted by a range of leading cultural commentators such as Andrew Marr, Tanya Byron and Will Self.

DVD VIEW

3A Ss discuss the statements in pairs. In feedback, elicit Ss' ideas but don't give any answers yet.

B Ss watch the DVD and check their answers. In feedback, elicit Ss' answers.

Answers: 1T 2T 3T 4T

4A Ss complete the extracts from memory in pairs. Monitor and help but don't give any answers yet.

B Play the DVD again for Ss to check their answers. In feedback, elicit Ss' answers.

Answers: 1 disorientating change 2 major fault lines 3 the lifestyle of the young 4 empowerment of young people 5 short trousers, a suit 6 take more holidays

5 Ss discuss the questions in small groups. In feedback, nominate Ss to share their ideas with the class and have a brief class discussion.

Alternative approach
Write: *old people* and *young people* on the board, and the following questions underneath: *What do they help each other with? What do they tell each other stories/anecdotes about? What kind of presents do they give each other (and when)? What do they give each other advice about? What things do they often talk about? What things do they not discuss?* Ss discuss the questions about their country/ies in small groups. In feedback, nominate Ss from each group to share their ideas with the class.

History of Now: The Story of the Noughties
VO=Voice-over JM=Julia Mango DD=Danny Dorling LE=Larry Elliott WS=Will Self SH=Sarah Harper

VO: The first decade of the new millennium saw waves of massive and, at times, disorientating change. Bewildering new words and phrases sprang up trying to make sense of it all. It was a decade of surprising connections, when what was really happening was often not as it appeared.
The story of the noughties is more than just the history of the last ten years. It tells us where the twenty-first century itself is heading.
In 2010 we already have a sense of the forces shaping Britain in our still new century. Some have been heavily discussed; others haven't. We begin this series with the most significant split to have emerged in our society in the last ten years.

JM: Age is to the twenty-first century what social class was to the twentieth century. It's one of the major fault lines in our society.

DD: Different generations became less aware of each other. Older people became more frightened of younger people. Younger people became less appreciative of older people.

LE: We had a situation where everybody wanted to be young, but the only people who could afford the lifestyle of the young were the old.

JM: Adults and young people are probably more divided now than they ever were in the past, partly because of the empowerment of young people and the role that youth culture has in dominating society.

WS: People say, 'Well, in the 1950s, you know, there was a transition. You went from having short trousers to wearing a suit and you were at work and you were an adult or you went down the pit and you became an adult.' And there was an absolute cut off point, there was none of this teen stuff. Now there's still a period of being a child, authentically a child. And then at the age of sexual maturity everybody's unloosed not into adulthood but to 'kidulthood'. You have the idea of this kind of perpetual childhood.

VO: In the noughties, 'kidulthood' was open to almost everyone. No longer did you have to be young to act young. In the early two thousands, the biggest club in Britain was School Disco.

SH: You have men and women in their mid thirties, even into their forties who are living the lifestyle that one would normally have presumed was that of a teenager or twenty-year-old.

DD: We looked recently at the spread of toys around the world, and the really interesting thing was that most of the toys weren't for children, they were actually toys for adults. And so the, the bulk of the world toy market, in terms of cash at least, isn't for toys being consumed by children anymore.

VO: The whole kidult accessory kit included a micro scooter or mountain bike, a pair of trainers, three-quarter-length trousers, t-shirts with carefully chosen pop culture references, an iPod, a game console and kid lit in your man bag.

DD: You've got used to playing, you've got used to going out, you've got used to having recreational time. And if you've got money, then why not have toys, why not take more holidays, why not carry on behaving like you might have behaved when you were eighteen, nineteen or twenty?

speakout talk about a decade

6A ▶ 6.6 Ss listen to the recording and make notes on the topics, then check in pairs. In feedback, elicit Ss' answers.

Answers: She talks about the 1990s
historical events: Nelson Mandela released from prison, Mad Cow disease – UK problem, but caused panic in rest of Europe, Mother Teresa died – she was affected by this
mobile phones / technology: internet took off – first heard about companies like Yahoo and EBay, she received her first email and bought first mobile phone (with changeable faces (yellow and strawberry)
economics: Mostly a prosperous decade where people were earning good money and enjoying themselves
music / clubbing: big bands like Take That and The Spice Girls were popular. She went to a Take That concert in '93 and it was the best night of her life – dance music and clubbing were also very popular.
fashion: looking back on it makes her cringe, shell-suits were in fashion, she had a purple one which she wore all the time, also flashing trainers were popular – people thought they were cool

B Focus attention on the **Key phrases**. Ss listen and choose the correct alternatives, then check in pairs. In feedback, elicit Ss' answers and drill the **Key phrases** chorally and individually.

Answers: 1 took off 2 prosperous 3 memorable
4 going 5 big 6 fashion 7 be a teenager in

Unit 6 Recording 6

W=woman

W: The nineties feels like such a long time ago now, but lots of important things happened in that decade. There were obviously some major historical events, like umm…well, Mandela was released from prison, and became President in 1990. There was Mad Cow disease throughout quite a lot of the nineties, which although it was a UK problem, caused a lot of panic certainly in the rest of Europe. I remember that really well. And then when Mother Teresa died. That was in '97, I think, and I remember it had quite an effect on me. The nineties was when the internet first took off as well, and we started to hear about companies like Ebay and Yahoo. I remember getting my first email in the nineties! And I got my first mobile phone then too. It had a changeable face, so that you could change the colour to suit your mood. I had a yellow face, and one with a strawberry on it. I'm not sure what that really says about me. Generally though, the nineties was quite a prosperous time, you know, lots of people were earning good money. So, I think the atmosphere was about enjoying yourself,

and having a good time. I think one of the most memorable things about the 1990s has to be the music. Big bands like *Take That* and *The Spice Girls* were around. I remember going to the *Take That* concert in '93 – it was amazing, it was the best night of my life, definitely. And clubbing was generally really big too. There were loads of big clubs. Dance music really took off during the nineties. Thinking about fashion back then makes me cringe, to be honest. Shell suits were all the rage at that time, and I had a purple one. I wore it all the time. It was my favourite, I absolutely loved it. Other fashion items I remember were light-up trainers, you know, when you walked the lights started flashing. Everyone thought they were really cool. It's funny to look back on it all really, but the nineties was a great decade to be a teenager in, definitely.

7A Arrange Ss in small groups to choose three factors and discuss their decade. Monitor and help with vocabulary, writing any new words and phrases on the board, and make notes on any common errors/good language for later feedback.

B Ss take it in turns to present their ideas to the class. When they have finished, give Ss feedback on their language.

writeback a review of a decade

8A Ss read the review then add things to each section in pairs. In feedback, elicit Ss' ideas.

B Ss write their reviews alone. Monitor and help with vocabulary, writing any new words and phrases on the board. When they have finished, Arrange Ss in small groups to read their reviews to each other. In feedback, nominate Ss to share their ideas with the class.

Alternative approach
If you have access to the internet, arrange Ss in pairs and assign a different decade of the 20th Century to each pair. Ss then research their decades on the internet in order to write a review. With *multilingual classes*, you could have the class research/write about the same decade but describe key events in their own countries.

Homework ideas
• Ex 7A: write about the decade you discussed.

LOOKBACK

Introduction

Ss revise and practise the language of Unit 6. The notes below provide ideas for exploiting the exercises and activities but your approach will depend on your aim, e.g. as a diagnostic or progress test or as revision and fluency practice. For example, if done as a test then it would not be appropriate to monitor or help them.

TRENDS AND PREDICTIONS

1 After explaining the activity, elicit the first answer as an example, in order to check Ss understand what to do. Ss complete the text alone then check in pairs. In feedback, elicit Ss' answers.

> **Answers:** 1 may/could 2 in 3 signs/chances 4 distant
> 5 gathers 6 be 7 thing

> **Optional extra activity**
> Draw the following chart on the board:
>
> | may | a thing of the past | the signs are |
> |---|---|---|
> | a distant memory | an explosion in | the chances are |
> | gather pace | be over | could |
>
> Arrange the Ss in two groups, and play noughts and crosses. Each group takes it in turn to choose a square, and must form a sentence correctly in order to gain that square. The winning group gets three squares in a row.

LANGUAGE

2A After explaining the activity, elicit the first answer as an example, in order to check Ss understand what to do. Ss rewrite the sentences alone then check in pairs. In feedback, elicit Ss' answers.

> **Answers:** 1 dead language 2 lingua franca 3 global language 4 mind their language 5 language barrier

B Ss discuss the statements in pairs. In feedback, nominate Ss from each group to share their ideas with the class.

FUTURE FORMS

3A After explaining the activity, elicit the first answer as an example, in order to check Ss understand what to do. (e.g. I Optimist: travelled the world, Pessimist: survived). Arrange the Ss in A/B pairs. Ss complete their sentences alone. Monitor and help with vocabulary, writing any new words and phrases on the board.

B Ss compare their ideas in pairs. In feedback, nominate Ss to share their ideas with the class, and decide who was the most optimistic and who the most pessimistic.

> **Alternative approach**
> Distribute a blank sheet of paper to each student in the class, and ask them to write their sentence completions on the paper in random order. Make sure they only write the completions, and not the first part of the sentence given on p 78. Monitor and help with vocabulary, writing any new words and phrases on the board. When they are ready, arrange Ss in pairs. Ss show their answers to their partner, who guesses which sentence each answer completes. Monitor and encourage them to ask follow-up questions to find out more information. In feedback, nominate Ss to share any new/interesting information with the class

CONCESSION CLAUSES

4A Ss complete the sentences alone then check in pairs. In feedback, elicit Ss' answers.

> **Answers:** 1 e) 2 b) 3 c) 4 f) 5 a) 6 d)

B Ss complete the sentences alone. Monitor and help with vocabulary, writing any new words and phrases on the board. When they are ready, Ss compare their sentences in pairs. In feedback, nominate Ss to share their ideas with the class.

DESCRIBING CAUSE AND EFFECT

5A After explaining the activity, elicit the first answer as an example, in order to check Ss understand what to do. Ss correct the sentences alone then check in pairs, and guess what trends they describe. In feedback, elicit Ss' corrections, but don't tell them which trends are described yet.

> **Answers:** 1 These can be **traced** back to the 1700s, …
> 2 This fashion item is often attributed **to** British designer Mary Quant in the 1960s, … 3 … but it has **its** origins in the 'talking' style of West African musician-poets. 4 These have their **roots** in Ancient China, …. 5 … it **led** to a new sport.
> 6 … This resulted **in** the brand name Gatorade. 7 … and gave rise **to** one of the most popular forms of electronic writing.

B Ss match the trends and sentences alone then check in pairs. In feedback, elicit Ss' answers.

> **Answers:** 1 roller skates 2 mini-skirt 3 hip-hop
> 4 sunglasses 5 snowboarding 6 energy drinks 7 blog

> **Optional extra activity**
> If you have access to the internet, ask Ss to investigate a past trend in pairs. They then write a similar short description. When they are ready, Ss read out their descriptions for the class to guess what it is.

> **Homework ideas**
> • **Workbook** Review and check 3, p42–44
> • **Workbook** Test 3, p45

OVERVIEW

THE GREAT ESCAPE

Introduction

Ss learn and practise cleft sentences in the context of escape stories. They also revise and practise suffixes.

SUPPLEMENTARY MATERIALS

Resource bank p166, p167

Warm up: Prepare the situation below.

Warm up

Explain the following situation to Ss: *You are locked in a room with two doors. One leads to a dungeon and the other leads to freedom. You don't know which is which. There are two prison guards, one guarding each door, and they will let you choose only one door to open and walk through.*

You can ask one question to one of the guards. However, one guard always lies, and the other always tells the truth. You don't know which is which. What question do you ask? Ss work in pairs to solve the puzzle. When they have finished, elicit the answer. (You ask: *If I asked the other guard which door leads to freedom, what would he say? Then open the **other** door*).

READING

1 Focus attention on the photos and elicit what Ss can see. Elicit/check: *amnesia* (loss of memory), *raise the alarm* (warn people that something bad is happening), *shattered* (broken into small pieces) and *an open verdict* (an official decision by the court saying that the exact cause of death is unknown). Ss read the text (the first part of the story), then discuss what they think happened in pairs. In feedback, elicit Ss' ideas and write them on the board.

B Ss discuss the questions in pairs. In feedback, elicit their ideas, but don't give any answers yet.

C Ss turn to p161 to check their ideas about what happened then check in pairs. In feedback, elicit what happened.

Suggested answers: 1 He was tanned because he had been living in Panama. 2 He'd pushed his canoe out to sea. 3 He had been hiding in his house for most of the time, but later travelled to Greece and Panama. 4 His deception was uncovered and he and his wife were sent to prison.

2A Ss complete the sentences alone, then check in pairs. In feedback, elicit Ss' answers.

Answers: 1 financial difficulties (debts). 2 hiding in the next door house when people visited, rarely leaving the house and changing his appearance. 3 start a new life, running a hotel business selling canoe holidays. 4 a colleague of Anne's who had become suspicious. 5 were sent to prison and their assets were taken from them.

B Ss discuss the questions in pairs. In feedback, elicit Ss' ideas and have a brief class discussion.

Teaching tip

When discussing controversial or shocking topics such as that discussed in the text, it's important to deal with the issues sensitively, in case Ss have had similar experiences. At this level, Ss should have the language to be able to talk about such topics appropriately, but if they don't wish to discuss topics like this at length it's important not to force them to.

Optional extra activity

Arrange Ss in pairs, and assign roles: one student is either John or Anne Darwin, and the other is one of their children. Ss write a dialogue, imagining that they are meeting for the first time after John and Anne have been released from prison. Monitor and help with ideas where necessary. When they are ready, Ss take it in turns to perform their dialogues to the class.

GRAMMAR cleft sentences

3A Ss cover the text and rewrite the sentences alone, then check in pairs. Don't elicit any answers yet.

B Ss check their answers in the texts on pages 80 and 161. In feedback, elicit Ss' answers.

Answers: 1 What police didn't initially realise was that the man standing in front of them was John Darwin, 'the missing canoe man'. 2 It was only when he failed to arrive at work for a night shift that the alarm was raised. 3 What he did then was spend the next few years hiding inside the house and rarely leaving. 4 It was a colleague of Anne Darwin's who eventually put the pieces of the puzzle together.

C Ss discuss the question in pairs, then read the rule to check. In feedback, check understanding and be prepared to provide further explanations and examples where necessary.

⟹ LANGUAGEBANK 7.1 p140–141

Stronger classes can read the notes and do the exercises at home. Otherwise, check the notes with Ss, especially the order of words in cleft sentences. In each exercise, do the first sentence as an example. Ss complete the exercises alone, then check their answers in pairs. Ss can refer to the notes to help them.

Answers: 1 1 The reason he lost his job was that he kept breaking the rules. 2 It was only when he left the theatre that he recognised her. 3 What I want to do is persuade them to come with us. 4 All I worry about/I'm worried about is whether she will have enough money. 5 What is amazing is that they have such a fantastic range of spices.
2 1 a) What elections have done is…give these people their first real opportunity to decide who will govern them. b) The thing that …has given these people their first real opportunity to decide who will govern them is the elections. c) It's the elections that have given these people their first real opportunity to decide who will govern them. 2 a) It was the airports, roads and rail systems that suffered widespread disruption due to the heavy snow and severe weather. b) It was heavy snow and severe weather that caused widespread disruption to the country's airports, roads and rail systems. c) What caused disruption to the country's airports, roads and rail systems was the heavy snow and severe weather. 3 a) What caused students to march through the city centre in protest were the new laws. b) The reason hundreds of students marched through the city centre was to protest against the new laws. c) What happened was hundreds of students marched through the city centre to protest against the new laws.

PRACTICE

4 Ss rewrite the sentences alone then check in pairs. In feedback, elicit Ss' answers.

Answers: 1 What I don't understand is why Anne Darwin didn't tell her sons about their father. 2 The place where they planned to start a new life was Panama. 3 It was the photograph of the couple buying a house in Panama that revealed the deception. 4 The thing that she couldn't understand was why Anne had decided to emigrate to Panama. 5 The reason why John Darwin flew back to the UK from Panama was that he was missing his sons. 6 What he found difficult was coming to terms with what his parents had done.

5A Give Ss five minutes to complete the sentences. Monitor and help with vocabulary, writing any new words and phrases on the board.

B Ss discuss their sentences in pairs. Monitor and encourage Ss to ask follow-up questions to find out more information. In feedback, nominate Ss to share their ideas with the class.

VOCABULARY escape

6A Ss match the sentence halves alone then check in pairs. In feedback, elicit Ss' answers and check understanding of the phrases. Be prepared to give further explanations and examples where necessary.

Answers: 1 b) 2 d) 3 f) 4 a) 5 h) 6 g) 7 e) 8 c)

Watch out!

Ss often have difficulty pronouncing –ed endings in verbs and adjectives. You can help raise awareness of how to pronounce these with the following procedure. Write the following letters on the board:

ay m n dg v

f sh ch k s

t d

Drill the sounds with the class, and ask them to place a finger on their throat. They should notice that the first line of sounds are voiced, and the second line are unvoiced. Repeat the process but add a 'd' sound after each letter. With the sounds in the first line, it sounds like /d/ and in the second line it sounds like /t/. With the sounds in the last line elicit that it's difficult to produce the sound, and so we add a vowel sound to produce /ɪd/. Use this to point out that this is what happens when we pronounce –ed endings.

Alternative approach

Write the sentence halves on slips of paper. Distribute the slips of paper to the class, one per student. Ss mingle and find their 'partner', with the other half of their sentence, then stick the corresponding halves on the board/wall, so others can see. In feedback, check answers with the class.

B Ss complete the sentences alone then check in pairs. In feedback, elicit Ss' answers.

Answers: 1 stranded 2 trapped 3 make a break for it/escape 4 an escape plan 5 fled 6 released

C Give Ss two or three minutes to think about their answers, and make notes if they want. Ss discuss the questions in pairs. In feedback, nominate Ss to share their ideas with the class.

Teaching tip

If you have Ss who are reluctant to speak, giving them a few mins to think about their answer/make notes means that when they start the discussion, they have more to say and so will be more comfortable.

SPEAKING

7A Focus attention on the questions. Elicit Ss' answers and have a brief class discussion. Ss turn to p159 and read the rules of the game. Check understanding by asking: *Where are you? What do you have with you? What have you already tried?*

B Arrange Ss in small groups to compile their lists and devise an escape plan. Monitor and help with vocabulary, writing any new words and phrases on the board.

C When Ss are ready, nominate Ss from each group to share their plan with the class. When all groups have finished, take a vote on the best plan.

VOCABULARY *PLUS* suffixes

8A Introduce the activity by writing the word *secret* on the board. Elicit the adjective and adverb and write them on the board (*secretive, secretively*). Ss complete the box alone then check in pairs. In feedback, elicit Ss' answers.

B Ss underline the suffixes alone then check in pairs. In feedback, elicit Ss' answers.

Answers:

verbs	nouns	adjectives	adverbs
emig<u>rate</u>	emigra<u>tion</u> / emig<u>rant</u>	xxx	xxx
dece<u>ive</u>	decep<u>tion</u>	decep<u>tive</u>	deceptive<u>ly</u>
pret<u>end</u>	pret<u>ence</u>	pret<u>end</u>	xxx
susp<u>ect</u>	susp<u>icion</u>	susp<u>icious</u>	suspicious<u>ly</u>

9A With *weaker classes*, elicit the first answer as an example first. Ss correct the sentences alone then check in pairs. In feedback, elicit Ss' answers and write them on the board.

B Ss discuss the questions in pairs. In feedback, elicit Ss' answers.

Answers to A and B: 1 emigrate (vb) 2 pretence (n) 3 recollection (n) 4 suspicious (adj) 5 massive (adj) 6 realise (vb) 7 extensively (adv) 8 supposedly (adv)

10A Elicit the first answer as an example. Ss work alone to complete the groups then check in pairs. In feedback, elicit Ss' answers. Then give Ss two or three minutes to read the different groups of suffixes and underline any new words. Ss first discuss the meanings of the new words in pairs, then check with you if necessary.

Answers: 1 emigrate 2 realise 3 recollection 4 pretence 5 suspicious 6 massive 7 extensively 8 supposedly

speakout TIP

Read the **speakout tip** with the class, then give Ss two minutes to discuss the questions in pairs. In feedback, elicit Ss' answers (*-like*: similar to, *-worthy*: deserving of/suitable for, *-ible/-able*: has this ability/feature) and ask if they know any other suffixes like this.

B Read the example with the class. With *weaker classes*, give them five minutes to write their questions first, and monitor and check they are forming questions correctly. Ss ask their questions in pairs. Monitor and encourage Ss to ask follow-up questions to find out more information. In feedback, nominate Ss to share their ideas with the class.

➡ VOCABULARYBANK p 154 SUFFIXES

1A Ss complete the table alone then check in pairs. In feedback, elicit Ss' answers and check understanding of the words. Drill the words chorally and individually, making sure Ss stress the words correctly.

B Ss complete the sentences alone then check in pairs. In feedback, elicit Ss' answers.
Stronger classes can do the exercises at home.

Answers: 1A verbs: fabricate, glorify; nouns: censorship, nationalist, governor, senility, likelihood, kindliness, repetition, sarcasm, expertise, remission; adjectives: exorbitant, nationalist, responsive, personable, identical, troublesome, classy, anxious, heroic
B 1 sympathise 2 effective 3 imposition 4 frivolity 5 enviable 6 hesitant 7 enthusiasm 8 chauvinistic

Homework ideas
• Ex 7B: Write about your escape plan.
• Vocabulary bank p154
• Language bank 7.1 Ex 1–2, p141
• Workbook Ex 1–6, p46–47

GETTING AWAY FROM IT ALL

Introduction

Ss learn and practise participle clauses in the context of relaxing. They also practise writing a leaflet.

SUPPLEMENTARY MATERIALS

Resource bank: p165, p168

Warm up: Write the words below on the board.

Ex 8 (alternative approach): Write the sentences on slips of paper.

Ex 10A: bring some leaflets and brochures to class.

WARM UP

Write on the board: *doing a job you enjoy, playing a computer or video game, studying English, using public transport, sitting in a park in summer, having breakfast, driving* and *reading a good book*. Ss discuss how they feel when doing each of these activities in pairs. In feedback, nominate Ss to share their ideas, and elicit which they find most relaxing/stressful.

VOCABULARY idioms: relaxing

1 Focus attention on the photos and elicit what Ss can see. Ss discuss the questions in pairs.

2A Ss discuss the questions in pairs. Monitor and help where necessary. In feedback, elicit Ss' answers and be prepared to provide further explanations and examples where necessary.

Answers: 1 switch off 2 slow down 3 unwind 4 take your mind off (something) 5 hang out 6 let your hair down 7 have a breather 8 take it easy

B Ss complete the sentences alone then check in pairs. In feedback, elicit Ss' answers.

Answers: 1 have a breather, take it easy 2 hang out 3 slow down 4 unwind, switch off 5 let your hair down 6 switch off 7 take your mind off 8 take it easy

3A ▶ 7.1 Read the questions with the class and check Ss understand what to listen for. Ss listen to the recording and answer the questions, then check in pairs.

Answers: 1 hang out, slow down, switch off, unwind – the second syllable is stressed 2 the stress is on the third word, on the noun or adjective

Unit 7 Recording 1

1 hang <u>out</u>
2 take it <u>easy</u>
3 have a <u>breather</u>
4 slow <u>down</u>
5 take your <u>mind</u> off it
6 switch <u>off</u>
7 let your <u>hair</u> down
8 un<u>wind</u>

B Play the recording again for Ss to repeat. If necessary, drill the phrases chorally and individually.

C Give Ss five minutes to write three true sentences about themselves. Monitor and help with vocabulary, and check Ss are using the expressions correctly. When they are ready, Ss compare their sentences in pairs.

Alternative approach

Ss write a mixture of true and false sentences about themselves in Ex 3C (i.e. 2 true and 1 false or 1 true and 2 false). When they are ready, Ss read them to their partner who guesses which are true and which are false.

▶ VOCABULARYBANK p154 WORK AND LEISURE IDIOMS

2A Focus attention on the pictures and elicit what Ss can see. Ss match the idioms and pictures alone then check in pairs. In feedback, elicit Ss' answers and be prepared to provide further explanations/examples where necessary.

B Ss discuss the questions in pairs. In feedback, elicit Ss' answers.

C Ss write their answers alone then compare in pairs. In feedback, elicit Ss' ideas.
Stronger classes can do the exercises at home.

Answers: 2A 1 C 2 A 3 E 4 B 5 D 6 F
B 1 burning the candle at both ends 2 take time out 3 while away (time), chill out, 4 working all hours and burning the midnight oil mean you are working extremely hard. They usually have a positive connotation (the person is working hard to achieve something useful).

LISTENING

4 Give Ss a few minutes to think about their answers to the questions alone and make notes if they want. When they are ready, arrange Ss in small groups to discuss the questions. In feedback, nominate Ss from each group to share their ideas with the class.

5A ▶ 7.2 Read the questions with the class. Ss listen to the recording and identify which of the questions each speaker answers, then check in pairs. In feedback, elicit Ss' answers.

B Ss listen to the recording again and make notes on the speakers' answers, then check in pairs.

Answers to A and B: speaker 1: 1 he practises Qigong 2 for a few years 3 your thoughts are truly in the present and so you're not worrying about the past or future
Speaker 2: 1 she visits an island on the Thames and then stays on her boat 3 it's another world, she's surrounded by nature and sleeping on the boat is peaceful
Speaker 3: 1 gardening 3 you have to be patient and watching things grow makes her feel very happy, free and peaceful

C Ss discuss the questions in pairs. In feedback, nominate Ss to share their ideas with the class.

Unit 7 Recording 2

M=Man W1=Woman 1 W2=Woman 2

M: The best way for me to switch off from my day to day routine is a series of very relaxing and healing movements called Qigong. Qigong it means literally moving the energy and I find that it's the only way to ease my mind after a stressful day. Uh I've been doing it for a few years now and the more I practise it the more effective it is for me. Um those movements, very slow movements with the hands and arms just pull the focus inwards rather than outwards towards the distractions and worries of the day.
And um you're not thinking about what's happened or what will happen, your thoughts are truly in the present and my mind is totally freed up.

W1: I'm a teacher and my week is usually very busy and very stressful. When I come home from school I don't stop, I still have a lot of marking and preparation so it's not until the weekend that I'm able to begin to switch off.

On a Saturday morning I drive to - Trowlock Island, a little island on the Thames, takes me about ten minutes by car to get there. I then go across on the ferry to the island. There's a little five minute walk to the end of the island, no cars, beautiful flowers, Spring flowers at the moment, trees, it's very peaceful, lovely, the sound of birds and then I get onto my boat, turn on the engine and chug away.

And instantly I am in another world and completely relaxed with the water, the swans around, the ducks, the sky. It is instant relaxation.

It's very peaceful at night sleeping on board, getting up early and I just completely forget about all the worries and stresses of the school and the pupils there and it's a, it's a very, very quick, very instant way of relaxing.

W2: Um I think the only thing I find really relaxing on a day to day basis is gardening. Um I try and get out in the garden most days, mainly because if I don't I'll probably start shouting at, at people. Um I think one of the disadvantages of being a mum is that you never, you're never on your own, someone always walks in when you're in the middle of just thinking about something, you can't finish a thought.

So if I go out and garden I can finish a thought plus being a very impatient person um you can't be impatient in the garden, you have to wait and you have to watch and you have to, you can just be in the moment planting things and, and watching things happen and, and I find it incredibly peaceful and relaxing and - almost meditative.

The thing is it can't be hurried and there's nothing else to do except watching, waiting and, and as a result my mind is free. Um yes I have a great sense of freedom in the garden um both physically and mentally um and I think it's that sense of freedom, I think, that sense of getting away from everything. Uh and the sense of peace that comes with it, with the activity and the slow, gradual process of things growing and changing and um blossoming. It's, it's a very joyful and very freeing activity.

GRAMMAR participle clauses

6A Elicit/check: *jaded, take matters into my own hands, get the hang of (something)*. Ss read the text and answer the question alone then check in pairs. In feedback, elicit Ss' answers.

Answer: She learned the tango by taking classes and practising at home.

B Focus attention on the examples and elicit which is a present participle and which is a past participle. Ss underline the other examples in the text then check in pairs. In feedback, ask a stronger student to read out the text, while other Ss tell them to stop when they reach a present or past participle.

Answers: Having listened to the music as a child, I felt I already knew the rhythms. However, the tango was harder than it looked. After the first class, my feet were sore, and my knees ached. Not wanting to give up, I decided to take matters into my own hands (and feet!). Using a CD lent to me by a friend, I practised at home and after a while, I improved. Encouraged by my teacher, I went to a café where you could hear the music, and eventually, having struggled with it for months, I got the hang of it. People looking for something a bit different always love the tango. When you're doing it, you feel completely free: the world disappears – it's just you, your partner, and the music.

7A Ss match the rules and example alone then check in pairs. In feedback, elicit Ss' answers and be prepared to provide further explanations and examples where necessary.

Answers: 1 c) 2 b) 3 a) 4 d)

B Ss find the examples in the text then check in pairs.

Answers: e) Having listened to the music as a child, I felt I already knew the rhythms. f) armed with nothing but a love of Argentinian culture,

➡ **LANGUAGEBANK** 7.2 p140–141
Stronger classes can read the notes and do the exercises at home. Otherwise, check the notes with Ss, especially the use of *Having + past participle* and how we form negatives. In each exercise, do the first sentence as an example. Ss complete the exercises alone, then check their answers in pairs. Ss can refer to the notes to help them.

Answers: 1 a Making b Made 2 a Told b Telling 3 a Paying b Paid 4 a worn b wearing 5 a written b Writing 2 ~~Arming~~ Armed, ~~graduate~~ graduated, ~~to discuss~~ discussing, ~~Giving~~ Given, ~~Asking~~ Asked

PRACTICE

8 With *weaker classes*, elicit the first answer as an example. Ss combine the sentences alone then check in pairs.

Answers: 1 While staying in Toulouse she learnt French cooking. 2 Having honed my technique, I spent all my free time painting. 3 Not knowing how to relax, I always felt tense until I discovered Pilates. 4 Given a/the chance to go to a dance school in Colombia, Paul learnt salsa. 5 Proven by experts to be a stress buster, jogging is great exercise. 6 Bought for me by my brother, my rollerblades are a great way for me to get around. 7 Not being a 'natural' at sports, he had to work incredibly hard. 8 Alternative lifestyles are practised by many people looking for freedom from modern life.

Alternative approach
Write the sentences (with *weaker classes*, choose 5 sentences) on slips of paper, and the corresponding words in brackets on the board, in random order. Pin the slips of paper to a wall outside the class, or at the back. Arrange Ss in A/B pairs. As sit with their notebooks, and Bs run to the wall and remember one sentence at a time. They then return to their partner, and tell them the sentence, and together they rewrite it as a participle clause, using one of the words on the board. The first pair to complete all the sentences wins.

SPEAKING

9A Read the question with the class, and explain they have no financial or physical limits. Ss discuss the question in pairs. In feedback, elicit Ss' ideas with the class.

B Read the list of activities with the class and check understanding. Arrange Ss in small groups to discuss the questions. Monitor and make notes on any common errors and good language used for later feedback. In feedback, nominate Ss from each group to share their ideas with the class and give Ss feedback on their language.

WRITING a leaflet

10A If you have brought some leaflets and brochures to class, distribute them for Ss to look at. Ss discuss the questions in pairs. In feedback, elicit Ss' ideas and write some common features on the board.

B Ss read the notes and check their ideas. In feedback, elicit Ss' ideas and tick any of the features mentioned on the board.

11 Ss read the leaflet then answer the questions in pairs. In feedback, elicit Ss' answers and deal with any new vocabulary from the text.

Answers: 1 Anyone who wants to stay somewhere where they can relax in a luxurious environment. 2 Yes.

LEARN TO use subheadings

12A Ss identify the subheadings used in pairs.

Answers: c) d) e)

B Ss discuss the questions in pairs. In feedback, elicit Ss' answers.

Answers: Heading: Sparngall Spa Retreat
Slogan: *Relax, Rejuvenate, Recharge*
The heading is the name of the place and the slogan uses verbs that are not informational but are designed to attract the reader (e.g. as here, through alliteration).

C Elicit Ss' ideas as to why subheadings are important in leaflets. Ss read the ideas then discuss in pairs. In feedback, elicit Ss' answers.

Answers: 4 is false

D Ss think of a subheading alone then compare in pairs. In feedback, elicit Ss' ideas.

Suggested answer: Directions

13A Read the information with the class, and elicit a few ideas. Ss prepare their ideas and make notes. Monitor and help with vocabulary, writing any new words and phrases on the board.

B When they are ready, Ss write their leaflets. Monitor and help where necessary. Then, arrange Ss in small groups to read each other's leaflets and choose their favourite.

Optional extra activity
Arrange the Ss in pairs to choose their best leaflet out of the two. When they are ready, one student stays with the leaflet they chose, and the other walks round the class, looking at other Ss' leaflets and asking questions. When they have asked about all the other leaflets, they return to their original partner and describe as much as they can remember.

Homework ideas
- Ex 13B: write a final draft of your leaflet. Download pictures to include.
- Language bank 7.2 Ex 1–2, p141
- Workbook Ex 1–5, p48–49

FREE TO MAKE MISTAKES

Introduction
Ss learn and practise phrases for exchanging opinions, and how to convince someone.

SUPPLEMENTARY MATERIALS
Resource bank p169

Warm up: Write the phrases below on the board.

WARM UP
Write on the board: *travel by bus, go to school, go on holiday, earn money, buy something in a shop* and *go to the cinema*. Tell Ss which of these you can remember doing for the first time without your parents. Encourage Ss to ask you questions. Ss discuss which of these they can remember in pairs. In feedback, nominate Ss to share their ideas with the class.

VOCABULARY risk

1 Ss discuss the questions in pairs. In feedback, nominate Ss to share their ideas with the class and have a brief discussion.

2A Elicit/check *unleashed a media frenzy* (started an exaggerated response), *nagging* (asking over and over again) and *stifle* (stop from developing). Ss read the article and answer the questions alone then check in pairs. In feedback, elicit Ss' answers.

Answers: 1 She let him travel home on the subway in New York alone when he was nine years old. 2 Because he had been nagging her for weeks to be allowed out on his own and because she believes in encouraging independence. 3 She received support from some, and a lot of negative reactions from others. She was accused of being 'crazy' and 'America's worst mom'. 4 She thinks that if you are too over-protective then your children do not learn about danger and about how to take risks, which then becomes a danger in itself.

B Ss discuss the meanings of the words and phrases in pairs. Monitor and encourage Ss to use the context to help guess the meanings, but don't give any answers yet. Ss complete the sentences in pairs. In feedback, elicit Ss' answers, and be prepared to give further explanations or examples where necessary.

Answers: 1 independence 2 mollycoddle 3 deliberately, expose 4 reasonable risks, unsupervised 5 over-protective 6 risk-averse

Optional extra activity
If you have access to the internet, ask Ss to do a search (using different search engines) for each of the words/phrases in Ex 2B, and write down the sentences in which they are used in the first two results. When they are ready, arrange Ss into small groups to share the sentences they found. In feedback, nominate Ss from each group to share their ideas with the class.

C Ss discuss the statements in pairs. In feedback, nominate Ss to share their ideas with the class and have a brief discussion.

Teaching tip
Personalisation is a very effective tool when learning new language such as in Ex 2B. Engaging with new language in a personalised way helps Ss internalise the phrases, which in turn helps Ss move the language from receptive to productive vocabulary. At this level, Ss should be able to easily integrate new language into their repertoire through personalisation.

FUNCTION exchanging opinions

3 ▶ 7.3 Read the statements with the class and check Ss know what they are listening for. Ss listen to the recording and match the statements with the speakers alone, then check in pairs. In feedback, elicit Ss' answers.

Answers: 1 W 2 M 3 W 4 W 5 W 6 M 7 M 8 M

4A Ss complete the phrases alone from memory then check in pairs. Play the recording again for Ss to check their answers. In feedback, elicit Ss' answers.

Answers: a) joking b) right c) point d) think e) judgement f) say g) sense h) ridiculous

Alternative approach
Arrange Ss in A/B pairs. Student A listens to complete phrases a), c), e) and g), and student B listens to complete phrases b), d), f) and h). After listening, they show each other their answers. In feedback, elicit Ss' answers for all the phrases and write them on the board.

Unit 7 Recording 3
M=Man W=Woman

M: Did you read that article recently about um, uh I can't remember her name, a New York journalist who …

W: Oh the one about the nine year old child?

M: Yeah who left her son uh in Central New York and left him to come back on his own, to make his own way back at the age of nine.

W: Brilliant!

M: Brilliant?

W: Yes!

M: Oh come on, you must be joking.

W: I'm absolutely serious.

M: Well in what way brilliant? I mean he could have got lost, he could have been attacked, he could have been mugged, he could have …

W: That's absolutely right and we have …

M: What and that's good?

W: Look we have to, as parents now take a stand against all this mollycoddling, cotton wool rubbish. I was allowed to do a lot at a very young age and it helped me make the right decisions about how to protect myself and learn to be street wise. These kids don't know anything these days.

M: Well I agree with you up to a point but I mean you can't think that a nine year old should be left alone to kind of grow up in the course of two hours.

W: Surely you don't think that he should never make his own way home then and never learn?

M: Of course not but not at the age of nine!

W: Right, well that goes against my better judgement because I actually think it's, it's more responsible as a parent to show them by chucking them in at the deep end.

M: Right so it's, you think it's more responsible to abandon your child, you can't think that surely?

W: She didn't abandon the child.

M: Well effectively she did.

W: The, you know he lives in New York and anyway …

M: What, so who, well that's one of the most dangerous places in the world!

W: How can you say that? There are far worse places in the world. It's all relative.

M: Of course it's all relative but if you look at the muggings and the crime rate in New York it's horrendous and a nine year old wouldn't have a clue how to deal with all of that. It's a, it just doesn't make sense to me.

W: Look, it, it wasn't from what I know at two o'clock in the morning so you know you have to take it with a pinch of salt a bit.

M: Right.

W: Right, so

M: Because all crime happens at two o'clock in the morning?

W: Well surely you don't think then that it's terribly dangerous to leave a child in a, in a city in the middle of the morning, that they know and they're not four.

M: I do at the age of nine, he didn't even have a mobile phone!

W: He's probably a nine year old that's really got a lot going on you know, that's the whole point I think to take the child as an individual.

M: I understand the, wanting the empowerment, I just think we're in a hurry to, to push our kids to grew, grow up too soon

W: Oh come on.

M: … these days, I don't understand it

W: Oh please!

M: What's the hurry?

W: You know everybody feels that, if everybody feels like that we're never going to get anybody that stands up for themselves.

M: Oh that's ridiculous! We're talking about a nine year old!

W: Well that's absolutely right.

B Ss categorise the phrases alone then check in pairs. In feedback, elicit Ss' answers and drill the phrases chorally and individually.

Answers: 1 b) 2 c) 3–6 d), e), f), g) 7–8 a), h)

⟹ LANGUAGEBANK 7.3 p140–141

Stronger classes could read the notes and do the exercise at home. Otherwise, drill the phrases from the chart, checking Ss are using natural intonation. Ss work alone to complete the conversations, then check their answers in pairs. In feedback, elicit Ss' answers. Ss practise the conversations in pairs.

Answers: 1 sense 2 suppose 3 100% 4 Where 5 honestly 6 more

---

speakout TIP

Read the **speakout tip** with the class and practise saying the expressions. Ss turn to p171 and find more examples in the audio script, then compare in pairs.

LEARN TO convince someone

5A ▶ 7.4 Ss listen to the recording, paying attention to the intonation used to sound polite. In feedback, elicit how the intonation is used.

Answer: Speakers use a slightly higher pitch, keep their voice level and don't strongly emphasise any particular words.

B Play the recording again and pause after each phrase for Ss to repeat. If necessary, drill the phrases chorally and individually.

6A Ss write the response alone then check in pairs. In feedback, elicit Ss' answers and drill the responses chorally and individually, focusing on polite intonation.

Answers: 1 Surely you don't think people should never eat meat? 2 All I'm trying to say is that children need to learn at some stage. 3 The point is that exams are a useful way to measure progress. 4 Oh, come on! That doesn't make any sense.

B Ss practise the dialogues in pairs. Monitor and check Ss are using polite intonation. In feedback, nominate Ss to perform the dialogues for the class.

SPEAKING

7A Read the situations with the class and check understanding. Give Ss five minutes to think about their answers alone and make notes. Monitor and help with vocabulary, writing any new words and phrases on the board.

B When they are ready, arrange Ss in small groups to discuss the situations. Monitor and make notes on any common errors and good language for later feedback. Nominate Ss from each group to share their ideas with the class, and give Ss feedback on their language.

Teaching tip

In group discussions, it's useful to choose a stronger student in each group to act as chairperson. The job of the chairperson is to make sure the discussion stays focused and that everyone has a chance to speak.

Homework ideas
• Language bank 7.3 Ex 1, p141
• Workbook Ex 1–4, p50

LITTLE DORRIT

Introduction
Ss watch an extract from the BBC drama *Little Dorrit*, in which William Dorrit receives some good news after being in prison for a long time. Ss learn and practise how to develop a plot, and write a story.

SUPPLEMENTARY MATERIALS
Warm up: Bring or download pictures from Victorian times, showing e.g. clothes, transport, working life, etc.

Warm up
Write on the board: *What do you think life was like in the 19th Century in Britain? What about in your country? Would you like to have lived during this time? Which period from history would you most like to experience?* Show Ss the pictures and arrange them in small groups to discuss the questions on the board. In feedback, nominate Ss from each group to share their answers with the class and have a brief class discussion.

▶ DVD PREVIEW

1 Focus attention on the photo and elicit what Ss can see. Ss discuss the questions in pairs. In feedback, elicit Ss' answers but don't give any answers yet.

2A Give Ss two minutes to read the programme information and check their predictions/discuss the question in pairs. In feedback, elicit Ss' answers, and write their predictions for the good news on the board.

B Ss work alone to find the words/phrases in the text, then check in pairs. In feedback, elicit Ss' answers and be prepared to provide further examples/explanations where necessary.

Answer: 1 prosperous 2 a fortune 3 (is) confined in 4 to compose (himself)

Culture notes
Little Dorrit was originally a serial novel by Charles Dickens, published between 1855 and 1857. It is a satirical work which focuses on debtors' prisons, where people were kept in Victorian times until they had repaid their debt. Charles Dickens is regarded by many as the greatest English novelist of the Victorian period, and many of his works are considered classics. A recurring theme in his books was the need for social reform at the time.

▶ DVD VIEW

3 Ss watch the DVD and say what the two pieces of good news are. In feedback, elicit Ss' answers.

Answers: The 'good news' is that William will be set free and will inherit a fortune.

4A Ss discuss who said each sentence from memory in pairs.

B Play the DVD again for Ss to check their answers. In feedback, elicit Ss' answers.

Answers: 1 PW 2 A 3 C 4 C 5 A 6 C 7 W 8 W

Optional extra activity
Before Ss watch the DVD in Ex 3, divide the class into two groups, group A and group B. Send group B out of the class, and ask them to brainstorm a list of what they think the two pieces of good news are. While they are doing that, play the DVD to the group A, and explain that after watching, they will describe what they saw to a partner, but with one 'small lie' (e.g. change the colour of one of the character's clothes, or what they say). When they are ready, bring group B back in, and arrange Ss in A/B pairs. Student Bs explain the list they brainstormed to student As, and students As confirm any correct answers. Student As then describe the clip to student Bs with their one 'small lie'. When they are ready, play the DVD again for student Bs to watch and identify the lie, then check with their partner. In feedback, elicit what 'lies' Ss told.

5 Ss discuss the questions in pairs. In feedback, nominate Ss to share their ideas with the class.

Alternative approach
Write the following topics on the board: *transport, work/ job, food, home, holidays, family and friends* and *shopping*. Ask Ss to consider each of these topics in turn when discussing the questions in Ex 5.

Little Dorrit
Mr C=Mr Chivery   JC= John Chivery   WD=William Dorrit
AD=Amy Dorrit   AC=Arthur Clennam
Mr C: There's something up, John. I feel it in my bones.
JC: I feel it in my bones too Pa.
WD: Amy, my dear.
AD: Father, I have been made so happy this morning. Mr Clennam brought some wonderful news, about you. If he had not prepared me for it, I do not think I could have borne it.
WD: What is it? What is it sir?
AC: Compose yourself and think of the best surprise that could possibly happen to you, the very best. Do not be afraid to imagine it.
WD: The very best that could happen to me?
AC: Yes. What would it be?
WD: To, to be free.
AC: You shall be, and very soon. And there is more, you shall be prosperous. You are heir to a great fortune.
WD: I shall be free?
AD: You shall be free, Father.
WD: And rich?
AD: And you can be as you were again. Oh Father, Father, thank God.
WD: Uh and um I, I can leave the Marshalsea?
AC: As soon as you're ready to.
WD: Uh and rich? I shall be rich?
AC: No doubt of it.
WD: I shall be rich. Mr Clennam, am I to understand that I could pass through the gate at this very moment?
AC: I think not quite yet.
WD: So I am still confined?
AC: 'Tis but a few hours sir.
WD: A few hours. You talk easily of hours, sir. How long do you think an hour is to a man who is choking for want of air? No but, perhaps it's uh, uh perhaps it's uh for the best, yes, well yeah uh, yes perhaps it is as well.
AD: Father, I think you should rest now.
WD: Uh yes, yes, I'm uh. It's all been um, yes, very tired. Oh. Oh. I shall be rich. I shall be free.

speakout develop a plot

6A Focus attention on the pictures. Ss think of three questions about them in pairs. Monitor and help where necessary.

B ▶ 7.5 Ss listen to the recording and answer their questions (if possible) in pairs. In feedback, elicit what Ss found out about the story.

C Focus attention on the **Key phrases**. Ss listen and tick the phrases they hear, then check in pairs. In feedback, elicit Ss' answers and drill the **Key phrases** chorally and individually.

Answers: After this, he walked a while, No sooner had he got in than he realised …, Once he'd got the engine going, he drove, Having waited so patiently, he …

D Ss discuss the questions in pairs. In feedback, elicit Ss' answers.

Answers:
at or near the beginning of a story:
Once upon a time
in the middle of a story:
After this, he …, No sooner had he [done this] than … [this happened], Once he'd [done this], he …, Having [done this], he …,
at or near the end of a story:
And the moral of the story is …, And he lived happily ever after.

Unit 7 Recording 5

S=Samuel

S: After twenty long years he was finally free. He breathed deeply. The air smelled good. He thought to himself he would spend the rest of his days outside, by the ocean, at the foot of a mountain, in a valley, in a field, under the stars, it didn't matter as long as he could breathe the air and never be confined again. But before all that, he knew there was something else he had to do. He walked to the nearest town. He had some savings and the first thing he bought was a shovel. This is the best thing I'll ever spend my money on, he said to himself. After this, he walked a while until he came to a car rental office. Using his old ID card, he rented an old, blue Chevrolet. No sooner had he got in it than he realised he barely remembered how to turn on the ignition. He fiddled around for a while but once he'd got the engine going, he drove long into the night. He was sure he would remember the tree. How could he forget? It was burned into his memory like a scar. Even in the darkness he would remember the rise of the hill, the curve in the road, the thick branches hanging over a rusting iron gate. He'd been looking forward to this moment for twenty years. Having waited so patiently, he knew his moment was close.

7A Ss prepare their stories in pairs. Monitor and help with vocabulary, writing any new words and phrases on the board.

B Ss practise telling the story in pairs. Monitor and help where necessary, and make notes on any common errors/good language for later feedback.

C Rearrange Ss into small groups so that Ss are working with different Ss form Ex 7B. Ss tell their stories in groups then answer the questions. In feedback, elicit Ss' answers to the questions, and give Ss feedback on their language.

writeback a story

8A Ss read the story and in pairs, decide which sentence comes next. In feedback, elicit Ss' answers. Give Ss one minute to underline any new words from the story, then ask you about what they mean.

Suggested answer: The map was wrinkled but still intact or Wrapped in newspaper was a pair of rough leather boots.

B Ss write their stories alone. Monitor and help with vocabulary, writing any new words and phrases on the board. When they have finished, Arrange Ss in small groups to read their stories to each other. In feedback, nominate Ss to tell the class about their favourite story.

Optional extra activity
When Ss have finished their final drafts, get them to publish their stories. There are many different ways they can do this. It could be on a class blog, a social networking site, or a class collection of short stories, which can then be distributed to other Ss in the school. Giving Ss a real purpose for writing like this can be very motivating.

Homework ideas
• Ex 8B: write a final draft of your story.

LOOKBACK

Introduction

Ss revise and practise the language of Unit 7. The notes below provide ideas for exploiting the exercises and activities but your approach will depend on your aim, e.g. as a diagnostic or progress test or as revision and fluency practice. For example, if done as a test then it would not be appropriate to monitor or help them.

CLEFT SENTENCES

1A Focus attention on the phrases in the box, and elicit possible ways of finishing each one. Ss complete the sentences alone then check in pairs. In feedback, elicit Ss' answers. Listen carefully to how Ss are pronouncing the cleft sentences, and if necessary drill chorally and individually.

Answers: 1 The reason I've come 2 It was when I was reading that book 3 What most impresses me 4 One thing I've learned is that 5 The person who 6 What you should do is 7 All I want to say 8 What they do

Optional extra activity

Ss test each other on the sentences in pairs. One student reads out the first part of the sentence, and their partner tries to remember what the rest of the sentence is.

B Ss complete the sentences in pairs. Monitor and help with vocabulary, writing any new words and phrases on the board. When they are ready, Ss compare their sentences with another pair.

IDIOMS: RELAXING

2A Read the example with the class and make sure Ss understand what to do. Ss complete the sentences alone then check in pairs. In feedback, elicit Ss' answers and be prepared to provide further explanations and examples where necessary.

Answers: 2 let 3 mind 4 out 5 down 6 off

B Read the example with the class and make sure Ss understand what to do. Ss rewrite the sentences about their partner alone. Monitor and help with vocabulary, writing any new words and phrases on the board.

C Ss compare their sentences in pairs. In feedback, elicit how many sentences Ss guessed correctly and any new/interesting information they found out about their partner.

ESCAPE

3A After explaining the activity, elicit the first answer as an example, in order to check Ss understand what to do. Ss complete the sentences alone then check in pairs. In feedback, elicit Ss' answers and drill the words where necessary.

Answers: 1 stranded 2 escape 3 released 4 made a break 5 refuge 6 fled

B Ss discuss what they would do in pairs. When they have finished, join pairs into groups of four to compare their ideas. In feedback, nominate Ss from each group to share their ideas with the class.

Suggested answers: 1 You decide to flee the country. 2 You decide to make a break for it. 3 You take refuge in the cave until the storm passes.

Alternative approach

Books closed. Write the sentences on slips of paper, and on the board, write the corresponding words from the box, in random order. Pin the slips of paper to a wall at the back of or outside the class. Arrange Ss in A/B pairs. As sit with their notebooks, and Bs run to the wall and remember one sentence at a time. They then return to their partner, and tell them the sentence, and together they complete it, using one of the words on the board. The first pair to complete all the sentences wins.

PARTICIPLE CLAUSES

4A Demonstrate the activity by telling Ss about your perfect day, using some of the participle clauses. Ss write their paragraphs alone. Monitor and help with vocabulary, writing any new words and phrases on the board, and check Ss are using the participle clauses correctly.

B When they are ready, arrange Ss in pairs to compare their paragraphs and answer the questions. In feedback, nominate Ss to share their ideas with the class.

EXCHANGING OPINIONS

5A After explaining the activity, elicit the first answer as an example, in order to check Ss understand what to do. Ss correct the responses alone then check in pairs, and guess what trends they describe. In feedback, elicit Ss' answers. Ss practise the conversations in pairs.

Answers: 1 up to a point 2 That's ridiculous! 3 I couldn't agree more 4 I suppose you've got a point, ...

B Ss write their own response alone then compare in pairs. In feedback, elicit Ss' ideas.

OVERVIEW

8.1 HISTORY IN A BOX

GRAMMAR | future in the past
VOCABULARY | time expressions
HOW TO | describe plans you had in the past

COMMON EUROPEAN FRAMEWORK
Ss can recognise a wide range of idiomatic expressions and colloquialisms; can easily follow and contribute to complex interactions in group discussion even on abstract, unfamiliar topics.

8.2 I REMEMBER …

GRAMMAR | ellipsis and substitution
VOCABULARY | memories
HOW TO | describe a memory

COMMON EUROPEAN FRAMEWORK
Ss can use organisational patterns, connectors and cohesive devices; can write clear, detailed, well-structured and developed descriptions.

8.3 TIME SAVERS

FUNCTION | discussing ideas
VOCABULARY | collocations with time
LEARN TO | solicit information

COMMON EUROPEAN FRAMEWORK
Ss can express their ideas and opinions with precision; can help along the progress of the discussion by inviting others to join in.

8.4 WONDERS OF THE UNIVERSE ⊙ BBC DVD

speakout | a turning point
writeback | a major decision

COMMON EUROPEAN FRAMEWORK
Ss can give clear, smoothly flowing, elaborate and often memorable descriptions; can write clear, detailed, well-structured and developed descriptions.

8.5 LOOKBACK

Communicative revision activities

BBC VIDEO PODCAST
What is the best time of life?

This video podcast extends discussion of the unit topic to discussing age. Ss can view people talking about their favourite time of life. Use this video podcast at the start or end of Unit 8.

HISTORY IN A BOX

Introduction

Ss revise and practise future in the past in the context of time capsules. They also learn and practise proverbs and sayings.

SUPPLEMENTARY MATERIALS

Resource bank p171, p172

Warm up: Write the words below on the board.

Ex 1A: prepare a list of five things you would put in a time capsule to represent your culture.

Ex 7B: bring 4 or 5 personal objects to class which represent you.

Warm up

Write on the board: *food pills, domestic robots, space holidays* and *flying cars*. Explain that these are some predictions about the future from the past that never came true. In pairs, Ss discuss which of these might come true in the future, and which other 'future predictions' they remember from when they were young. In feedback, elicit Ss' ideas.

READING

1A Focus attention on the picture and elicit what Ss can see. Explain that a time capsule is a box in which you place objects to represent a time and a culture. It is then buried for future generations to dig up years later. Introduce the activity by describing five things you would put in a time capsule to represent your culture. Give Ss three or four minutes to prepare a list of five things. When they are ready, arrange Ss in small groups to compare their lists. With *multilingual classes*, try to include different nationalities in each group.

Alternative approach
Write the following objects on the board: *a car, a newspaper, some food, a mobile phone, an item of clothing, a book, some music, a piece of furniture, a photo/picture, some medicine, a DVD, a computer* and *some money*. Arrange Ss in pairs, and ask them to decide which three things from the list would be best to put in a time capsule, and why. In feedback, nominate Ss to share their ideas with the class.

B Ss read the text quickly to check their ideas from Ex 1A. In feedback, ask if any of their ideas were included.

Teaching tip
Research into the human brain shows that when we learn new information, we process it by 'attaching' it to schematic knowledge we already have about the world. When Ss read a text, prediction is a very effective tool to take advantage of this natural process. We can encourage this by using any visuals or the title to elicit predictions about what Ss will read, then asking them to compare the information in a text with what they predicted.

2A Ss read the article again and match the underlined words to the things/people/times in the article, then check in pairs. In feedback, elicit Ss' answers. After checking the answers, give Ss two minutes to underline new words from the text in Ex 1B that they want to ask about. When they are ready, Ss ask and answer in pairs. Help with any further explanations necessary.

Answers: 1 Antonio Carlos Jobim 2 Bulawayo, Zimbabwe 3 Ralph's Fine Dining 4 Bharatpur, India 5 France's National Library 6 Professor Thornwell Jacobs 7 Panasonic and Mainichi Newspapers 8 In 2025

B Ss discuss the question in pairs. In feedback, elicit Ss' answers and have a brief class discussion.

VOCABULARY time expressions

3A Ss read the extracts then answer the questions in pairs. In feedback, elicit Ss' answers and be prepared to provide further explanations and examples where necessary.

Answers: 1 at the dawn of (more literary and used only for very big occasions), the outset; 2 in years to come 3 on the verge of, was about to 4 for the foreseeable future

B Ss complete the sentences alone then check in pairs. In feedback, elicit Ss' answers.

Answers: 1 In years to come, we will remember this as a golden age. 2 Scientists are the on the verge of finding a cure for AIDS. 3 Humanity probably won't exist at the dawn of the next millennium. 4 We are about to enter an age of natural disasters. 5 From the outset, the internet was able to unite people around the world. 6 Poverty will be with us for the foreseeable future

C Ss discuss the statements in pairs. In feedback, elicit Ss' ideas and have a brief class discussion.

GRAMMAR future in the past

4A Ss find the sentences and answer the questions in pairs. In feedback, elicit Ss' answers and be prepared to provide further explanations and examples where necessary.

Answers: 1 a) The capsule was supposed to be opened in 2007; b) His capsule was to remain hidden for the foreseeable future; c) The other wasn't going to be touched for five thousand years. d) It was to have been the world's biggest time capsule. 2 a) was supposed to c) wasn't going to d) was to 3 They were going to leave these untouched; the crypt wasn't meant to be opened until 8113; One of them would be opened regularly; in years to come someone would find such glories of our time. (The first and second examples describe plans that did not become reality).

B Ss complete the table alone then check in pairs. In feedback, elicit Ss' answers and write them on the board.

Answers: 1 was/were 2 was/were 3 was/were 4 was/were

⟹ **LANGUAGEBANK** 8.1 p142–143

Stronger classes can read the notes and do the exercises at home. Otherwise, check the notes with Ss, especially the different use of *would* here and the other expressions. In each exercise, do the first sentence as an example. Ss complete the exercises alone, then check their answers in pairs. Ss can refer to the notes to help them.

Answers: 1 1 f) 2 d) 3 a) 4 c) 5 b) 6 e)
2 1 We **were** about to ascend the mountain when snow started to fall. 2 Correct. 3 Melissa meant **to** tell you about the dinner invitation, but she forgot. 4 We were to **have** taken the 6.02 train to Manchester, but it was cancelled. 5 She got sick when she was on **the** verge of becoming a superstar. 6 Correct. 7 Thompson then travelled to Bali, where he **would** later meet his sixth wife. 8 I was ~~but~~ hoping to work with Donna again, but she left the company. 9 Correct. 10 I was to **meet** Daley and his gang in the subway at midnight.

PRACTICE

5 With *weaker classes*, elicit the first answer as an example. Ss rewrite the sentences alone then check in pairs. In feedback, elicit Ss' answers.

Answers: 1 Our time capsule was to be opened in 2020. 2 The document wasn't to be seen until 2050. 3 The safe was supposed to be locked for ten years … 4 We were going to visit Montevideo … 5 It was to have been the world's biggest outdoor festival … 6 Jim went to Peru, where he would live for twenty years.

6A Demonstrate the activity by telling Ss one true and one false sentence about yourself. Encourage Ss to ask you questions to find out which is true/false. Ss write their own sentences. Monitor and help with vocabulary, writing any new words and phrases on the board.

B When they are ready, arrange Ss in pairs to read out their sentences. In feedback, nominate Ss to share any new information they found out about their partner with the class.

SPEAKING

7A Focus attention on the photo and elicit Ss' answers to the questions. Write any new vocabulary on the board.

B If you brought objects to class, then demonstrate the activity by showing them to Ss and explaining why they represent you. Give Ss five minutes to think about their answers and make notes. Monitor and help with vocabulary, writing any new words and phrases on the board.

C When they are ready, arrange Ss in groups to share their ideas. Monitor and make notes on any common errors and good language for later feedback. In feedback, nominate Ss from each group to share their ideas with the class. Give Ss feedback on their language.

VOCABULARY PLUS proverbs

8A Ss underline the proverb and answer the question in pairs. In feedback, elicit Ss' answers.

Answer: actions speak louder than words

B Give Ss one or two minutes to think of a definition and write it down. When they are ready, Ss compare their ideas in pairs. In feedback, elicit Ss' ideas and read the **speakout tip** with the class.

speakout TIP

Read the **speakout tip** with the class and elicit any proverbs they know in English. Find out if proverbs are common in the Ss' own language(s) and elicit one or two examples.

9A Arrange Ss in two groups: As and Bs. Groups As match the proverbs with the situations, and Bs match the pairs of similar proverbs. When they are ready, check answers with each group.

Answers: Group A: 1 d) 2 b) 3 e) 4 a) 5 c) 6 f)
Group B: 7 g) 8 l) 9 i) 10 k) 11 j) 12 h)

B Arrange Ss in A/B pairs. Each student takes it in turns to show their list of proverbs to their partner while hiding the definitions, and, in a random order, explain the meanings, while their partner guesses which proverbs they are describing. In feedback, check understanding of the proverbs and be prepared to provide further explanations and examples where necessary.

10 ▶ 8.1 Ss listen to the recording, paying attention to the rhythm of each proverb. Play the recording again for Ss to mark the stressed syllables, then check in pairs. In feedback, elicit Ss' answers and drill the proverbs chorally and individually.

Answers: 1 A picture is worth a thousand words.
2 Better safe than sorry. 3 Out of sight, out of mind.
4 Home is where the heart is. 5 Practise what you preach.
6 Rome wasn't built in a day. 7 There's no place like home.
8 Nothing ventured, nothing gained. 9 Don't judge a book by its cover. 10 Actions speak louder than words.
11 Practice makes perfect. 12 Absence makes the heart grow fonder.

Watch out!

English is a stress-timed language. This means that the rhythm of speech is dictated by the number of stressed syllables, and unstressed syllables shorten to fit this rhythm. In syllable-timed languages, stressed and unstressed syllables take around the same amount of time to say. You can demonstrate this by drilling: *ME – YOU – HIM – HER*. Keeping the same rhythm, add the unstressed syllables: *ME and then YOU and then HIM and then HER.* An awareness of stress-timing can help Ss sound more natural when they speak, and also help when listening.

11 Read the example with the class. Ss discuss the questions in pairs. In feedback, elicit Ss' ideas and have a brief class discussion.

⫸ **VOCABULARYBANK** p155 PROVERBS

1A Ss match the phrases and meanings alone then check in pairs. In feedback, elicit Ss' answers and be prepared to provide further explanations and examples where necessary.

B Ss discuss which proverbs have equivalents in their own language(s) in pairs. With *multilingual classes*, try to arrange Ss so that each pair includes different nationalities. In feedback, elicit Ss' ideas.

C Read the examples with the class. Ss write situations alone then compare in pairs. In feedback, elicit Ss' ideas. *Stronger classes* can do the exercises at home.

Answers: 1A 1 f) 2 j) 3 d) 4 c) 5 i) 6 e) 7 a) 8 g)
9 b) 10 h)

Optional extra activity

Ss choose one of the proverbs and write a short paragraph describing a situation where they could use it e.g. *Much as I love travelling, I found that after 3 months away, I really missed my family (home is where the heart is).* When they are ready, Ss read out their situations for other Ss to guess the proverb in small groups.

Homework ideas

• Ex 7C: Write about your 'Museum of Me'.
• Vocabulary bank p155
• Language bank 8.1 Ex 1–2, p143
• Workbook Ex 1–6, p51–52

I REMEMBER …

Introduction

Ss learn and practise ellipsis and substitution in the context of memories. They also practise writing a competition entry.

SUPPLEMENTARY MATERIALS

Resource bank: p170, p173

Speakout tip (optional extra activity): Write the verbs on cards and make enough copies for one set of cards per group

Warm up

Elicit the five senses and write them on the board: *see* (or *sight*), *smell, hear* (or *hearing*), *taste* and *touch*. Read out the following things and ask Ss to write down the sense they most closely associate with each one: *1 bus 2 baby 3 coffee 4 city 5 football 6 work 7 summer 8 English*. Ss compare their answers in pairs. In feedback, elicit, via a show of hands, which senses Ss wrote for each thing and explain that this shows we absorb information in different ways.

LISTENING

1 Focus attention on the words in the box ad check understanding. Give Ss three or four minutes to think about their answers and make notes. When they are ready, Ss discuss their ideas in pairs. In feedback, nominate Ss to share their ideas with the class.

2A Ss read the listing and answer the questions in pairs. In feedback, elicit Ss' answers.

Answers: Childhood memories. The effect is called 'the Proust phenomenon'.

B ▶ 8.2 Ss listen to the programme and tick the smells that are mentioned, then compare answers in pairs and discuss what the people said about each one. In feedback, elicit Ss' answers.

Answers: disinfectant: reminds him of school; cigarettes: horrible smell, reminds her of when she could smell cigarettes on her clothes, and would try to hide the smell so her parents wouldn't find out; candles: when they have just been snuffed out, reminds him of when he used to sing in church choir
Also mentioned: vinegar and paint

3A Check Ss understand they are looking for factual errors, not grammatical ones. Ss correct the sentences alone then check in pairs.

B When they are ready, play the recording again for Ss to check their answers. In feedback, elicit Ss' answers.

Answers: 3 Psychologists think memories associated with smells are stronger than those evoked by **photos**.
4 Professor Chu uses **familiar** smells to trigger autobiographical memories. 6 When the man smells candles he is reminded of when he **sang in the church choir**.

4A Focus attention on the phrases in the box and check understanding. Ss complete the sentences alone then check in pairs. Don't elicit any answers yet.

B Ss turn to p171 and check their answers with the audio script. In feedback, answer any questions Ss have about the phrases.

Answers: 1 carried back in time 2 evoking memories 3 takes me back in time 4 evocative smell

Unit 8 Recording 2

G=Geoff Watts M1=Man 1 M2=Man 2 C =Claudia Hammond
S= Simon Chu L=Louise J= John Aggleton

G: Hello. We're looking back quite a bit in this week's programme, back to childhood for a start.
Now, ever had that feeling of being suddenly carried back in time by a particular odour? You probably have because it's a common experience. The smell of coal does it for me, and even more specifically mint sauce. One whiff of that, and it's back to Sunday lunch in the house where I was born. There is, it seems, something special about smells when it comes to evoking memories. Now, as Claudia Hammond reports, psychologists think they may be getting to the root of it.

M1: The smell that always really takes me back in time is the smell of disinfectant, and kind of cedary wood. And for some bizarre reason it reminds me of being at school when I was about seven.

M2: Whenever I smell Privet, walk past a hedge or something, it takes me instantly back to my kindergarten, to the rather smelly passage through from the garden to the school restaurant, where we had our lunches. It takes me straight back there.

C: For some reason, the memories evoked by smells seem to be stronger than memories that come back to you, say from looking at a photo. In the field of psychology, they call it the Proust phenomenon, after the famous incident with the madeleines in *Remembrance Of Things Past*. One of the people studying the Proust Effect is Doctor Simon Chu, a lecturer in psychology at Liverpool University. The link between smell and memory has hardly been touched by researchers, because until recently, it's been very difficult to prove in the lab. Using familiar smells, like vinegar and talcum powder, Simon Chu tries to trigger autobiographical memories.

C: So, what have you got here? You've got about eight little plastic boxes.

S: Here we've got things like raw mixed herbs, we've got … um … some cigarette ash, some vinegar, ketchup, got some paint. What I'm going to do is I'm going to give you a word, and I'm going to ask you to tell me as much as you can about a particular experience that the word reminds you of.

C: First, he gives his volunteer Louise a word, like cigarette. And she has to come up with an event from her past linked to the word. Once she's remembered everything she can, he lets her sniff the real thing from one of his special boxes.

S: I'd like you to sniff gently at this, and tell me anything else you can remember about that particular experience.

L: Oooh … um … stale cigarette smoke … that's a horrible smell … I can still smell it from here. I just remember … just the smell of it … and the fact that it, you can still smell it on yourself ages later. And then when you go home, you suddenly realise that your parents are probably going to be able to smell it on you as well. And then you get that fear inside you that they're going to know that you were smoking, and … you know there were the polos, and the perfume and that kind of thing – desperately trying to cover up the smell, so that your parents don't know what you've been up to.

C: Confronted by the actual smell of cigarettes, Louise remembers far more about the event than she did when she was simply given the word 'cigarette'. In particular, she remembered the fear that her parents would find out she'd been having a sneaky cigarette. It seems that smell is very good at bringing back the emotional details like this.

S: There is something quite unusual, and special about the relationship between smells and memory.

J: For me, the most evocative smell is that smell you get when candles have just been snuffed out. And it takes me back to my childhood when I was a chorister in a church choir, in a village in Berkshire. And towards the end of the service, one of the servers used to come out and extinguish the big candles up by the altar. And if I just smell that smell, of candles being snuffed out, I'm instantly back at that time and the memories of the music of my boyhood, the church music of the time.

G: Odours that prompt the memories of times past.

C Demonstrate the activity by telling Ss about smells which bring back strong memories for you. Arrange Ss in small groups to discuss the questions. In feedback, nominate Ss from each group to share their ideas with the class.

GRAMMAR ellipsis and substitution

5A Ss read the conversations and answer the questions alone then check in pairs. In feedback, elicit Ss' answers.

> **Answers to a) and b):** 1 A: (Do you/Can you) remember any special smells from your childhood? B: Yes, I **do** (remember special smells from my childhood) actually. (I remember) the smell of my grandmother's perfume. 2 B: Does it (remind you of holidays in Greece)? I've never been **there** (to Greece). 3 A: (Have you) got any photos of your family? B: Yes, (I have got) **lots** (of photos of my family).

B Read the rules with the class. Ss answer the questions alone then check in pairs. In feedback, elicit Ss' answers.

> **Answers:** 1 (Have you) ever been to Spain?, (I'll) see you (later/tomorrow/on Monday, etc.). 2 So = I've got everything I need.

> **Watch out!**
>
> Ellipsis is very common in spoken English, and very informal. While it's very useful for Ss to recognise this when conversing with native speakers, they shouldn't be encouraged to use it when writing, as it will look too informal.

> ⇒ **LANGUAGEBANK** 8.1 p142–143
>
> *Stronger classes* can read the notes and do the exercises at home. Otherwise, check the notes with Ss, especially the words we use for substitution. In each exercise, do the first sentence as an example. Ss complete the exercises alone, then check their answers in pairs. Ss can refer to the notes to help them.
>
> **Answers:** 1 1 one 2 do 3 so 4 not 5 ones 6 there 7 mine 8 some
> 2 1 I'm not sure if they've finished, but I think they have (finished). 2 We could have met them later, but I didn't want to (meet them later). 3 (Do you) want a coffee? I've just made some (coffee). 4 I'd be happy to help if you need me to (help). 5 A: What time were we supposed to arrive? B: (We were supposed to arrive) at six. 6 Erica had ice cream for dessert and Bill (had) chocolate cake. 7 They'll be here soon, but I don't know exactly when (they'll be here). 8 A: (Have you) got the time? B: (The time is) half past two.

PRACTICE

6A Ss underline the correct alternative alone then check in pairs. In feedback, elicit Ss' answers.

B ▶ 8.3 Ss cross out the unnecessary word in pairs. When they are ready, play the recording for Ss to check their answers. In feedback, check Ss' answers and drill the elliptted phrases chorally and individually. Note that it is also possible to delete the subject in the examples below.

> **Answers to A and B:** 1 A: ~~Are~~ you coming to the party? B: Yes, I think **so**. 2 A: Did you just delete the file? B: ~~I~~hope **not**. 3 A: ~~Do you~~ want to try this perfume? B: No, but I'll try that **one**. 4 A: ~~Do~~ you think we'll have enough time to discuss this later? B: We'll have **a little** ~~time~~. 5 A: ~~Are you~~ going away on holiday this year? B: No. Ann Marie doesn't have enough money and ***nor*** do I. 6 A: ~~Are~~ you sure you've got enough copies for everyone? B: Yes, ~~I've got~~ **lots**.

7 Arrange the class in two groups: group A and group B. Ss cross out the unnecessary words. When they are ready, check each group's answers. Arrange Ss in A/B pairs. Ss read out their sentences for their partners to respond. Monitor and help where necessary. In feedback, nominate Ss to read out their conversations to the class.

> **Answers:** Student A: 1 ~~Have you~~ ever been to China? – b)
> 2 ~~I~~ don't know why I can't get this camera to work. – c)
> 3 I love olives. – d) 4 ~~Have~~ they nearly finished? – e)
> 5 What's that? ~~It~~ looks wonderful. – a)
> Student B: 1 ~~Have you~~ been in the job for long? – c) 2 ~~Are~~ you sure she's coming today? – a) 3 Someone called you earlier and left a message. – d) 4 ~~Do you want a~~ tea or coffee? – e) 5 ~~Did you~~ see the film last night? – b)

VOCABULARY memories

8A With *weaker classes*, elicit the first answer as an example. Ss complete the sentences alone then check in pairs. In feedback, elicit Ss' answers.

> **Answers:** 1 This place **holds** lots of memories for us
> 2 … it **brings** back a lot lf memories. 3 It's one of my **earliest** memories. 4 I have very **vague** memories …
> 5 I only have a very **hazy** recollection 6 … I remember it **vividly** 7 /I remember her dress **distinctly** 8 … the memories come **flooding** back

B Ss answer the questions in pairs. In feedback, elicit Ss' answers and be prepared to answer any questions they have about the words.

> **Answers:** Not strong: vague, hazy; Very strong: distinctly, vividly, flooding

➠ VOCABULARYBANK p155 MEMORIES

2A Ss underline the expressions alone then check in pairs. In feedback, elicit Ss' answers and be prepared to provide further explanations/examples where necessary.

B Ss discuss the questions in pairs. In feedback, elicit Ss' answers.

C Ss match the meanings with expressions alone then check in pairs. In feedback, elicit Ss' answers.
Stronger classes can do the exercises at home.

Answers: 2A 1 nothing springs to mind 2 a once-in-a-lifetime experience 3 a day to remember 4 it's on the tip of my tongue 5 I can't for the life of me remember 6 I clean forgot 7 That's going back 8 I remember it like it was yesterday 9 I've had a complete memory lapse 10 It's etched on my memory
B remembering/forgetting: 1, 4, 5, 6, 8, 9, 10 past experiences: 2, 3, 7, 8
C a) etched on my memory; remember it like it was yesterday b) day to remember; once-in-a-lifetime experience, c) it's on the tip of my tongue d) I clean forgot; I can't for the life of me remember e) that's going back

SPEAKING

9A Ss read the text and choose a stage of their lives to talk about.

B Focus attention on the word webs and check understanding. Give Ss five minutes to think about their answers and make notes. Monitor and help with vocabulary, writing any new words and phrases on the board.

C When they are ready, arrange Ss in small groups to share their memories. Monitor and make notes on any common errors and good language for later feedback. In feedback, nominate Ss from each group to share their ideas with the class and give Ss feedback on their language.

WRITING a personal story

10A Elicit/check: *sap* (the substance that carries food through a plant), *beckoning* (making a signal that someone should come nearer) and *bark* (the outer layer of a tree). Ss read the story and answer the questions alone then check in pairs. In feedback, elicit Ss' answers.

Answers: 1 Because the writer had special memories of playing in the tree with her cousins as a child. 2 It became a doctor's surgery.

B Ss read the advice then discuss if the writer follows it in pairs. In feedback, elicit Ss' answers.

Answer: The writer follows all the advice.

LEARN TO improve descriptive writing

11 Read the advice and examples with the class. Ss follow the instructions alone then check in pairs. In feedback, elicit Ss' answers.

Answers: 1 adjectives: huge (house), ancient (tree), sticky (sap), green / lush (leaves), crunchy (apples), juicy (figs), smooth (bark), verbs: Chatter / stood / feast / beckon / sprinting 2 onomatopoeia: crunchy apple, sticky sap, smooth bark Texture: smooth bark, sticky sap 3 The writer uses the contrast of the house nowadays (as a doctor's surgery) with her memory of the house in the past. Her happy memories, with her feeling (sad) of seeing how the house and gardens had been changed. 4 personification of an object: 'The tree knew all our secrets.' 'The branches beckoned…' metaphor: Memories … flooding back'

Teaching tip
Writing meaningful, colourful descriptions is a difficult skill to achieve, even in your first language, At this level, however, Ss should be encouraged to push the boundaries of their existing knowledge of English in order to produce illustrative texts. Improving their writing using the methods described in Ex 11 can lead to Ss producing texts which are above and beyond the level of their day-to-day English use, and can be very fulfilling.

speakout TIP

Read the **speakout tip** with the class, then elicit Ss' answers to the questions.

Optional extra activity
Write the following verbs on cards or pieces of paper, and make one copy for each group of three Ss: *whisper, mumble, scream, exclaim, murmur, slur, announce, burst out* and *gossip*. Elicit/check the meaning of each of the words and write them on the board, along with the sentence: *Our teacher is great.* Arrange Ss in groups of three, and distribute one set of cards to each group, and place them face down in the middle. Ss take it in turns to pick up a card, and say the sentence on the board in the style of the verb on the card. Other Ss listen and guess which verb the student is using.

In feedback, nominate Ss from each group to demonstrate one or two of the verbs.

12 Read the instructions with the class and check understanding. Ss write their stories alone. Monitor and help with vocabulary, and encourage Ss to use descriptive language as in Ex 11. When they have finished, Ss swap stories with a partner and discuss what they like about each other's stories.

Homework ideas
• Ex 12: write a final draft of your story.
• Language bank 8.2 Ex 1–2, p143
• Workbook Ex 1–5, p53–54

TIME SAVERS

Introduction

Ss learn and practise phrases for discussing ideas, and how to solicit information.

> **SUPPLEMENTARY MATERIALS**
>
> Resource bank p174
>
> Warm up: Write the questions below on the board.

Warm up

Write the following questions on the board: *Do you have enough leisure time? What things would you like to have more time for in your life? Do you have less leisure time nowadays than when you were younger? Why (not)?* Ss discuss the questions in small groups. In feedback, nominate Ss from each group to share their ideas with the class.

VOCABULARY collocations with *time*

1 Focus attention on the photos and elicit what Ss can see. Arrange Ss in small groups to discuss the questions. In feedback, nominate Ss from each group to share their ideas with the class.

2A Books closed. Write on the board: *time*. Elicit any phrases Ss know with *time* and write them on the board. Ss complete the expressions alone then check in pairs. In feedback, elicit Ss' answers and check understanding of the expressions.

> **Answers:** 2 pushed 3 hands 4 to 5 the 6 in, spare

B Ss discuss the questions in the same groups as Ex 1. In feedback, nominate Ss from each group to share their ideas with the class.

FUNCTION discussing ideas

3 Elicit/check: *tantrums*. Ss read the list alone then answer the questions in pairs. In feedback, elicit Ss' ideas.

> **Alternative approach**
> Arrange Ss in A/B pairs. Student A reads the first three tips and student B reads the last three. When they are ready, Ss cover the text and explain what they read to their partner.

4A ▶ 8.4 Read the expressions in the box with the class and check understanding. Ss listen to the recording and tick the ideas mentioned. In feedback, elicit Ss' answers.

> **Answers:** read only the conclusion, phone first, divide up your day, bring in an expert, use the microwave, make lists, read the instructions first

B Ss mark the statements true or false in pairs. Play the recording again for Ss to check their answers. In feedback, elicit Ss' answers.

> **Answers:** 1 T 2 T 3 T 4 F (but she thinks it would be a good idea) 5 F (she thinks it's a good idea) 6 F (but he does say that making all your phone calls at once saves time)

Unit 8 Recording 4

M1=Man M2=Man 2 W1=Woman 1 W2=Woman 2

M1: Okay so uh what ideas do we have for saving time?

M2: Well like for example at university, if we've got a lot to read, there's like a massive reading list um, I'll like take a report or an analysis that someone else has written and I just simply haven't got time to read the whole thing, so I just often just skip to the conclusion and just like make bullet point notes of what I read there.

M1: Right okay.

M2: Well it's not ideal obviously but it does save time.

W1: Yeah, yeah

M1: Sure, sure.

W2: And I find when I'm really busy and I just have to um have a very, very quick lunch to save time. I just bring something in, in a Tupperware, put it in the microwave on a plate.

M1: Ah that's a good idea.

W1 Yeah and certainly …

W2: Five minutes, my lunch is over in ten.

W1: … I mean with the kids like, you know I'll try and make something at the beginning of the week um. You know if everyone's eating at different times, going out in different things, microwave, I don't really like them but they, they really save a lot of time. You can just put a small portion in the microwave, heat it up, a couple of minutes, they can eat it and go.

M2: Yeah makes sense.

W2: Yeah, it's a real short cut.

M1: Does anyone else make lists? 'Cos I find that really helps if I, I have lists …that help me divide up the day and know what I'm doing when.

W2: Yes I …

M2: Cos you can focus on particular tasks then assign particular times.

M1: Exactly.

W2: Yes, yes, yes. To do all your phone calls in one go …

M1: Exactly, I know I've got that amount of time and that's it.

W2: … all your emails in, in one after the other.

W1: Yeah it's nice to be able to tick things off and know ….

M2: Mind you, if the list becomes too long then I'll procrastinate for so long about which to do first, that it actually wastes time.

M1: Yeah … it has to be realistic

W2: I also think when, I don't know if any of you have had to make up um furniture from a flat pack.

M2: Oh yes.

W2: I think. I often don't read the instructions properly. I glance at them and then I really wish that I had taken some time and really studied it before I embarked.

M1: Yes, cos in the long run that would've helped.

M2: I am with you there.

M1: Absolutely

M2: I've been caught out like that many times.

W1: Yeah but I mean when it comes to something like… I mean I found one of the most time consuming things is trying to sort out a computer problem myself, when I don't really know what I'm doing. And I have had to conclude that paying someone for an hour of their time is gonna save about 3 hours of mine.

M1: Absolutely.

W1: Ultimately.

M1: That's true.

W2: Absolutely, yeah I, I certainly believe in bringing in the expert. There's a wonderful organisation called Tech Friend, that you ring up, you pay a yearly fee and you can ring then at any time with your computer problems.

M1: Oh that's interesting.

W1: Brilliant - a very good idea.

M1: Okay well anything to add? I mean to sum up we, we've talked about the idea that you use the microwave, you make lists, you read the instructions first properly and divide up your day so you have things sort of more organised um. Can you think of anything else? Any other suggestions?

M2: Actually yes recently, for my birthday, I knew of this restaurant in town that I'd been to on like a Friday or Saturday night one time. And I was gonna have a Sunday lunch there, so I got everybody to meet there and it was closed. I did not realise it would be closed on a Sunday so …

M1: Ah

M2: You know the telephone was invented many years ago, why do we not use it? Phone first.

W1: Yes, yeah, yeah.

M1: That's true. Yeah, good idea.

W1: Good one.

5A Read the examples with the class. Ss turn to p172 and find examples in the audio script to complete the chart alone, then check in pairs. In feedback, elicit Ss' answers and write them on the board.

B Ss work alone to add the expressions to the table then check in pairs. In feedback, elicit Ss' answers, and drill the expressions chorally and individually.

acknowledging an idea	introducing an alternative
Answers to A:	
Yeah.	Yeah but I mean …
That's a good idea.	
Makes sense.	
Exactly.	
I am with you there.	
That's very true.	
Absolutely.	
Good one.	
Answers to B:	
Definitely.	But looking at it another way, …
I know what you mean.	Alternatively, …
I never thought of that.	(Although) having said that, …
	On the other hand, …
	Yes and no.

6 Ss cross out the incorrect alternative alone then check in pairs. In feedback, elicit Ss' answers.

Answers: Incorrect: 1 That's true 2 But looking at it another way 3 I never thought of that 4 Yes and no. 5 Having said that 6 Alternatively

⇒ LANGUAGEBANK 8.3 p142–143

Stronger classes could read the notes and do the exercise at home. Otherwise, drill the phrases from the chart, checking Ss are using natural intonation. Ss work alone to complete the conversation, then check their answers in pairs. In feedback, elicit Ss' answers. Ss practise the conversation in groups of three.

Answers: 1 I never thought of that 2 I'm with you there 3 That makes sense 4 But looking at it another way 5 I know what you mean 6 on the other hand 7 Having said that

LEARN TO solicit more information

7 Ss underline the expressions then check in pairs. In feedback, elicit Ss' answers.

Answers: Okay, well anything to add?
Can you think of anything else?
Any other suggestions?

8A Ss discuss what words are missing in pairs. In feedback, elicit Ss' ideas, but don't give any answers.

B Ss complete the expressions with the words in the box. In feedback, elicit Ss' answers and drill the phrases chorally and individually.

Answers: 2 more 3 detail 4 missed 5 come

speakout TIP

Read the **speakout tip** with the class and explain that because *any* means 'all possibilities', it is useful for soliciting information. Elicit Ss' answers to the question.

9A ▶ 8.5 Read the questions with the class and check Ss understand what to listen for. Play the recording for Ss to listen and answer the questions, then check in pairs. In feedback, elicit Ss' answers.

Answers: 1b) 2a)

B Play the recording again for Ss to listen and repeat.

10 Ss order the words alone then check in pairs. In feedback, elicit Ss' answers. Ss practise the conversations in pairs.

Answers: 1 Can you tell us more? 2 Can you go into more detail? 3 Is there anything we've missed? 4 Can you think of anything else? 5 Anyone managed to come up with other ideas?

SPEAKING

11A Write the following headings on the board: *working, studying, travelling* and *doing housework*. Elicit an example of ways to save time under each, and write it under the correct heading. Give Ss five minutes to brainstorm their ideas alone. Monitor and help with vocabulary, writing any new words and phrases on the board. In feedback, elicit Ss' answers under each heading and write them on the board.

B Arrange Ss in small groups. Read the instructions with the class and check understanding. Ss share their ideas in their groups. Monitor and make notes on any common errors and good language for later feedback. In feedback, ask each group to present their ideas to the class and ask other Ss to choose their favourite ideas. Give Ss feedback on their language.

Teaching tip

Brainstorming can be a very effective way of generating ideas. However, in order to be successful, it's important that everyone involved feels comfortable enough to share their ideas. Make sure when setting up activities like this that Ss understand that all input is useful, and shouldn't be discouraged from suggesting ideas they feel aren't valuable.

Homework ideas

• Ex 11B: write a report on your group's ideas.

• Language bank 8.3 Ex 1, p143

• Workbook Ex 1–4, p55

WONDERS OF THE UNIVERSE

Introduction

Ss watch an extract from the BBC documentary *Wonders of the Universe*, in which Professor Brian Cox investigates the nature of time. Ss learn and practise how to talk about a turning point, and write a forum entry about a major decision.

SUPPLEMENTARY MATERIALS

Warm up: Prepare the riddle below.

Warm up

Read out the following riddle to the class: *I never was, am always to be. No-one ever saw me, nor ever will. And yet I am the confidence of all, to live and breathe on this terrestrial ball. What am I?* Ss discuss the answer in pairs. When they are ready, elicit Ss' answers (tomorrow or the future).

DVD PREVIEW

1A Ss complete the sentence alone. Monitor and help with vocabulary if necessary.

B Ss compare their answers in pairs and discuss the question. In feedback, elicit Ss' ideas and have a brief class discussion.

Suggested answers: art, science

2 Give Ss two minutes to read the programme information then discuss the question in pairs. In feedback, elicit Ss' answers.

Answer: The concept of the arrow of time, which describes how time is characterised by irreversible change.

Culture notes

The BBC documentary *Wonders of the Universe* was first screened in 2011. This four-part series focuses on a different aspect of the universe in each episode, and follows on from the 2010 documentary *Wonders of the Solar System*. Professor Brian Cox is a British particle physicist at the University of Manchester, and is currently involved with the ATLAS experiment at the Large Hadron Collider at CERN. He also found fame in the 1990s as keyboard player for the pop group *D:Ream*.

▶ DVD VIEW

3 Read the sentences with the class and check understanding. Ss watch the DVD and put the ideas in order, then check in pairs. In feedback, elicit Ss' answers.

Answers: 1 b) 2 d) 3 a) 4 c)

Teaching tip

When doing visually-based tasks such as in Ex 3, it's important to make sure that Ss are very clear about what to do before they view, so they can maximise their viewing without having to look down at the page too often. One way of making the task clearer/more memorable is to give Ss one or two minutes to predict the answers before they watch. Even if they have no idea, the cognitive challenge of engaging with the exercise in this way will enable them to recall it more easily when viewing.

4A Ss complete the extracts from memory, then check in pairs. Monitor and help but don't give any answers yet.

B Play the DVD again for Ss to check their answers. In feedback, elicit Ss' answers.

Answers: 1 jumbled up 2 onto glaciers 3 future 4 change 5 tragedy 6 irreversibly changing

5 Ss discuss the questions in small groups. In feedback, nominate Ss to share their ideas with the class and have a brief class discussion.

Wonders of the Universe

BC = Brian Cox

BC: Why are we here? Where do we come from? These are the most enduring of questions and it's an essential part of human nature to want to find the answers.

The glacier is such a massive expanse of ice that at first sight, just like the cycles of the heavens, it appears fixed and unchanging. Yet seen close up, it's continually on the move, as it has been for tens of thousands of years. As time passes, snow falls, ice forms, the glacier gradually inches down the valley and huge chunks of ice fall into the lake below.

But even this simple sequence contains a profound idea. Events always happen in the same order. They're never jumbled up and they never go backwards.

Now that is something that you would never see in reverse, but interestingly there's nothing about the laws of physics that describe how all those water molecules are moving around, that prevent them from all getting together on the surface of the lake, jumping out of the water, sticking together into a block of ice and then gluing themselves back onto the surface of the glacier again.

But interestingly, we do understand why the world doesn't run in reverse. There is a reason, we have a scientific explanation, and it's called the arrow of time.

We never see waves travelling across lakes, coming together and bouncing chunks of ice back onto glaciers. We are compelled to travel into the future. And that's because the arrow of time dictates that as each moment passes things change.

And once these changes have happened, they are never undone.

Permanent change is a fundamental part of what it means to be human. And we all age as the years pass by; people are born, and they live, and they die. I suppose it's kind of the joy and tragedy of our lives. But out there in the universe, those grand and epic cycles appear eternal and unchanging. But that's an illusion.

See in the life of the universe, just as in our lives, everything is irreversibly changing.

speakout a turning point

6A ▶ 8.6 Ss listen to the recording then answer the questions in pairs. In feedback, elicit Ss' answers.

Answers: 1 1) to go to theatre school 2) to leave theatre school and go to a normal school and get an education 3) to have children 2 Not really, although she wonders what might have happened had she made different decisions 3 Her sister had a more successful career from an earlier stage.

B Focus attention on the **Key phrases**. Ss listen and choose the correct alternative, then check in pairs. In feedback, elicit Ss' answers and drill the **Key phrases** chorally and individually.

Answers: 1 go to a specialised theatrical school 2 no pressure either way … 3 go to a theatre school 4 it's panned out 5 another decision 6 have children or not 6 what would have happened if …

Unit 8 Recording 6

W=woman

W: When I was about nine or ten and everybody uh from primary school was moving up to secondary school my parents gave me the option to go to a specialised theatrical school or a regular comprehensive. And um it was very important, cos I remember being sat down and shown brochures of everything. And there was no pressure either way. And at that young age I made the decision to go to a theatre school. And luckily for me I, I, it's panned out and I've had a career in that um, that line of work.

But I then found myself faced with another decision, because we were moving house and uh we had to leave school, and did we want to continue with theatre school or did we want to go to a normal school? And at that point I was about 14, and I decided actually I want to get an education and leave the theatrical world at that point, still very, very young to make those decisions.

And I did, I left and went to a regular comprehensive and got some uh you know qualifications behind me and everything, and my sister didn't she carried on at theatre school and she went straight into work, very early, and was really successful. I've always wondered if perhaps I should have chosen the other option cos it was a longer road for me, and I'm still very much on it.

And um, and I suppose that the next major decision, the final decision was whether to have children or not or take this huge job that was offered to me, and I chose my children, in that case. So I'm very grateful I've got two lovely boys um, and I've still got my career but I just um, kind of wonder what would have happened if …

7A Read the instructions with the class and check understanding. Give Ss five minutes to answer the questions and make notes. Monitor and help with vocabulary, writing any new words and phrases on the board.

B Arrange Ss in small groups to share their ideas. Encourage Ss to make notes and answer questions. Monitor and note any common errors and good language for later feedback. In feedback, nominate Ss from each group to share their ideas with the class. Give Ss feedback on their language.

Alternative approach

Arrange Ss in small groups. When talking about their turning points in Ex 7B, Ss describe their answers to the questions in Ex 7A, without actually mentioning what the decision was. Other Ss in the group ask follow-up questions to find out more information, then try to guess what the decision was. In feedback, nominate Ss from each group to share any new/interesting information with the class.

writeback a major decision

8A Elicit/check: *forum entry* (something you write to share with a group of people with a common interest on the internet), *pivotal moment* (very important) *and blood is thicker than water* (expression meaning that family relationships are the strongest ones). Ss read the forum entry and discuss the question in pairs. In feedback, elicit Ss' answers.

B Write on the board: *Relationships, Career, Moving, Education* and *Travel*. Ss choose one of the topics (or think of another one) and make notes on the main events. When they are ready, Ss write their forum entries. Monitor and help with vocabulary, writing any new words and phrases on the board. When they have finished, Arrange Ss in small groups to read each other's entries and ask questions. In feedback, nominate Ss to tell the class about any interesting information they found out about other Ss.

Optional extra activity

Visit http://www.forumotion.com/ and create a forum for Ss to post a final draft of their entries. After writing a first draft in class, Ss type up a second draft at home then post it on the forum. Next class, if you have access to the internet, open up the forum to show the class. Ss can read the entries and vote for their favourite one.

Homework ideas

- Ex 7B: write about the turning point you described.
- Ex 8B: write a final draft of your forum entry.

LOOKBACK

Introduction

Ss revise and practise the language of Unit 8. The notes below provide ideas for exploiting the exercises and activities but your approach will depend on your aim, e.g. as a diagnostic or progress test or as revision and fluency practice. For example, if done as a test then it would not be appropriate to monitor or help them.

TIME EXPRESSIONS

1A After explaining the activity, elicit the first answer about a student in the class as an example, in order to check Ss understand what to do. Ss complete the sentences about other Ss in the class. Monitor and check Ss are forming the sentences correctly.

B Arrange Ss in small groups. Check Ss understand that they shouldn't say the Ss' names. Ss read out their sentences for others to guess who they are describing. In feedback, nominate one or two Ss to read out their sentences for the class to guess.

FUTURE IN THE PAST

2A Ss choose the correct sentences alone then check in pairs. In feedback, elicit Ss' answers.

Answers: 1 meant to 2 was to have 3 were meant
4 going to 5 was planning 6 were supposed 7 was going to

Optional extra activity

Ss choose the best, worst, funniest and lamest excuses from Ex 2A in pairs. In feedback, nominate Ss to share their ideas with the class and find out how many had the same answers.

B Ss write their excuses alone. Encourage Ss to be as creative as possible with their excuses. Monitor and help with vocabulary, writing any new words and phrases on the board. When they are ready, Ss compare their excuses in pairs. In feedback, nominate Ss to choose their best excuses to share with the class.

ELLIPSIS AND SUBSTITUTION

3A After explaining the activity, elicit the first answer as an example, in order to check Ss understand what to do. Ss complete the sentences alone then check in pairs. In feedback, elicit Ss' answers.

Answers: 1 not 2 have 3 so 4 there 5 can't 6 not, one

B Ss discuss and cross out the words in pairs. In feedback, elicit Ss' answers.

Answers: 1 Do you, No I 2 Are you 3 Do you, Yes I
4 It's 5 Will we 6 Do you

C Ss practise the conversations in pairs. In feedback, nominate Ss to read out the conversations to the class.

Alternative approach

Arrange Ss in pairs. Ss choose one of the conversations in Ex 3A and write a dialogue which occurs immediately before or after the conversation in the book. Monitor and help with vocabulary, writing any new words and phrases on the board. When they are ready, Ss look back at their dialogues and cross out any words which could be omitted in casual conversation. Monitor and help where necessary. When they are ready, pairs take it in turns to perform their dialogues for the class, who guess which conversation from Ex 3A it goes with.

MEMORIES

4 Ss complete the sentences alone then check in pairs. In feedback, elicit Ss' answers.

Answers: 1 holds 2 brings 3 vague 4 distinctly 5 flooding
6 earliest

Optional extra activity

Ss choose three of the expressions and write sentences which are true for them. When they are ready, Ss compare their sentences in pairs.

DISCUSSING IDEAS

5A After explaining the activity, elicit the first answer as an example, in order to check Ss understand what to do. Ss complete the conversation alone then check in pairs. In feedback, elicit Ss' answers. Ss practise the conversation in pairs.

Answers: 1 a good 2 thought of 3 makes perfect
4 having said 5 that's true 6 another way 7 know what
8 other hand 9 I'm with 10 Mind you

B Ss work in pairs to make notes and use the expressions. Monitor and help where necessary. When they are ready, Ss use their notes to practise the conversation. In feedback, nominate Ss to perform their conversation for the class.

Homework ideas
• **Workbook** Review and check 4, p56–58
• **Workbook** Test 4, p59

OVERVIEW

9.1 LIVING ART
GRAMMAR | tenses for unreal situations
VOCABULARY | the arts
HOW TO | describe unreal situations

COMMON EUROPEAN FRAMEWORK
Ss can summarise information from written sources; can argue a position convincingly.

9.2 FEELING INSPIRED
GRAMMAR | adverbials
VOCABULARY | ideas
HOW TO | give a review

COMMON EUROPEAN FRAMEWORK
Ss can understand extended speech; can write reviews of literary works.

9.3 LOVE IT OR HATE IT
FUNCTION | ranting/raving
VOCABULARY | express yourself
LEARN TO | use comment adverbials

COMMON EUROPEAN FRAMEWORK
Ss can give clear, detailed descriptions of complex subjects; can use a broad lexical repertoire.

9.4 TATE MODERN ◎ BBC DVD
speakout | recommend a cultural place
writeback | a recommendation

COMMON EUROPEAN FRAMEWORK
Ss can present clear, detailed descriptions of complex subjects; can write clear, detailed, well-structured and developed descriptions.

9.5 LOOKBACK
Communicative revision activities

BBC VIDEO PODCAST
Do you do anything creative in your life?

This video podcast extends discussion of the unit topic to creativity. Ss can view people talking about creative things they do. Use this video podcast at the start or end of Unit 9.

LIVING ART

Introduction
Ss revise and practise tenses for unreal situations in the context of modern art. They also learn and practise three-part multi-word verbs.

SUPPLEMENTARY MATERIALS
Resource bank p175, p176 and p177
Warm up: Write the questions below on the board.
Ex 1B: bring dictionaries to class for Ss to use.

Warm up
Write the following questions on the board:
How many types of art can you think of?
Which is your favourite?
In general, do you like art?
How often do you go to galleries/exhibitions?

Ss discuss the questions in small groups. In feedback, nominate Ss from each group to share their opinions with the class.

VOCABULARY adjectives: the arts

1A Focus attention on the photos and elicit what Ss can see. Ss discuss the question in pairs. In feedback, elicit Ss' ideas and have a brief class discussion.

B Divide the class into two groups: group A and group B. If you've brought dictionaries to class, distribute them for Ss to use. Ss discuss the questions in their groups and use the dictionaries to look up any new words. Monitor and help where necessary. When they are ready, check understanding of the words with each group.

Answers: 1 A unconventional: very different from the way people usually behave, think, dress, etc.; thought-provoking: making people think seriously about a particular subject; moving: making you feel strong emotions, especially sadness or sympathy; bleak: without anything to make you feel happy or hopeful; impressive: makes you admire it because it is very good, large, important, etc.; compelling: very interesting or exciting, so you have to pay attention; charming: very pleasing or attractive; well-received: accepted with enthusiasm, e.g. by critics; poignant: making you feel sad or full of pity;
B overrated: not as good or important as some people think or say; offbeat: unusual and not what people normally expect, especially in an interesting way; stylish: attractive in a fashionable way; amusing: funny and entertaining; striking: attractive in an unusual way that is easy to notice; dramatic: exciting or impressive, so that people notice; stunning: extremely attractive or beautiful; heart-breaking: making you feel extremely sad or disappointed; subtle: not easy to notice or understand unless you pay careful attention
2 Most of the words can describe most art forms, e.g. film, art, music.
3 Adjectives to describe people: unconventional, impressive, charming, offbeat, stylish, amusing, striking, stunning. We can use the other adjectives when we want to describe people's performances.

Teaching tip
Training Ss to use dictionaries when looking up unfamiliar words is very useful in helping Ss become more autonomous in their learning outside class. Make sure that when looking up words, Ss don't just read the definition, but also look for and note down any other relevant information such as part of speech, pronunciation and example sentences.

C Arrange Ss in pairs, with one person from each group. Ss take it in turns to explain their words and think of examples. Monitor and help where necessary. In feedback, nominate Ss to share their examples with the class, and answer any questions Ss have about new vocabulary.

D ▶ 9.1 Ss practise saying the words aloud then answer the question in pairs. When they are ready, play the recording for Ss to check. In feedback, elicit Ss' answers and drill the words chorally and individually.

Answers: poignant, subtle

speakout TIP
Read the **speakout tip** with the class and elicit the silent letters in the words. Elicit any other words Ss know with silent letters and write them on the board (e.g. *invasion, socialise, daughter*). Drill the words chorally and individually.

READING

2A Focus attention on the title of the text and elicit Ss' ideas as to what the text is about. Write their ideas on the board in note form.

B Give Ss three or four minutes to read the text quickly and check their ideas. Tell them not to worry about new vocabulary yet, as they'll have a chance to work on this later. In feedback, elicit what the text is about and compare against Ss' previous ideas on the board.

Answer: The text is about an art project that took place on the fourth plinth in Trafalgar Square: members of the public were invited to 'perform' on the plinth.

3 Read the headings with the class and check understanding. Ss match the headings and paragraphs alone then check in pairs. In feedback, elicit Ss' answers.

Answers: a) 4 b) 5 c) 6 d) 2 e) 1 f) 3

Alternative approach
Ss cover the headings in Ex3 and write their own headings alone, then check in pairs. In feedback, elicit Ss' ideas. Ss then match the headings in Ex 3 to the paragraphs.

4 With *weaker classes*, elicit the first answer as an example. Ss find the words and expressions alone then check in pairs. In feedback, elicit Ss' answers and check understanding of the words and expressions.

Answers: 1 depict 2 engendering 3 orchestrate 4 preoccupations 5 onlookers 6 at random 7 spectrum 8 overran 9 serene/peaceful 10 voyeuristic

5 Ss discuss the questions in pairs. In feedback, nominate Ss to share their ideas with the class and have a brief class discussion.

GRAMMAR verb tenses for unreal situations

6A Give Ss one or two minutes to read the comments and prepare their answers. Monitor and check understanding. When they are ready, Ss discuss which they agree with in pairs. In feedback, nominate Ss to share their ideas with the class.

B Ss answer the questions in pairs. In feedback, elicit Ss' answers and be prepared to provide further explanations/examples where necessary.

Answers: 1 The final verbs in the underlined phrases are in the Past Simple, except for 6, which is Past Perfect. 2 b)

Watch out!
In English, it's useful to think about present and past tenses as representing 'distance'. Present tenses can be 'close' and past tenses 'distant' to us in terms of time (e.g. *I have a car.* or *When I was younger, I had a bike*) or in terms of reality (e.g. *I'm not brave* or *I wish I was brave*).

⟹ LANGUAGEBANK 9.1 p144–145
Stronger classes can read the notes and do the exercises at home. Otherwise, check the notes with Ss, especially the use of the infinitive with *would rather/would sooner*. In each exercise, do the first sentence as an example. Ss complete the exercises alone, then check their answers in pairs. Ss can refer to the notes to help them.

Answers: 1 Incorrect: 1 prefer 2 as were 3 How about 4 the 5 want that 6 Rather 7 one time 8 as 2 1 It's high time you spoke to your mother. 2 Suppose I pressed this button, what would happen? 3 They treat that girl as though she were a princess. 4 Given the choice, I'd sooner learn Chinese than German. 5 What if there were a volcanic eruption in a densely populated area? 6 It's about time she stopped smoking. 7 They behave as if they own/owned the place. 8 I'd rather you didn't go there.

PRACTICE

7 Ss complete the sentences alone then check in pairs. In feedback, elicit Ss' answers.

Answers: 1 was 2 hadn't 3 time 4 had 5 rather 6 imagine 7 if 8 would

8 Give Ss three or four minutes to think about their answers to the questions. Monitor and help with vocabulary, writing any new words and phrases on the board. When they are ready, arrange Ss in small groups to discuss the questions. In feedback, nominate Ss from each group to share their ideas with the class.

Optional extra activity
Read out the following information to the class: *The mayor of your city has awarded you a grant to create a cultural space in your city. It can be a sculpture, a mural on the side of a building, or a piece of music to be played through speakers during the day. Choose and design something which you feel will reflect the culture of your city, and decide where it will be installed.* Ss work alone to think of an idea and make notes. Monitor and help with vocabulary, writing any new words and phrases on the board. When they are ready, arrange Ss in small groups to share their ideas and choose the best one. In feedback, nominate Ss from each group to share their best ideas with the class.

SPEAKING

9A Ss read about the clients and look at the sculptures on p162. Monitor and help with new vocabulary, and check understanding of the client information. Ss choose a sculpture for each client, and think of reasons for their choices.

B When they are ready, arrange Ss in small groups to discuss their choices and try to agree. Monitor and take notes on any common errors and good language for later feedback. In feedback, nominate Ss from each group to share their ideas with the class and give them feedback on their language.

VOCABULARY *PLUS* three-part multi-word verbs

10A Ss read the sentences and answer the questions alone then check in pairs. In feedback, elicit Ss' answers and be prepared to provide further explanations and examples where necessary.

Answers: 1 a) stand up for (talk in support of) b) came up with (thought of ideas, plans, etc.) c) put up with (tolerated) 2 It is not possible to split three-part multi-word verbs. 3 The stress is on the first particle i.e. *up*.

B Books closed. Elicit Ss' ideas as to what they usually do to learn/remember multi-word verbs, and write their ideas on the board. Ss read the advice and decide which they agree with, then compare ideas in pairs. In feedback, elicit Ss' ideas and have a brief class discussion.

Answer: The only piece of advice which is not a good idea is point 2.

11 With *weaker classes*, check the meaning of the multi-word verbs in the options first. Ss choose the correct options alone then check in pairs. In feedback, elicit Ss' answers and be prepared to provide further explanations/examples where necessary.

Answers: 1 get away with 2 get round to 3 go in for 4 go along with 5 come down to 6 come up with 7 put up with 8 put down to 9 stand up to 10 stand up for 11 catch up with 12 catch on to

12 Give Ss five minutes to choose three questions and think about their answers. Monitor and help with vocabulary, writing any new words and phrases on the board. When they are ready, Ss compare their answers in pairs. In feedback, nominate Ss to share their ideas with the class.

> **VOCABULARYBANK** p156 THREE-PART MULTI-WORD VERBS
>
> **1A** Ss complete the definitions alone then check in pairs. In feedback, elicit Ss' answers and be prepared to provide further explanations and examples where necessary.
>
> **B** Give Ss five minutes to finish the sentences however they want. Monitor and help with vocabulary, writing any new words and phrases on the board. When they are ready, arrange Ss in small groups to compare their ideas. In feedback, nominate Ss from each group to share their ideas with the class.
> *Stronger classes* can do the exercises at home.
>
> **Answers:** a) cut down on b) go through with c) go back on d) go down with e) do away with f) look down on g) keep up with h) watch out for i) look in on j) get up to

Homework ideas
- Ex 5: Write about what you would do if you were given 60 mins on the plinth.
- Vocabulary bank p156
- Language bank 9.1 Ex 1–2, p145
- Workbook Ex 1–6, p60–61

FEELING INSPIRED

Introduction

Ss learn and practise adverbials in the context of memories. They also practise writing a review.

SUPPLEMENTARY MATERIALS

Resource bank p178

Warm up: Prepare some ways in which you are creative in your day-to-day life to explain to the class.

speakout tip p107: Bring dictionaries for Ss to use.

Warm up

Tell the class all the ways in which you are creative in your day-to-day life. Try to include some usual activities such as writing emails, making excuses for being late, etc. Encourage Ss to ask you follow-up questions to find out more information. Give Ss three or four minutes and to list all the ways in which they are creative in their lives. Monitor and help with vocabulary, writing any new words and phrases on the board. When they are ready, Ss discuss their ideas in pairs. In feedback, nominate Ss to share their ideas with the class.

LISTENING

1A Focus attention on the picture and elicit what Ss can see. Ss discuss the questions in pairs. In feedback, elicit Ss' answers and write them on the board.

B ▶ 9.2 Write the following headings on the board: *Job, Where they get their inspiration* and ask Ss to copy them in their notebooks. Ss listen and take notes alone then check in pairs. In feedback, elicit Ss' answers.

Answers: 1 writer: switching off, doing something mundane like washing up 2 artist: old photographs, poems, people around her (what they are wearing, etc.) 3 chef: old recipe books 4 fashion designer: exhibitions and museums, sketches, postcards, inspiration board

C Refer Ss back to the list of their ideas from Ex 1A on the board, and elicit which of their ideas were mentioned.

2A Ss answer the questions from memory in pairs. Don't elicit any answers yet.

B Play the recording again for Ss to check their answers. In feedback, elicit Ss' answers.

Answers: 1 It takes his mind off his work, and that is when he often gets ideas. 2 She likes photos because they're a good starting point for her work. She uses the photos to build a story around them, a collage for her artwork. 3 They hold memories of enjoyable meals. 4 Images, photos, sketches, quotes, cards – things that she likes the look of. Just looking at things which are aesthetically pleasing helps to make her feel creative and give her ideas.

C Ss discuss the questions in pairs. In feedback, nominate Ss to share their ideas with the class.

Unit 9 Recording 2

Speaker 1

People always ask me that, and it's a very difficult question to answer. One thing is that it's no good just sitting around waiting for an idea to come. If I'm stuck for an idea, I have to switch off and do something else for a while. If I'm stuck with the plot, or I need to work out how a particular character should behave, then I'll go off and do something else for a bit. Doing the washing up is quite good, doing something mundane, that you don't have to think too hard about. So, I like to invite lots of people round to dinner, so that in the morning there are lots of plates to wash, and that gets me thinking. When you free the mind it helps spark creative connections. So you're doing the washing up, or having a shower, and suddenly an idea might come to you. You actually have to take your mind off the writing, off the task in hand. And that's when you think of something creative. It's funny how our brains work. Sometimes, I'll go out into the garden, or go for a run to clear my head. When I get back to my desk, the ideas flow a lot more easily.

Speaker 2

I use a lot of mixed media, so I get my ideas from all over the place. But one place I often start is with a photograph. I really like old black and white photographs, so I might start with a photo of someone, and then I'll gradually build up a story around the photo, using a collage of different ideas and colours. Sometimes I read poems, or write them, and I put quotes on the pictures to help tell the story. But it usually starts with the photo. Sometimes when I'm out with a group of people, I get very inspired just watching what's happening. I look at the colours, the clothes people are wearing, how the colours change in the candlelight, things like that. I might take a photo, or I just try to keep the image in my head – take a mental picture of what it looks like, and the feeling I have, and then I'll use that in a painting that I'm working on.

Speaker 3

Um books mainly, old recipe books … like Margaret Costa, a classic. I'll look through old recipes and then try to recreate the same idea but with a modern, more contemporary twist. Yes, old tomes. Larousse is another one, with plenty of ideas, or sometimes I'll go to the Michelin guides, you know the restaurants with stars – they have books, so I look there too. Unfortunately, I rarely eat out myself, so I don't get ideas that way, but books are a great inspiration. And there's something about having big, heavy books in the kitchen that have been with you a long time. They inherit your character a little, and hold in them so many memories of enjoyable meals.

Speaker 4

I sometimes go to museums or exhibitions, and I'll go and look at some Picasso, or Van Gogh, someone who used big bold colours, and I'll just sit in the gallery with my notebook, and do a few sketches, or try out some colours. Or if I don't have time, I'll buy some postcards, and then when I get home I'll choose from the various patterns and shades. I have an inspiration board at home – a wall in my studio where I put images, photos, things I like the look of. If I go into a shop and see a design I like, then I'll try to take a picture of it (or do a quick sketch) and that will go onto the board. I won't copy it exactly, but it might feed into something I'm working on. There are all sorts of things there, quotes I read, cards that people send me. The idea is that I can use the board as a starting point for a new design. It's important that I can see and touch lots of different textures, and materials. These are very important in fashion. Sometimes just looking at something aesthetically pleasing helps to get the creative juices flowing, and gives you a few ideas to reflect on.

VOCABULARY ideas

3A Write: *idea* in the middle of the board. Give Ss two minutes to come up with any phrases they know with *idea* in pairs. In feedback, elicit Ss' ideas and write them on the board.

B Ss compare the phrases with their ideas from Ex 3A in pairs. In feedback, elicit Ss' ideas and check understanding of the phrases.

Suggested answers: 1 He's always **coming up with novel ideas**. – having new/original ideas 2 I'm **toying with the idea** of going back to college. – considering the idea (but not in a very serious way) 3 What **gave you the idea for** the book? – was your inspiration 4 **The idea came to me** while I was having a bath. – I had the idea when … 5 We had a meeting **to brainstorm ideas for** the new advertising campaign. – to quickly come up with as many ideas as possible (good and bad) without rejecting any 6 We **hit on the idea of** renting a cottage. – suddenly had the idea 7 **Whose bright idea was it** to leave the washing out in the rain? – good idea (ironic, ie it was a bad idea) 8 The company is looking for people who can **come up with original ideas**. – have new ideas (that other people haven't thought of) 9 **It seemed like a good idea** at the time. – We thought it was a good idea, but it wasn't 10 Camping in the middle of winter was a **ridiculous idea**. – bad/laughable idea

C Ss answer the questions alone then check in pairs. In feedback, elicit Ss' answers and be prepared to provide further explanations and examples where necessary.

Answers: a) 7 b) 1, 3, 4, 5, 6, 8 c) 2 d) 7, 9, 10

4A Ss work alone to match phrases to the situations then check in pairs. In feedback, elicit Ss' answers.

Answers: 1 He's toying with the idea of going to university. 2 You need to brainstorm some ideas for selling the product. 3 You hit on an idea / An idea came to you for what to do for your birthday. 4 It seemed like a good idea at the time.

B Give Ss five minutes to write their situations. Monitor and help with vocabulary, writing any new words and phrases on the board. When they are ready, Ss read out their situations in pairs for their partner to guess the phrase. In feedback, nominate one or two Ss to read their situation out for the class to guess.

speakout TIP

Read the **speakout tip** with the class and explain that dictionaries are useful for finding phrases as well as words. If you have brought dictionaries to class, give them out for Ss to use to look up phrases with *creativity*. In feedback, elicit Ss' answers and check understanding with the class.

➡ VOCABULARYBANK p156 COLLOCATIONS WITH IDEAS

2 Focus attention on the phrases and definitions, and check understanding. Ss complete the sentences alone then check in pairs. In feedback, elicit Ss' answers and be prepared to provide further explanations/examples where necessary. *Stronger classes* can do the exercises at home.

Answers: 1 have an idea 2 get the wrong idea 3 someone's idea of a joke 4 a clear idea 5 full of bright ideas 6 don't have the faintest idea

GRAMMAR adverbials

5A Elicit/check: *to bear fruit, to spark*. Ss read the article and tick the ideas they like. In feedback, elicit Ss' answers.

B Arrange Ss in pairs, and ask them to cover the article. Ss try to remember the suggestions in pairs.

6A Focus attention on the underlined adverbials in the article. Ss work alone to replace them with the words in the box then check in pairs. In feedback, elicit Ss' answers and be prepared to provide further explanations and examples where necessary.

Answers: 1 for his ideas: to keep track of his observations 2 simultaneously: at the same time 3 a year: annually 4 readily: willingly 5 on your own: alone 6 almost certainly: most probably

B Ss read the rule and answer the questions alone then check in pairs. In feedback, elicit Ss' answers.

Answers: 1 readily, on your own 2 simultaneously 3 a year 4 almost certainly 5 for his ideas

C Ss find more examples alone then check in pairs. In feedback, elicit Ss' answers and check understanding of the adverbials.

Possible answers: Para 1: frequently, to keep track of interesting ideas and websites you come across Para 2: by extending your sphere of interest with hobbies Para 3: just to read, to do nothing but read Para 4: both online and offline Para 5: every once in a while, to just relax and be by yourself Para 6: every day

➡ LANGUAGEBANK 9.2 p144–145

Stronger classes can read the notes and do the exercises at home. Otherwise, check the notes with Ss, especially the word order in sentences with adverbials. In each exercise, do the first sentence as an example. Ss complete the exercises alone, then check their answers in pairs. Ss can refer to the notes to help them.

Answers: 1 1 c) 2 b) 3 b) 4 a) 5 c) 6 b) 7 c) 8 a) 9 c)
2 1 I just grab a sandwich to eat quickly at lunchtime if I'm in a hurry. 2 In the evenings my husband and I generally sit in front of the television too tired to talk. 3 I always carefully plan anything I write in English to reduce the number of mistakes. 4 Unfortunately, I consistently spend too much time in front of the computer. 5 They met online and enjoyed each other's company for a while. 6 I took up painting about six months ago to help me relax. 7 I left my things on the kitchen table when I left this morning. 8 I'll probably have more time to see my friends when my exams are finished.

PRACTICE

7A Read the example with the class. Ss expand the sentences alone then check in pairs. *Early finishers* can write the sentences on the board. In feedback, nominate Ss to read out their sentences to the class.

Answers: 2 f) We regularly go walking in the mountains near our house during the holidays. 3 a) I can easily change the appointment for you to make it more convenient. / I can easily change the appointment to make it more convenient for you. 4 b) I generally like to facebook friends in the evenings when I'm at home to find out what they've been doing. 5 e) I usually like to take things easy at the weekends. 6 c) I'll probably try to visit my family next time I'm in the area.

B Give Ss five minutes to choose their sentences and expand them in different ways. Monitor and help with vocabulary, writing any new words and phrases on the board. When they are ready, Ss compare their sentences in pairs. In feedback, nominate Ss to share their sentences with the class.

SPEAKING

8A Read the examples with the class. Arrange Ss in small groups, and give them five minutes to write as many questions as they can. Encourage Ss to be creative and think of unusual questions, or those which might reveal what kind of person someone is. Make sure each student in the group writes the questions, as they'll need them later. Monitor and help with ideas and vocabulary, writing any new words and phrases on the board.

B Rearrange Ss into different groups. Ss ask and answer their questions, making their answers as interesting as possible. Monitor and make notes on any common errors/good language for later feedback.

Teaching tip

When rearranging Ss into groups, it's useful to ask them to stand up first, before allocating groups. This avoids confusion caused by Ss not remembering their groups when they move and makes the process quicker.

C Nominate all the Ss in turn to share their information with the class. Give Ss feedback on their language.

WRITING a review

9A Elicit/check: *Venus fly trap* (a plant which catches insects) and *gill* (the part of the fish that lets it breathe). Ss read the review and answer the questions alone then check in pairs. In feedback, elicit Ss' answers.

Answers: 1 A science programme (about inventions inspired by the natural world) 2 Children and adults too 3 Positive

B Ss read the guidelines then discuss which ones the review follows in pairs. Monitor and help where necessary. In feedback, elicit Ss' answers.

Answer: Review meets the guidelines 1–3, but doesn't demonstrate the clear structure suggested in 4

LEARN TO use a range of vocabulary

10A Ss discuss the synonyms in pairs. When they have finished, elicit Ss' ideas and write them on the board.

B Ss work alone to find synonyms in the review then check in pairs. In feedback, elicit Ss' answers and check understanding.

Answers: 1 eccentric 2 highly intelligent 3 delighted 4 fascinating 5 initially 6 escapades 7 pleasantly 8 humorous 9 stunning

speakout TIP

Read the **speakout tip** with the class. Ss find examples in the review. In feedback, elicit Ss' answers.

11 Give Ss five minutes to read the exhibition information and the notes on p163, and check understanding. Ss write their reviews alone. Monitor and help with vocabulary, writing any new words and phrases on the board. When they've finished, Ss swap reviews with a partner, who reads it and suggests where synonyms could be used to vary the vocabulary.

Homework ideas
- Ex 11: write a final draft of your review.
- Language bank 9.2 Ex 1–2, p145
- Workbook Ex 1–5, p62–63

LOVE IT OR HATE IT

Introduction

Ss learn and practise phrases for ranting and raving, and how to use comment adverbials.

SUPPLEMENTARY MATERIALS

Resource bank p179

Warm up: Prepare something to rant about and something to rave about.

Ex 1A: if possible, load up rantrave.com to introduce the topic.

Warm up

Describe your rant and your rave to the class, but don't say what it is you're describing. Ss listen, then discuss in pairs what you described. In feedback, elicit Ss' answers and see how many guessed correctly.

VOCABULARY express yourself

1A If possible, load up rantrave.com on to a computer for Ss to see. Ss read the website extract and answer the questions alone then check in pairs. In feedback, elicit Ss' answers.

Answers: 1 It is a review website. **2** You can read people's reviews of, for example, music albums and about their general opinion on things.

B Ss discuss the meanings in pairs. Monitor and help where necessary. In feedback, elicit Ss' answers.

Answers: 1 rave: say wonderful things about **2** rant: say terrible things about **3** crave a fresh perspective: desire a different opinion or new way of looking at things **4** speak their mind: say what they think **5** let your feelings fly: allow your emotions to show **6** (give somebody) a piece of your mind: express your opinion loudly about something you disapprove of

C Ss complete the sentence alone then check in pairs. In feedback, elicit Ss' answers.

Answers: 1 crave a fresh perspective **2** rant **3** a piece of your mind **4** speak their mind **5** let your feelings fly **6** rave

FUNCTION ranting/raving

2A Give Ss five minutes to choose three of the topics and prepare their ideas. When they are ready, arrange Ss in small groups to compare their ideas. In feedback, nominate Ss from each group to share their ideas with the class.

> **Alternative approach**
> Ss work alone to think of something people might rant or rave about for each of the topics. Monitor and help with vocabulary, writing any new words and phrases on the board. When they are ready, arrange Ss in pairs to read out their ideas for their partner to guess which topic they are describing.

B ▶ 9.3 Elicit/check: *Rayburn* (old-fashioned style cooker which also acts as a boiler), *grossly overpriced* (ridiculously expensive). Ss listen and work alone to match the topics to the extracts then check in pairs. In feedback, elicit Ss' answers.

Answers: 1 travel **2** food **3** arts and entertainment **4** travel **5** food **6** products

C Ss discuss what each person said in pairs. If necessary, play the recording again for Ss to check their answers. In feedback, elicit Ss' answers.

Unit 9 Recording 3

Speaker 1

If there's one thing I cannot stand it's getting off a tube train on the London underground and lots of people on the platform try to get on the carriage before I have gotten off. Honestly it drives me up the wall. Don't they understand that if I can't get off then they can't get on, so they need to let me off. And I have in the past actually raised my voice at tourists.

Speaker 2

The last time we went to Cornwall we went to the lovely little town of Fowey, and I discovered what I could describe for me as paradise, it's a tearoom which somebody could describe in a book and it still wouldn't be as good as, as the actual experience when you go in it, beautifully decorated. It's got those little um cake plates with, piled up with the most beautiful sumptuous cupcakes. And then in the back part they've got a lovely Rayburn, and if you decided you wanted sardines on toast or scrambled egg or something they'll just whip it up for you. Every single thing you could imagine on your dream menu. I could have sat there for a week and worked my way through the menu. It was the most wonderful, delicious and, and, the people were so friendly. And they'd gone to such sort of trouble to make this gorgeous place to eat. And um I'd definitely go back there again.

Speaker 3

The other night I saw the best show ever, it was a show called Dirty Dancing, it's on in the West End, absolutely fantastic. The acting was brilliant, the dancing was brilliant, the songs were terrific. I mean uniformly they were absolutely terrific. And I don't know who played the mother but she was especially good, honestly, really the best show ever, you must see it.

Speaker 4

I cannot recommend highly enough a trip to one of the beautiful islands of Thailand. I went there last year and there is absolutely nothing better than finding yourself on a private beach with a cool drink in hand and having a dip in tropical warm waters. And I saw one of the most spectacular sunsets I've ever seen. And honestly I couldn't believe my luck when I saw turtles in the water, I've always wanted to see turtles. It was idyllic.

Speaker 5

The worst meal I ever had was quite recently. It was absolutely horrendous. The restaurant was grossly overpriced, honestly it was a total waste of money. But it's also you know minutes of my life that I won't get back um. The service was appalling, and the waiter just seemed like he'd rather be doing anything else. Clearly it's hard to cook for a lot of people, I understand that, at the same time. But you know meals were coming out at all different times. We had appetisers arriving and then the main course and then nothing for about an hour. It was horrendous.

Speaker 6

I bought the 'one-touch can opener' and it has changed my life, seriously, and I'm not even over stating how amazing it is. It's an all-time classic of products, you have to get one, and I couldn't believe my luck when it arrived in the post, just for me, and it does exactly what it says it will. You touch it once and you leave it alone. It's incredible! It's the most incredible thing. You don't have to, you can do something else if you want. It's one of the most spectacular life changing products you can buy, because all of that mess and effort taken away um. So if you're ever thinking about it, just do it, it's awesome, seriously, the best product.

3A Ss try to complete the phrases from memory in pairs. When they are ready, play the recording again for them to check their answers. In feedback, elicit Ss' answers.

Answers: 1 fantastic 2 ever 3 better 4 spectacular 5 luck
6 classic 7 stand 8 wall 9 horrendous 10 waste

B ▶ 9.4 Ss listen to the recording, paying attention to
the intonation. Play the recording again for Ss to repeat the
phrases using correct intonation.

4 Ss match the sentence halves alone then check in pairs. In
feedback, elicit Ss' answers.

Answers: 1 c) 2 f) 3 a) 4 e) 5 b) 6 d)

⟹ **LANGUAGEBANK** 9.3 p144–145

Stronger classes could read the notes and do the exercise
at home. Otherwise, drill the phrases from the chart,
checking Ss are using natural intonation. Ss work alone to
correct the mistakes, then check their answers in pairs. In
feedback, elicit Ss' answers. Ss practise the conversations
in pairs.

Answers: 1 It was awesome – really the best concert
ever. 2 It wasn't my **cup** of tea. 3 … if there's one
thing I can't stand ~~for~~ it's violence. 4 Yes, it's an **all-time**
classic. 5 Oh, I thought it was **absolutely** incredible. 6 It
was a total waste of money.

LEARN TO use comment adverbials

5A ▶ 9.5 Ss listen to the extracts and complete the
sentences then check in pairs. In feedback, elicit Ss' answers
and drill the phrases chorally and individually.

Answers: 1 Honestly 2 actually 3 definitely 4 especially
5 grossly 6 Clearly

speakout TIP

Read the **speakout tip** with the class and emphasise the use of
comment adverbials to give you thinking time. Explain this is
something native speakers do, too.

B Ss choose the correct alternatives alone then check in pairs.
In feedback, elicit Ss' answers.

Answers: 1 Honestly 2 Basically 3 Clearly 4 surprisingly
5 simply 6 Undoubtedly

Optional extra activity
Ss choose three of the adverbials, and write an example
sentence for each one. Monitor and help with vocabulary,
writing any new words and phrases on the board. When
they are ready, arrange Ss in pairs. Ss take it in turns to read
out their sentences, substituting the adverbials by saying
'blank'. Their partner guesses which adverbial they used.

C Ss discuss the questions in pairs. Elicit Ss' answers. Ss
work in pairs to develop a conversation including two more
comment adverbials. Monitor and help with vocabulary,
writing any new words and phrases on the board. In feedback,
nominate Ss to perform their conversations to the class.

Answers: 1 rave 2 rant 3 rave 4 rant 5 rant 6 rave

SPEAKING

6A Give Ss five minutes to choose their topics and prepare
their rants and raves. Monitor and help with vocabulary,
writing any new words and phrases on the board.

B When they are ready, arrange Ss in small groups to share
their rants and raves. Give each student one minute to rant
or rave about their topic. In feedback, nominate Ss from each
group to share their rants/raves with the class.

Homework ideas
• **Ex 6B:** write about one of your rants or raves as a post
  for rantrave.com.
• **Language bank** 9.3 Ex 1, p145
• **Workbook** Ex 1–4, p64

TATE MODERN

Introduction

Ss watch an extract from the BBC programme *The Culture Show*, in which an art critic looks at the Tate Modern museum on its 10th birthday. Ss learn and practise how to recommend a cultural place, and write a recommendation.

SUPPLEMENTARY MATERIALS

Warm up: Bring or download photos of modern art.

Warm up

Display some photos of modern art round the class (you can find out about current exhibitions at the Tate Modern at http://www.tate.org.uk/modern/). Review the adjectives for describing art from Ex 1B in Unit 9.1. Ss look at the photos in pairs and discuss which they like/don't like, and think of adjectives from Unit 9.1 to describe each one. In feedback, elicit Ss' ideas.

DVD PREVIEW

1 Ss discuss the questions in pairs. In feedback, nominate Ss to share their ideas with the class.

2 Give Ss two minutes to read the programme information then discuss the question in pairs. In feedback, elicit Ss' answers.

Answer: The programme will attempt to say why the gallery has been so popular and how it has changed the public's perception of art.

Culture notes

The *Tate Modern* is a modern art gallery in central London. It is part of the Tate group, which includes Tate Britain, Tate Liverpool, Tate St Ives and Tate Online. It opened in 2000, and since then has been very popular, ranking as the third most visited art gallery in Britain. Entry is free, except for some exhibitions.

DVD VIEW

3 Read the phrases with the class and check understanding. Ss watch the DVD and tick the works they see, then check in pairs. In feedback, elicit Ss' answers.

Answers: 1, 2, 3, 5, 7 and 8

4A Ss answer the questions from memory in pairs. Monitor and help but don't give any answers yet.

B Play the DVD again for Ss to check their answers. In feedback, elicit Ss' answers.

Answers: 1 5 million 2 Tate Modern's size 3 The Turbine Hall has temporary 'happenings'. The higher floors contain the permanent collection. 4 The last one hundred years.
5 Henri Matisse and his peers seem 'charmingly quaint' (old fashioned). Contemporary artists like Gerhard Richter seem incredibly contemporary. 6 Did art change or did Tate Modern change us?

5 Ss discuss the questions in pairs. In feedback, nominate Ss to share their ideas with the class and have a brief class discussion.

Optional extra activity

Write the following prompts on the board: *What's its name? Where is it? What can you see there (give examples)? How old is it? Are there any famous works there? Would you recommend visiting it?* Give Ss five minutes to think of a museum or art gallery in their city or cities, and work alone to think of answers to the questions and make notes. Monitor and help with vocabulary/ideas, writing any new words and phrases on the board. When they are ready, arrange Ss in small groups to share their ideas and choose which place they'd like to visit. In feedback, nominate Ss from each group to summarise their descriptions for the class.

Tate Modern is 10! A Culture Show Special

MC=Matthew Collings

MC: Tate Modern is ten. More people visit Tate Modern than any other comparable modern art museum in the world; a statistics-busting five million visitors a year. What do they get from it? One thing is size.

This is Tate Modern's turbine hall. It's as big as an aircraft hanger, so even when there's nothing in it, it's incredibly impressive.

It's here that Tate Modern's temporary 'happenings' go on; live performances, interactive conceptual art events, towering installations. It's a sort of 'make-you-think' theme park; people wondering what it means to fling themselves down giant slides and having a good think about the sight of a very large mechanical glowing sun.

The most recent attraction in the philosophy fairground was a metal container by Miroslaw Balka. Inside you could experience sheer darkness, as a mind expanding event.

Up here are the galleries that house Tate's permanent collection of modern and contemporary art. It's a collection that goes back in time a hundred years ago and ranges right up until today.

Modern art by modern artists who now seem quite charmingly quaint, like Matisse.

And work by contemporary artists who really do seem incredibly contemporary, like Gerhard Richter. And the collective of artists that calls itself No Ghost Just a Shell. What are they telling us? No idea, but we enjoy basking in contemporary art's lurid glow anyway.

This temple of the far out has become a fixture in ordinary people's lives. What happened? The kind of thing that goes on here used to be considered hatefully baffling. Now it's revered and loved. Did art change or did Tate Modern change us?

speakout recommend a cultural place

6A ▶ 9.6 Ss listen to the recording then answer the questions in pairs. In feedback, elicit Ss' answers.

> **Answers:** The shape of the roof and the size of the building. The students are studying architecture.

B Focus attention on the **Key phrases**. Ss listen and tick the phrases they hear, then check in pairs. In feedback, elicit Ss' answers and drill the **Key phrases** chorally and individually.

> **Answers:** It's one of the world's most recognisable landmarks.
> The most striking thing about it is …
> The best time to go is …
> The building itself is obviously admired all over the world …
> It's also been very influential …

Unit 9 Recording 6

I live in Sydney Australia and I'd recommend the Sydney Opera House. I'd say it's one of the world's most recognisable landmarks certainly for anyone interested in modern architecture. The most striking thing about it is the shape of the roof, which looks like … well, like a group of open shells, or maybe sails unfurling, just like a ship. Its size is quite dramatic as well – it's a lot bigger than it looks in pictures.

I think the best time to go is either really early in the morning when there's no one there or in the evening. If you go in the evening, you can watch the sun setting over the Sydney Harbour Bridge and you'll see the birds overhead circling the roof, which is just an amazing sight. And as it gets dark, there are the city lights reflected off the water and you can stroll along the harbour and pop into any of the great restaurants or bars there.

The building itself is obviously admired all over the world, but it's also been very influential in modern architecture. It was one of the first buildings to use computer aided design – back in the 1960s when it was being built, and a lot of the techniques involved in its construction have been copied by other architects. For example the use of reinforced concrete was very …

> **Watch out!**
>
> A very common mistake, even at higher levels, is to use the singular form after *one of the …* e.g. *It's one of the world's most recognisable landmark* (rather than *landmarks*)… Check understanding by explaining that we are referring to one of a group, and so we use the plural here.

7A Read the instructions with the class and check understanding. Give Ss five minutes to plan their ideas on their own. Monitor and help with vocabulary, writing any new words and phrases on the board.

B Arrange Ss in small groups to share their cultural places. Encourage Ss to make notes and answer questions. Monitor and note any common errors and good language for later feedback. In feedback, nominate Ss from each group to share their ideas with the class. Give Ss feedback on their language.

writeback a recommendation

8A Ss read the post and reply and discuss the question in pairs. In feedback, elicit Ss' answers.

> **Answer:** The writer recommends it because it's a wonderful place to browse, you can buy all kinds of things, and it has interesting architectural details.

> **Teaching tip**
>
> After Ss have read a text, give them 1 min to scan the text and underline three words they'd like to ask you the meanings of. When they are ready, arrange Ss in small groups to share their words and agree on three words for the group. In feedback, answer Ss' questions about the new vocabulary.

B Makes sure Ss choose a different place to the one they spoke about in Ex 7B. Ss write their recommendations alone. Monitor and help with vocabulary, writing any new words and phrases on the board. When they have finished, Arrange Ss in small groups to share their recommendations. In feedback, nominate Ss to tell the class which place they would most like to visit.

> **Homework ideas**
> • Ex 7B: write about the place you recommended.
> • Ex 8B: write a final draft of your recommendation.

LOOKBACK

Introduction

Ss revise and practise the language of Unit 9. The notes below provide ideas for exploiting the exercises and activities but your approach will depend on your aim, e.g. as a diagnostic or progress test or as revision/fluency practice. For example, if done as a test then it would not be appropriate to monitor or help them.

ADJECTIVES: THE ARTS

1 Ss choose the correct alternatives alone then check in pairs. In feedback, elicit Ss' answers.

> **Answers:** 1 impressive 2 compelling 3 poignant
> 4 overrated 5 offbeat 6 stylish

> **Optional extra activity**
> Ss write example sentences for the words which were not correct alternatives. When they are ready, Ss read their sentences to a partner, without saying the words, for their partner to guess.

TENSES FOR UNREAL SITUATIONS

2A Check understanding of *wish list* (all the things you would like to have or would like to happen in a particular situation) Ss find the six mistakes alone then check in pairs. In feedback, elicit Ss' answers and ask if they agree with the writer.

> **Answers:** It's high time art forms like opera **were** made accessible to the public; … and it's about time the public **had** a chance to enjoy them; I'd sooner TV **wasn't** overtaken by sites like YouTube; Finally, it's time schoolteachers **thought** outside the box; Supposing kids **had** a chance to learn how to juggle …? I'm sure millions of kinaesthetic learners would rather they **spent** their days doing this ….

B Ss write their sentences alone. Monitor and help with ideas and vocabulary, writing any new words/phrases on the board, and check Ss are using tenses correctly. When they are ready, arrange Ss in small groups to share their wish lists and find out if other Ss agree.

> **Alternative approach**
> When Ss have written their three 'wishes' for the arts in Ex 2B, arrange Ss in groups of four. Ss share their ideas, and together negotiate, then agree on a list of three 'wishes' for the group. In feedback, nominate Ss from each group to share their 'wishes' with the class.

IDEAS

3A Ss complete the sentences alone then check in pairs. In feedback, elicit Ss' answers.

> **Answers:** 1 c) 2 a) 3 b) 4 c) 5 a) 6 a)

B Read the example with the class, and elicit ideas for the second sentence in order to check Ss understand what to do. Ss test each other in pairs. In feedback, nominate Ss to share their ideas for the class to guess.

> **Optional extra activity**
> Write the following on the board: *someone's bright idea, an original idea* and *a ridiculous idea*. Ss work alone to think of an example of each from the real world. When they are ready, arrange Ss in small groups to read out their examples for other Ss to guess the phrase.

ADVERBIALS

4A Read the example with the class, and elicit ideas for the the second sentence in order to check Ss understand what to do. Ss expand the sentences in pairs. Monitor and check Ss are forming sentences correctly.

B Nominate Ss to share their longest sentences with the class.

RANTING/RAVING

5A Ss complete the conversations alone then check in pairs. In feedback, elicit Ss' answers.

> **Answers:** 1 amazing 2 all-time 3 ever 4 thing 5 luck
> 6 horrendous 7 idyllic 8 waste

B Ss practise the conversations in pairs. In feedback, nominate Ss to perform their conversations for the class.

> **Optional extra activity**
> Write the following questions on the board:
> *How was your last holiday?*
> *What did you think of the last film you saw?*
> *Have you ever read 1984 by George Orwell?*
> *Have you ever been to the Tate Modern?*
> *Did you like the last restaurant you went to?*
> *Have you ever tried Indian food?*
>
> Ss work alone to write 3 true and 3 false rants/raves in order to answer the questions. Monitor and help with vocabulary, writing any new words and phrases on the board. When they are ready, Ss mingle and ask other Ss the questions. Ss should reply with the rants and raves they prepared, for their partner to guess if it's true or false.

OVERVIEW

10.1 LONG WAY ROUND
GRAMMAR | inversion
VOCABULARY | collocations
HOW TO | describe a memorable journey

COMMON EUROPEAN FRAMEWORK
Ss can quickly identify the content and relevance of articles; can give a clear, detailed description of how to carry out a procedure.

10.2 DREAMS COME TRUE?
GRAMMAR | comparative structures
VOCABULARY | ambition
HOW TO | talk about your ambitions

COMMON EUROPEAN FRAMEWORK
Ss can understand extended speech even when relationships are only implied and not signalled explicitly; can write detailed expositions of complex subjects in an essay, underlining what he/she considers to be the salient issues.

10.3 MAKING A PLAN
FUNCTION | negotiating
VOCABULARY | negotiation
LEARN TO | stall for time

COMMON EUROPEAN FRAMEWORK
Ss can argue a formal position convincingly, responding to questions and answering complex lines of counter argument fluently; can preface their remarks appropriately in order to gain time and keep the floor whilst thinking.

10.4 WILDEST DREAMS ◉ BBC DVD
speakout | a dream job
writeback | a job application

COMMON EUROPEAN FRAMEWORK
Ss can use language flexibly and effectively for professional purposes; can express themselves with clarity and precision, using language flexibly and effectively.

10.5 LOOKBACK
Communicative revision activities

BBC VIDEO PODCAST
What are your goals in life?

This video podcast extends discussion of the unit topic to life goals. Ss can view people talking about their goals in life. Use this video podcast at the start or end of Unit 10.

LONG WAY ROUND

Introduction
Ss learn and practise inversion in the context of travel experiences. They also learn and practise using synonyms.

SUPPLEMENTARY MATERIALS
Resource bank p181, p182
Warm up: Think of a long journey you've been on and prepare to describe it to the class.
Speakout tip Ex 8B: Bring a thesaurus for Ss to use

Warm up
Describe a long journey you've been on to the class. Encourage them to ask follow-up questions to find out more information. Give Ss three or four minutes to think of a long journey they've been on and prepare to talk about it. Monitor and help with vocabulary, writing any new words and phrases on the board. Ss describe their journeys in pairs. In feedback, nominate Ss to share any interesting information they found out about their partner with the class.

READING AND VOCABULARY

1 Focus attention on the photo and elicit what Ss can see. Ss discuss the questions in small groups. In feedback, nominate Ss from each group to share their ideas with the class.

2A Ss match the phrases alone then check in pairs. Monitor and help where necessary. In feedback, elicit Ss' answers and be prepared to give further explanations and examples where necessary.

Answers: 1c) 2d) 3e) 4g) 5b) 6a) 7f)

Optional extra activity
Ss take it in turns to test each other in pairs. One student covers the left-hand column and the other reads out phrases from the right-hand column at random, for their partner to guess the first word or phrase.

Teaching tip
At Advanced level, it's often thought that Ss should be taught more 'advanced' vocabulary (i.e. longer words). However, it's equally important to encourage Ss at this level to make the most of what they already know. Teaching collocations enables Ss to do what native speakers do – use words they already know to generate new meanings with collocations.

B Write: an epic journey on the board and elicit how this might relate to the story (e.g. perhaps they travelled across a continent). Ss work through the rest of the phrases in pairs and discuss their possible relevance to the story. In feedback, elicit Ss' ideas and write them on the board.

3A Elicit/check: *ride pillion* (on the back of someone's motorbike). Ss read the text quickly to check their ideas from Ex 2B and answer the question in pairs. In feedback, tick any of the ideas on the board that were mentioned, and elicit the good and bad things about the journey.

> **Answers: Good things:** close, open friendship; kind strangers; becoming more open to strangers; beautiful landscapes; range of extraordinary experiences; feeling of achievement
> **Bad things:** missing family; physical privations; rehydrated food; poor or no washing facilities; being held up at borders

B Ss insert the sentences alone then check in pairs. In feedback, elicit Ss' answers.

> **Answers:** 1 d) 2 b) 3 g) 4 e) 5 c) 6 a) Extra sentence: f)

4 Ss answer the questions in pairs, referring back to the text if they need to. In feedback, elicit Ss' answers.

> **Answers:** 1 They were both British actors, with young families and an obsession with motorbikes. 2 Both had ridden bikes when they were younger. Charley had grown up riding a bike on a farm, whereas Ewan didn't have much off-road experience. 3 They realised people were just being curious and friendly, so they started to relax and be less suspicious. 4 They spoke on the phone most nights. It helped them to enjoy the trip, knowing that their families were OK. 5 He offered them a bedbug-free room, which turned out to be a luxury mansion with a lot of gun-wielding mobsters.

SPEAKING

5A Arrange Ss in small groups. Focus attention on the titles of the leaflets, and elicit Ss' predictions about what they think each involves. Ss read the leaflets and discuss which they'd like to go on. In feedback, elicit Ss' ideas.

B Read the instructions with the class. Ss plan their trips in groups, using the questions to help with ideas. Monitor and help with vocabulary, writing any new words and phrases on the board.

C When Ss are ready, different groups take it in turns to present their plans to the class. When all the groups have presented their plans, take a class vote on the most interesting trip.

> **Optional extra activity**
> Ss design/write a leaflet for their trip. Monitor and help with vocabulary, writing any new words and phrases on the board. When they are ready, arrange the Ss in pairs to choose their best leaflet out of the two. One student stays with the leaflet they chose and acts as a 'travel agent', trying to 'sell' their trip. The other student walks round the class, looking at other Ss' leaflets and asking questions. When they have asked about all the other leaflets, they return to their original partner and describe as much as they can remember. When they have finished, hold a class vote to see which trip is the most popular.

GRAMMAR inversion

6A Ss read the text and answer the question alone, then check in pairs. In feedback, elicit Ss' answers.

> **Answers:** It was the same people, long journey on motorbikes, experience of a lifetime, (but different journey – down through Europe and Africa, rather than around the world)

B Ss read the sentences and answer the questions alone then check in pairs. In feedback, elicit Ss' answers, and explain that the change in word order is the same as when we form questions.

> **Answers:** The word order has been inverted (auxiliary + subject + verb clause)
> 1 **If the first journey had not been** such a success, they never would have considered the second.
> 2 **If he had been** a more experienced rider, he might not have fallen so often.

C Ss complete the rule and find another example alone then check in pairs. In feedback, elicit Ss' answers.

> **Answers:** formal; Had they known how difficult the journey would prove, they might never have started.

D Explain that conditionals are only one structure that we use inversion with, and that we can also use it after beginning a sentence with a negative adverbial, for emphasis. Read the examples with the class, then Ss find two more examples in the text. In feedback, elicit Ss' answers.

> **Answers:** Not only did *The Long Way Round* journey challenge their view of the world, it also tested their physical endurance; Never before had they experienced such hospitality from complete strangers.

▸ **LANGUAGEBANK** 10.1 p146–147

Stronger classes can read the notes and do the exercises at home. Otherwise, check the notes with Ss, especially the inversion in the second clause after *Not until* and *Only now*, and the use of *but also* after *Not only*. In each exercise, do the first sentence as an example. Ss complete the exercises alone, then check their answers in pairs. Ss can refer to the notes to help them.

> **Answers:** 1 1c) 2e) 3a) 4d) 5f) 6b)
> 2 1 Seldom **have I** seen him looking so miserable.
> 2 Correct. 3 Under no circumstances **should you** leave the office. 4 **Had we** known there would be a water shortage, we would have been more prepared. 5 Only later **did she** realise her mistake. 6 Correct. 7 Correct. 8 Were they to **have** apologised more quickly, I might have forgiven them.

PRACTICE

7A With *weaker classes*, elicit the first answer as an example. Ss complete the sentences alone then check in pairs. In feedback, elicit Ss' answers.

> **Answers:** 1 Not until they were ready to depart did he think about leaving his family. 2 Only then did I see the danger that we were in. 3 No sooner had we left the tent than it collapsed. 4 Had we thought about it more, we would have taken extra fuel. 5 Never before had they ridden motorbikes for such extended distances. 6 At no point did they consider giving up the expedition.

B Give Ss five minutes to think of a journey and write their sentences. Monitor and help with vocabulary, and check Ss are forming inversions correctly. When they are ready, Ss share their sentences with a partner. In feedback, nominate Ss to share their ideas with the class.

VOCABULARY *PLUS* synonyms

8A Ss read the extracts alone then discuss the synonyms in pairs. In feedback, elicit Ss' ideas and write them on the board.

> **Alternative approach**
> Do it as a team game. Groups have three minutes to write as many as possible, then award points in feedback.

B Elicit the first answer as an example. Ss find the word with a different meaning alone then check in pairs. In feedback, elicit Ss' answers and check understanding of the words with different meanings.

> **Answers:** 1 dull 2 tracker 3 overemphasise 4 complete 5 train 6 excite
> Other possible synonyms: 1 exciting, riveting 2 voyage, excursion 3 emphasise, underscore 4 launch, commence 5 comprehend, succeed 6 annoy, peeve

> **Teaching tip**
> It could be argued that there is no such thing as a true synonym. Even words with very similar meanings often have subtle semantic differences. At this level, it's useful to discuss what those differences are, and Ss should have the language to do so.

speakout TIP

Read the **speakout tip** with the class. Ss look up the word in a thesaurus, or an online thesaurus, then share their answers.

9 Ss complete the sentences alone then check in pairs. In feedback, elicit Ss' answers.

> **Answers:** 1 bugs 2 exhilarated 3 emphasised 4 embarked 5 mastered 6 expedition

10 Encourage Ss to look back at their notes from the lesson and write down five words. Ss think of synonyms in pairs. When they have finished, rearrange Ss in new pairs to share their words and synonyms. In feedback, elicit Ss' answers and write any new words and phrases on the board.

> ➤ **VOCABULARYBANK** p157 SYNONYMS
> **1A** Ss find the different words alone then check in pairs. In feedback, elicit Ss' answers and check understanding of the words with different meanings.
>
> **B** Ss choose the correct alternatives alone then check in pairs. In feedback, elicit Ss' answers.
> *Stronger classes* can do the exercises at home.
>
> **Answers:** 1A 1 impure 2 welcome 3 hypothetical 4 admit 5 run 6 lightweight 7 minimal 8 dishonest
> B 1 admit 2 stroll 3 cumbersome 4 straightforward 5 ignore 6 assume

> **Homework ideas**
> • Ex 5B: Write a leaflet for the trip you planned.
> • Vocabulary bank p157
> • Language bank 10.1 Ex 1–2, p147
> • Workbook Ex 1–6, p65–66

DREAMS COME TRUE?

Introduction

Ss revise and practise comparative structures in the context of ambitions. They also practise writing a 'for and against' essay.

SUPPLEMENTARY MATERIALS

Resource bank p180, p183

Warm up: Write the adjectives below on the board.

Warm up

Write the following adjectives on the board: *independent, sensible, rich, carefree, stressed, shy, happy-go-lucky, optimistic, prepared to take risks, happy, hard to please* and *interested in things around me.* Ss use the adjectives to compare their lives now to when they were children, giving reasons for each statement. Monitor and gauge how well Ss are using comparative structures. In feedback, nominate Ss to share their ideas with the class.

SPEAKING

1 Arrange Ss in groups to discuss question 1. When they have finished, nominate Ss from each group to share their ideas with the class. Ss read the texts alone then discuss if any of their ideas were mentioned.

GRAMMAR comparative structures

2A Ss answer the questions alone then check in pairs. In feedback, elicit Ss' answers.

Answers: 1 Hurst's 2 Brockovich's 3 Brockovich's

B Ss answer the question in pairs. In feedback, elicit Ss' answers.

Answers: small difference: barely any different, big difference: significantly more, far more

3A With *weaker classes*, check understanding of the words in the box first. Ss categorise the words alone then check in pairs. In feedback, elicit Ss' answers.

Answers: 1 much, far, considerably, slightly, infinitely, a bit, a lot, marginally, miles, not, way, a good deal, decidedly, significantly, barely any, loads 2 just, nothing like, nowhere near, not, every bit

B Ss discuss the questions in pairs. In feedback, elicit Ss' answers.

Answers: 1 small difference: slightly, a bit, marginally, barely any; big difference: much, far, nothing like, considerably, infinitely, a lot, nowhere near, miles, a good deal, decidedly, significantly, way, loads no difference: just, every bit (*not* can be a small or a big difference.)
2 formal: considerably, infinitely, marginally, every bit, a good deal, decidedly, significantly;
informal: much, just, far, nothing like, slightly, a bit, a lot, nowhere near, miles, way, barely any, loads (*way* and *loads* are very informal and only used in spoken English; *not* is neutral)

Watch out!

Comparative structures are a much wider area of language in English than many Ss realise. Ss may be familiar with a lot of the language presented here, but may not use it naturally. Encourage Ss to be precise when comparing by using as much of this language as possible.

C Ss match the rules and examples alone then check in pairs. In feedback, elicit Ss' answers and be prepared to provide further explanations and examples where necessary.

Answers: 1b) 2 a)

⟫ LANGUAGEBANK 10.2 p146–147

Stronger classes can read the notes and do the exercises at home. Otherwise, check the notes with Ss, especially which structures are more formal/informal. In each exercise, do the first sentence as an example. Ss complete the exercises alone, then check their answers in pairs. Ss can refer to the notes to help them.

Answers: 1 1 like 2 a 3 barely (or hardly) 4 deal 5 every 6 faster 7 the 8 near 2 1 just gets better and better 2 nowhere near as famous as 3 is every bit as remarkable 4 little more than a year 5 would be far greater than 6 come a good deal closer 7 nothing like as flamboyant as his hero 8 considerably more money than

PRACTICE

4 Ss complete the sentences alone then check in pairs. Monitor and check Ss are using comparative structures correctly. In feedback, nominate Ss to share their ideas with the class.

Optional extra activity

Ss change parts of the sentences and make them true for their real lives. When they are ready, Ss compare in pairs.

5A ▶ 10.1 Ss listen to the recording and notice the emphasis. If necessary, play the recording again for Ss to listen and repeat. Ss practise reading their own sentences aloud with the correct emphasis.

Unit 10 Recording 1

1 My life would be considerably better if I had a normal job.
2 Being a celebrity is nothing like as glamorous as it seems.
3 One good thing about fame is that it's far easier to book a table in a restaurant.
4 Even for a celebrity, it's every bit as difficult to enjoy life.

Teaching tip

When emphasising a point in English, *how* we say something is just as, if not more, important than *what* we say. Help Ss to use stress naturally by exposing them to examples such as those in Ex 5A and encouraging them to use appropriate emphasis when speaking.

B ▶ 10.2 Ss discuss the meanings in pairs. In feedback, elicit Ss' answers. Ss listen to the expressions and repeat.

Answers: Meanings: 1 The more the merrier: If more people are involved in something, it will be more enjoyable. We often use this expression to say everyone is welcome. 2 The sooner the better: You should do something as soon as possible. 3 The bigger they come, the harder they fall: If people or things are powerful and successful, they will suffer more when they are defeated. This expression is often used to say you should not be scared because your opponent is big or well-known.

LISTENING

6A Focus attention on the pictures and ask: *Do you know who this writer is? Have you read any of his books?* Ss read the text then discuss the questions in pairs. In feedback, elicit Ss' ideas, but don't give any feedback yet.

B ▶ 10.3 Ss listen to the extract and check their answers. Elicit Ss' answers in feedback.

Answers: 1 He was busy teaching full-time. 2 He became a celebrity, appeared on lots of shows, met famous people and was suddenly listened to. 3 He met other famous people such as actors, politicians, the Pope and the Duchess of York. He also met lots of the general public when he toured.

7A Ss discuss the significance of the numbers and names from memory in pairs. When they are ready, play the recording again for Ss to check their answers. In feedback, nominate a different student for each number/name to share their answers with the class.

Answers: 1 the number of years he taught in New York high schools 2 the number of copies he expected to sell of *Angela's Ashes* 3 the number of languages *Angela's Ashes* was translated into 4 The year it was published. 5 The number of classes he taught a day. 6 How often his photo was taken. 7 He met President Clinton and Hillary Rodham Clinton. 8 He met the Duchess of York and was interviewed by her. 9 He nearly met Elton John. 10 He was asked for his opinion on William Butler Yeats (an Irish poet) as he was suddenly considered an expert on everything

Unit 10 Recording 3

When I taught in New York City high schools for thirty years no one but my students paid me a scrap of attention. In the world outside the school I was invisible. Then I wrote a book about my childhood and became mick of the moment. I hoped the book would explain family history to McCourt children and grandchildren. I hoped it might sell a few hundred copies and I might be invited to have discussions with book clubs. Instead it jumped on the best-seller list and was translated into thirty languages and I was dazzled. The book was my second act.

In the world of books I am a late bloomer, a johnny-come-lately, new kid on the block. My first book, *Angela's Ashes*, was published in 1996 when I was sixty-six, the second, *'Tis*, in 1999 when I was sixty-nine. At that age it's a wonder I was able to lift the pen at all. New friends of mine (recently acquired because of my ascension to the best-seller lists) had published books in their twenties. Striplings. So, what took you so long?

I was teaching, that's what took me so long. Not in college or university, where you have all the time in the world for writing and other diversions, but in four different New York City public high schools. (I have read novels about the lives of university professors

where they seemed to be so busy with adultery and academic in-fighting you wonder where they found time to squeeze in a little teaching.) When you teach five high school classes a day, five days a week, you're not inclined to go home to clear your head and fashion deathless prose. After a day of five classes your head is filled with the clamour of the classroom.

I never expected *Angela's Ashes* to attract any attention, but when it hit the best-seller lists I became a media darling. I had my picture taken hundreds of times. I was a geriatric novelty with an Irish accent. I was interviewed for dozens of publications. I met governors, mayors, actors. I met the first President Bush and his son, the governor of Texas. I met President Clinton and Hillary Rodham Clinton. I met Gregory Peck. I met the Pope and kissed his ring. Sarah, Duchess of York, interviewed me. She said I was her first Pulitzer Prize winner. I said she was my first duchess. She said, Ooh, and asked the cameraman, Did you get that? Did you get that? I was nominated for a Grammy for the spoken word and nearly met Elton John. People looked at me in a different way. They said, Oh, you wrote that book, This way, please, Mr. McCourt, or Is there anything you'd like, anything? A woman in a coffee shop squinted and said, I seen you on TV. You must be important. Who are you? Could I have your autograph? I was listened to. I was asked for my opinion on Ireland, conjunctivitis, drinking, teeth, education, religion, adolescent angst, William Butler Yeats, literature in general. What books are you reading this summer? What books have you read this year? Catholicism, writing, hunger. I spoke to gatherings of dentists, lawyers, ophthalmologists and, of course, teachers. I travelled the world being Irish, being a teacher, an authority on misery of all kinds, a beacon of hope to senior citizens everywhere who always wanted to tell their stories.

They made a movie of *Angela's Ashes*. No matter what you write in America there is always talk of The Movie. You could write the Manhattan telephone directory, and they'd say, So, when is the movie?

B Ss turn to the audio script on p174 and find the words, then discuss their meanings in pairs.

C Ss turn to p163 and check their answers. In feedback, elicit Ss' answers and be prepared to provide further explanations and examples where necessary.

Answers: a scrap (of attention) (n) = a very small amount, dazzled (adj) = amazed, ascension (n) = rise, clamour (n) = continuous loud noise, geriatric (adj) = old (person), a beacon (of hope) (n) = a shining light

8 Ss discuss the questions in pairs. Monitor and help where necessary. In feedback, elicit Ss' answers.

Suggested answers: 1 It was a second phase in his life. His first act was as a teacher. 2 Frank didn't feel he had become important or was any different from before. 3 He is amused by the idea of his new 'expertise' because it seems to be related to his celebrity status. Previously nobody wanted his opinions on anything. His tone of voice is ironic. 4 The book is about Ireland and the hardship of life there.

VOCABULARY ambition

9A Ss choose the correct alternatives alone then in pairs, and discuss the meanings. In feedback, elicit Ss' answers and be prepared to provide further explanations/examples where necessary.

Answers: 1 *crave* and *hanker(ed) after* mean you have an extremely strong desire for something 2 *be in the spotlight* and *be the centre of attention* mean receive a lot of attention, e.g. on TV 3 *serve an apprenticeship* and *pay your dues* mean you spend a lot of time learning how to do something well – observing others, practising, etc. 4 *be held in high esteem* and *be renowned* mean you are well-known for being good at something 5 *become an overnight success* and *shoot to fame* mean you become suddenly famous 6 *be set on* something and *have aspirations* mean you have an ambition to do something

B Ss read the sentences again and tick the ones they agree with. When they are ready, Ss compare their opinions in pairs. Monitor and encourage Ss to ask follow up questions to find out more information. In feedback, elicit Ss' opinions and have a brief class discussion.

⇒ **VOCABULARYBANK** p157 AMBITION

2A Focus attention on the pictures and elicit what Ss can see in each one. Ss complete the captions alone then check in pairs. In feedback, elicit Ss' answers.

B Ss cover the captions and retell the story in pairs. Monitor and help where necessary by prompting Ss with the first word of each phrase. In feedback, nominate Ss to retell the story to the class, choosing a different student to describe each picture.
Stronger classes can do the exercises at home.

Answers: 2A 1 desire 2 heart 3 hogging 4 big 5 stroke 6 off 7 wonder 8 lifetime

SPEAKING

10 Give Ss three or four minutes to read the questions and think about their answers alone. Monitor and help with vocabulary, writing any new words and phrases on the board. When they are ready, arrange Ss in small groups to discuss the questions. Monitor and make notes on any common errors and good language for later feedback. In feedback, nominate Ss from each group to share their ideas with the class and give Ss feedback on their language.

WRITING a 'for and against' essay

11A Read the quotes with the class and check understanding. Ss discuss the questions in pairs. In feedback, elicit Ss' answers and have a brief class discussion.

B Elicit/check: *posterity* (all the people in the future who will be alive when you are dead), *fill a void* (an empty place or situation where something is needed) and *mediocrity* (the quality of being below average or second-rate). Ss read the essay and make notes on the arguments for and against celebrity culture, then check in pairs. In feedback, elicit Ss' answers.

Answers: arguments 'for': it gives us insights into the rich and famous. Following them is fun. Most of us enjoy gossip. It's good to hear about some superstar getting what he deserves. Fame has become democratised; you don't need talent to be famous.
arguments 'against': people now idolise mediocrity. Teenagers want to be famous for its own sake without making any effort to learn a skill. Fame can be confused with achievement.

12 Read the structure notes with the class. Ss discuss the question in pairs. In feedback, elicit Ss' answers.

Answer: The essay follows the same structure.

LEARN TO describe pros and cons

13A Focus attention on the table. Ss refer back to the essay and decide which phrases were not used, then check in pairs. In feedback, elicit Ss' answers.

Answers: While … is true, it is also true to say …, One of the benefits is …, One of the drawbacks is …

B Ss categorise the phrases alone then check in pairs. In feedback, elicit Ss' answers.

Answers: contrasting arguments: In contrast to this, …, We also need to take … into consideration;
pros: One advantage is …, The arguments for … include …, On the positive side, …;
cons: One disadvantage is …, The arguments against … include …, On the negative side, …

14 Ss choose a topic and plan their pros and cons arguments alone. Monitor and help with vocabulary, writing any new words and phrases on the board. When they are ready, Ss write their essays. Encourage them to use the phrases from Ex 13B. When they have finished, Ss swap their answers with a partner and read them.

Homework ideas
• Ex 14: write a final draft of your essay.
• Language bank 10.2 Ex 1–2, p147
• Workbook Ex 1–5, p67–68

MAKING A PLAN

Introduction

Ss learn and practise phrases for negotiating, and how to stall for time.

SUPPLEMENTARY MATERIALS

Resource bank p184

Warm up

Arrange Ss in A/B pairs, and explain the following situation: *As are teachers, and need to collect homework from all Ss by the end of the week, or the school director won't be happy. Bs are Ss, and have an important university exam on Friday. It's really important to study for this exam, and so they won't be able to do the homework until next Monday. In pairs, Ss discuss the situation and try to find a mutually agreeable solution. In feedback, elicit Ss' solutions.*

VOCABULARY negotiation

1 Give Ss three or four minutes to read the questions and think about their answers. Monitor and help where necessary. When they are ready, arrange Ss in small groups to discuss the questions. In feedback, nominate Ss from each group to share their ideas with the class.

Optional extra activity
Read out the following information to the class: *A parent and child are negotiating what time the child should go to bed. The child is 7 years old, and wants to go to bed at 10 p.m. so that they can watch a TV programme they like. The parent thinks this is too late and thinks they should be in bed before 9 p.m.* Arrange the class in two groups: parent and child. Ss work together in their groups to brainstorm a list of reasons why they should get what they want, and also a list of possible concessions (e.g. the child promises to eat their vegetables, the parent promises to take the child to the zoo, etc.). Monitor and help with ideas where necessary. When they are ready, arrange Ss in pairs with one student from each of the previous groups. Ss act out their negotiation and try to reach an agreement. In feedback, ask Ss if they managed to agree and what concessions they gave.

2A Ss read the tips and choose the three most important alone then check in pairs. In feedback, elicit Ss' answers.

B Ss think of more tips in pairs. Monitor and help with vocabulary, writing any new words and phrases on the board. In feedback, elicit Ss' ideas and write them on the board.

C Ss match the words and expressions and definitions alone then check in pairs. In feedback, elicit Ss' answers.

Answers: a) 7 make concessions b) 4 tactful c) 6 bluff d) 5 defer e) 3 make compromises f) 1 establish common goals g) 2 haggling

FUNCTION negotiating

3A Ss put the stages in the correct order alone then check in pairs. Don't elicit any answers yet.

B ▶10.4 Ss listen to the recording and check their answers. In feedback, elicit Ss' answers and write them on the board in the correct order.

Answers: 1 name your objectives 2 establish common goals 3 make an offer 4 refuse or accept the deal 5 follow up the deal

4A Ss discuss the questions in pairs. Don't elicit any answers yet.

B Play the recording again for Ss to check their answers. In feedback, elicit Ss' answers.

Answers: 1 asking questions to find out what the other person wants and then really listening to what they say 2 *if* 3 ask about it 4 refusing 5 *no* 6 consult a more senior colleague 7 to keep the conversation open

Unit 10 Recording 4

M=Man

M: Much of negotiating is in body language and gesture, but it's also vital that you use the right words. So you're at the beginning of some kind of negotiation. The first thing you want to do is name your objectives. So you can use a phrase such as 'we want to sort this out as soon as possible'. This makes it clear to everybody what you want from the discussion. Another thing you need to do is explore positions. What does that mean? Well, it means asking questions like 'Can you tell me more about this?' 'What do you have in mind?' Exploring positions is all about asking what the other guy wants and then really listening. In this way you can establish common goals. Um, so then you need to make an offer. And this is where the real negotiating starts, and the 'if' word becomes so important because your offer is going to be conditional on certain terms being met, concessions and compromises being made. So you might say, 'If you do this for me, I'll do this for you.' 'We'd be prepared to help you if you help us.' And, as for questions, again we can use 'if'. 'What if'? 'What if we gave you access to this?' 'What if we gave you a helping hand?' 'What if we supported your idea?' In negotiating, the word 'if' is the biggest word in the language.
   OK. Check that you understand. Negotiations can be long and tiring, but you cannot switch off for a moment. If you missed something, don't bluff. You have to ask about it. Go over the points more than once. Be sure. Ask 'Have I got this right?' 'Are you saying this or that?' 'If I understand you correctly, you mean this.'
   OK, so then you get towards the endgame. The haggling is over. It's decision time and you need to refuse or accept the deal. Refusing is always delicate. You really don't want to close off all further discussion, so you need to be tactful and phrase the refusal carefully. You never just say no. 'No' is a word that closes doors. Instead, you give reasons and explanations. For example, you might say, 'That's more than I can offer'. 'That would be difficult for me because of my situation'. 'I'm not sure I can do that because I promised something else'. In other words, you refuse without saying no. It's at this stage you might want to stall for time, or defer the decision, or if you're in business, consult a more senior colleague.
   The next stage is when you've reached agreement. You say something like, 'good. That sounds acceptable to me.' Or 'Great, we've got a deal.' But that's not it. It isn't over. You need to follow up the deal. Be polite and civil. Say something like, 'We can talk about it again and review the situation in a few months'. If it's a more formal deal, we can say 'Let me know if you have any queries.' 'If there are any other points, I'll email you.' The thing is to follow up the deal. Always keep the conversation open.

C Ss discuss the questions in pairs. In feedback, elicit Ss' answers and have a brief class discussion.

5A Read the phrases with the class. Ss turn to p175 and check which ones were used in the audio script. In feedback, elicit Ss' answers.

> **Answers:**
> naming your objectives
> We want to sort this out as soon as possible.
> exploring positions
> What do you have in mind?
> conditional offers
> If you do this for me, I'll do this for you.
> What if we supported your idea?
> refusing an offer
> That would be difficult for me because …
> I'm not sure I can do that because …,
> accepting an offer
> Good. That sounds acceptable to me.
> Great. We've got a deal
> following up on the deal
> Let me know if you have any queries.

> **Optional extra activity**
> Arrange Ss in pairs. One student closes his/her book, and the other student reads out phrases from the table at random. The student with his/her book closed guesses which function the phrase relates to. When they have finished, Ss swap roles and repeat the activity.

B Ss think of other expressions in pairs. In feedback, elicit Ss' ideas and write them on the board.

> ⇒ **LANGUAGEBANK** 10.3 p146–147
>
> *Stronger classes* could read the notes and do the exercise at home. Otherwise, drill the phrases from the chart, checking Ss are using natural intonation. Ss work alone to correct the word order, then check their answers in pairs. In feedback, elicit Ss' answers. Ss practise the conversations in pairs.
>
> > **Answers:** 1 A: We want to sort this out as soon as possible. B: So do we. Can you go into more detail about your proposal? 2 A: By the end of the meeting we want to have a concrete plan. B: What do you have in mind? 3 A: If you do this for me, I'll help you with the project. B: I'm not sure we can do that because of our contract. 4 A: Good, that sounds acceptable to me. B: Let me know if you have any queries.
> > 5 A: Great! we've got a deal. B: Get in touch if anything needs clarifying. 6 A: What if we supported your idea for the pension scheme? B: OK, but the rest of the proposal would be difficult for us as it still means cutting jobs.

6 Elicit the first answer as an example. Ss complete the sentences alone then check in pairs. In feedback, elicit Ss' answers.

> **Answers:** 1 We want to sort this **out** as soon as possible. 2 Can you go **into** more detail? 3 Great! We've got **a** deal. 4 What **do/did** you have in mind? 5 If you sponsor this idea for me, I **can/will** make concessions for you. 6 What **if** we supported your project from the beginning? 7 I'm not sure I **can** do that because of what I told my friend. 8 That **might/may/could/will** be difficult for me because I already agreed something else. 9 Let me know **if** you have any queries about the arrangements. 10 Get **in** touch if anything needs clarifying.

> **Alternative approach**
> Books closed. Write the missing words on the board in random order. Arrange Ss in small groups, elicit a name for each group and write it on the board. Read out each sentence one by one, and Ss call out the missing word. The first team to call out the correct missing word receives a point. The team with the most points at the end wins. When you have finished, erase the missing words from the board, and Ss complete the sentences as in Ex 6.

LEARN TO stall for time

7A Ss read the expressions and discuss the questions in pairs. In feedback, elicit Ss' answers.

> **Answers:** 'Stalling for time' means delaying something because you are not ready. 4 is not used to stall for time.

B ▶ 10.5 Ss listen to the recording and repeat the expressions, copying the intonations. If necessary, drill the expressions chorally and individually.

> **Teaching tip**
> Stalling for time is a very useful tool when participating in a group discussion, and one which native speakers use all the time in order to keep their turn. Teaching Ss phrases such as those in Ex 6 can equip them with a very valuable tool for giving them more thinking time when discussing.

SPEAKING

8A Ss read the notes and discuss the question in pairs. In feedback, elicit Ss' answers.

B Arrange the Ss in two groups, and ask them to turn to the relevant pages. Give Ss enough time to read their roles and prepare their answers to the questions. Monitor and help where necessary.

C When they are ready, arrange Ss in pairs to carry out the negotiation. Encourage Ss to use the phrases for negotiating from Ex 5A and the expressions for stalling for time from Ex 7A. Monitor and make notes on any common errors and good language for later feedback.

D Ask each group to present the results of their negotiations to the class. Give Ss feedback on their language.

> **Homework ideas**
> • Language bank 10.3 Ex 1, p147
> • Workbook Ex 1–3, p69

WILDEST DREAMS

Introduction

Ss watch an extract from the BBC programme *Wildest Dreams*, in which contestants compete to produce a wildlife documentary. Ss learn and practise how to describe a dream job, and write a job application.

SUPPLEMENTARY MATERIALS

Warm up: Prepare your own ideas for a wildlife documentary.

Warm up

Explain the following situation to the class: *You have been given the opportunity to make a wildlife documentary. There are no limits to distance, travel or expense. What would you make your documentary about, and why?* Describe your own ideas to the class and encourage them to ask you questions. Give Ss three or four minutes to prepare their ideas. When they are ready, arrange Ss in small groups to share what they decided. In feedback, elicit Ss' ideas.

▶ DVD PREVIEW

1 Elicit/check: *put someone through their paces* and *swamp*. Give Ss three minutes to read the programme information then discuss the question in pairs. In feedback, elicit Ss' answers.

Answer: 1 They travel to Botswana's Okavanga Delta to film wildlife for a BBC TV competition **2** They can win a job at the BBC's Natural History Unit. If they are not good enough, they get sent home.

Culture notes
The BBC reality show *Wildest dreams* was first screened in 2009. It is presented by Nick Knowles and award-winning wildlife filmmaker James Honeyborne. The programme follows the progress of a group of amateur wildlife enthusiasts as they compete for a job with the BBC's Natural History Unit.

▶ DVD VIEW

2 Read the phrases with the class and check understanding. Ss watch the DVD and put the statements in the order they hear them, then check in pairs. In feedback, elicit Ss' answers.

Answers: 1 c) **2** a) **3** e) **4** f) **5** d) **6** b)

3A Ss complete the extracts from memory in pairs. Monitor and help but don't give any answers yet.

B Play the DVD again for Ss to check their answers. In feedback, elicit Ss' answers.

Answers: 1 determination, dedication **2** killer bees **3** pushed, predator **4** crash course **5** escape, ticket **6** life-changing

4 Arrange Ss in small groups to discuss the questions. In feedback, nominate Ss to share their ideas with the class and have a brief class discussion.

Wildest Dreams

NK=Nick Knowles M1=Man W1=Woman W2=Woman 2
SK=Simon King A=Alan SR=Sadia Ramzan

NK: Wildlife film-making is one of the most difficult jobs on earth.
M1: This is not good.
NK: To get shots like these you have to track dangerous animals.
W1: Oi!!
NK: Then get close to them without being attacked. It takes people with a very special mix of determination and dedication.
SK: Unbelievable!
NK: Thousands try but very few can do it. Now the BBC has chosen nine animal lovers from ordinary backgrounds to see if any of them have what it takes to become a wildlife film-maker.
W2: We've got to throw ourselves into it. We've got to put ourselves on the line.
NK: How will this factory worker from Rotherham cope filming thousands of killer bees?
A: The bees are obviously getting a bit more angry now. Please don't sting me.
NK: Can an ex-burger bar manageress deal with everything that the natural world can throw at her?
W1: I'm feeling really under pressure and I'm gonna lose my temper in a minute.
NK: And when pushed to the limits, how does it feel to track the most powerful predator on earth?
W2: It's exhilarating, but it's made my day, I can't stop smiling.
NK: Which of these nine people has what it takes to win one amazing job filming some of the best wildlife shows in the world? For the winner this will be their wildest dream.
    The BBC is renowned around the world for its natural history programmes, like *Blue Planet*, *Big Cat Diary* and *Life In Cold Blood*. Today, nine ordinary people are on a journey to one of the world's remotest spots, the Okavango Delta in Botswana, to start a crash course in wildlife film-making.
    East London mum Sadia Ramzan dreams of escape and loves animals, so this could be just the ticket.
SR: I've never been anywhere like this in my life, so this is all really, really amazing experience for me.
NK: For warehouse worker Alan, who's normally on the night shift, it's already an adventure.
A: I've never even been on a plane before, so to be going over African wilderness is just absolutely amazing.
NK: After a three-day journey they finally touchdown. I'm Nick Knowles and I'm here to see how they cope with the rigorous challenges ahead and to look after them during their time in Africa. Make no mistake, this is gonna be tough.
NK: Welcome to Africa.
All: Thankyou.
NK: We've brought you to the ends of the earth. Ahead of you lies, I guarantee, an experience of a lifetime and for one of you this will be a life changing experience. Are you ready to start your adventure?
All: Yes!

speakout a dream job

5A ▶ 10.6 Ss listen to the recording then answer the questions in pairs. In feedback, elicit Ss' answers.

> **Answers:** 1 film-maker 2 He's doing a degree in time-based art and digital film, and he has made a series of short films before. 3 It's important to be open-minded / forward-thinking / have good business sense / be organised / flexible 4 doing as much creative work as he can / getting work experience with an advertising company

B Focus attention on the **Key phrases**. Ss listen and choose the correct alternatives, then check in pairs. In feedback, elicit Ss' answers and drill the **Key phrases** chorally and individually.

> **Answers:** 1 would have to be 2 relish having the opportunity 3 I'm doing a degree in … 4 creative 5 try out new ideas 6 things that are going to work 7 open-minded 8 some work-experience

Unit 10 Recording 6

T=Tom

T: I guess my dream job would have to be a film-maker. Making short films, well, making full-length films too – that would be wonderful. The kind of films I'm interested in are those realistic animation films. What appeals to me is that it's wonderfully creative. There's so much you can do. You can do anything. I'd relish having the opportunity to work in an environment like that.

I'm fairly qualified in that, well I'm doing a degree in time-based art and digital film at University so we do a lot of work on film, image, sound and performance. I've made a series of short films, using various different techniques, so I've got a bit of experience behind me. And I'd like to think that I'm a fairly creative individual. I have lots of ideas about how to do things, and I'm not afraid to try out new ideas, to experiment. I'd say I've got quite a good eye for things that are going to work. Like an instinct. I can sense if something is working or not visually, or if we need to change it.

I think it's essential to be open-minded and forward thinking. There are a lot of people now doing fantastically creative things, and making films, so it's quite hard to be able to stand out from the crowd. So you need good business sense too, to make sure your film is successful. It's not just about having the ideas. You need to be a good organiser, so you can manage a project. And you have to be flexible.

As for moving towards getting my dream job, as I said, I'm still studying at the moment, but I try to do as much creative work as I can in my spare time. I'm also doing some work experience with an advertising company, looking at how we can use short films in advertising. I'm hoping that this experience will help me to find a job when I graduate.

6A Give Ss five minutes to plan their answers to the questions in Ex 5A. Monitor and help with vocabulary, writing any new words and phrases on the board.

B Arrange Ss in small groups to present their ideas. Monitor and note any common errors/good language for later feedback. In feedback, nominate Ss from each group to describe the winning presentation to the class. Give Ss feedback on their language.

writeback a job application

7A Ss read the post and discuss the question in pairs. In feedback, elicit Ss' answers and answer any questions about new vocabulary in the text.

> **Answer:** ice cream taster

B Ss write their paragraphs alone. Monitor and help with vocabulary, writing any new words and phrases on the board. Make sure Ss don't name the job in their descriptions.

C When they are ready, arrange Ss in small groups to read out their paragraphs for others to guess, making sure they work with different Ss from the ones they worked with in Ex 6B. In feedback, nominate Ss to read out their paragraphs for the class to guess.

> **Homework ideas**
> • Ex 7B: write a final draft of your paragraph.

LOOKBACK

Introduction

Ss revise and practise the language of Unit 10. The notes below provide ideas for exploiting the exercises and activities but your approach will depend on your aim, e.g. as a diagnostic or progress test or as revision and fluency practice. For example, if done as a test then it would not be appropriate to monitor or help them.

COLLOCATIONS

1 Ss complete the sentences alone then check in pairs. In feedback, elicit Ss' answers.

Answers: 1 an obsession 2 the depths 3 an epic 4 held up 5 humbled by

Optional extra activity
Ss write sentences about people they know using the collocations. When they are ready, Ss compare their sentences in pairs.

INVERSION

2A After explaining the activity, elicit the first answer as an example, in order to check Ss know what to do. Ss put the words in order alone then check in pairs. In feedback, elicit Ss' answers.

Answers: 1 No sooner had she sat down than there was a knock at the door. 2 Not only did you eat the last chocolate, but you also didn't buy any more. 3 Had I realised what was going to happen, I would have called you earlier. 4 Never again would they see anything like it. 5 Only now can I appreciate how difficult it must have been. 6 Had they gone to bed earlier, they might not have overslept.

B Read the example with the class. Ss write their stories in pairs. Monitor and help with vocabulary, writing any new words and phrases on the board.

C Ss read out their stories to the class. When they have finished, hold a class vote to choose the best story.

Alternative approach
After Ss have written their story, they draw five simple pictures to illustrate each sentence, in the style of a comic strip. Ss then pass their pictures to another pair, who write the corresponding sentence under each picture. When they have finished, Ss return their sentences to the original pair to compare their stories.

COMPARATIVE STRUCTURES

3A After explaining the activity, elicit the first answer as an example, in order to check Ss know what to do. Arrange Ss in pairs to write their sentences. Monitor and check Ss are using the structures correctly.

B Ss compare their sentences in the same pairs. In feedback, nominate Ss to share their sentences with the class.

AMBITION

4A Ss complete the sentences alone then check in pairs. In feedback, elicit Ss' answers.

Answers: 1 shot 2 overnight 3 centre 4 held in high 5 serve 6 for 7 on 8 crave 9 aspiration 10 after

B Read the example with the class. Ss write their sentences alone then check in pairs. Monitor and help with vocabulary, writing any new words and phrases on the board. In feedback, nominate pairs to share any similar sentences with the class.

NEGOTIATING

5A After explaining the activity, elicit the first answer as an example, in order to check Ss know what to do. Ss cross out the extra words alone then check in pairs. In feedback, elicit Ss' answers.

Answers: a) the b) to c) time d) that e) for f) taken g) of (after *not*)

B Ss put the phrases in order in pairs. In feedback, elicit Ss' answers.

Answers: 1 c) 2 f) 3 a) 4 g) 5 d) 6 e) 7 b)

C Ss discuss possible responses in pairs. In feedback, elicit Ss' ideas. Ss practise the negotiation in pairs.

Alternative approach
Ss write possible responses alone. Monitor and help with vocabulary, writing any new words and phrases on the board. When they are ready, arrange Ss in pairs to read out their responses in random order for their partner to guess which sentences they are the responses to.

Homework ideas
• **Workbook** Review and check 5, p70–72
• **Workbook** Test 5, p73

PAGE	UNIT	PHOTOCOPIABLE	LANGUAGE POINT	TIME
135	1	Quality people	**Vocabulary: personality** • practise using personality adjectives • practise speaking skills by asking and answering questions about people you know	25–30
136	1	Pictures of you	**Vocabulary plus: idioms for describing people** • review idioms for describing people in the context of a card game	25–30
137	1	Pick a shape	**Grammar: the continuous aspect** • review the continuous aspect • practise speaking skills by guessing and explaining personal information	30
138	1	Former selves	**Grammar: describing habits** • practise using forms to describe present and past habits	30
139	1	Original names	**Functional language: speculating** • practise language for speculating by discussing names and their origins	30
140	2	Rags to riches	**Vocabulary: learning and opinions** • review phrases connected with learning and opinions in the context of a story • practise reading skills by putting a story in order	25–30
141	2	Over the hill and far away	**Vocabulary plus: metaphors** • review metaphors • practise speaking skills by describing pictures and discussing ideas	25–30
142	2	Hexagonal regrets	**Grammar: conditionals and regrets** • review conditional forms and regrets in the context of a board game • give freer practice of the forms by discussing real regrets	30–40
143	2	Something in common	**Grammar: verb patterns** • practise forming and using verb patterns in the context of a questionnaire	25–30
144	2	What's your opinion?	**Functional language: introducing opinions** • practise functional language for giving opinions for or against statements	30–40
145	3	Describing places	**Vocabulary: landscapes and descriptive adjectives** • review vocabulary for landscapes and descriptive adjectives in a crossword	25
146	3	Fix it!	**Vocabulary plus: prefixes** • review prefixes by building words and putting them in sentences	30
147	3	Descriptions	**Grammar: noun phrases** • review noun phrases in the context of a board game • practise speaking skills by describing real places, events, activities, etc.	30–40
148	3	The job that I do	**Grammar: relative clauses** • review relative clauses by describing jobs	30
149	3	A better place	**Functional language: making a proposal** • practise functional language for making proposals to improve a school	40
150	4	Election time	**Vocabulary: social issues** • review vocabulary of social issues • practise speaking skills in the context of an election campaign roleplay	30–40
151	4	The perfect crimes?	**Vocabulary plus: lexical chunks** • practise lexical chunks in the context of completing a story • practise speaking skills by asking and answering questions	25–30
152	4	What is it?	**Grammar: introductory _it_** • review the introductory _it_ by completing a partner's sentences • practise speaking skills by discussing opinions on statements	30
153	4	Perfect classmates	**Grammar: the perfect aspect** • review the perfect aspect in the context of a questionnaire • practise speaking skills by asking and answering about personal experiences	30
154	4	What would you do?	**Functional language: expressing hypothetical preferences** • practise functional language for expressing hypothetical situations in the context of discussing moral responses	30
155	5	Guess the phrase	**Vocabulary: secrets, truths and myths** • review vocabulary of secrets, truths and myths in the context of a game • practise making definitions	25–30
156	5	Mini bingo	**Vocabulary plus: multi-word verbs** • review multi-word verbs by forming personalised sentences • practise speaking skills by asking and answering questions	30
157	5	Mistakes and advice	**Grammar: modal verbs and phrases** • review forms for expressing general advice and past regrets in the context of discussing hypothetical situations	30–40
158	5	I can't believe it!	**Grammar: the passive** • review passive forms in different tenses in the context of true/false statements	30
159	5	It's up to you	**Functional language: making a point** • practise functional language for making a point in the context of a roleplay on the freedom of speech	30

RESOURCE BANK

Index of photocopiables

PAGE	UNIT	PHOTOCOPIABLE	LANGUAGE POINT	TIME
160	6	Tomorrow's world	**Vocabulary: trends and predictions** • review vocabulary of trends and predictions by completing a partner's sentences • practise speaking skills by discussing opinions on statements	30
161	6	Prepositional dominoes	**Vocabulary plus: prepositional phrases** • review prepositional phrases in the context of a dominoes game • practise speaking skills by discussing opinions on statements	25–30
162	6	What does your future hold?	**Grammar: future forms** • practise future forms in the context of a questionnaire on your real opinions about the future	30
163	6	Duelling	**Grammar: concession clauses** • review concession clauses in the context of completing and sequencing statements about language skills • practise speaking skills by 'duelling' on other issues	20–25
164	6	Roots and results	**Functional language: describing cause and effect** • practise functional language for describing cause and effect in the context of defining and guessing situations	30
165	7	Escape!	**Vocabulary: escape and relaxing** • review vocabulary of escape and relaxing in the context of a board game	30
166	7	In a fix	**Vocabulary plus: suffixes** • review suffixes in the context of completing a partner's word within a sentence	30
167	7	Great escapes	**Grammar: cleft sentences** • review cleft sentences beginning with *What* and *It* in the context of texts describing historical events	30
168	7	It was a cold, dark night …	**Grammar: participle clauses** • review participle stories in the context of building a story using prompts • practise speaking skills by building new stories	30–40
169	7	Controversial slips	**Functional language: exchanging opinions** • practise functional language for giving opinions and agreeing and disagreeing in the context of a roleplay on controversial issues	30
170	8	False memory?	**Vocabulary: memories** • review vocabulary of memories in the context of sharing and inventing memories	30
171	8	A thousand words	**Vocabulary plus: proverbs** • review proverbs and sayings by finding ways to describe them to a partner • practise speaking skills by exchanging opinions on the proverbs	20–25
172	8	It nearly happened	**Grammar: future in the past** • review forms for talking about the future in the past in the context of true/false statements about plans	25–30
173	8	Nice to meet you	**Grammar: ellipsis and substitution** • review ellipsis and substitution in the context of a questionnaire asking and answering about personal experiences	30
174	8	Solutions	**Functional language: discussing ideas** • practise functional language for giving suggestions and discussing solutions for problems	25–30
175	9	Rave reviews	**Vocabulary: the arts** • review adjectives to describe films, books, etc. • practise speaking skills by asking and answering questions	30
176	9	Questions, questions	**Vocabulary plus: three-part multi-word verbs** • review three-part multi-word verbs by forming questions • practise speaking skills by asking and answering questions	30–40
177	9	Imagine	**Grammar: verb tenses for unreal situations** • review verb tenses for unreal situations in the context of a questionnaire • practise speaking skills by discussing statements	25–30
178	9	How did you do it?	**Grammar: adverbials** • review adverbials by placing them correctly in a partner's sentence	25–30
179	9	Just a minute!	**Functional language: ranting and raving** • practise functional language for speaking enthusiastically or critically about a topic	25–30
180	10	Cross words	**Vocabulary: ambition** • review vocabulary of ambition in the context of a crossword	20–25
181	10	Synonym rummy	**Vocabulary plus: synonyms** • review synonyms for words and phrases in the context of a card game	25–30
182	10	Complaints	**Grammar: inversion** • review inverted forms in the context of a roleplay making and responding to complaints in a hotel	20–25
183	10	The unbelievable truth	**Grammar: comparative structures** • review comparative structures by making statements describing facts and myths	25–30
184	10	Negotiating a documentary	**Functional language: negotiating** • practise functional language for negotiating a deal in a roleplay about making a film	30–40

Worksheet A

1 Read out your sentences for your partner to correct the underlined words.

1 _____ dislikes people from other parts of the country. There's no real reason for it, I think he's/she's just <u>neurotic</u>.

2 _____ is always cleaning the house, even when it's already clean! He's/She's a bit <u>obstinate</u>, I think.

3 _____ is a truly <u>thoughtful</u> person. So many people have gone on to create great things after hearing him/her speak.

4 _____ often has a lot of 'big' ideas, which always end up being too big to work. He's/She's a bit <u>perceptive</u>, I think.

5 _____ always considers and listens to our ideas, even if he/she doesn't agree with them. It's good that he's/she's so <u>insensitive</u>.

6 _____ is naturally <u>conscientious</u>. He's/She's always asking questions about where I've been, things I've bought, etc. I think he's/she's just nosy!

7 _____ is a very <u>rebellious</u> person. He/She always likes being on his/her own, and whenever you invite him/her out, he/she always finds an excuse not to come.

8 _____ is so <u>mature</u> when it comes to studying/working. I sometimes wonder what he's/she's doing in that position if he's/she's not interested!

2 Complete the sentences with the names of people you know outside of the class who the sentences are true for. Share your answers with a partner.

Worksheet B

1 Read out your sentences for your partner to correct the underlined words.

1 _____ is so <u>apathetic</u>. Even when she's/he's clearly wrong, she/he won't change her/his mind!

2 _____ is quite a <u>solitary</u> person. She/he always knows when I'm having a problem, even when I've hidden it well from everyone else.

3 _____ is so <u>obsessive</u>. She's/He's always panicking and thinking there's something wrong with her/his health, at the slightest sign of anything unusual.

4 _____ is very <u>over-ambitious</u> for her/his age. We often have conversations about things I can usually only speak to other adults about.

5 _____ can be really <u>inspirational</u> at times. Whenever she/he sees someone upset, she/he just ignores them.

6 _____ is the kind of person who would take work with them to do on holiday, if it wouldn't get done otherwise. She's/He's really <u>open-minded</u>.

7 _____ often does things just to be 'different', and as a consequence often gets into trouble for it. She's/He's just a <u>prejudiced</u> person, I think.

8 _____ always considers how other people will be affected before making a decision, and always seems to say the right thing. I think she's/he's a really <u>inquisitive</u> person.

2 Complete the sentences with the names of people you know outside of the class who the sentences are true for. Share your answers with a partner.

Worksheet A

1   I never knew he had a wife and two kids. He's such a dark sheep.

2   'Who's that woman in the corner surrounded by people?' 'That's Jane, she's always the life and soul of the ways.'

3   If you want to find out something about anyone at work, ask Paula, she knows everything, she's the office busybox.

4   Don't ask Mike to represent our case to management, he'll just agree with them – he's such a yes-kid.

5   Every time I sit down to try and concentrate, Judith starts chatting to me. She's becoming a right pain in the hand!

Worksheet B

1   Does she ever stop talking? She's such a chatterbody!

2   If you have any questions, you're best off asking Margaret – she's been here for years and she's an old neck.

3   My brother was always getting into trouble when we were younger, he was always the black horse of the family.

4   If you have a problem with your computer, ask John from IT to have a look. He's a real whiz man and will get it working in seconds.

5   I love the new system, it saves me so much time – not like some people here who hate anything different, they're so set in their party.

1 **Write answers to some of these sentences in the shapes below. Choose the shapes at random.**

- a hobby/interest you're thinking of taking up

- something you've been trying to learn for months

- what you were doing when the lesson started today

- someone who's always getting on your nerves

- something in your life which is getting easier

- something nice you're always saying to other people

- where you are thinking of going for your next holiday

- how long you've been studying English

- something you were hoping to borrow from a friend

- what other people in your house/flat were doing when you got home yesterday

- something you were thinking of doing next weekend

- something your teacher is always telling you to do

- a place in your country that's becoming nicer

- what you were doing on your way to class today

- a problem you've been thinking about for a long time

Fold

2 **Look at your partner's answers and guess what they refer to.**

1

FORMER SELVES

Grammar: describing habits

You are hard-working.	**You used to be lazy.**	**You are thoughtful.**
I'll _____	I'd _____	I'll _____
I'm always _____	I was always _____	I'm always _____
I keep _____	I kept _____	I keep _____

You used to be insensitive.	**You are mature.**	**You used to be childish.**
I'd _____	I'll _____	I'd _____
I was always _____	I'm always _____	I was always _____
I kept _____	I keep _____	I kept _____

You are inquisitive.	**You used to be apathetic.**	**You are sociable.**
I'll _____	I'd _____	I'll _____
I'm always _____	I was always _____	I'm always _____
I keep _____	I kept _____	I keep _____

You used to be solitary.	**You are calm.**	**You used to be neurotic.**
I'd _____	I'll _____	I'd _____
I was always _____	I'm always _____	I was always _____
I kept _____	I keep _____	I kept _____

You are interesting.	**You used to be boring.**	**You are conscientious.**
I'll _____	I'd _____	I'll _____
I'm always _____	I was always _____	I'm always _____
I keep _____	I kept _____	I keep _____

You used to be rebellious.	**You are open-minded.**	**You used to be obstinate.**
I'd _____	I'll _____	I'd _____
I was always _____	I'm always _____	I was always _____
I kept _____	I keep _____	I kept _____

138 PHOTOCOPIABLE © Pearson Education Limited 2012

Names	Origins	Meanings
1 Ashlee	Indonesian	*victorious*
2 Alton	Hawaiian	*beautiful*
3 Nadya	Russian	*field of ash trees*
4 Gwendolen	Traditional English	*hope*
5 Boipelo	Tswana (Southern African)	*nobleman*
6 Indah	Modern English	*white ring or bow*
7 Asha	Mongolian	*calm heavens*
8 Tural	Swahili	*old town*
9 Venka	Japanese	*clear mist*
10 Sarangerel	Chinese	*worthy man*
11 Somchai	Thai	*life*
12 Kasumi	Irish	*proud*
13 Zhou	Esperanto	*to be alive*
14 Patrick	Azerbaijani	*boat*
15 Nalani	Welsh	*moonlight*

'ash' is a type of tree in English	'ton' means town in older English	'nadyezhda' means hope in Russian
'gwen' means white in Welsh	a word that begins with 'B' and means proud in an African language	a word that begins with 'I' and means 'beautiful' in a South-East Asian language
a word that begins with 'A' and means 'life' in an African language	a word that begins with 'T' and means 'be alive' in an Asian language	a word that begins with 'V' and means victorious in an invented language
a word that begins with 'S' and means 'moonlight' in an Asian language	a word that begins with 'S' and means 'worthy' man in a South-East Asian language	'sumi' means 'clear' in Japanese
a word that begins with 'Z' and means 'boat' in an Asian language	'Patricius' meant 'nobleman' in Roman, and was later adapted when used in an island country	a word that begins with 'N' and means 'calm heavens' on a group of islands

2

RAGS TO RICHES
Vocabulary: learning and opinions

Worksheet A

1 Work in pairs and put the story in the correct order.

A   She listened while he explained the secret. At first it was so simple, she couldn't believe it and _____ – maybe this old man was mad and she should leave.

B   One day, an elderly man stopped and talked to her. He had a kind face, and gave her some food and money. He explained that he had once been homeless, cold and hungry, just like her, but he _____ someone had given him. Now he was living a comfortable life and had his own house.

C   One day, a woman who worked for a well-known design company visited the market, and noticed Mia's designs. She fell in love with Mia's unique style, and offered her a top design job. Mia proved to be an instant success, and the woman was glad she'd _____ by hiring Mia.

D   She went back to the streets, but this time with hope burning in her heart. Her idea was to create jewellery and ornaments from the things she found on the street. She collected normal, everyday things which most people threw away, and turned them into objects of beauty. Soon, she began selling these in the local market. She remembered the man's secret and _____ .

E   He promised to show her his secret, but said she would need to listen carefully – she would be _____ .

F   Mia was alone, homeless and sad. She'd lost her parents when she was young, run away and was living on the cold, unwelcoming streets. The people who passed her every day were cruel, she always _____ from their comments, they all had the same _____ about homeless people.

2 Use the phrases below in the correct form to complete the gaps in student B's parts of the story.

> have a profound effect on
> learn the ropes   a convincing argument
> believe in yourself
> challenge the stereotypes
> keep an open mind
> from a new perspective

Worksheet B

1 Work in pairs and put the story in the correct order.

G   His words _____ her, and she just wanted to know more.

H   And so Mia became successful, and lived the life she'd always wanted. One day, she was walking along the dark, cold streets, when she saw a young, homeless man, looking lonely and tired. She sat down and said; 'Let me tell you a secret.'
What was that secret?
Always _____ .

I   But the old man insisted she _____ , and so she went on listening. He made such _____ that eventually she began to believe him.

J   They said she was lazy, and should find a job. It was hard to _____ people had, when the city offered almost no opportunities to work for someone sleeping rough.

K   Mia enjoyed the work, even though she didn't make much money. Eventually, she had enough to rent a small apartment and began to see life _____ .

L   They went back to his house, and he poured hot soup into a bowl for her. They talked about many things, then he described his experience to her. He described how he had worked selling newspapers on the street, but because of a secret he had been told, he _____ quickly, and soon moved up to run his own newspaper. He then revealed the secret to her.

2 Use the phrases below in the correct form to complete the gaps in student A's parts of the story.

> on a steep learning curve
> preconceptions   have second thoughts
> never give up   come under attack
> trust her instincts
> take advantage of an opportunity

140 PHOTOCOPIABLE © Pearson Education Limited 2012

Worksheet A

1 Describe your pictures to your partner and write the correct metaphor below each one.

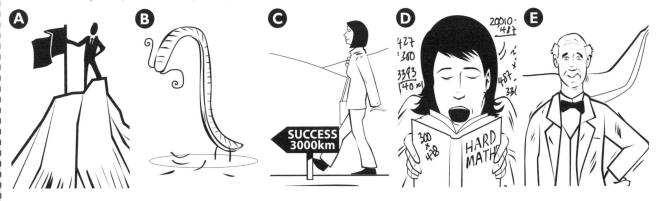

A   B   C   D   E

_____   _____   _____   _____   _____

2 Listen to your partner's descriptions and say the correct metaphor.

a half-baked idea   hard to swallow   find yourself at a crossroads
food for thought   start to go downhill

Worksheet B

1 Listen to your partner's descriptions and say the correct metaphor.

regurgitate   reach the peak of your profession   be over the hill
on its last legs   you'll go far

2 Describe your pictures to your partner and write the correct metaphor below each one.

A   B   C   D   E

_____   _____   _____   _____   _____

3 Work in pairs. Discuss the questions.

1 What ideas have you heard recently that you found hard to swallow?

2 What events beyond your control might cause your career to start to go downhill?

3 Have you ever found yourself at a crossroads? What did you decide to do, and how did you decide?

4 Do you think you'll go far in your career? What will help you do this?

5 What would it mean in real terms to be at the peak of your profession?

6 Can you think of an idea you heard recently that gave you food for thought?

Team B ◄──────►

Team A

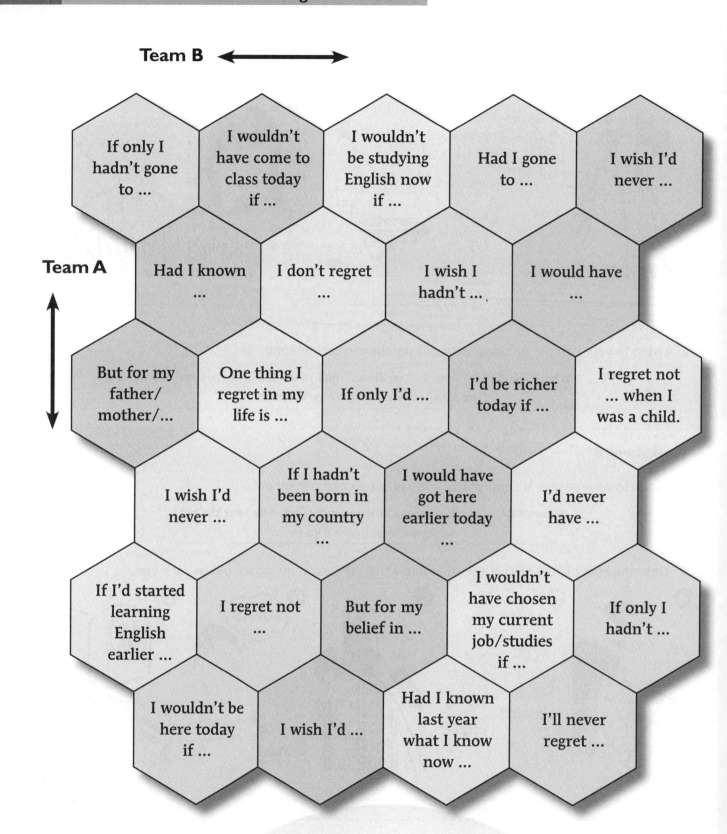

If only I hadn't gone to …

I wouldn't have come to class today if …

I wouldn't be studying English now if …

Had I gone to …

I wish I'd never …

Had I known …

I don't regret …

I wish I hadn't … ,

I would have …

But for my father/mother/…

One thing I regret in my life is …

If only I'd …

I'd be richer today if …

I regret not … when I was a child.

I wish I'd never …

If I hadn't been born in my country …

I would have got here earlier today …

I'd never have …

If I'd started learning English earlier …

I regret not …

But for my belief in …

I wouldn't have chosen my current job/studies if …

If only I hadn't …

I wouldn't be here today if …

I wish I'd …

Had I known last year what I know now …

I'll never regret …

	My answer	Classmate 1	Classmate 2
1 a place you recall _____ when you were very young			
2 something you often worry about _____ when you go out			
3 something you love _____ on a Sunday			
4 something you never fail _____ every morning when you wake up			
5 _____ happy, for me, is about …			
6 something you are determined _____ this year			
7 something you would like _____ by the time you are 60			
8 something you would like the opportunity _____ for the first time			
9 something other people always have to remind you _____			
10 an emotion you find it hard to admit to _____ in front of others			
11 something you are embarrassed _____ to other people			
12 something you enjoy _____ in class			
13 where you expect _____ this time next year			
14 a place you want _____ by the time you are 60			
15 something you can't stand _____ at the weekend			

lose   experience   visit x 2   say   feel   do x 5   achieve x 2   be x 2

Worksheet A

1 Think of two reasons why someone might <u>agree</u> with each of the statements below.
  They do not necessarily need to represent your true opinions.

Statement	Reason 1	Reason 2
1 Politicians should receive high salaries.		
2 The internet is a reliable source of information.		
3 Newspapers should always be impartial.		
4 Access to information is a basic human right.		
5 Teachers should always pay equal attention to all their students.		
6 Rich people should always pay more tax.		
7 War is always wrong.		
8 Education should be free for everyone.		

2 Argue the case <u>for</u> each of the statements with student B.

Worksheet B

1 Think of two reasons why someone might <u>disagree</u> with each of the statements below.
  They do not necessarily need to represent your true opinions.

Statement	Reason 1	Reason 2
1 Politicians should receive high salaries.		
2 The internet is a reliable source of information.		
3 Newspapers should always be impartial.		
4 Access to information is a basic human right.		
5 Teachers should always pay equal attention to all their students.		
6 Rich people should always pay more tax.		
7 War is always wrong.		
8 Education should be free for everyone.		

2 Argue the case <u>against</u> each of the statements with student A.

Crossword A

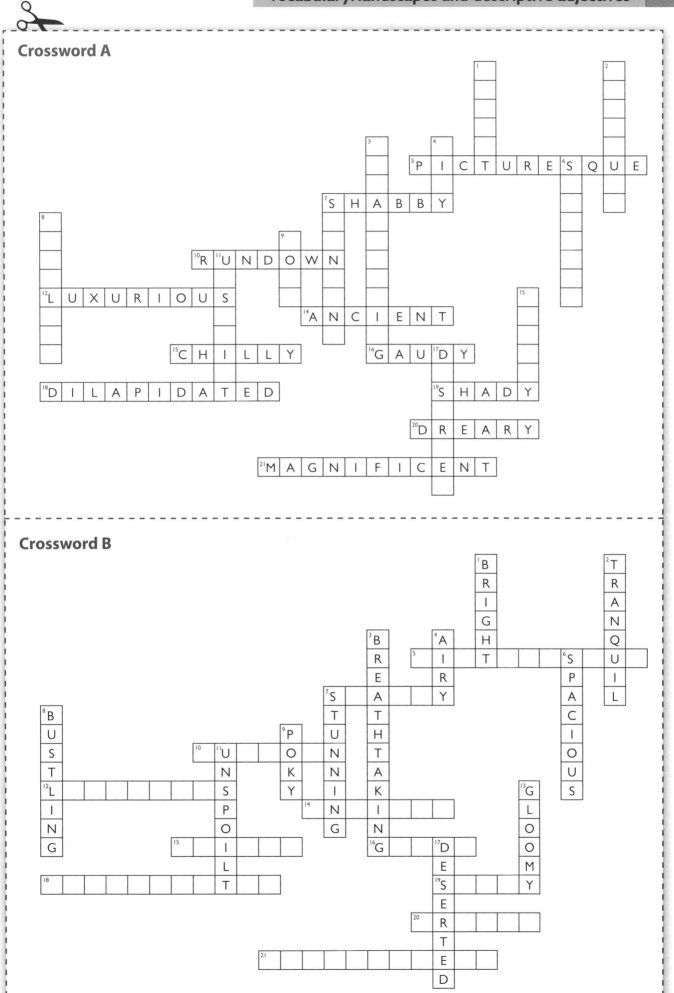

5 PICTURESQUE
7 SHABBY
10 RUNDOWN
12 LUXURIOUS
14 ANCIENT
15 CHILLY
16 GAUDY
18 DILAPIDATED
19 SHADY
20 DREARY
21 MAGNIFICENT

Crossword B

1 BRIGHT
2 TRANQUIL
3 BREATHTAKING
4 AIRY
5 IT
6 SPACIOUS
7 STUNNING
8 BUSTLING
9 POKY
11 UNSPOILT
13 GLOOMY
16 G
17 DESERTED
19 S

Worksheet A

1 Read out your sentences for your partner to complete.

1 When I was young I used to _____ a lot at school. I was always getting into trouble!

2 The history of my country is very _____ . It seems nothing exciting has ever happened there!

3 In my country there are a lot of _____ organisations which help the poorest people.

4 In the future I plan to study for a _____ degree.

5 I think a lot of football players these days behave _____ in their private lives. They should set a good example for children both on and off the pitch.

6 I think it's very important to be _____ in your work. You can't just wait for opportunities to come about on their own.

7 I think that nowadays we _____ the importance of celebrities in society. They're not as important as we make them out to be.

8 Many parts of my hometown have started to _____ in recent years – in some places the buildings are falling apart.

2 Which sentences are true for you? Discuss with your partner.

Prefixes

pre-	under-	non-	im-
anti-	mal-	ir-	un-

Words

conformist   reversible
eventful   polite   statement
nutrition   government   date

Worksheet B

1 Read out your sentences for your partner to complete.

1 To say my country has had an interesting history would be an _____ . It's had quite a colourful past!

2 I think it's important to be _____ . You shouldn't just be like everyone else.

3 One of the biggest problems in my country these days is _____ , mainly because there aren't enough different types of food available.

4 Some of the damage we have caused to the world through pollution is _____ . We may never be able to go back to how things were in the past.

5 There are some very old cities in my country. They even _____ the Roman Empire.

6 There have been several _____ protests in my country in recent years.

7 My life has been very _____ recently. Nothing worth talking about has happened to me!

8 I really hate _____ people. Manners don't hurt, and they don't cost anything!

2 Which sentences are true for you? Discuss with your partner.

Prefixes

ir-	un-	over-	pro-	mis-
post-	non-	de-		

Words

behave   active
governmental   generate
interesting   estimate
graduate   responsibly

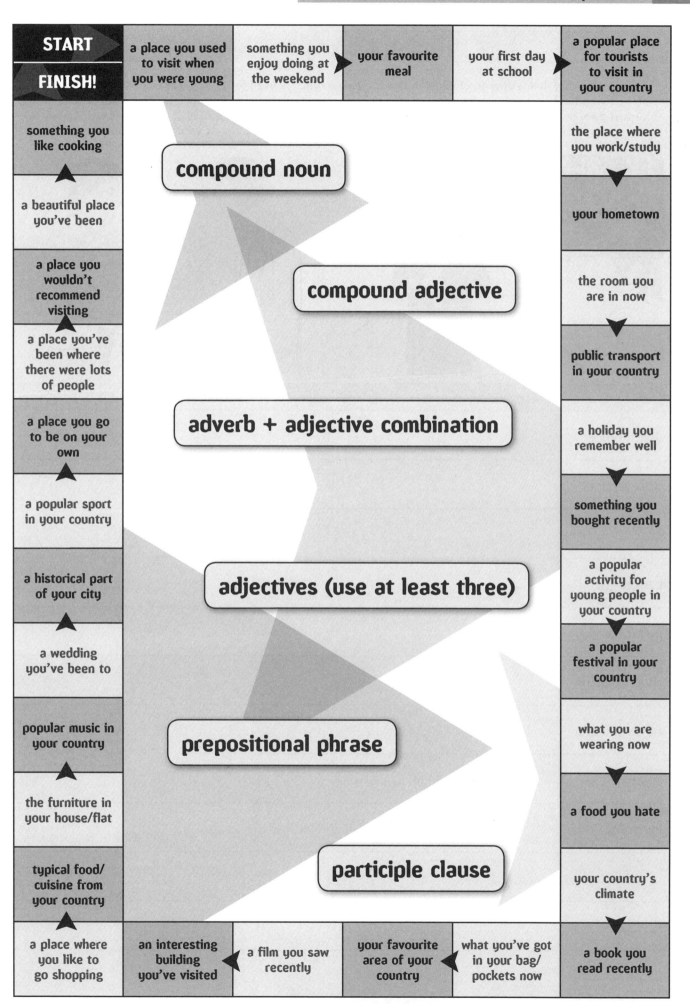

START

FINISH!

a place you used to visit when you were young

something you enjoy doing at the weekend

your favourite meal

your first day at school

a popular place for tourists to visit in your country

something you like cooking

a beautiful place you've been

a place you wouldn't recommend visiting

a place you've been where there were lots of people

a place you go to be on your own

a popular sport in your country

a historical part of your city

a wedding you've been to

popular music in your country

the furniture in your house/flat

typical food/ cuisine from your country

a place where you like to go shopping

the place where you work/study

your hometown

the room you are in now

public transport in your country

a holiday you remember well

something you bought recently

a popular activity for young people in your country

a popular festival in your country

what you are wearing now

a food you hate

your country's climate

an interesting building you've visited

a film you saw recently

your favourite area of your country

what you've got in your bag/ pockets now

a book you read recently

compound noun

compound adjective

adverb + adjective combination

adjectives (use at least three)

prepositional phrase

participle clause

Clauses

... some/all/a few/none of which ...	... a thing which is used for ... ... at which point ...
... who have to ... ... who are ... ... which is ...	... none of whom ... ... that they use ...
... most people that ... ... where you can find ...	... it can be anywhere that ... ... where they visit ...
... at/on/in which they sit every day ...	... that they use for ... ... who they work for ...

Job	Description
police officer	
web designer	
pilot	
banker	
politician	
shop assistant	
office manager	
actor	
journalist	
_____	
_____	
_____	

The _____ Project

Background information (current situation, problems, why it's needed):

Overall purpose of the project:

Main changes and stages of the project (could include a picture here):

Main benefits:

1 _____

2 _____

3 _____

4 _____

Closing statement:

Manifesto for the _____ Party

1	human	immigration
2	child	development
3	economic	control
4	intellectual	punishment
5	capital	rights
6	religious	labour
7	environmental	trade
8	illegal	speech
9	civil	freedom
10	free	awareness
11	freedom of	liberties
12	gun	property

Our four main issues:

1 _____

2 _____

3 _____

4 _____

If elected, we plan to:

1 _____

2 _____

3 _____

4 _____

5 _____

6 _____

7 _____

8 _____

9 _____

10 _____

11 _____

12 _____

A wasn't even in the vicinity	F has previous convictions
B protested their innocence	G fresh evidence came to light
C placed him under arrest	H was brought to justice
D escape justice	I breaking into a school at the time
E he had the perfect alibi	J a security camera shop

1 Listen to your partner's chunks and write them in the correct places in the stories below.

Poor dog

A woman in Florida **1** _____ after a surveillance video showed she'd trained her children to steal a puppy.

The best place to steal from?

Two burglars in Texas still **2** _____ after being caught on security camera, stealing from **3** _____ .

Solid evidence

One Belgian man thought **4** _____ when he was suspected of robbing a jewellery store. He said he **5** _____ as he was busy **6** _____ . The police promptly **7** _____ for the new crime.

A guilty conscience

A man who stole a road sign in England was cautioned by the police after **8** _____ . He had felt guilty and taken it to the police station.

Discounts galore

A woman in the USA who used a stolen credit card to pay for groceries, didn't **9** _____ as she made the mistake of also using her own discount card. She also **10** _____ for fraud.

2 Work in pairs. Discuss the questions.

1 Which crime was the most stupid? Which was the worst?
2 Do you know of any other 'stupid' crimes?
3 What should the punishments be for the crimes above?

Worksheet A

1   Read out your sentence starters for your partner to complete.

1   I really hate it when I hold a door open …

2   It's often said that people from my country …

3   It's no wonder that people who've had a bad upbringing …

4   It rains a lot in my country …

5   It appears that the more I study English grammar, …

6   It always amazes me when I read about how some people …

7   I think it's important …

8   It's pointless for me to try and remember …

2   Listen to your partner's sentence starters and complete them with the correct phrase below.

A   going for a walk.

B   new vocabulary.

C   over in the street.

D   it helps to be in an English-speaking country.

E   on Sunday.

F   is increasing in my country.

G   to my house/flat.

H   I thought I'd failed!

3   Do you agree with the sentences? Why (not)? Discuss with your partner.

Worksheet B

1   Listen to your partner's sentence starters and complete them with the correct phrase below.

A   are warm.

B   people's birthdays – I always forget!

C   for people and they don't say 'thank you'.

D   to remember people's names.

E   often become criminals.

F   the less I understand!

G   survive natural disasters.

H   in April.

2   Read out your sentence starters for your partner to complete.

1   I find it easy to learn …

2   I couldn't believe it when I passed the last exam I took – …

3   It's not far from my English school …

4   When it's sunny, I like …

5   I always find it funny when I see people fall …

6   When learning English, …

7   It's a shame we can't have English classes …

8   It's been reported that crime …

3   Do you agree with the sentences? Why (not)? Discuss with your partner.

Name		Details
1 _____	hopes (learn) something new by the end of the year.	
2 _____	(meet) a famous person.	
3 _____	(think) about what he/she was going to have for dinner tonight when he/she started this activity.	
4 _____	(meet) the teacher before he/she joined this class.	
5 _____	(work) for 20 years by 2020.	
6 _____	(finish) reading a book by the end of the month.	
7 _____	(work) really hard recently.	
8 _____	(learn) a lot of new vocabulary this week.	
9 _____	(dream) about something nice when they woke up this morning.	
10 _____	(study) English for more than ten years by the end of this year.	
11 _____	expects (achieve) something important by the end of next year.	
12 _____	(just, eat) something when the class started today.	
13 _____	(think) about the future a lot recently.	
14 _____	(make) more than five phone calls by the end of the day.	
15 _____	(know) their best friend since they were very young.	

Your friend has a 15-year-old son. Walking home one night you see him in the park with a group of friends, painting graffiti on a wall.	Leaving the supermarket in a hurry to get back to work, you accidentally hit a parked car. You have only scratched the paint a little.	Working late one night, you see a colleague stealing stationery from a supply cupboard.	You see a T-shirt you really like in a shop, and it's very cheap. You know that the company who makes this T-shirt treats their workers very badly.
Checking your bank account, you realise the bank has made a mistake and there is more money in your account than you should have.	Visiting a family in another country, you are offered a food that you really don't like. You know this food is very expensive and you will appear rude if you don't eat it.	You are robbed on holiday and fill out your insurance form stating that your camera was stolen. You later find your camera in another bag.	Paying for something in a supermarket, the shop assistant gives you too much change.
A close friend asks you to lie in court and say they were with you when a crime happened. They weren't with you at the time.	A friend who you work with is going for promotion. You know he/she really wants the job. Your boss offers you the promotion instead.	You are a doctor. Your colleague, another doctor, asks you to write them a prescription for a drug 'to help them relax'.	You borrow your partner's laptop. While using it, an instant message program pops up and someone says 'Hi gorgeous'.
Your friend gives you a lift and crashes their car. While waiting for the police to arrive, he/she asks you to say you were driving, as they already have a record and will lose their licence.	You're cooking dinner for friends, and you've spent four hours making the dish. At the last minute, while your guests are waiting, you drop the food on the floor.	It's your friend's birthday, and you've forgotten to get them a present. When you left your last job (where you worked with the same friend), you were given an mp3 player that you didn't want as you already had a better one.	You're at a party, and someone starts talking to you – it's clear they know who you are. You can't remember their name (or where you know them from), but you're sure you've met them before.
You find a large amount of money in the street.	You travel home on the same train from work every day. Because you work late, there are never any ticket inspectors to check your ticket at the station.	A friend gives you a 'hot tip' that the company they work for is about to launch a successful new product, and offers you shares in the company.	You see someone shoplifting in a supermarket.

keep yourself to yourself	behind closed doors	between you and me	give the game away
let it slip	spill the beans	stay schtum	let the cat out of the bag
conventional wisdom	a commonly held perception	a fallacy	uncover the truth
verify	intuitively true	debunk a myth	disprove a myth
keep a secret	your innermost thoughts	keep it quiet	divulge a secret
forgive someone	reveal the truth	in confidence	speak openly

a room in your house/flat which needs brightening up _____	the last thing you switch off before you go to bed at night _____	what you would do to jazz up your classroom _____	something you might pore over when doing research _____
something you've been mulling over recently _____	a reason you might hang around the classroom after the lesson has finished _____	something you'd like to find out about your teacher _____	something the government should crack down on in your country _____
a piece of news you heard recently which blew you away _____	a time in your life you always have good memories of _____	an event that you were planning to go to but it was called off _____	a tradition in your country you would like to carry on _____
something you like doing when you're messing around at home _____	an old TV programme you would like to see them bring back _____	the thing that you put away most recently at home _____	a famous person you think should slow down and be less crazy _____
something you do to keep on using English outside class _____	a crime you would speak out against _____	something you need to think over at the moment _____	the last plan you made where you had to cry off _____

General advice	Past mistakes
1 Starting a new job You ought to _____ . You don't need to _____ . You'd better (not) _____ . _____ is allowed. You can _____ . You're (not) supposed to _____ .	**1 You lied to someone about something important and they found out.** I should never have _____ . I had to _____ . I didn't have the courage to _____ . I couldn't _____ . I needn't have _____ . I was forced to _____ .
2 Starting a family You ought to _____ . You don't need to _____ . You'd better (not) _____ . _____ is allowed. You can _____ . You're (not) supposed to _____ .	**2 You let a close friend's secret slip. Now everyone knows and he's/she's upset.** I should never have _____ . I had to _____ . I didn't have the courage to _____ . I couldn't _____ . I needn't have _____ . I was forced to _____ .
3 Getting on with your English teacher You ought to _____ . You don't need to _____ . You'd better (not) _____ . _____ is allowed. You can _____ . You're (not) supposed to _____ .	**3 You left something important on a plane and can't get it back.** I should never have _____ . I had to _____ . I didn't have the courage to _____ . I couldn't _____ . I needn't have _____ . I was forced to _____ .
4 Situation: _____ You ought to _____ . You don't need to _____ . You'd better (not) _____ . _____ is allowed. You can _____ . You're (not) supposed to _____ .	**4 Situation:** _____ I should never have _____ . I had to _____ . I didn't have the courage to _____ . I couldn't _____ . I needn't have _____ . I was forced to _____ .
5 Situation: _____ You ought to _____ . You don't need to _____ . You'd better (not) _____ . _____ is allowed. You can _____ . You're (not) supposed to _____ .	**5 Situation:** _____ I should never have _____ . I had to _____ . I didn't have the courage to _____ . I couldn't _____ . I needn't have _____ . I was forced to _____ .

1 Danish pastries (originally make) in Denmark.	2 Meteorites (cool) when they enter the Earth's atmosphere.	3 Bats (born) blind.	4 Coffee (make) from beans.
False – they actually originated in Austria.	**True** – they are cool inside, and the outer layer burns off.	**False** – they actually have good eyesight, they just use their hearing more.	**False** – coffee 'beans' are actually seeds.
5 Before Christopher Columbus travelled to America, it (already think) that the Earth was round.	6 The red juice that (often find) in uncooked red meat is blood.	7 The Sun is white, but (see) as yellow through the atmosphere.	8 By 2024, a permanent base (build) on the moon by NASA.
True – people knew the Earth was round, but miscalculated the distance to India.	**False** – it's actually meat 'juice' – this is why you don't see blood in white meat.	**True.**	**True.**
9 Body temperature (lower) by alcohol.	10 Milk and dairy products should (avoid) by a person with a cold or flu.	11 Sleepwalkers (not harm) by (wake up).	12 The same place (never strike) by lightning twice.
True – alcohol causes blood vessels to move to the skin which makes you feel warm, but actually makes you colder.	**False** – milk and dairy products do not increase mucus production and so don't make a cold worse.	**True** – conversely, sleepwalkers can injure themselves by hitting furniture.	**False** – The Empire State Building is struck by lightning around 100 times a year.
13 The car (invent) by Henry Ford.	14 The universe (create) in an explosion.	15 English (speak) by most people in the world.	16 Alcohol remains in food when (cook).
False – though he was one of the first to mass-produce them.	**False** – it was a sudden expansion, but not an explosion.	**False** – Mandarin Chinese is the world's most spoken language.	**True** – not all of it evaporates.
17 Different tastes can (detect) on all parts of the tongue – not only on certain parts.	18 Damaged hair can (not repair) by shampoo.	19 No scientist (ever kill) because of their scientific opinions.	20 The world (not affect) by climate change until some time in the distant future.
True.	**True** – though it can help prevent damage.	**True** – as far as scientific historians know.	**False** – climate change is already occurring now.

Student A

You are part of the government, involved in a discussion about whether to change the freedom of speech laws in your country. In a recent court case, a newspaper was brought to court accused of tapping celebrities' phone lines. Several celebrities were involved, and the newspaper was fined heavily. The newspaper stated in their defence that they should be able to use whatever means possible to find out information, in accordance with freedom of speech.

You represent the Freedom Party. Your members strongly believe that the public has a right to know what celebrities get up to in private, and want the law to safeguard the rights of newspapers in obtaining information using whatever means possible. Before you begin the discussion, plan your reasons below:

Reason 1 _____ .

Reason 2 _____ .

Reason 3 _____ .

Student B

You are part of the government, involved in a discussion about whether to change the freedom of speech laws in your country. In a recent court case, a newspaper was brought to court accused of tapping celebrities' phone lines. Several celebrities were involved, and the newspaper was fined heavily. The newspaper stated in their defence that they should be able to use whatever means possible to find out information, in accordance with freedom of speech.

You represent the Privacy Party. While you believe freedom of speech is important, you believe that it doesn't apply to journalists who report on celebrities' private lives. You want the new law to safeguard people's right to privacy in their private lives. Before you begin the discussion, plan your reasons below:

Reason 1 _____ .

Reason 2 _____ .

Reason 3 _____ .

Student C

You are part of the government, involved in a discussion about whether to change the freedom of speech laws in your country. In a recent court case, a newspaper was brought to court accused of tapping celebrities' phone lines. Several celebrities were involved, and the newspaper was fined heavily. The newspaper stated in their defence that they should be able to use whatever means possible to find out information, in accordance with freedom of speech.

You represent the Balance Party. While you think freedom of speech for journalists is important, you also believe that people (including celebrities) have the right to a private life. Before you discuss the case with the other students in your group, think of reasons for each side's arguments below:

A law which grants newspapers absolute freedom:

Reason 1 _____ .

Reason 2 _____ .

A law which protects the privacy of celebrities:

Reason 1 _____ .

Reason 2 _____ .

Worksheet A

1 Use the words in the box and read out your sentence starters for your partner to complete.

days	explosion	signs	bound	gather	distant	thing

I The _____ are that English will no longer …

2 Medical research is _____ to …

3 Changes in technology will _____ …

4 The _____ of the USA being the world's most powerful …

5 Nuclear power will become a _____ of …

6 There will be an _____ …

7 Using a mouse and keyboard will become a _____ …

2 Listen to your partner's sentence starters and complete them with the correct phrase below.

A   common at home and at work.

B   the past.

C   30 million+ will be common.

D   global languages.

E   memory.

F   new forms of diseases/viruses.

G   in the frequency of natural disasters.

3 Do you agree with the sentences? Why (not)? Discuss with your partner.

Worksheet B

1 Listen to your partner's sentence starters and complete them with the correct phrase below.

A   country are over.

B   memory.

C   be the 'Lingua Franca'.

D   pace.

E   the past.

F   find a cure for cancer.

G   in personalised space travel.

2 Use the words in the box and read out your sentence starters for your partner to complete.

point	well	explosion	signs	likely	distant	thing

I Spanish or Mandarin Chinese may _____ become …

2 Robots are _____ to become more …

3 The figures _____ to an increase …

4 Religion will become a _____ of …

5 There will be an _____ in …

6 War will become a _____ …

7 The _____ are that cities of …

3 Do you agree with the sentences? Why (not)? Discuss with your partner.

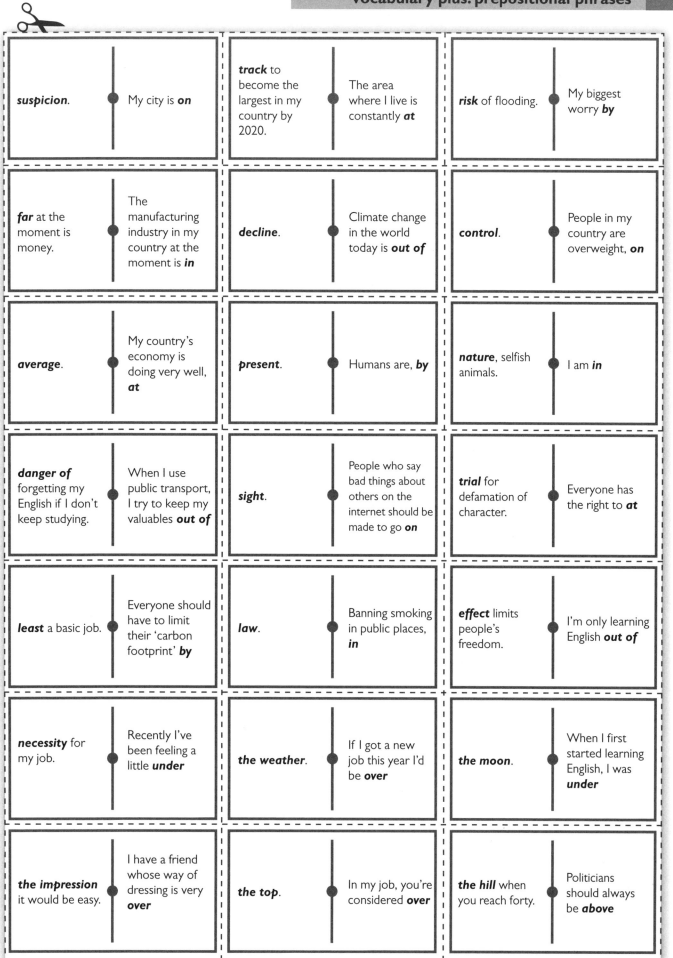

suspicion.	My city is **on**	*track* to become the largest in my country by 2020.	The area where I live is constantly **at**	*risk* of flooding.	My biggest worry **by**
far at the moment is money.	The manufacturing industry in my country at the moment is **in**	*decline*.	Climate change in the world today is **out of**	*control*.	People in my country are overweight, **on**
average.	My country's economy is doing very well, **at**	*present*.	Humans are, **by**	*nature*, selfish animals.	I am **in**
danger of forgetting my English if I don't keep studying.	When I use public transport, I try to keep my valuables **out of**	*sight*.	People who say bad things about others on the internet should be made to go **on**	*trial* for defamation of character.	Everyone has the right to **at**
least a basic job.	Everyone should have to limit their 'carbon footprint' **by**	*law*.	Banning smoking in public places, **in**	*effect* limits people's freedom.	I'm only learning English **out of**
necessity for my job.	Recently I've been feeling a little **under**	*the weather*.	If I got a new job this year I'd be **over**	*the moon*.	When I first started learning English, I was **under**
the impression it would be easy.	I have a friend whose way of dressing is very **over**	*the top*.	In my job, you're considered **over**	*the hill* when you reach forty.	Politicians should always be **above**

		Details
1 _____	thinks he/she (live) in another country this time next year.	
2 _____	thinks his/her country (do) well in the next World Cup.	
3 _____	(study) another language next year.	
4 _____	(get) married by the end of the decade.	
5 _____	's government (make) an important announcement soon.	
6 _____	(go) somewhere nice at the weekend.	
7 _____	's favourite TV programme (start) before they arrive home.	
8 _____	(definitely arrive) home late tonight.	
9 _____	's birthday (be) next month.	
10 _____	(go) to the supermarket on their way home tonight.	
11 _____	(have) lunch/dinner with friends this week.	
12 _____	(complete) an important project by the end of the year.	
13 _____	thinks he/she (probably travel) somewhere nice in the near future.	
14 _____	(still study) English this time next year.	
15 _____	(go) out tonight.	
16 _____	(definitely sleep) well tonight.	

Worksheet A

1 **You start. Read out sentence A to student B, then choose the correct sentence and concession clause to continue the 'duel'.**

   A I am excellent at English grammar.

   B That may well be true. N_____ , my English is better than yours.

   C Much a_____ I appreciate your use of these phrases, I feel that being able to speak fluently is more important.

   D Even t_____ you have a good English accent, I can use concession clauses like a native speaker.

2 **Use the starters below and concession clauses to 'duel' with student B. Add two ideas of your own.**

   1 I can drive really well.

   2 My country has a brilliant football/rugby/(other sport) team.

   3 I can speak three languages.

   4 _____ .

   5 _____ .

Worksheet B

1 **Student A starts. Listen to their first sentence, then choose the correct sentence and concession clause to continue the 'duel'.**

   E D_____ the fact that fluency is important, you can't express yourself without being accurate.

   F W_____ your grammar is good, my pronunciation is excellent.

   G Important t_____ concession clauses are, it's better to know prepositional phrases, like me.

   H Hmm, let's just agree to disagree!

2 **Use the starters below and concession clauses to 'duel' with student A. Add two ideas of your own.**

   1 I can sing really well.

   2 I've got lots of friends.

   3 I'm very good at Maths.

   4 _____ .

   5 _____ .

Worksheet A

1 **You start. Read out sentence A to student B, then choose the correct sentence and concession clause to continue the 'duel'.**

   A I am excellent at English grammar.

   B That may well be true. N_____ , my English is better than yours.

   C Much a_____ I appreciate your use of these phrases, I feel that being able to speak fluently is more important.

   D Even t_____ you have a good English accent, I can use concession clauses like a native speaker.

2 **Use the starters below and concession clauses to 'duel' with student B. Add two ideas of your own.**

   1 I can drive really well.

   2 My country has a brilliant football/rugby/(other sport) team.

   3 I can speak three languages.

   4 _____ .

   5 _____ .

Worksheet B

1 **Student A starts. Listen to their first sentence, then choose the correct sentence and concession clause to continue the 'duel'.**

   E D_____ the fact that fluency is important, you can't express yourself without being accurate.

   F W_____ your grammar is good, my pronunciation is excellent.

   G Important t_____ concession clauses are, it's better to know prepositional phrases, like me.

   H Hmm, let's just agree to disagree!

2 **Use the starters below and concession clauses to 'duel' with student A. Add two ideas of your own.**

   1 I can sing really well.

   2 I've got lots of friends.

   3 I'm very good at Maths.

   4 _____ .

   5 _____ .

electronic music	terrorism	climate change	human rights
advances in medical science	the internet	T-shirts	computer games
Coca-Cola®	space exploration	physics	smart phones
an ageing population	personal computers	fast food	modern farming techniques
cheap flights	high-heeled shoes	the electric guitar	downloading music
blogs	unemployment	radio	reality TV

16 You t_____ r_____ in an abandoned house.

Miss a turn.

FREE SQUARE

17 You are spotted by the border guards, but f_____ from their lights.

Go forward one square.

18 Decide which country you would like to e_____ to.

FREEDOM!

15 People think you are acting s_____ and call the police.

14 In a forest you decide you can t_____ i_____ e_____ .

Go back one square.

3 You h_____ an escape plan.

Move forward one square.

FREE SQUARE

4 When your plan is ready you m_____ a b_____ for it.

Move forward one square.

5 Describe how you like to l_____ y_____ h_____ d_____ at the weekend.

FREE SQUARE

2 Describe a time when you have felt t_____ in a situation.

6 Running away is hard work, so you stop to h_____ a b_____ .

Move back one square.

13 Describe what you do to s_____ o_____ in the evening.

Miss a turn.

1 After your appeal fails, the authorities decide you will never be r_____ .

Move back one square.

START

FREE SQUARE

12 Local people recognise you, but you manage to e_____ .

Go forward one square.

7 You reach the local village, which seems safe, so you decide to h_____ o_____ there for a while.

Miss a turn.

11 Stop at a café to t_____ y_____ m_____ o_____ the escape.

Go back one square.

FREE SQUARE

10 Trying to cross a river, you become s_____ on a small island.

Go back two squares.

9 After days on the run you're tired and need to s_____ d_____ .

Go back one square.

8 Describe things that you like to do to u_____ .

FREE SQUARE

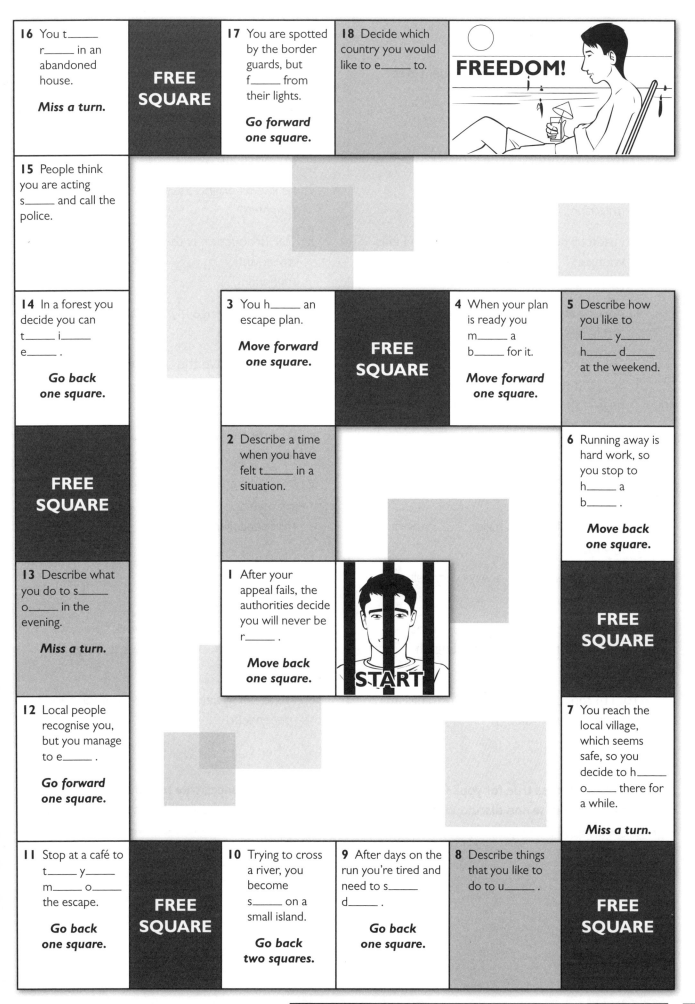

Worksheet A

1 **Read out your sentences for student B to complete.**

1 I would never emigr_____ – I like my country too much.
(emigrate)

2 I'd love to be a famous music_____ .
(musician)

3 I used to be quite rebel_____ when I was younger.
(rebellious)

4 My language is suppos_____ difficult for foreigners to learn.
(supposedly)

5 Sometimes when I don't understand an English speaker, I pretend I do to avoid embarrass_____ .
(embarrassment)

6 Lone_____ is a problem in big cities.
(Loneliness)

7 I don't like films which glor_____ violence.
(glorify)

8 I have a friend who's always very help_____ .
(helpful)

9 Accur_____ of grammar is the most important thing when using English.
(Accuracy)

10 I'm cap_____ of doing many things at once (multi-tasking).
(capable)

2 **Are the sentences true for you? Correct the ones that are false and discuss with student B.**

Worksheet B

1 **Read out your sentences for student A to complete.**

1 I have no recollect_____ of my life before I was five years old.
(recollection)

2 I'd like to bright_____ up our classroom.
(brighten)

3 Car production is the dom_____ industry in my country.
(dominant)

4 I'd like to change my appear_____ .
(appearance)

5 I'd love to have the opport_____ to visit Antarctica.
(opportunity)

6 I'd hate to be an account_____ .
(accountant)

7 Things in my country have changed dramatic_____ over the last twenty years.
(dramatically)

8 My country has an extens_____ rail network.
(extensive)

9 When you have a lot of work to do, it's best to priori_____ the easiest things first.
(prioritise)

10 I hate being depend_____ on other people.
(dependent)

2 **Are the sentences true for you? Correct the ones that are false and discuss with student A.**

Worksheet A

1 Read about the two famous escapes below.

The Tower of London
Under the reign of Elizabeth I, in 16th-century England, Catholics were persecuted, and priests were often captured and imprisoned. One such priest was John Gerard, who was arrested in 1594 for his missionary work. He was eventually sent to the Tower of London, where he was cruelly tortured and later sentenced to death. One night, in 1597, a friend managed to throw a rope to him in his tower, and he made a break for it. Despite his hands being very badly injured from the torture, he was able to climb down and escape. He later fled to Rome, where he spent the rest of his life.

Libby Prison
Libby Prison was one of the most infamous of the jails used to hold captured Union soldiers during the US civil war. On the night of 9th February, 1864, over 100 prisoners, led by Colonel Rose and Major Hamilton, managed to escape by tunnelling through the prison's cellar. The cellar was known as 'Rat Hell' by the inmates, because of the number of rats that lived in this dark, unforgiving place. Of the 109 escapees, two drowned, 48 were recaptured, and 59 reached the safety of Union lines. It was considered the most successful escape of the US civil war.

2 Ask your partner the questions below about their text and write the answers using cleft sentences with *what* or *it*.

1 Was Alcatraz used as a factory?

_____

2 Were petty criminals held at Alcatraz?

_____

3 Did the three prisoners use heavy industrial equipment to cut the walls?

_____

4 Did the three prisoners escape by helicopter?

_____

5 Did the soldiers escape on Christmas Day?

_____

6 Did the soldiers use ropes to escape from the prisoner-of-war camp?

_____

7 Were the soldiers caught because the tunnels were too long?

_____

8 Was the 70th prisoner seen by a guard?

_____

3 Discuss with student B. Which escape do you think was the easiest/most daring/riskiest/cleverest?

Worksheet B

1 Read about the two famous escapes below.

Alcatraz
Alcatraz prison was a high security US federal prison located on Alcatraz island in San Francisco Bay. It was used to hold the most serious criminals from 1933–1963. In 1961, three inmates, Frank Morris and John and Clarence Anglin, hatched an escape plan. They spent months making very simple tools, and by late May 1962 they had cut through the walls of their cells. They then climbed a ventilation shaft to the roof, made their way down the outside of the building, and quickly assembled a raft to cross the bay to the mainland. Their escape wasn't discovered until the morning, as they'd used soap, toilet paper and hair to make 'dummies' which they put in their beds. The trio have never been caught, though it is thought they drowned in the bay.

The Great Escape
This famous escape gets its name from the scale of the operation and the risk, planning and sheer daring involved. 76 soldiers escaped from a prisoner-of-war camp on 24th March 1944. Their escape was the result of a year's work, involving 600 prisoners, and via three tunnels dug 30 feet below the camp. Unfortunately, they underestimated the distance to the nearby forest and the 77th prisoner was seen by the guards. Most of the escapees were later recaptured – only three made it to safety – but the bravery of the soldiers was remarkable.

2 Ask your partner the questions below about their text and write the answers using cleft sentences with *what* or *it*.

1 Did Elizabeth I escape from the Tower of London?

_____

2 Was John Gerard arrested for burglary?

_____

3 Did John Gerard use a ladder to escape?

_____

4 After he escaped, was John Gerard captured and tortured?

_____

5 Were Confederate soldiers held in Libby Prison?

_____

6 Did Colonel Rose and Major Hamilton take control of the local town?

_____

7 Did snakes live in the prison cellar?

_____

8 Did 109 prisoners escape by jumping out of the windows?

_____

3 Discuss with student A. Which escape do you think was the easiest/most daring/riskiest/cleverest?

Walking carefully …

… and knowing he/she …

Not wanting to appear afraid …

Relieved, …

Exhausted …

… resulting in …

Having _____ , …

Moving quickly …

Having finished early, …

… the _____ burning in the distance …

Not knowing what to expect …

Surprised at what he/she saw, …

Charmed by _____ , he/she …

Feeling cautious, …

Realising what had happened, …

Not wanting to seem rude, …

… satisfied that he'd/she'd done her best. …

Thrilled by the thought of _____ , he/she …

The man/woman smiling at him/her was …

Crying with joy, …

The man/woman holding the _____ was …

Not being _____ , …

Knowing what was to come, …

Feeling eyes staring at him/her, …

Men are better drivers than women.

Women can 'multi-task'. Men can't.

Voting in elections should be compulsory.

Sportsmen and women receive too much money.

Climate change is the world's most serious problem.

Capital punishment is a good way to punish serious crimes.

All guns should be banned.

Children should learn more useful subjects in schools.

Everyone should pay less tax.

Politicians never tell the truth.

Classical music is the best music that has ever been written.

People who live in cities shouldn't drive big cars.

Student A	**Student B**	**Student C**	**Student D**
You are the initiator. Begin each discussion by agreeing with the statement on the slip.	Disagree with everything anyone else in the group says, unless they agree with you.	Be as 'controversial' as possible, making statements which you think will shock the other people in the group.	Keep changing your opinion during each discussion.

a TV programme from your childhood	a place you went on holiday	a smell	a piece of music
an item of clothing	a toy	a surprise	a party you went to
one of your birthdays	your first day at school	a journey	starting to learn English
a member/ friend of your family	someone you went to school with	an argument	a time when you felt sad
a food	a teacher	a book you read	the first time you rode a bike
a game you played	a special place	your first mobile phone	a time when you felt proud

Worksheet A

1 Describe each proverb/saying to your partner but do not use the words in italics.
  Your partner will try and guess the proverb/saying.

Actions speak louder than words *do – say – promise – never*	Nothing ventured, nothing gained *try – like – scared – careful*
Absence makes the heart grow fonder *miss – away – gone – close*	Better safe than sorry *careful – dangerous – try –risky*
There's no place like home *live – house – best – away*	Practice makes perfect *try – again – repeat – until*

Worksheet B

1 Describe each proverb/saying to your partner but do not use the words in italics.
  Your partner will try and guess the proverb/saying.

Rome wasn't built in a day *slow – fast – progress – time*	Don't judge a book by its cover *thought – but – actually – very*
A picture is worth a thousand words *represent – show – see – express*	Home is where the heart is *house – live – place – family*
Practise what you preach *do – say – same – actions*	Out of sight, out of mind *miss – love – forget – here*

Worksheet A

1 **Read out your sentences with the correct future in the past for others to guess if they are true or false.**

1 On 26th September 1983, a Soviet Lieutenant General received a computer message saying that a nuclear missile (*about / strike*) the Soviet Union. Though he was (*point / launch*) nuclear missiles to retaliate, he decided it was a computer error and avoided a nuclear war. *True*

2 In the early 20th Century, the then US President Roosevelt (*going / build*) a national network of high-altitude monorails. Construction (*about / start*) when the car was invented. *False*

3 Madonna (*originally / plan / become*) a lawyer, but she dropped out of university after forming a band. *False*

4 Jack Black (*about / accept*) a part in the original *Star Wars* film in the 1970s, when he changed his mind, saying he 'didn't think it (*going / be*) successful'. *False*

5 Games giant Nintendo considered creating the 'Nintendolphin' for the 3DS – a game whereby players (*would / raise*) a virtual dolphin. *True*

Worksheet B

1 **Read out your sentences with the correct future in the past for others to guess if they are true or false.**

1 When John Lennon was 5 years old, he had to choose between moving with his father to New Zealand or staying with his mother in Liverpool. He was (*point / leave*) with his father when his mother started crying, and he ran back to her. Had he moved with his father, The Beatles (*would / never / have / happen*). *True*

2 Tatlin's Tower (*meant / be*) a utopian monument built in St. Petersburg. It (*would / dwarf*) the Eiffel Tower and rotated once every year, but was never built. *True*

3 In 1975, a US Major (*verge / start*) a nuclear war after seeing an approaching missile on his radar screen. He was (*about / order*) an attack, when he realised that the 'missile' he had seen was actually a bit of the sandwich he'd been eating. *False*

4 Christopher Columbus, en route to discover America, (*supposed / stop*) on the way in Africa, to pick up supplies for the Italian royal family. He (*about / stop*) there, when he changed his minded and continued his journey in order to save time. Had he stopped, he would have hit a terrible storm and never discovered America. *False*

5 The singer Bob Dylan (*originally / going / use*) his given name Robert Allen, but changed his mind after he read some of Dylan Thomas's poems. *True*

Worksheet C

1 **Read out your sentences with the correct future in the past for others to guess if they are true or false.**

1 X-Seed 4000 (*going / be*) a 4 km-high building. It (*mean / hold*) a city within its structure and it (*would / be*) the world's tallest building, but it was never built. *True*

2 Ancient Greeks planned to build an underwater city in the Mediterranean Sea. It (*supposed / provide*) protection from attacks, as it couldn't be seen from a ship. *False*

3 Stalin (*going / build*) a huge tunnel between Moscow and Leningrad (now St. Petersburg). It (*mean / allow*) travel between the two cities in the event of a nuclear war. *False*

4 On departing from Southampton on its maiden voyage, the *Titanic* caused huge waves in the harbour, which caused the *SS New York* to move and break free of its ropes. The *SS New York* (*about / crash*) into the *Titanic*, when it was rescued by smaller boats. *True*

5 The British government (*plan / build*) the London Ringways as a series of circular motorways expanding from the city centre in the 1960s. Parts of it were (*verge / be*) completed, when a campaign to build more homes meant it was cancelled. *True*

		Short answer	Details
1	Have you ever cooked a meal for more than six people?		
2	Have you got any plans for your next holiday?		
3	Was there anything you wanted to do when you were younger, but couldn't do when you were younger?		
4	Have you learnt much vocabulary recently?		
5	Did you have a nice weekend?		
6	Do you know many English-speaking people?		
7	If you won the lottery, would you spend a lot of money or would you save a lot of money?		
8	Will you have to take any exams soon?		
9	Do you like the room we are studying in?		
10	Do you know anyone outside the class who thinks they're always right but they're not always right?		
11	Do you plan to continue studying English after this course?		
12	Do you have any great memories from your childhood?		
13	Do you know anyone outside the class who thinks they're funny but they're not funny?		
14	Who in your family taught you the most things?		
15	Would you like to be rich or would you like to be healthy?		
16	Do you get much time to yourself these days?		

Problem	Ideas	Solution
1 You have to give a presentation in English.	1 _____ 2 _____	
2 You've moved to a new city and want to make friends.	1 _____ 2 _____	
3 You've got an exam next week and you haven't revised yet.	1 _____ 2 _____	
4 You've just started learning a new language and want to improve quickly.	1 _____ 2 _____	
5 You want to find a new job.	1 _____ 2 _____	
6 You are a manager of a team which isn't working well together – they're demotivated.	1 _____ 2 _____	
7 You want to lose weight.	1 _____ 2 _____	
8 You want to buy a birthday present for someone who has everything they need.	1 _____ 2 _____	
9 Your friend has invited you to his/her wedding, but you can't go.	1 _____ 2 _____	
10 You have an important project to finish for work this week, and you don't have enough time to do it.	1 _____ 2 _____	
11 Your boyfriend/girlfriend has bad breath.	1 _____ 2 _____	
12 You want to impress your new boss.	1 _____ 2 _____	

Name	Adjectives	Real example(s)
Film: Three Weeks in Tuscany	_____ and _____	
Book: Dark Days of the Apocalypse	_____ and _____	
Artwork: The Scheme	_____ and _____	
Play: The Last Lieutenant	_____ and _____	
Film: 7 Days to Get Home	_____ and _____	
Book: The River	_____ and _____	
Album: Fireflies	_____ and _____	
Sculpture: Victim	_____ and _____	
Artwork: Lisa	_____ and _____	

Film: **Three Weeks in Tuscany**
moving, charming

This film will make you feel very emotional, so be prepared! The setting is beautiful, old-fashioned and pleasing on the eye.

Book: **Dark Days of the Apocalypse**
bleak, overrated

This book has received a lot of praise in the media, which I feel is undeserved. The ending will rob you of any hope in humanity, leaving you feeling very negative.

Artwork: **The Scheme**
offbeat, stylish

This piece is not what you expect, but it's unusual in an interesting and very contemporary way.

Play: **The Last Lieutenant**
poignant, heart-breaking

Most plays about the war are sad, but this production goes one step further. You'll feel deep compassion for all those involved, and the ending will make you cry, I can guarantee it!

Film: **7 Days to Get Home**
amusing, dramatic

Although primarily a comedy which will make you laugh throughout, the story is exciting and full of twists and turns. It will have you on the edge of your seat.

Book: **The River**
subtle, compelling

The clever storyline keeps you guessing until the end, with many facts not obvious until the last few pages. The suspense will make you hungry to read on, and you won't be able to put this book down.

Album: **Fireflies**
well-received, impressive

The first album by new band 'The Orknies' has had a lot of praise in the media, and rightly so. Some of the songs here are so good, you'll be truly amazed.

Sculpture: **Victim**
striking, thought-provoking

Inspired by the 2010 earthquake in Haiti, this sculpture immediately stands out and demands attention. It will also make you reflect on the strength of the human spirit.

Artwork: **Lisa**
unconventional, stunning

More than a simple portrait, the artist breaks all the normal rules for the genre. The result is something so beautiful you won't be able to take your eyes off it.

1 Use a word from each circle to replace the underlined words in questions 1 and 2 below with three-part multi-word verbs.

2 Use a word from each circle to make ten more three-part multi-word verbs, and form a question with each.

come   put
stand   get   go
do   catch

with   for
to

up   away
round   along
in   down
on

3 Ask your questions to three other students.

	Student 1	Student 2	Student 3
1 Is there anyone you haven't seen for a long time, that you'd like to <u>find out what's been happening with</u> him/her? _____ ?			
2 Do you find it easy to <u>think of</u> new ideas? _____ ?			
3 _____ ?			
4 _____ ?			
5 _____ ?			
6 _____ ?			
7 _____ ?			
8 _____ ?			
9 _____ ?			
10 _____ ?			
11 _____ ?			
12 _____ ?			

Worksheet A

1 Read the sentences and write your own opinions/answers in the second column.

2 Read out your sentences using the correct verb forms and write student B's opinions/answers in the third column. How many are the same as yours?

		✓, X or answer	My partner's answers
I	It's high time the government (do) more for the disadvantaged in society.		
2	What if you (have) the chance to redesign the school. What changes (make)?		
3	Suppose you (go) to live on a desert island alone. What three books (take) with you?		
4	I'd rather my teacher (not give) us any homework today.		
5	I'd sooner (eat) fish than meat, given the choice.		
6	My father always tells jokes as if he (be) the best comedian in the world, but he's not funny.		
7	It's about time I (settle down) and started a family.		
8	I feel as though I (know) this grammar very well now.		

Worksheet B

1 Read the sentences and write your own opinions/answers in the second column.

2 Read out your sentences using the correct verb terms and write student A's opinions/answers in the third column. How many are the same as yours?

		✓, X or answer	My partner's answers
I	It's about time I (start) eating more healthily.		
2	What if you (not start) this course. What (do) now?		
3	I hate it when people treat me as though I (not exist).		
4	It's high time I (find) a new job.		
5	Supposing you (live) in another country. How your life (be) different now?		
6	I'd sooner my teacher (correct) me when I made mistakes.		
7	I'd rather (travel) by train than bus, given the choice.		
8	I'm really tired today. I feel as if I (not sleep) well for a long time.		

Worksheet A

1 Read out your sentences for student B to match and place the adverbials.

1	I started learning English.	A slowly
2	I used to find it difficult to come up with new ideas. I'm much more creative.	B yesterday
3	Cigarette advertising is a ridiculous idea.	C to feel fresh at the start of the week
4	I had to apologise. It had seemed like a good idea at the time, but it turned out it wasn't!	D aimlessly; in my free time
5	I speak in public.	E definitely; at the weekend
6	I find some English grammar difficult.	F always; quickly
7	I try to learn new vocabulary.	G Fortunately for me; cleverly
8	I see original ideas for TV programmes.	H recently

**2 Discuss with your partner. Which of the sentences are true for you?
Change the others so they are true for you.**

Worksheet B

1 Read out your sentences for student A to match and place the adverbials.

1	I had a good day.	A when I was younger; nowadays
2	Someone came up with a time-saving device.	B impossibly
3	I hate it when people walk in front of me.	C recently; for doing something
4	I've been toying with the idea of taking up a new interest.	D pretty much every day
5	I'll be going out with my friends.	E hardly ever; nowadays
6	I like to rest on Sundays.	F without a doubt
7	I get ready when I go out.	G ten years ago
8	I like to wander around the shops.	H sometimes; too loudly

**2 Discuss with your partner. Which of the sentences are true for you?
Change the others so they are true for you.**

public transport in your country	supermarkets	a film you've seen recently	an actor
people who speak too loudly	drivers in your or another country	a band or musician	a place you've visited
English grammar	a book you've read recently	a gadget	a meal you've had/restaurant you've eaten in recently
a past teacher you've had	an artist	political correctness	a company you love/hate
computers	a website you use/have used	a sport	a subject you studied at school

Crossword A

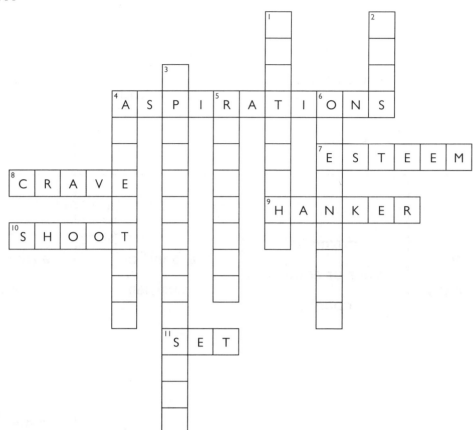

Crossword B

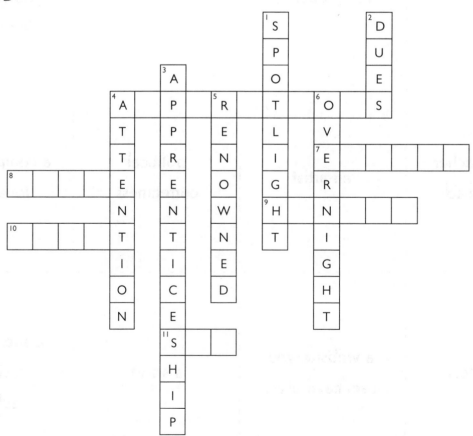

gripping	**thrilling**	**exhilarating**
journey	**trip**	**expedition**
highlight	**stress**	**accentuate**
master	**grasp**	**get the hang of**
bug	**irritate**	**get on (my) nerves**
embark on	**undertake**	**set off**

Student A

You are a guest at a hotel, checking out after an unpleasant stay. You're not happy at all, and want a discount on the cost of the room. Your specific complaints are:

1 You've never seen a room as dirty as that one before.

2 If you'd known the food was so bad, you wouldn't have ordered from room service.

3 You didn't realise the toilet was broken until you'd used it.

Try to find a solution with the receptionist.

Student B

You work on reception at a hotel. One of the guests has come to check out, but is refusing to pay the full price for their room and food they ordered through room service. Listen to their complaints, but state the following:

1 Your hotel never gives discounts in *any* situation – it's company policy.

2 People don't often complain, guests are usually very happy.

3 If they'd mentioned these problems before, you could have moved them to another room.

Try to find a solution with the guest.

Student A

You work at the check-in desk of an airline. A passenger approaches with some very large suitcases which will need to be checked in. The flight they are on is currently delayed for 4 hours. Don't tell them, but the reason is the pilot is sick, and since you have no other pilots available, you're waiting for him to feel better before the flight can leave. While listening to their complaints, state the following:

1 If they had no baggage to check in, you could put them on another flight with a smaller plane.

2 It's not just your airline, but other airlines are experiencing delays, too (you're not sure if this is true, but don't tell the passenger).

3 You can't pay for them to travel with another airline, in any situation.

Try to find a solution with the passenger.

Student B

You are travelling to the other side of the country for an important business meeting which could potentially be very lucrative. However, your flight is delayed by 4 hours, and as far as you can see, all other airlines have no delays. At the check-in desk, make the following complaints:

1 You've never had a flight that was delayed for that long before.

2 If they paid for you to travel with another airline, you could arrive on time.

3 There's no way you can arrive late for your meeting.

Try to find a solution with the airline staff.

Game 1 – student A
Bananas

- As bananas ripen, the starch in the fruit turns to sugar. Therefore, the riper the banana, the sweeter it tastes.
- Pears are nowhere near as popular as bananas in the USA.
- India produces significantly more bananas than any other country in the world.
- Bananas have become longer and longer in the last 200 years.

- _____
  _____
  _____
- _____
  _____

Game 1 – student B
The human body

- As we get older, we have fewer and fewer bones. A baby has 300, whereas the average adult has 206.
- A human being has far fewer chromosomes than a crayfish, and only slightly more than a pea.
- In general, people in the UK are decidedly more obese than people in France.
- The longer a person lives, the smaller their eyes become.

- _____
  _____
  _____
- _____
  _____

Game 1 – student C
The Earth

- The world consumes way more wood than 100 years ago.
- Parts of Antarctica are getting drier and drier – they haven't had any rain for 2 million years.
- The Atlantic Ocean is nowhere near as deep as the Pacific Ocean.
- The Earth is considerably larger than it was 1,000 years ago.

- _____
  _____
  _____
- _____
  _____

Game 2 – student A
Football

- Football stadiums might be getting bigger and bigger, but most modern attendances are nothing like as large as the 1950 World Cup final, with almost 200,000 fans present.
- Soccer, as football is known there, is becoming more and more popular in the USA, but only over the last ten years.
- Most footballers are nowhere near as unlucky as one Chelsea player, who broke his leg when celebrating a goal – before the season had started!
- In Tahiti, football teams are way bigger than usual, with 20 players on each team.

- _____
  _____
- _____

Game 2 – student B
Coffee

- Arabica coffee is significantly more common than any other type of coffee, making up around 75 per cent of all the coffee in the world.
- Beethoven was just as precise about his coffee as his music, and would only drink coffee that had been made with exactly 60 beans per cup.
- Most coffee production is nowhere near as strange as a type from Indonesia, which is passed through the digestive system of a small animal before being dried in the sun and roasted.
- Galactica coffee, grown in Zimbabwe, has a strange quality – the longer you brew it, the spicier it becomes.

- _____
  _____
- _____

Game 2 – student C
Wildlife

- By far the biggest freshwater fish is the Giant Mekon Catfish, which can weigh over 300 kg.
- Jellyfish have been around for millions of years, and they've got bigger and bigger. However, most jellyfish are nothing like as big as the Arctic Lion's Mane, which has been known to grow up to 37 m long.
- No other animal in the world is as fast as a type of falcon, which normally flies around 50 mph. However, the higher they are, the faster they fall – when diving they can reach speeds of over 200 mph!
- Most mushrooms grow nowhere near as fast as the Eyelon mushroom, found in New Guinea, which grows so fast you can hear it!

- _____
  _____
- _____

Team A

You represent a group of film-makers who have been commissioned by 'Quark Productions', a well-known production company, to produce a feature-length wildlife documentary about the rare Tree Kangaroo. Its habitat is in a remote part of Papua New Guinea, which will be difficult to travel to.

Before you begin the negotiation to agree the final contract, prepare which concessions you feel able to make in order to reach agreement.

Demands	Concession	Agreed
1 Production time – 1 year (9 months filming and 3 months for the edit)		
2 70 per cent of all profits		
3 To direct the film yourselves		
4 All expenses (flights, accommodation, food and equipment) paid for by Quark Productions		
5 An advance of 50% of estimated profits when filming begins		
6 Film produced in digital format only		
7 Indemnity – film-makers not responsible for any legal claims brought against the film		
8 Intellectual property – film-makers keep full rights to the work		

Team B

You represent 'Quark Productions', a well-known production company specialising in wildlife documentaries. After the recent discovery of the rare Tree Kangaroo in a remote part of Papua New Guinea, you have commissioned a group of young, inexperienced film-makers to produce a feature-length documentary on the animal.

Before you begin the negotiation to agree the final contract, prepare which concessions you feel able to make in order to reach agreement.

Demands	Concession	Agreed
1 Production time – 6 months (4 months filming and 2 months for the edit)		
2 70 per cent of all profits		
3 To bring in a another, more experienced director		
4 All expenses (flights, accommodation, food and equipment) paid for by film-makers themselves		
5 No advance paid when filming begins		
6 Film produced in two formats – digital and analogue, so it can be shown in cinemas		
7 Indemnity – film-makers responsible for any legal claims brought against the film		
8 Intellectual property – Quark Productions keep full rights to the work		

Unit 1

QUALITY PEOPLE

Materials: One copy of worksheet A and worksheet B per pair of students

Arrange Ss into A and B pairs and distribute the worksheets. Explain that in each of their sentences, the underlined word is wrong, and their partner has a sentence with the correct word in it. They take it in turns to read out a sentence, while their partner finds the correct word and reads it out so that the sentence can be completed correctly. Encourage Ss to add *He* (or *She*) to the start of the sentences to make them read grammatically. Ss then discuss why the original word is wrong, e.g. *Neurotic doesn't work here because it means … .* Demonstrate the activity by reading out student A's first sentence and asking a student B to give you the correct word. When Ss have finished, go through the answers.

Answers: Student A: 1 prejudiced   2 obsessive
3 inspirational   4 over-ambitious   5 open-minded
6 inquisitive   7 solitary   8 apathetic
Student B: 1 obstinate   2 perceptive   3 neurotic
4 mature   5 insensitive   6 conscientious   7 rebellious
8 thoughtful

Ss work alone to complete the sentences with the names of people they know outside of the class who the sentences are true for. Allow them to change the wording of the sentences if necessary, but not the adjective. Ss discuss their sentences in pairs. Monitor and encourage them to ask follow up questions to find out more information.

PICTURES OF YOU

Materials: One set of picture cards per pair; One copy of worksheet A and worksheet B per pair of students

Arrange Ss into A and B pairs and distribute the A and B worksheets. Ss work alone to read their sentences and correct the mistakes in the idioms. Monitor and help where necessary, but don't give any answers yet.

When Ss are ready, give each pair a set of the picture cards and place them face down between the Ss. Ss take it in turns to turn over the cards and decide who each card belongs to. Ss can now show each other their worksheets and check their answers are correct.

Alternatively, if you don't have time to cut up the picture cards, then just give them a copy of all the pictures, and ask them to work with it face-up between them.

When Ss have finished, check answers with the class.

Answers: Student A: 1 dark horse   2 life and soul of the party   3 busybody   4 yes-man   5 pain in the neck
Student B: 1 chatterbox   2 old hand   3 black sheep of the family   4 whizz kid   5 set in their ways

As a follow up, Ss can discuss people they know who can be described with the idioms (avoid having them make comments on other Ss in the class, though).

PICK A SHAPE

Materials: One worksheet per student

Distribute the worksheets and ask Ss to read the sentences at the top and write short answers, at random, in the shapes below. Tell Ss that they should write only one or two words for each answer. They should not look at each other's answers yet. Monitor and help Ss with any vocabulary they need.

When they are ready, ask the Ss to fold their worksheet in half. Arrange Ss into pairs. Tell Ss to show each other their answers. Their partner tries to guess which sentences their answers refer to. If they get stuck and need help, they can have another look at the sentences at the top of the worksheet. *Early finishers* can discuss the sentences they didn't provide answers to. When they have finished, elicit any interesting answers from the pairs.

FORMER SELVES

Materials: One card per student

Make a copy of the worksheet and cut up the cards so there is one for each student. At the top of the board, write: *You are cheerful.* and next to it write: *You used to be depressed.* Underneath the first sentence write: *I'll …, I'm always …,* and *I keep …* Under the second sentence write: *I'd …, I was always …,* and *I kept …* and elicit possible continuations from the class e.g. *I'll just smile when I have a problem, I'm always singing to myself, I keep telling jokes.*

Distribute a card to each student, and make sure they don't show their card to anyone else. If you don't have an even number of Ss, give two cards to a stronger student.

Ss work alone to complete the sentences. They should describe habits that a person with this characteristic might do, or have done (if their sentence is in the past). Monitor and check Ss are producing the forms correctly.

Explain that the cards are in pairs, with one describing a person's past, and the other describing what that person is like now. When they are ready, Ss mingle and read out their habit but NOT the adjective. They should find their partner, who has the opposite characteristic. In feedback, elicit some habits from pairs and write all the adjectives on the board.

Answers: lazy / hard-working   insensitive / thoughtful
childish / mature   boring / interesting
conscientious / rebellious   neurotic / calm
solitary / sociable   apathetic / inquisitive
obstinate / open-minded

As a follow up, Ss describe past and present habits for other adjectives in pairs. In feedback, nominate one or two Ss and ask them to share the habits they came up with with the class.

ORIGINAL NAMES

Materials: One worksheet per group of three Ss

Arrange the Ss in groups of three and distribute one copy of the top half of the worksheet to each group.

Review the language from unit 1.3 for speculating, and drill the phrases. Ss work together to try and match the names to their origins and meanings. Monitor and encourage Ss to give reasons for their choices, e.g. by saying the names aloud and speculating as to what language they sound like.

After a while elicit some of their guesses, but don't give any answers yet. Give out the cards to each group and place them face down in the middle. Each student takes turns to take a card and read out the clue, and the rest of the group check their answers. Alternatively, if you don't have time to cut up the cards, fold each worksheet in half before you distribute them and ask Ss not to look at the other side until this stage.

While they are doing this, write the following questions on the board; *Which of these names do you like? Which do you dislike? Do you know what your name means? What are some common names in your country? What do you think they mean?*

When Ss have finished, check answers with the class.

> **Answers:** 1 Modern English, field of Ash trees
> 2 Traditional English, old town   3 Russian, hope   4 Welsh, white ring or bow   5 Tswana (Southern African), proud
> 6 Indonesian, beautiful   7 Swahili, life   8 Azerbaijani, to be alive   9 Esperanto, victorious   10 Mongolian, moonlight
> 11 Thai, worthy man   12 Japanese, clear mist   13 Chinese, boat   14 Irish, nobleman   15 Hawaiian, calm heavens

After checking the answers, Ss discuss the questions from the board in their groups.

Unit 2

RAGS TO RICHES
Materials: One copy of worksheet A and worksheet B per pair of students

Arrange Ss into pairs and distribute the A and B worksheets. Ss work together to put the parts of the story in order. With *weaker classes*, give them the first part before they begin. When they have finished, elicit the order, but don't go into the missing phrases yet. Ss then take it in turns to read out their sections with the gaps, for their partner to supply the missing phrase. Monitor and help where necessary.

When Ss have finished, ask one pair to read out the complete the story to the class.

> **Answers:** Order: 1 F   2 J   3 B   4 G   5 E   6 L   7 A
> 8 I   9 D   10 K   11 C   12 H
>
> Student A: A had second thoughts   B took/had taken advantage of an opportunity   C trusted her instincts
> D never gave up   E on a steep learning curve
> F came under attack, preconceptions
>
> Student B: G had a profound effect on   H believe in yourself   I kept/keep an open mind, a convincing argument
> J challenge the stereotypes   K from a new perspective
> L learnt the ropes

OVER THE HILL AND FAR AWAY
Materials: One copy of worksheet A and worksheet B, and one set of discussion questions per pair of students

Arrange the Ss into pairs and distribute the A and B worksheets. Don't give out the discussion questions yet. Explain that each worksheet has pictures which illustrate metaphors. Student A describes each of his/her pictures in turn, while student B listens and supplies the correct metaphor from their list. When they have finished, pairs swap and repeat the process. When they have finished, elicit Ss' answers.

> **Answers:** Student A: A reach the peak of your profession
> B on its last legs   C you'll go far   D regurgitate   E be over the hill
>
> Student B: A find yourself at a crossroads   B hard to swallow   C start to go downhill   D food for thought
> E a half-baked idea

Distribute the discussion questions. Ss discuss in pairs.

HEXAGONAL REGRETS
Materials: One worksheet per student

Arrange Ss into groups of four and form teams of two Ss. They take it in turns to choose a hexagon, then make a correct sentence with the sentence frame in the hexagon. The other team decides if it is correct. If it is, the first team 'take' the hexagon. If not, then the other team has a chance to 'take' that hexagon before having their turn. Monitor and help where necessary, adjudicating the teams' sentences in case of any disputes. Team B must start and finish on one of the outermost hexagons in rows 1, 3 or 5.

The object of the game is to connect the top and bottom of the grid (team A), or the left and right sides of the grid (team B). Teams can work their way around the board (and the other team's line) in order to reach the other side. The first team to do this wins the game. Teams can also play 'strategically by trying to block the other team's progress.

As a follow up (or for *early finishers*), Ss can discuss their real regrets using the sentence frames on the grid.

SOMETHING IN COMMON
Materials: One worksheet per student

Distribute the worksheets. Ss work in pairs to complete the sentences with the correct form of the verbs in the box. When they have finished, check answers with the class.

> **Answers:** 1 visiting   2 losing   3 doing   4 to do   5 being
> 6 to achieve   7 to have achieved   8 to experience
> 9 to do   10 feeling   11 to say   12 doing   13 to be
> 14 to have visited   15 doing

Ss work alone to write their answers in the *My answer* column. Monitor and help with vocabulary where necessary.

When Ss are ready they should ask their questions to another student and complete the *Classmate 1* column. They then change partners and ask a different student, using the *Classmate 2* column.

In feedback, elicit any answers Ss have in common.

WHAT'S YOUR OPINION?
Materials: One copy of worksheet A and worksheet B per pair of students

Arrange the Ss into pairs and distribute the A and B worksheets. Ss work alone to read the statements, and write two reasons why someone who is 'for' (student A) or 'against' (student B) each statement might agree or disagree with them. Encourage Ss to be creative, and make it clear that this doesn't have to reflect their true opinions. Monitor and help where necessary.

Review the language from unit 2.3 for introducing opinions.

Ss discuss the statements and share their reasons for/against, trying to convince their partner with their 'opinions/reasons'. When they have finished, nominate Ss from each group to share their ideas with the class, and ask who gave the most convincing arguments.

As a follow up, Ss can discuss their real opinions on the statements in small groups.

Unit 3

DESCRIBING PLACES

Materials: One copy of crossword A and crossword B per pair of students

Arrange Ss into pairs, and distribute the worksheets. Sit Ss face to face and tell them not to show their worksheets to each other. Tell Ss that they each have half of the answers to a crossword and they are going to work together to complete it. Elicit the questions they need to ask, e.g. *What's 4 across? What's 12 down?* Each student takes it in turns to ask for clues and to describe the word for their partner to guess, until they have completed the crossword. With *weaker classes*, give them some time before you pair them off to allow them to prepare clues for their words.

When they have finished, check answers with the class, giving further examples if necessary

FIX IT!

Materials: One copy of worksheet A and worksheet B per pair of students

Arrange Ss into A and B pairs and distribute the worksheets. Demonstrate the activity by reading out student A's first sentence and asking a student B to form the correct word to fill the gap by combining a prefix and a word from the right-hand column of their worksheet. Ss take it in turns to read out a sentence, while their partner forms the correct word to fill the gap, and reads it to them so that the sentence can be completed.

When Ss have finished, go through the answers, checking understanding of the words by giving further examples where necessary.

> **Answers:** Student A: 1 misbehave   2 uninteresting
> 3 non-governmental   4 postgraduate   5 irresponsibly
> 6 proactive   7 overestimate   8 degenerate
> Student B: 1 understatement   2 non-conformist
> 3 malnutrition   4 irreversible   5 pre-date
> 6 anti-government   7 uneventful   8 impolite

Ss discuss whether their sentences are true or false for them, in pairs. Monitor and encourage them to change the false sentences to make them true.

DESCRIPTIONS

Materials: One worksheet, a dice and counters per group of students

Arrange Ss in small groups. Distribute one worksheet, a dice and counters to each group.

Ss place their counter on the START square, and take it turns to throw the dice and move their counter that number of squares, clockwise. When they land on a square, they describe what is in the square, using one or more noun phrases, and choosing at least two of the features from the boxes in the middle to incorporate, e.g. *My first day at school was a surprisingly happy event. We had special cards for learning the alphabet with funny little pictures on them.* If they choose to use adjectives, they should use at least three somewhere in their description, making sure they are in the correct order. Monitor and check they are forming noun phrases correctly, and help where necessary. The winner is the first student to reach the FINISH square.

THE JOB THAT I DO

Materials: One worksheet per student

Distribute the worksheets. Focus attention on the sentence frames at the top, and write *scientist* on the board. Elicit some example sentences to describe the job and where they work, e.g. *People who do this job, all of whom are very well qualified, work long hours,* etc.

Ss work alone to write similar sentences for the jobs on the worksheet, using the sentence frames to help with ideas (they don't have to use these, as long as they use relative clauses). Ss then think of three more jobs and write descriptions at the bottom. Point out that we use *they* in order to avoid using *he/she*. Make sure Ss don't show their answers to anyone, or write the name of the job in their descriptions. Monitor and check Ss are forming relative clauses correctly, and help where necessary.

When Ss have finished, put them in pairs. Ss take it in turns to read out their descriptions at random, while their partner guesses which job/place of work they are describing. When they have finished, they read out the descriptions of the three jobs at the bottom for their partner to guess the jobs.

A BETTER PLACE

Materials: One worksheet per pair of students

Arrange the class in pairs (groups of three for large classes), and review the language for making a proposal from unit 3.3. Explain the following situation:

The directors of your school have decided to allocate a large amount of money to creating a new space in the school. The space should be primarily for the benefit of the students, and should have an educational purpose. The directors have asked for proposals to be submitted by all students, and the best proposal will be allocated the money.

Distribute the worksheets, and explain that Ss are going to make a proposal for how the money should be spent. Ss work in their pairs to complete the necessary information on the worksheet. If they wish, they can also draw a simple picture to illustrate what the space would look like. They should also provide a 'catchy' closing statement in the last section of the worksheet. Monitor and make sure they provide as much information as possible.

When they are ready, give groups a few more minutes to decide how they are going to present their proposal, i.e. who will present each part.

Ss then take turns to present their proposals to the class. After each proposal, encourage other Ss in the class to ask further questions. At the end, ask Ss to choose their favourite one.

Unit 4

ELECTION TIME
Materials: One worksheet per group of three Ss

Arrange Ss into groups of three, and give one worksheet to each group. Ss work together to match the words in the first two columns to form social issues. When they have finished, elicit Ss' answers and check understanding of the phrases.

> **Answers:** 1 human rights   2 child labour   3 economic development   4 intellectual property   5 capital punishment   6 religious freedom   7 environmental awareness   8 illegal immigration   9 civil liberties   10 free trade   11 freedom of speech   12 gun control

Explain that you are going to hold a 'class election', and the Ss' groups represent the different political parties. Ss choose four of the issues that they would like to focus on, and write them in the box. They then think of possible measures they will introduce (if elected), and write them in the spaces provided. Ss can write three measures for each issue, or more for some and fewer for others. Monitor and help with vocabulary where necessary, and ask them to think of a name for their party.

When they have finished, Ss read out their manifestoes to the class. When all groups have finished, Ss vote for one of the parties (not their own), to see who wins the election.

As a follow up, Ss can discuss (in their groups) which of the issues are most important in their country/ies today, and why.

THE PERFECT CRIMES?
Materials: One copy of the cut up cards; one copy of the bottom half of the worksheet per pair of Ss

Before class, cut up one copy of the cards with the chunks and attach them to the wall outside the classroom or in a corner.

Arrange Ss in pairs, and ask them to choose a 'runner' and a 'writer'. Distribute one copy of the worksheet to each 'writer'. The 'runners' go to where the chunks are displayed, choose a phrase, memorise it, and then repeat it to their partner. The 'writer' then writes it in the correct gap on their worksheet.

N.B. It's important that the 'runner' remembers the whole phrase, in order to help with chunking. If they forget one word or part, they must go back and memorise it again.

When Ss have finished, check answers with the class.

> **Answers:** 1 H   2 B   3 J   4 E   5 A   6 I   7 C   8 G   9 D   10 F

Give Ss a few minutes to read through the completed stories, then they discuss the questions in pairs. In feedback, nominate Ss to share their ideas with the class.

WHAT IS IT?
Materials: One copy of worksheet A and worksheet B per pair of students

Arrange Ss in pairs, and distribute one copy of the worksheets per pair of Ss. Make sure Ss don't show their worksheet to their partner.

Student A reads out their sentence starters for student B to complete with their phrases. When they've finished, Ss repeat the process with student B's sentence starters. When they've finished, check answers with the class.

> **Answers:** Student A: 1 C   2 A   3 E   4 H   5 F   6 G   7 D   8 B
> Student B: 1 B   2 H   3 G   4 A   5 C   6 D   7 E   8 F

Ss discuss if they agree or disagree with the statements and why, in pairs. If they disagree, encourage Ss to change the sentences so they are true for them. Encourage them to personalise the sentences where possible.

PERFECT CLASSMATES
Materials: One worksheet per student

Distribute one worksheet to each student in the class. With *weaker classes*, give them time to write the verbs in the correct form first, and check answers with the class.

> **Answers:** 1 to have learnt   2 has met   3 had been thinking   4 had met   5 will have been working/will have worked   6 will have finished   7 has been working/has worked   8 has learnt   9 had been dreaming   10 will have been studying   11 to have achieved   12 had just eaten   13 has been thinking   14 will have made   15 has known

Ss mingle and ask questions to find people who the sentences are true for. Elicit the first two questions as an example e.g. *Do you hope to have learnt something new by the end of the year? Have you (ever) met a famous person?*

When they find a student who answers 'yes', they write their name in the first column. Ss ask a follow up question to find out more, and write notes in the *Details* column. Monitor and help where necessary, and encourage Ss to ask as many people as possible.

When Ss have finished, arrange them into groups of four to share their answers. In feedback, nominate Ss from each group to share any interesting answers with the class.

WHAT WOULD YOU DO?
Materials: One set of cards per group of students

Arrange Ss in small groups. Give one set of cards to each group, and place them face down in the middle of each group. Ss take turns to pick up a card and read out the situation to their group. Ss then discuss what they would do in each situation, then agree on the best course of action. Monitor and encourage Ss to use the functional phrases.

When they have finished, nominate Ss from each group to share their decisions with the class, and ask other groups if they agree.

Unit 5

GUESS THE PHRASE
Materials: One set of cards per group of students

Arrange Ss into small groups, and place one set of cards, face down, in the middle of the group.

Demonstrate the activity by saying: *I'm thinking of a word which means 'check something is true'*… and elicit the answer *(verify)*.

Each student in the group takes it in turn to take a card, and define the word or phrase on it. The first student in the group to get the answer wins the card. At the end of the activity, the student in the group with the most cards wins. Monitor and help where necessary.

MINI BINGO
Materials: One worksheet per student

Distribute one worksheet to each student. Ss work alone to complete each box with an answer which is true for them. Monitor and check Ss understand the multi-word verbs in each box.

When they have finished, arrange Ss in small groups. Each student takes it in turn to read out a sentence including their answer, e.g. *I've recently been mulling over whether to look for a new job*, and see if any other group members have the same answers. Encourage Ss to ask follow up questions to find out more information. In feedback, nominate Ss from each group to share any common answers with the class.

MISTAKES AND ADVICE
Materials: One worksheet per student

Distribute the worksheets. Write the following situations on the board: *1 Using public transport, 2 You failed an important exam*. Using the sentence frames on the worksheet, elicit possible advice and regrets Ss might have in each situation, e.g. *1 You ought to leave plenty of time, You don't need to worry about parking, You'd better not listen to loud music, Using your mobile quietly is allowed, You can read a book, You're not supposed to push other people if they're in your way, 2 I should never have gone to that party the night before, I had to answer difficult questions, I didn't have the courage to guess the answers, I couldn't remember anything, I needn't have arrived so early, I was forced to give up*, etc.

Ss work alone to complete the sentences under *General advice 1–3* and *Past mistakes 1–3*. Monitor and help where necessary, and make sure Ss don't show their sentences to anyone else.

When Ss have finished, arrange them in pairs. Ss take it in turns to read out their sentences for each situation randomly, while their partner listens and guesses which situation is being described.

When Ss have finished, they work alone again to think of two more situations for *General advice* and two more situations for *Past mistakes*, and write relevant sentences for each. When they are ready, they read their sentences for each situation to their partner, who listens and guesses the situation.

I CAN'T BELIEVE IT!
Materials: One set of cards per group of students

Arrange Ss in groups of three. Distribute one set of cards per group of Ss, and place them face down in the middle of each group. Don't worry about keeping the cards in order, the numbers are just for reference when checking answers.

Ss take it in turns to take a card, and use the prompts to form a sentence using the correct passive form of the verb in brackets and read it out. Other Ss listen and decide if the sentence is true or false. Every student who guesses correctly wins a point. If no one guesses correctly, the student who read out the sentence gets a point. Monitor and help Ss form the sentences where necessary. The student with the most points in each group at the end wins.

Answers: 1 were originally made   2 are cooled   3 are born   4 is made   5 was already thought   6 is often found   7 is seen   8 will have been built   9 is lowered   10 be avoided   11 are not harmed, being woken up   12 has never been struck/is never struck   13 was invented   14 was created   15 is spoken   16 it's cooked   17 be detected   18 can't be repaired   19 has ever been killed   20 will not be affected

IT'S UP TO YOU
Materials: One set of rolecards per group of three Ss

Arrange Ss in groups of three. If you have an even number of Ss, have one or two groups of four, and double up role C.

Ss work alone to read their roles and plan their reasons. Monitor and help with ideas where necessary. Review the language for making a point, as well as the language for managing a conversation in unit 5.3.

Ss discuss the situation in groups of three of four, by taking turns to make their point. They need to agree on what the law should look like, and if necessary make compromises. In feedback, nominate Ss from each group to share their ideas with the class.

Unit 6

TOMORROW'S WORLD
Materials: One copy of worksheet A and worksheet B per pair of students

Arrange Ss in pairs, and distribute one copy of the worksheets per pair of Ss. Make sure Ss don't show their worksheet to their partner.

Student A reads out their sentence starters for student B to complete with their phrases, completing the missing word as they read them out. They choose from the words in the box to complete the gaps. With *weaker classes*, give them 3–4 minutes before they begin to complete the gaps in their sentence halves first, and check answers. When they've finished, Ss repeat the process with student B's sentence starters. Check answers with the class.

Answers: Worksheet A: 1 signs C   2 bound F   3 gather D   4 days A   5 thing E   6 explosion G   7 distant B
Worksheet B: 1 well D   2 likely A   3 point G   4 thing B   5 explosion F   6 distant E   7 signs C

Ss discuss if they agree or disagree with the statements and why, in pairs. If they disagree, encourage Ss to elaborate/change the sentences so they are true for them.

PREPOSITIONAL DOMINOES
Materials: One set of cards per group of students

Preteach *carbon footprint* and *defamation of character*. Draw a simple sketch of a domino on the board and ask Ss if they know this game and what it's called in their language. Put Ss in groups of three or four, depending on your class size, give them a set of 'Prepositional Dominoes' and ask them to divide them between the group, face down.

Ss take it in turns to lay down their cards, forming correct sentence halves and prepositional phrases. If they can't go they miss a turn. The winner is the first student to use all their cards. While they are playing, go round and check they are forming correct phrases, and answer any questions they have.

When all groups have finished, check answers and, in the same groups, Ss discuss how far they agree/disagree with the statements.

WHAT DOES YOUR FUTURE HOLD?

Materials: One worksheet per student

Distribute one worksheet to each student in the class.

Ss mingle and ask questions to find people who the sentences are true for. Elicit the first two questions as an example, e.g. *Do you think you'll be living in another country this time next year? Do you think your country will do well in the next World Cup?*

When they find a student who answers 'yes', they write their name in the first column, and ask a follow up question to find out more details, and write these as notes in the *Details* column. Monitor and help where necessary, and encourage Ss to ask as many people as possible.

N.B. Sometimes more than one future form is possible, depending on how we see an event, or how we want others to see it. Therefore, when Ss are mingling and asking their questions, monitor carefully, and allow anything that sounds natural, but make a note of any forms which are used incorrectly, and correct them with the class before moving on to the next stage.

When Ss have finished, arrange them into pairs to share their answers. In feedback, nominate Ss from each group to share any interesting answers with the class.

> **Suggested answers:** 1 will be living   2 will do
> 3 is going to study   4 will have got   5 is to make
> 6 is going   7 will have started   8 will definitely arrive
> 9 is   10 will be going   11 is having   12 will have
> completed   13 will probably travel   14 will still be studying
> 15 is going   16 will definitely sleep

DUELLING

Materials: One copy of worksheet A and worksheet B per pair of students

Arrange Ss in pairs. Distribute one copy of the worksheets per pair of Ss, and make sure Ss don't show their worksheet to their partner. Explain that Ss will 'duel' in pairs, using concession clauses to respond to what their partner says. Student A starts, and reads out their sentence A. Student B replies using the correct response and concession clause. Ss continue until they reach the last sentence (student B's sentence H). Monitor and check Ss are using the correct concession clauses.

> **Answers:** A → F (While) → D (though) → G (though) → C (as) → E (Despite) → B (Nevertheless) → H

Ss then continue 'duelling' by taking it in turns to use their sentence starters at the bottom of the worksheet, and 'duel' for as long as possible in the same way. Monitor and check Ss are using the clauses correctly.

N.B. It is important to treat this topic in a light-hearted manner. Make it clear that the statements themselves are probably not true, but what's more important is that they keep the discourse going and find something to say. They should try and use a range of phrases.

ROOTS AND RESULTS

Materials: One set of cards per group of students

Arrange Ss into small groups, and place one set of cards, face down, in the middle of the group. Demonstrate the activity by saying: *It has its origins in the popularity of radio. It all started in the UK with the BBC. It has led to thousands of programmes being made. What is it? (TV).*

Each student in the group takes it in turn to take a card, and tell the rest of the group some causes and effects of the thing on their card. The first student in the group to name what's on the card wins it. If no one can guess what it is, the student who picked it up keeps it. At the end of the activity, the student in the group with the most cards wins. Monitor and help where necessary.

As a follow up, Ss can choose two or three of the cards to research further for homework. Ss bring their information to the next lesson and share with the class.

Unit 7

ESCAPE!

Materials: One worksheet, a dice and counters per group of students

Arrange Ss in small groups. Distribute one worksheet, a dice and counters to each group. If you don't have dice, Ss can use a coin (heads = move one square, tails = move two).

> **Answers:** 1 released   2 trapped   3 hatch   4 make a break   5 let your hair down   6 have a breather
> 7 hang out   8 unwind   9 slow down   10 stranded
> 11 take your mind off   12 escape   13 switch off
> 14 take it easy   15 suspiciously   16 take refuge
> 17 flee   18 emigrate

Ss place their counter on the START square, and take it in turns to throw the dice and move their counter that number of squares. When they land on a square, they complete the gapped phrase and follow the instructions on the square. Ss should only follow the instructions for the square they land on first. For example, if they land on a square which tells them to go back three spaces, and they move to a square which tells them to go forward one square, then they should ignore the second instruction. On their next turn, they throw the dice to get their next instruction. If they land on a grey square, they should answer the question. If they land on a free square, they don't need to do anything for that turn. The winner is the first student to reach the FREEDOM! square.

IN A FIX

Materials: One copy of worksheet A and worksheet B per pair of students

Arrange Ss in pairs. Distribute one copy of the worksheets per pair of Ss, and make sure Ss don't show their worksheet to their partner. Ss take it in turns to read out their sentences to their partner, who listens and completes the word stem with the correct suffix. If their partner completes it correctly, they win a point. The winner is the one with the most points at the end.

When they have finished, Ss discuss which of the sentences are true for them, and change any which are false. In feedback, nominate Ss to share their opinions with the class.

GREAT ESCAPES

Materials: One copy of worksheet A and worksheet B per pair of students

Arrange Ss in pairs. Distribute one copy of the worksheets per pair of Ss, and make sure Ss don't show their worksheet to their partner. Give them enough time to read their texts. Monitor and help with vocabulary, writing any new words/phrases on the board.

When they are ready, each student introduces each of their stories by saying where and when it happened, though make sure they don't give away too much information about their stories here, e.g. *I've got a story about two men who escaped from Alcatraz in the 1960s.* Ss take it in turns to read out their questions to their partner, who answers it using a cleft sentence with *what* or *it*. The student who asked the question then writes the answers as a cleft sentence. Monitor and check Ss are forming cleft sentences correctly.

When Ss have finished, check answers with the class – note that more than one version may be correct.

Suggested answers: Worksheet A: 1 What Alcatraz was used as was a prison. 2 It was the most serious criminals that/who were held there. 3 What they used were very simple tools to cut the walls. 4 What happened/What they did was they cut through the walls, climbed to the roof, then climbed down the building and assembled a raft to cross the bay. 5 It was 24th March that they escaped. 6 What they used were three tunnels. 7 What happened was they built the tunnels too short because they thought the forest was closer. 8 It was the 77th prisoner who/that was seen by a guard.

Worksheet B: 1 It was John Gerard who/that escaped from the Tower of London. 2 What he was arrested for was his missionary work. 3 What he used to escape was a rope. 4 What happened/What he did was he fled to Rome. 5 It was Union soldiers who/that were held in Libby Prison. 6 What they did was lead the escape. 7 It was rats that lived in the cellar. 8 What happened was the soldiers escaped by tunnelling through the cellar.

Ss discuss question 3 in pairs. In feedback, nominate Ss to share their ideas with the class.

IT WAS A COLD, DARK NIGHT …

Materials: One worksheet per pair of students

Arrange Ss in pairs, and distribute one copy of the worksheet per pair of Ss. Explain that you are going to read the first part of the story to them:

Respected by everyone in the local village, John was a good father and husband. Being the local doctor, he knew all the villagers well and they often came to him for advice. One night, realising he had left some important documents at his surgery, he went back to pick them up. When he entered the surgery and switched the lights on, there was a woman sitting in the corner of the room, smiling at him. "Hello John," she said, "I bet you didn't expect to see me here."

After reading out the introduction, Ss continue the story, line by line, using one of the participle clauses on the worksheet. Each time they add a sentence, Ss cross out the prompt on the worksheet. Encourage Ss to continue the story as long as they can, and monitor and help where necessary.

When they've finished, nominate one or two pairs to retell their story to the class.

As a follow up, write the following prompts on the board, and ask Ss to repeat the process with the prompts on the worksheet to start another story: *Hated by everyone, … Not wanting to appear rude, … Having finished dinner, … Driving very slowly, … Not having been there before, …*

CONTROVERSIAL SLIPS

Materials: One set of slips and role cards per group of students

Arrange Ss into groups of three or four. Cut up and place one set of slips, face down, in the middle of the group, and give one role card to each student in the group, making sure they don't show them to other Ss in the group (for groups of three, don't use the 'student D' card).

Each turn, student A picks up a slip and starts discussing the statement with the group. Other students give 'their' opinions, following the instructions on the role cards, and give reasons for their opinions. When they have discussed all the statements, Ss guess what the other Ss' instructions were.

As a follow up, if you think Ss can handle the topics sensitively, groups can discuss their real opinions regarding the statements. In feedback, nominate a student from each group to share their group's ideas with the class.

Unit 8

FALSE MEMORY?

Materials: One set of cards per group of students

Arrange Ss in small groups. Review the vocabulary for describing memories from unit 8.2. Place one set of cards face down in the middle of each group.

Ss take it in turns to take a card and show it to the group. They then either tell the group about a real memory, or invent one, using at least one of the phrases for describing memories. The other group members then ask questions to find out more details, and decide if he/she is telling the truth or lying. Each correct guess wins a point, but if no one guesses correctly, the student who picked up the card gets a point.

Monitor and check Ss are using the phrases correctly. The winner is the student with the most points. When they have finished, nominate Ss from each group to share any interesting facts they discovered.

N.B. If you think Ss need more preparation time before describing memories, don't cut up the cards but give one copy to each student. Ask them to choose six of the topics in the boxes, and give them time to prepare three true memories and three false memories to tell the group before they start.

A THOUSAND WORDS

Materials: One copy of worksheet A and worksheet B per pair of students

Arrange Ss in pairs. Distribute one copy of the worksheets per pair of Ss, and make sure Ss don't show their worksheet to their partner. Give Ss time to work alone to think of situations which explain the proverbs and sayings, without using the words in italics. Monitor and help where necessary.

Ss take it in turns to read out their situations to their partner (without using the words in italics), who listens and guesses the proverb/saying.

When they have finished, Ss discuss which of the proverbs/sayings they agree with, using examples from their own lives.

IT NEARLY HAPPENED

Materials: One copy of worksheet A, B and C per group of three students

Arrange Ss in groups of three. Distribute one copy of the worksheets per group of Ss, and make sure Ss don't show their worksheet to the other members of the group.

Ss take it in turn to read out their sentences, using the correct future in the past. With *weaker classes*, give them time to write the correct forms first, then check answers. Other Ss in the group listen and say if they think the sentences are true or false. If they guess correctly, they win a point. If no one guesses correctly, then the student who read out the sentence gets a point. Monitor and check they are using the forms correctly. The winner is the student with the most points at the end.

Answers: Worksheet A: 1 was about to strike, on the point of launching   2 was going to build, was about to start   3 was originally planning to become   4 was about to accept, was going to be   6 would raise/would have raised

Worksheet B: 1 on the point of leaving, would never have happened   2 was meant to be, would dwarf/would have dwarfed   3 was on the verge of starting, about to order   4 was supposed to stop, was about to stop   5 was originally going to use

Worksheet C: 1 was going to be, was meant to hold, would be/would have been   2 was supposed to provide   3 was going to build, was meant to allow   4 was about to crash   5 was planning to build, on the verge of being

As a follow up, Ss discuss which of the facts they found the most surprising.

NICE TO MEET YOU

Materials: One worksheet per student

Distribute one worksheet to each student in the class. Write the following questions on the board: *Have you ever visited Antarctica? Do you like tea or do you like coffee?* Elicit which words can be omitted (*Ever visited Antarctica? Do you like tea or coffee?*) and elicit possible short answers, e.g. *Maria has. Sergei likes tea.* Do a quick review of how we use ellipsis and substitution from unit 8.2 of the Students' Book. Give them time to cross out the words which can be omitted from the questions on the worksheet first, and check their answers.

Suggested answers: 1 Ever cooked for more than six people?   2 Any plans for your next holiday?   3 Anything you wanted to do when you were younger, but couldn't?   4 Learnt much vocabulary recently?   5 Nice weekend?   6 Know many English-speaking people?   7 If you won the lottery, would you spend a lot (of money) or save a lot?   8 Have to take any exams soon?   9 Like the room we're studying in?   10 Know anyone outside the class who thinks they're always right but they're not/but aren't?   11 Plan to continue studying English after this course?   12 Any great memories from your childhood?   13 Know anyone outside the class who thinks they're funny but (they) aren't?   14 Who in your family taught you the most?   15 Would you like to be rich or healthy?   16 Get much time to yourself these days?

Ss mingle and ask questions to find people who the sentences are true for. When they find a student who can answer the question, they write a short answer in the second column (like the examples on the board), and ask a follow up question to find out more details, and write these as notes in the *Details* column. Monitor and help where necessary, and encourage Ss to ask as many people as possible.

When Ss have finished, arrange them into pairs to share their answers.

In feedback, nominate Ss from each group to share any interesting answers with the class.

SOLUTIONS

Materials: One worksheet per student

Arrange Ss in pairs, and distribute one worksheet to each student. Give Ss one minute to read through the list of problems and check understanding.

Ss work in pairs to come up with two suggestions to deal with each problem, and write them in the *Ideas* column. Monitor and help with vocabulary, writing any new words/phrases on the board. Make sure that both Ss in each pair write down their ideas, as they will need to discuss them on their own later.

Review the language for discussing ideas from unit 8.3. When they are ready, rearrange Ss into groups of three or four, making sure that Ss from the same pair are now working in different groups. Ss discuss their ideas for each problem, then try to agree on one solution for each problem.

In feedback, nominate Ss from each group to share their solutions with the class.

Unit 9

RAVE REVIEWS

Materials: One copy of the chart and one cut-up card per student

Distribute one copy of the chart and one 'review card' to each student. If you have more than nine Ss, then double up as necessary. Make sure Ss don't show their 'review cards' to other Ss. Give Ss one minute to write the adjectives from their own 'review card' in the corresponding place in their chart.

Ss mingle and read out their reviews (but NOT the two adjectives) to other Ss, who should listen and guess the two adjectives, then write them in the correct place in their chart.

When they have finished, Ss compare answers in pairs. Check answers with the class.

Ss then work alone to think of real examples of films, books, etc. for each pair of adjectives. If they can't think of one example for each pair, then they can write two different examples, one for each pair. When they are ready, Ss share their ideas in pairs. Encourage Ss to ask follow up questions to find out more information.

In feedback, nominate Ss to share their ideas with the class.

QUESTIONS, QUESTIONS

Materials: One worksheet per student

Distribute one worksheet to each student. Give them a few minutes to replace the underlined words in the first two questions with three-part multi-word verbs, made up from a word from each of the circles at the top. Check answers with the class.

Answers: 1 catch up with   2 come up with

Ss work alone to write ten more questions, using a word from each circle to form three-part multi-words verbs. Monitor and help where necessary.

When they are ready, Ss ask their questions to three other Ss, and write their answers in the corresponding columns. Monitor and encourage Ss to ask follow up questions to find out more information.

In feedback, nominate Ss to tell the class who they have most in common with.

IMAGINE

Materials: One copy of worksheet A and worksheet B per pair of students

Arrange Ss in pairs. Distribute one copy of the worksheets per pair of Ss, and make sure Ss don't show their worksheet to their partner. Give Ss a few minutes to read the sentences, decide if they agree or disagree with them (or what their answers are), and write them in the second column. With *weaker classes*, ask Ss to write out the verb forms first.

Answers: Worksheet A: 1 did   2 had, would you make
3 went, would you take   4 didn't give   5 eat   6 was
7 settled down   8 know

Worksheet B: 1 started   2 hadn't started; would you be
doing   3 didn't exist   4 found   5 lived; would your life be
6 corrected   7 travel   8 haven't slept

When they have finished, Ss take it in turns to read out their sentences to their partner, who listens and says if they agree, disagree or what their answers are. Monitor and check Ss are forming the sentences correctly, and encourage them to ask follow up questions to find out more information.

In feedback, nominate Ss to share their opinions with the class.

HOW DID YOU DO IT?

Materials: One copy of worksheet A and worksheet B per pair of students

Arrange Ss in pairs. Distribute one copy of the worksheets per pair of Ss, and make sure Ss don't show their worksheet to their partner.

Ss take it in turns to read out their sentences. Their partner listens and chooses the missing adverbials. They then say the sentence with the adverbials in the correct place. For example, student A reads out: *I started learning English.* Student B finds the adverbial (*ten years ago*), and reads the complete sentence back: *I started learning English ten years* ago. The first student then writes the adverbials in the correct place.

When they have finished, check answers with the class. If there is more than one possible position for the adverbial in the sentence, Ss should choose the most neutral.

Answers: Worksheet A: 1 I started learning English *ten years ago*. (G)   2 I used to find it difficult to come up with new ideas *when I was younger*. *Nowadays* I'm much more creative. (A)   3 Cigarette advertising is, *without a doubt*, a ridiculous idea. (F)   4 I *recently* had to apologise *for doing something*. It had seemed like a good idea at the time, but it turned out it wasn't! (C)   5 I *sometimes* speak *too loudly* in public. (H)   6 I find some English grammar *impossibly* difficult. (B)   7 I try to learn new vocabulary *pretty much every day*. (D)   8 I *hardly ever* see original ideas for TV programmes *nowadays*. (E)
Worksheet B: 1 I had a good day *yesterday*. (B)
2 *Fortunately for me,* someone *cleverly* came up with a time-saving device. (G)   3 I hate it when people walk *slowly* in front of me. (A)   4 I've been toying with the idea of taking up a new interest *recently*. (H)   5 I'll *definitely* be going out with my friends *at the weekend*. (E)   6 I like to rest on Sundays *to feel fresh at the start of the week*. (C)   7 I *always* get ready *quickly* when I go out. (F)   8 I like to wander *aimlessly* around the shops *in my free time*. (D)

Ss discuss which of the statements are true for them in pairs. For the ones that aren't true, they change them so that they are. Monitor and encourage them to ask follow up questions to find out more information.

In feedback, nominate Ss to share any interesting ideas with the class.

JUST A MINUTE!

Materials: One set of cards per group of three Ss.
A stopwatch, timer or phone with this function

Arrange Ss into groups of three or four. Place one set of cards with statements, face down, in the middle of the group. Review the language for ranting and raving and using comment adverbials from unit 9.3.

Ss take it turns to pick up a card and decide if they want to rant or rave about the topic on the card. They then rant or rave for one minute, using as many of the phrases/comment adverbials as possible. Other Ss in the group time the student and note each time he/she uses a rant or rave phrase/comment adverbial. If the student who is speaking pauses for a considerable length of time (don't let other Ss be too harsh about this), then their turn ends.

Ss repeat the process until they've used all the cards.

In feedback, nominate Ss from each group to share any interesting information with the class.

Unit 10

CROSS WORDS

Materials: One copy of crossword A and crossword B per pair of students

Arrange Ss into pairs, and distribute the worksheets. Sit Ss face to face and tell them not to show their worksheets to each other. Tell Ss that they each have half of the answers to a crossword and they are going to work together to complete it. Elicit the questions they need to ask, e.g. *What's 4 across? What's 12 down?* Each student takes it in turns to ask for clues and to describe the word for their partner to guess, until they have completed the crossword. With *weaker classes*, give them some time before you pair them off to allow them to prepare clues for their words.

When they have finished, check answers with the class, giving further examples if necessary.

SYNONYM RUMMY

Materials: One set of cards per group of three students

Arrange students in groups of three (it can also be played in pairs or groups of four). Distribute one 'pack of cards' per group, and lay them face down in the middle of the group.

Explain the rules to the class. First, the cards are shuffled well. One student deals four cards to each player, and places the remaining cards face down in the middle, but turns over the top card and places it, face up, next to the pile. This is the discard pile. Players must begin each turn by picking up a card either from the face-down pile or from the discard pile. They must finish every turn by placing one of their cards on the discard pile. When a student has a pair or trio of synonyms in their hand, they must place it face up in front of them. If the face-down pile runs out during the game, Ss turn over the discard pile and place the top card face up to begin a new discard pile. During their turn, a student may get rid of additional cards by adding them to their own or another player's pair on the table. The aim of the game is for Ss to use all their cards by putting them all in pairs or trios. The winner is the first student to get rid of all their cards.

COMPLAINTS

Materials: One copy of worksheet A and worksheet B per pair of students

Arrange Ss in pairs and distribute one set of cards to each pair. Give them enough time to read their roles and check Ss understand what they have to do. Tell the Ss that all of their points should be expressed as inversions, and give them time to think about (with *weaker classes*, ask them to write them out) the inversions they need to use first. In feedback, nominate pairs to describe what solutions they came up with to the class.

Suggested answers: First situation: Student A: 1 Never before have I seen such a dirty room. 2 Had I known the food was so bad, I wouldn't have ordered from room service. 3 Not until I'd used the toilet did I realise it was broken.

Student B: 1 Under no circumstances/On no account can we give discounts – it's not company policy. 2 Rarely do guests complain – they're usually very happy. 3 Had you mentioned these problems before, I could have moved you to another room.

Second situation: Student A: 1 Were you to have no baggage to check in, I could put you on a flight with a smaller plane. 2 Not only is our flight delayed, but other airlines are also experiencing delays. 3 On no account/Under no circumstances can we pay for you to travel with another airline.

Student B: 1 Never before have I been delayed for this long. 2 Were you to pay for me to travel with another airline, I could arrive on time. 3 Under no circumstance/On no account can I arrive late for my meeting.

THE UNBELIEVABLE TRUTH

Materials: One set of cards per group of three students

Arrange Ss in groups of three and review the language for comparative structures from unit 10.2.

Explain the rules of the game. Each student takes it in turn to give a short talk on a topic, with three facts and three myths. Each time the rest of the group thinks they've heard a fact, they say 'buzz!'. If they are correct, the person who said it gets a point. If they're incorrect, they lose a point. If the student giving the talk manages to say a fact with no one else calling out, they get a point. The winner is the student with the most points (or the least negative points!).

Distribute the cards for game 1. Ss have three facts and one myth on their cards – the first three sentences are facts, and the fourth is a myth. Give Ss enough time to think of and write two further myths, using a comparative structure in each one. Encourage them to be inventive, including false statistics to make them sound more plausible. When they read out their 'facts', make sure they mix up the order of facts and myths. Monitor and help where necessary.

When they have finished, Ss repeat the above process with the game 2 cards.

In feedback, elicit which facts Ss found surprising.

NEGOTIATING A DOCUMENTARY

Materials: One set of negotiation cards per pair of Ss

Arrange Ss into pairs, and give out an equal number of team A and team B cards with one group of three if necessary. Review the language for negotiating from unit 10.3.

Give Ss enough time to read their role cards and think about what concessions they are prepared to make for each point of the contract. Monitor and check understanding.

When Ss are ready, arrange them in groups of four to carry out the negotiation. If you have an odd number of Ss, have one or two groups of three, with stronger Ss working on their own against a pair. Monitor and note any common errors for later class feedback.

In feedback, nominate groups who agreed a contract to share what they agreed on with the class.

TESTS INDEX

LISTENING

1 ▶ 33 **Listen to six recordings. Which speaker is describing …**

1 someone who is set in their ways?	_A_
2 a dark horse?	___
3 a busybody?	___
4 a black sheep?	___
5 the life and soul of the party?	___
6 a chatterbox?	___

☐ **10**

PRONUNCIATION

2 ▶ 34 **Listen to six extracts and mark the breaks in each sentence.**

1 It is of the utmost importance | that we take action now.

2 A surprising number of people are completely unaware of the threat to the environment.

3 Nothing I read in the papers could have prepared me for what I witnessed yesterday.

4 Not for the first time have I been reminded just how fragile our planet really is.

5 In her own way, Gemma is a remarkable woman who has always followed her dreams.

6 I've always tried to lead by example.

☐ **5**

VOCABULARY AND GRAMMAR

3 **Complete the sentences.**

1 Tom really thinks he's a big __cheese__ in the company even though his role is minor.

2 Don't worry about Stella – she's a _____ cookie who can look after herself.

3 Peter is a total _____ potato. I don't know how he can just lounge around all day doing nothing.

4 You can be such a wet _____ sometimes. Why do you always have to spoil my fun?

5 That Sally's a rotten _____ to be sure. She always manages to spoil the atmosphere.

6 Greg's a bit of a _____ cannon. You can't ever be sure how he's going to react to things.

☐ **5**

4 **Correct the underlined prefixes.**

1 Do you believe in <u>sub</u>natural forces? ___super___

2 Our team was <u>over</u>played and we lost 10–1! _____

3 It's hard to read the <u>under</u>titles when the screen's so small. _____

4 The terms of this contract are <u>un</u>-negotiable I'm afraid. _____

5 Your trust in Tom is completely <u>im</u>placed as he's nothing but a fraudster. _____

6 There were thousands of people on the <u>pro</u>-government rally. The President is nervous. _____

☐ **5**

5 **Unscramble the words.**

1 the *Wi-ocrall remic* happens in the business world.
   ___White-collar crime___

2 The level of *itricallye* in some developed countries is quite shocking.
   _____

3 It's hard to believe that *greden iquatenliy* still exists where men earn more than women for doing the same work.
   _____

4 Although Simon is still able to work, at 68 he has been a victim of *ismage*.
   _____

5 If you are brought up in *tropyev*, you don't have enough money to cover even your basic needs.
   _____

6 Our neighbours have been repeatedly warned about their *ascoltinai avirbouhe* but they take no notice.
   _____

☐ **5**

6 **Match sentence beginnings 1–6 with endings a)–f) below.**

1 The meeting was held _b_

2 Phil almost let ___

3 I can't believe Sam gave ___

4 Perhaps Mark has ___

5 Come on, spill ___

6 Steve finally divulged ___

a) the game away without even realising.

b) behind closed doors for security reasons.

c) the beans and tell us what's going on.

d) his secret and felt much better afterwards.

e) something to hide. He's looking guilty.

f) it slip that he was leaving his job.

☐ **5**

7 Complete the sentences with the words in the box.

~~wouldn't~~ always inclined kept will tends

1 My parents __would__ allow me to stay out late when I was a teenager.
2 John _____ always tell you the truth even if it's unpalatable.
3 I _____ trying to get hold of Pat but in the end I gave up.
4 Lucy's _____ complaining about something.
5 Max _____ to sulk if he doesn't get his own way.
6 Phil's _____ to get headaches when he has too much to do.

[5]

8 Complete the second sentence so that it means the same as the first. Use the word in capitals.

1 I overslept because I went to bed late. IF

   If I hadn't gone to bed late, I wouldn't have overslept.

2 I'm sorry that I didn't follow my dream. WISH

   _____

3 It's a shame Stephen isn't here today. ONLY

   _____

4 I lost my wallet. I don't have my credit cards. IF

   _____

5 Fred feels bad about being angry with you. REGRETS

   _____

6 We didn't listen to you so we got lost. HAD

   _____

[10]

9 Underline the correct alternative.

1 William will have been _teaching_ / _taught_ for ten years by the end of this academic year.
2 How long have you _been waiting_ / _waited_?
3 Maria _has_ / _had_ been working as a teacher for years before I met her.
4 When do you think you'll have _finished_ / _been finishing_ the book I lent you?
5 I appear to have _mislaid_ / _been mislaying_ my glasses again!
6 I didn't realise that you've _been knowing_ / _known_ each other for years.

[5]

SPEAKING

10 Put the phrases in italics in the correct order.

1 Kevin _being_ / _gives_ / _impression_ / _of_ / _the_ in control, but he's quite uptight underneath.

   gives the impression of being

2 I'd / to / had / that / a / If / make / I / guess / say Luke's in his early thirties.

   _____

3 you're / reckon / about / I ten years older than you look.

   _____

4 guess / I'd / that / a / hazard Sarah will resign any day now.

   _____

5 maybe / me / makes / that / It / think Paul and Jackie are having a few problems.

   _____

6 look / say / doesn't / she / I'd a day over thirty.

   _____

[5]

11 Complete the text with the words in the box.

~~background~~ long-term feasible instance plan objective

Just to give a bit of [1] _background_ information, I represent local small businesses. The main [2]_____ of our proposal is to raise our profile so what we [3]_____ to do is set up a series of networking events. This idea is [4]_____ because we have been given an excellent venue for free. In the first [5]_____ this would mean that we only have to advertise in the local press but once the events are established, there will be [6]_____ benefits for all concerned.

[5]

12 Match sentence beginnings 1–6 with endings a)–f) below.

1 Given the choice __b__
2 This would be by ____
3 If I found myself in ____
4 I'd just as soon ____
5 My preference would be ____
6 If it was up to ____

a) this situation, I'd call my parents.
b) I would stop working.
c) me, I'd call the meeting off.
d) to avoid confrontation.
e) far the best option.
f) watch a DVD as listen to music.

[5]

READING

13 Match quotations a)–f) with paragraphs 1–6.

Words *of* wisdom

by Anita Drake

1 *Years teach us more than books.*

I have always been interested in self-development and have a huge library of so-called self-help books on subjects ranging from the power of positive thinking and visualisation through to yoga and meditation. All of them have given me comfort to a greater or lesser extent but I realise that there is no substitute for experience and as I grow older, I become more aware of the value of that experience.

2 _____

When you are young, it's very easy to think that your way is the best or only way. We look at others and wonder why they're behaving the way they are. How could they be so silly? How come they don't see what they're doing? And of course, we don't stop to apply the same rules to our own behaviour.

3 _____

As we grow older, however, we realise that we worry unnecessarily about a lot of things. We fret about the past, we worry about the future and we neglect the present. It is clear that there are certain things over which we have no control and yet we persist in stressing. What a waste of energy and time. The key is to spend that energy on making changes to areas of our lives that we can indeed affect: personal relationships, work and the local environment, for example.

4 _____

Society today is very much a left-brain society with more attention and focus being placed on science and fact rather than intuition and creativity, which come from right-brain existence. This in turn has led to a certain distance growing up within communities and many people are now rather emotionally aloof.

5 _____

In order to become a wiser, more rounded, person, I believe it is important to find people from whom you can learn. Everyone has something to teach so you don't need to find a guru as such but by surrounding yourself with those who've thought deeply about life, you can certainly benefit.

6 _____

Humans are by their very nature fallible so it's important that as we go through life we learn to admit to our mistakes and move on. If we didn't make mistakes, we wouldn't evolve but the key is to acknowledge the error and to be forgiving of others and ourselves.

a) Years teach us more than books.

b) The more a man knows, the more he forgives.

c) It is easier to be wise for others than for ourselves.

d) By associating with wise people you will become wise yourself.

e) The art of being wise is knowing what to overlook.

f) The seat of knowledge is in the head; of wisdom, in the heart.

10

WRITING

14 Underline the correct alternative.

1 We're trying to revise for exams, <u>hence</u> / *therefore* the need for silence.

2 What you believe is up to you. I would, *however* / *thus*, prefer you to keep your thoughts to yourself.

3 I'm really happy for you. *Nevertheless* / *In fact*, I'm over the moon.

4 George works more productively in the morning. Sam, *in addition* / *conversely*, prefers the afternoons.

5 There are a lot of empty shops in town and *what is more* / *as a result*, the number is going up all the time.

6 As you will realise, we *obviously* / *accordingly* need to rethink our strategy.

[| **5**]

15 Complete the sentences with the words in the box.

> ~~eventually~~   subsequently   immediately   afterwards
> meanwhile   ever since

1 Although I was initially apprehensive, I _eventually_ grew to like Paul.

2 Laura, _____, had decided to stay at home and study.

3 I was affected by what I'd seen for ages _____.

4 Dan started out at the bottom and _____ went on to become CEO.

5 When Greg saw the blaze he _____ called the fire brigade.

6 I've been afraid of wasps _____ I was stung as a child.

[| **5**]

16 A discursive essay: Fast food is to blame for rising levels of obesity. Write 200–250 words.

_____

_____

_____

_____

_____

_____

_____

_____

_____

_____

_____

_____

_____

_____

_____

_____

_____

_____

_____

_____

_____

_____

_____

_____

_____

_____

_____

_____

_____

_____

_____

_____

_____

_____

[| **10**]

[**Total:** | **100**]

LISTENING

1 ▶ 33 **Listen to six recordings. Which speaker is describing …**

1 someone who is set in their ways?   _A_

2 a black sheep?   ___

3 a chatterbox?   ___

4 a busybody?   ___

5 a dark horse?   ___

6 the life and soul of the party?   ___

| 10 |

PRONUNCIATION

2 ▶ 34 **Listen to six extracts and mark the breaks in each sentence.**

1 It is of the utmost importance | that we take action now.

2 A surprising number of people are completely unaware of the threat to the environment.

3 Nothing I read in the papers could have prepared me for what I witnessed yesterday.

4 Not for the first time have I been reminded just how fragile our planet really is.

5 In her own way, Gemma is a remarkable woman who has always followed her dreams.

6 I've always tried to lead by example.

| 5 |

VOCABULARY AND GRAMMAR

3 **Complete the sentences.**

1 Tom really thinks he's a big __cheese__ in the company even though his role is minor.

2 You can be such a _____ blanket sometimes. Why are you always so negative?

3 That Ben's a _____ apple to be sure. He always manages to create a bad atmosphere.

4 Greg's a bit of a loose _____. You can't ever be sure how he's going to react to things.

5 Don't worry about Stella – she's a tough _____ and is pretty scary when under attack.

6 Peter is a total couch _____. I don't know how he can just lounge around all day doing nothing.

| 5 |

4 **Correct the underlined prefixes.**

1 Do you believe in subnatural forces? ___super___

2 I'm afraid the decision is unreversible. _____

3 These jackets are co-changeable so take whichever one you want. _____

4 There were thousands of people on the pro-government rally. The President is nervous. _____

5 Your plan is ridiculously unpractical but I wish you luck. _____

6 That restaurant is really rather underrated in my opinion. I can't see what all the fuss is about. _____

| 5 |

5 **Unscramble the words.**

1 *theWi-ocrall remic* happens in the business world.
   ___White-collar crime___

2 We're lucky to be able to say what we think as there's little *sporsniche* in this country.
   _____

3 It's hard to believe that *greden iquatenliy* still exists where men earn more than women for doing the same work.
   _____

4 There's a lot of *adsnogire micer* in countries with a culture of bribery and corruption.
   _____

5 If you live in *tropyev*, you don't have enough money to cover even your basic needs.
   _____

6 Our neighbours have been repeatedly warned about their *ascoltinai avirbouhe* but they haven't changed.
   _____

| 5 |

6 **Match sentence beginnings 1–6 with endings a)–f) below.**

1 The meeting was held _b_

2 Phil has always kept ____

3 I can't believe Sam gave ____

4 Perhaps Mark has ____

5 What was said yesterday ____

6 Steve finally blurted ____

a) the game away without even realising.

b) behind closed doors for security reasons.

c) must remain between you and me.

d) out his secret and felt much better afterwards.

e) something to hide. He's looking guilty.

f) himself to himself.

| 5 |

7 Complete the sentences with the words in the box.

> ~~wouldn't~~   always   inclination   kept on   will   prone to

I My parents ___would___ allow me to stay out late when I was a teenager.

2 John _____ always tell you the truth even if it's unpalatable.

3 I _____ taking painkillers even though they didn't really help.

4 Lucy's _____ complaining about something or other.

5 Max is _____ driving too fast especially when he's on the motorway.

6 Phil has an _____ to spend money when he knows he shouldn't.

☐ **5**

8 Complete the second sentence so that it means the same as the first. Use the word in capitals.

I I overslept because I went to bed late. IF

  If I hadn't gone to bed late, I wouldn't have overslept.

2 It's annoying that you don't tidy up. WISH

  _____

3 It's a shame Stephen isn't here today. ONLY

  _____

4 I forgot my keys. I'm locked out of my house. IF

  _____

5 Laura feels bad about being so impatient. REGRETS

  _____

6 Sarah had a bad back so she couldn't go to work. BUT FOR

  _____

☐ **10**

9 Underline the correct alternative.

I William will have _been teaching_ / _taught_ for ten years by the end of this academic year.

2 When do you think you'll have _heard_ / _been hearing_ about your application?

3 Hannah claims not to have _known_ / _been knowing_ about the meeting.

4 I can't believe that you've _been making_ / _made_ so many friends since you moved here.

5 How long have you _waited_ / _been waiting_ for the bus?

6 Maria _has_ / _had_ been working as a teacher for years before I met her.

☐ **5**

10 Put the phrases in italics in the correct order.

I Kevin _being_ / _gives_ / _impression_ / _of_ / _the_ in control but underneath it all, he's quite uptight.

  gives the impression of being

2 _you're_ / _reckon_ / _about_ / _I_ as fit as I am.

  _____

3 _I'd_ / _to_ / _had_ / _that_ / _a_ / _If_ / _make_ / _I_ / _guess_ / _say_ Luke's about to retire.

  _____

4 _maybe_ / _me_ / _makes_ / _that_ / _It_ / _think_ I should reconsider your offer.

  _____

5 _guess_ / _I'd_ / _that_ / _a_ / _hazard_ the prime minister will resign soon.

  _____

6 _look_ / _say_ / _doesn't_ / _she_ / _I'd_ a day over twenty-five.

  _____

☐ **5**

11 Complete the text with the words in the box.

> ~~background~~   long-term   feasible   instance   plan objective

Just to give a bit of [1] _background_ information, I represent local small businesses. The main [2] _____ of our proposal is to raise our profile so what we [3] _____ to do is set up a series of free events. This idea is [4] _____ because we have been given an excellent venue for our sole use. In the first [5] _____ this would mean that we only have to advertise in the local press but once the events are established, there will be [6] _____ benefits for all concerned.

☐ **5**

12 Match sentence beginnings 1–6 with endings a)–f) below.

I Given the choice, _b_

2 This would be by ____

3 If I found myself in ____

4 I'd just as soon ____

5 My preference would be ____

6 If it was up to ____

a) this situation, I'd just walk out.

b) I would stop working.

c) me, I'd call the meeting off.

d) to encourage everyone to participate.

e) far the most interesting alternative.

f) stay in as go out.

☐ **5**

READING

13 Match quotations a)–f) with paragraphs 1–6.

Words of wisdom

by Anita Drake

1 *Years teach us more than books.*

I have always been interested in self-development and have a huge library of so-called self-help books on subjects ranging from the power of positive thinking and visualisation through to yoga and meditation. All of them have given me comfort to a greater or lesser extent but I realise that there is no substitute for experience and as I grow older, I become more aware of the value of that experience.

2 _____

When you are young, it's very easy to think that your way is the best or only way. We look at others and wonder why they're behaving the way they are. How could they be so silly? How come they don't see what they're doing? And of course, we don't stop to apply the same rules to our own behaviour.

3 _____

As we grow older, however, we realise that we worry unnecessarily about a lot of things. We fret about the past, we worry about the future and we neglect the present. It is clear that there are certain things over which we have no control and yet we persist in stressing. What a waste of energy and time. The key is to spend that energy on making changes to areas of our lives that we can indeed affect: personal relationships, work and the local environment, for example.

4 _____

Society today is very much a left-brain society with more attention and focus being placed on science and fact rather than intuition and creativity, which come from right-brain existence. This in turn has led to a certain distance growing up within communities and many people are now rather emotionally aloof.

5 _____

In order to become a wiser, more rounded, person, I believe it is important to find people from whom you can learn. Everyone has something to teach so you don't need to find a guru as such but by surrounding yourself with those who've thought deeply about life, you can certainly benefit.

6 _____

Humans are by their very nature fallible so it's important that as we go through life we learn to admit to our mistakes and move on. If we didn't make mistakes, we wouldn't evolve but the key is to acknowledge the error and to be forgiving of others and ourselves.

a) Years teach us more than books.

b) The art of being wise is knowing what to overlook.

c) The more a man knows, the more he forgives.

d) It is easier to be wise for others than for ourselves.

e) The seat of knowledge is in the head; of wisdom, in the heart.

f) By associating with wise people you will become wise yourself.

`10`

WRITING

14 Underline the correct alternative.

1 We're trying to revise for exams, _hence_ / *therefore* the need for silence.

2 A lot of houses in the village are empty and *what is more* / *as a result* a lot of people are considering moving away.

3 What you believe is your own business. I would, *however* / *thus*, prefer you to keep your thoughts to yourself.

4 I'm so delighted for Harry. *Nevertheless* / *In fact*, I'm over the moon as he deserves a little happiness after all he's been through.

5 George works more productively in the afternoons. Holly, *in addition* / *conversely*, prefers early mornings.

6 In view of this new information, we'll need to plan our course of action *obviously* / *accordingly*.

[ ] 5

15 Complete the sentences with the words in the box.

eventually   subsequently   immediately   afterwards
meanwhile   ever since

1 Although I was initially apprehensive, I _eventually_ grew to like Paul.

2 I've been afraid of the dark _____ I was a child.

3 I was affected by what I'd seen for ages _____ the accident.

4 Fred started out as a chef and _____ went on to open his own restaurant.

5 When Greg saw the blaze he didn't panic but _____ called the fire brigade.

6 Laura, _____, had decided to stay at home and study.

[ ] 5

16 A discursive essay: Fast food is to blame for rising levels of obesity. Write 200–250 words.

[ ] 10

Total: [ ] 100

LISTENING

1 ▶ 30 **Listen to six recordings. Which speaker …**

1 goes jogging to take their mind off their work? _A_
2 is burning the candle at both ends? ____
3 whiles away their time in the garden? ____
4 has been burning the midnight oil? ____
5 lets their hair down at the weekends? ____
6 likes to put their feet up with a good book? ____

| | 10 |

PRONUNCIATION

2 ▶ 31 **Listen to six extracts and underline the stressed syllables.**

1 Better <u>safe</u> than <u>sorry</u>.
2 Out of sight, out of mind.
3 Home is where the heart is.
4 Practise what you preach.
5 Rome wasn't built in a day.
6 A picture is worth a thousand words.

| | 5 |

VOCABULARY AND GRAMMAR

3 Add the letters to complete the words.

1 It's amazing how quickly mobile phone technology has taken o _f_ _f_.
2 I don't think that vintage cars will ever lose their a _ _ _ _ _.
3 What's the latest t _ _ _ _ _ in computer games?
4 This new diet is just a passing t _ _ _ _, I'm sure.
5 The fashions of the 1950s have captured the i _ _ _ _ _ _ _ _ _ _ _ of young people today.
6 The number of designer labels for children has r _ _ _ _ _ dramatically in recent years.

| | 5 |

4 Complete the sentences. Use the correct form of the words in brackets.

1 I can't get over your _stupidity_. What were you thinking?! (stupid)
2 Ken is an _____ to his parents. Why do they put up with him? (embarrass)
3 I'm afraid this is not my area of _____. (expert)
4 This film _____ everything that is good about modern cinema today. (example)
5 I've always been _____ and non-conformist. (rebel)
6 Sally can be so _____ sometimes. (sarcasm)
7 How many _____ were there for the job? (apply)
8 We are fortunate to have little _____ in our country. (censor)
9 _____ speaking, I'm far worse off this year than I was last year. (finance)
10 Most state companies have now been _____. (private)
11 I've brought you some flowers to _____ up your day. (bright)

| | 10 |

5 Complete the sentences.

1 I've always believe that the ___pen___ is mightier than the sword.
2 Be grateful for what you have. After all, _____ can't be choosers.
3 There's always so much to do – no rest for the _____!
4 As long as you make an effort and put your best foot _____, we'll be proud of you.
5 The early bird catches the _____, so get up early if you want to succeed.
6 Everything looks promising but let's not _____ our chickens just yet.

| | 5 |

6 Underline the correct alternative.

1 I think I'<u>m going to</u> / will be sick.
2 Where will you be going / have gone for your holiday this year?
3 We aren't to / due to meet until six o'clock so there's no rush.
4 This time next week they'll have heard / be hearing the good news.
5 I don't think the government might / will be re-elected.
6 The break starts / is starting in ten minutes, so we can have a good chat then.

| | 5 |

7 Complete the sentences with the correct form of the verbs in the box.

~~stand~~ know abandon spend consider manufacture

1 The girl _standing_ by the door is my cousin.
2 _____ many years in Madrid, Clare speaks fluent Spanish.
3 _____ anyone at the party, Paul felt very lonely.
4 Goods _____ in China are generally cheaper.
5 _____ a delicacy, truffles are incredibly expensive.
6 _____ as a puppy, our dog was quite nervous when we first got him.

☐ **5**

8 Complete the second sentence so that it means the same as the first. Use the word in capitals.

1 It would be good if Max paid his way. TIME
  It's time Max paid his way.

2 We should go home now. HIGH
  _____

3 I'd prefer it if you didn't call me at work. RATHER
  _____

4 Wouldn't you prefer to go for a pizza? SOONER
  _____

5 You really should know this grammar by now. ABOUT
  _____

6 Mark looks very tired; perhaps he's been working too hard. AS THOUGH
  _____

☐ **5**

9 Underline the correct alternative.

1 Meat is _just_ / _a good deal_ as expensive as fish these days.
2 I'm _a lot_ / _nothing like_ as fit as I used to be.
3 The harder you look for happiness, the _more_ / _loads_ elusive it seems to be.
4 My garden is _every bit_ / _miles_ more beautiful after all the rain we've had.
5 Our last holiday was only _significantly_ / _marginally_ more expensive than we'd anticipated.
6 There's _slightly_ / _barely_ any difference between these two jackets in terms of price.

☐ **5**

10 Complete the sentences with the words in the box.

~~sense~~ logic more think joking point

1 It just doesn't make _sense_ to me.
2 I couldn't agree _____.
3 I agree with you up to a _____.
4 Where's the _____ in that?!
5 Oh, come on, you must be _____!
6 Surely you don't _____ that.

☐ **5**

11 Match sentence beginnings 1–6 with endings a)–f) below.

1 That film was one of _e_
2 There's nothing better ____
3 It drives me up the wall ____
4 I couldn't believe my luck ____
5 If there's one thing I can't stand ____
6 Modern art exhibitions are not ____

a) my cup of tea at all.
b) when we got tickets for the concert.
c) when people turn up late for meetings.
d) it's bad language.
e) the best I've ever seen.
f) than a cup of tea and a good book.

☐ **5**

12 Complete the sentences with the correct preposition.

1 Your proposal sounds acceptable _to_ me.
2 I want to sort this mess ____ as soon as possible.
3 Please do get ____ touch if anything needs clarifying.
4 What do you have ____ mind?
5 ____ the end of the day, we'd like to have resolved this problem.
6 Can you go ____ more detail, please?

☐ **5**

READING

13 Match sentences a)–f) with gaps 1–6.

by Robin Stanley

Why are some people born lucky - or are they?

Have you ever looked at some people and wondered whether they were born under a lucky star? [1] *They seem to have it all, or at least all the things that you would like to have.* Well, actually, it's nothing to do with luck but all to do with positive thinking, visualisation, self-belief, call it what you will.

Looking at your own life, are there things you would like to change or improve?

[2] _____

If you want to know what your future holds, just take a look at your present thoughts, as they are the very thoughts that create your future. In some ways this is a frightening notion, but it is also very powerful because it means that we can actually take control of our existence and mould it into what we want for ourselves.

If you want to have a closer look at your belief system, then just look around you.

[3] _____

For example, if you believe there is never enough to go round and that life is a struggle, that you have to fight for what you want, then you will never have enough, and you will struggle and fight your way through life.

[4] _____

This is nothing less than a self-fulfilling prophecy because if you believe bad things will happen to you, then they surely will. If, on the other hand, you believe there is no limit to what you can do and you believe that adversity just serves to make you stronger, then your life will be one of achievement and resilience.

[5] _____

Although you will have been in the same place, you will inevitably have remembered different things and this 'filtering' of information is a reflection of the way we view the world. If, for example, you're feeling very negative, you will see only bad things around you. If, however, you're full of the joys of life, everyone will be smiling and happy.

So, if you want to shape your future into a happy, productive, fulfilling time, eliminate negative thoughts about what you don't want, in favour of positive ones about what you do.

[6] _____

Only you have the power, so what are you waiting for?

a) They seem to have it all, or at least all the things that you would like to have.

b) We all know people who say, 'Why do bad things always happen to me?'

c) You'll be amazed at how quickly your life will change.

d) The thoughts that go through your head every day, over and over again, have shaped your reality.

e) Consider how many times you've talked over a situation with someone.

f) I'm assuming that there probably are, otherwise you wouldn't be reading this article.

| 10 |

WRITING

14 Write present perfect sentences. Use the prompts.

1 a dramatic increase / use of mobile phones

There has been a dramatic increase in the use of mobile
phones.

2 number / people / learning English / grow / over the last few years

_____

_____

3 gradual decline / quality / language teaching

_____

_____

4 number / teenagers / leaving school without qualifications / rise sharply

_____

_____

5 steady increase / level of unemployment

_____

_____

6 value of property / UK / fall / steadily

_____

_____

| | 5 |

15 Match the synonyms.

| ~~initially~~   pleasantly surprised   eccentric   entertaining really fascinating   highly intelligent |

1 at first   _initially_
2 extremely interesting   _____
3 surprised and pleased   _____
4 funny and enjoyable   _____
5 very clever   _____
6 unusual / peculiar   _____

| | 5 |

16 Descriptive writing. Write a personal story in 200–250 words.

_____
_____
_____
_____
_____
_____
_____
_____
_____
_____
_____
_____
_____
_____
_____
_____
_____
_____
_____
_____
_____
_____
_____
_____
_____
_____
_____
_____
_____
_____
_____
_____
_____
_____
_____
_____
_____
_____
_____

| | 10 |

| **Total:** | 100 |

LISTENING

1 ▶ 30 **Listen to six recordings. Which speaker ...**

1 goes jogging to take their mind off their work? _A_
2 likes to put their feet up with a good book? ____
3 lets their hair down at the weekends? ____
4 is burning the candle at both ends? ____
5 has been burning the midnight oil? ____
6 whiles away their time in the garden? ____

| | 5 |

PRONUNCIATION

2 ▶ 31 **Listen to six extracts and underline the stressed syllables.**

1 Better <u>safe</u> than <u>so</u>rry.
2 Out of sight, out of mind.
3 Home is where the heart is.
4 Practise what you preach.
5 Rome wasn't built in a day.
6 A picture is worth a thousand words.

| | 5 |

VOCABULARY AND GRAMMAR

3 **Add the letters to complete the words.**

1 It's amazing how quickly mobile phone technology has taken o _f_ _f_.
2 I don't think that vintage cars will ever l _ _ _ _ their appeal.
3 What's the latest t _ _ _ _ _ in men's fashion?
4 This new diet is just a p _ _ _ _ _ _ _ trend, I'm sure.
5 The fashions of the 1950s have really c _ _ _ _ _ _ _ _ the imagination of young people today.
6 The number of designer labels for children has r _ _ _ _ dramatically in recent years.

| | 5 |

4 **Complete the sentences. Use the correct form of the words in brackets.**

1 I can't get over your _stupidity_. What were you thinking?! (stupid)
2 Ken is an excellent _____. I don't know why he doesn't play professionally. (music)
3 The price of oil has risen _____ in the last few months. (drama)
4 This play _____ everything that is good about modern theatre today. (example)
5 Hannah felt such _____ when she first moved to London. (lonely)
6 Sally can be so _____ sometimes. (sarcasm)
7 Steve is suffering from acute _____ after a frenetic year. (exhaust)
8 We are fortunate to have little _____ in our country. (censor)
9 _____ speaking, I'm far worse off this year than I was last year. (finance)
10 Happiness can prove to be quite _____ if you look too hard. (elude)
11 David does have a _____ to exaggerate, doesn't he? (tend)

| | 10 |

5 **Complete the sentences.**

1 I've always believe that the ____pen____ is mightier than the sword.
2 Be grateful for what you have. After all, beggars can't be _____.
3 If you have a good idea, you need to strike while the _____'s hot.
4 As long as you make an effort and put your best _____ forward, we'll be proud of you.
5 What time do you call this?! Mind you, better _____ than never.
6 Everything looks promising but let's not count our _____ just yet.

| | 5 |

6 **Underline the correct alternative.**

1 I think I'<u>m going to</u> / will be sick.
2 This time next week they'll have enjoyed / be enjoying a well-deserved break.
3 I don't think the president might / will be re-elected.
4 Tom will be leaving / have left by the time you get back.
5 We aren't to / due to meet until tomorrow so don't worry.
6 The break starts / is starting in ten minutes, so we can have a good chat then.

| | 5 |

7 Complete the sentences with the correct form of the verbs in the box.

| ~~stand~~   recognise   reject   study   consider   make |

1 The girl _standing_ by the door is my cousin.
2 _____ Spanish for many years, Clare was quite fluent.
3 _____ anyone at the party, Paul felt like an outsider.
4 Goods _____ in China are generally cheaper.
5 _____ a delicacy, truffles are incredibly expensive.
6 _____ by its mother, our dog was very nervous when we first got him.

☐ 5

8 Complete the second sentence so that it means the same as the first. Use the word in capitals.

1 It would be good if Max paid his way. TIME
_It's time Max paid his way._____

2 You should go to bed now. HIGH
_____

3 I'd prefer it if you didn't leave your clothes all over the floor. RATHER
_____

4 Wouldn't you prefer to have a pizza this evening? SOONER
_____

5 You really should know the rules by now. ABOUT
_____

6 Stephen looks exhausted; perhaps he's been working too hard. AS THOUGH
_____

☐ 5

9 Underline the correct alternative.

1 Meat *is just / a good deal* as expensive as fish these days.
2 I'm *a lot / nothing like* as slim as I used to be. I must get into shape.
3 There's *slightly / barely* any difference between these two sweaters so I'll take the cheaper one.
4 The harder you look for happiness, *the more / loads* elusive it seems to be.
5 Mary is *every bit / miles* more beautiful in the flesh than in her photos.
6 The new car was only *significantly / marginally* more expensive than we'd anticipated, so we're quite happy.

☐ 5

10 Complete the sentences with the words in the box.

| ~~sense~~   logic   more   think   joking   point |

1 It just doesn't make _sense_ to me.
2 Oh, come on, you must be _____!
3 Surely you don't _____ that.
4 I couldn't agree _____.
5 I agree with you up to a _____.
6 Where's the _____ in that?!

☐ 5

11 Match sentence beginnings 1–6 with endings a)–f) below.

1 That film was one of _e_
2 There's nothing better ____
3 It drives me up the wall ____
4 I couldn't believe my luck ____
5 If there's one thing I can't stand ____
6 Bustling markets are not ____

a) my cup of tea at all.
b) when I managed to get George Clooney's autograph.
c) when people don't do what they say.
d) it's arrogance.
e) the best I've ever seen.
f) than a leisurely walk with friends.

☐ 5

12 Complete the sentences with the correct preposition.

1 Your proposal sounds acceptable _to_ me.
2 Can you go ____ more detail, please?
3 Please do get ____ touch if you need any more information.
4 What does Mark have ____ mind?
5 Let's sort our finances ____ as soon as possible.
6 ____ the end of the day, we'd like to have come to some agreement.

☐ 5

READING

13 Match sentences a)–f) with gaps 1–6.

by Robin Stanley

Why are some people born lucky - or are they?

Have you ever looked at some people and wondered whether they were born under a lucky star? [1] *They seem to have it all, or at least all the things that you would like to have.* Well, actually, it's nothing to do with luck but all to do with positive thinking, visualisation, self-belief, call it what you will.

Looking at your own life, are there things you would like to change or improve? I'm assuming that there probably are otherwise you wouldn't be reading this article. [2] _____

In some ways this is a frightening notion, but it is also very powerful because it means that we can actually take control of our existence and mould it into what we want for ourselves.

[3] _____

The thoughts that go through your head every day, over and over again, have shaped your reality. For example, if you believe there is never enough to go round and that life is a struggle, that you have to fight for what you want, then you will never have enough, and you will struggle and fight your way through life. We all know people who say, 'Why do bad things always happen to me?'

[4] _____

If, on the other hand, you believe there is no limit to what you can do and you believe that adversity just serves to make you stronger, then your life will be one of achievement and resilience.

Consider how many times you've talked over a situation with someone. Although you will have been in the same place, you will inevitably have remembered different things and this 'filtering' of information is a reflection of the way we view the world.

[5] _____

If, however, you're full of the joys of life, everyone will be smiling and happy.

So, if you want to shape your future into a happy, productive, fulfilling time, eliminate negative thoughts about what you don't want, in favour of positive ones about what you do. You'll be amazed at how quickly your life will change.

[6] _____

a) They seem to have it all, or at least all the things that you would like to have.

b) This is nothing less than a self-fulfilling prophecy because if you believe bad things will happen to you, then they surely will.

c) If you want to know what your future holds, just take a look at your present thoughts, as they are the very thoughts that create your future.

d) If, for example, you're feeling very negative, you will see only bad things around you.

e) Only you have the power so what are you waiting for?

f) If you want to have a closer look at your belief system, then just look around you.

| 10 |

WRITING

14 Write present perfect sentences. Use the prompts.

1 a dramatic increase / use of mobile phones
There has been a dramatic increase in the use of mobile phones.

2 value of property / UK / fall / steadily / in the last couple of years
_____
_____

3 number / teenagers / leaving school without qualifications / rise sharply
_____
_____

4 steady increase / level of unemployment among young people
_____
_____

5 number / people / learning Chinese / grow / over the last few years
_____
_____

6 some people / believe / gradual decline / quality / language teaching
_____
_____

☐ **5**

15 Match the synonyms.

| initially   pleasantly surprised   funny and enjoyable |
| highly intelligent   extremely interesting   peculiar |

1 at first   *initially*
2 really fascinating   _____
3 surprised and pleased _____
4 entertaining   _____
5 very clever   _____
6 unusual / eccentric   _____

☐ **5**

16 Descriptive writing. Write a personal story in 200–250 words.

_____

☐ **10**

| Total: | **100** |

Mid-course Test A

LISTENING

1

Audioscript

A: Peter can be so incredibly frustrating sometimes. Maybe it's something to do with his age but he really is very rigid in his thinking and in his behaviour. He'll always have his tea at the same time every day and nothing will get in the way of that. All his friends know, so they wouldn't dare call him then.

B: There's a woman in our street who makes it her business to know everything that's going on, so if you want to know anything about anyone I'd ask her. Well, actually, you don't need to ask her as she'll tell you anyway. I'm often tempted to tell her something that's not true to see how long it'll be before it comes back to me. I certainly wouldn't tell her anything I didn't want the world to know.

C: Frankly, you can't get a word in edgeways with Christine. I've never known anyone talk so much. She barely pauses to draw breath and then she's off again. I guess her husband must just turn off because it would drive you mad otherwise. And it's not as if she's saying anything particularly interesting. You know what I mean … you can't have a conversation as such, as she tends to make observations about stuff. I know it's mean, but when she calls, I sometimes don't answer the phone.

D: You know, I had no idea that Fred played the piano so well. He's always kept it very quiet and I only found out because other friends were talking about a festival they'd been to and he was one of the performers. I don't know why he's so secretive about it. I'll ask him next time I see him, as I'd love to hear him play.

E: I feel very sorry for Maria. Nothing she does is good enough for her parents and then her brother can do no wrong in their eyes. I think it all started when she kind of disobeyed their wishes and dropped out of college to go travelling. I'd imagine they're not used to anyone not doing as they wish, so since then they've been very cool towards her. I hope they'll realise how hurtful they've been but at least Maria is happy doing her own thing.

F: I always enjoy it when Clare comes to stay as she's so much fun. It doesn't matter how tired she says she is, she'll always rise to the occasion. I don't know where she gets all her energy, or her jokes for that matter. The last time I saw her was at my brother's wedding and to be honest, she very nearly upstaged the bride.

2 D   3 B   4 E   5 F   6 C

PRONUNCIATION

2

2   A surprising number of people | are completely unaware | of the threat to the environment.

3   Nothing I read in the papers | could have prepared me | for what I witnessed yesterday.

4   Not for the first time | have I been reminded | just how fragile our planet really is.

5   In her own way, | Gemma is a remarkable woman | who has always followed her dreams.

6   I've always tried | to lead by example.

VOCABULARY AND GRAMMAR

3

2 tough   3 couch   4 blanket   5 apple
6 loose

4

2 out   3 sub   4 non   5 mis   6 anti

5

2 illiteracy   3 gender inequality   4 ageism
5 poverty   6 antisocial behaviour

6

2 f   3 a   4 e   5 c   6 d

7

2 will   3 kept   4 always   5 tends
6 inclined

8

2   I wish I'd followed my dream.

3   If only Stephen were here today.

4   If I hadn't lost my wallet, I would have my credit cards.

5   Fred regrets being angry with you.

6   Had we listened to you, we wouldn't have got lost.

9

2 been waiting   3 had   4 finished
5 mislaid   6 known

SPEAKING

10

2   If I had to make a guess, I'd say that

3   I reckon you're about

4   I'd hazard a guess that

5   It makes me think that maybe

6   I'd say she doesn't look

11

2 objective   3 plan   4 feasible   5 instance
6 long-term

12

2 e   3 a   4 f   5 d   6 c

READING

13

2 c   3 e   4 f   5 d   6 b

WRITING

14

2 however   3 In fact   4 conversely
5 what is more   6 obviously

15

2 meanwhile   3 afterwards   4 subsequently
5 immediately   6 ever since

16

(sample answer)

You can't walk down any main street in any city of the world now without coming across a fast food outlet. In fact, you will most probably be spoilt for choice: pizzas, burgers, chicken, kebabs or fish and chips, the list is endless. One thing that they all have in common, however, is a certain lack of nutritional value.

Much has been written about a worrying increase in the number of obese people in countries of the developed world. On the one hand, this has been put down to a sedentary lifestyle with most people working or playing at computers for hours every day, but on the other hand, we can attribute the increase to the ready availability of fast food.

There is no doubt that the levels of saturated fats, salt and sugar in fast food are higher than recommended in a normal diet, but surely we cannot lay the blame for being overweight solely at the door of the burger. We need to take responsibility for our eating habits.

In conclusion, I would say 'everything in moderation' is the best way forward. The occasional burger won't do you any harm but fast food should not be a major part of any diet.

(204 words)

Mid-course Test B

LISTENING

1

Audioscript

(*See test A.*)

2 E 3 C 4 B 5 D 6 F

PRONUNCIATION

2

2 A surprising number of people | are completely unaware | of the threat to the environment.

3 Nothing I read in the papers | could have prepared me | for what I witnessed yesterday.

4 Not for the first time | have I been reminded | just how fragile our planet really is.

5 In her own way, | Gemma is a remarkable woman | who has always followed her dreams.

6 I've always tried | to lead by example.

VOCABULARY AND GRAMMAR

3

2 wet 3 rotten 4 cannon 5 cookie
6 potato

4

2 ir 3 inter 4 anti 5 im 6 over

5

2 censorship 3 gender inequality
4 organised crime 5 poverty
6 antisocial behaviour

6

2 f 3 a 4 e 5 c 6 d

7

2 will 3 kept on 4 always 5 prone to
6 inclination

8

2 I wish you would tidy up.

3 If only Stephen were here today.

4 If I hadn't forgotten my keys, I wouldn't be locked out of my house.

5 Laura regrets being so impatient.

6 But for her bad back, Sarah would have been able to go to work.

9

2 heard 3 known 4 made
5 been waiting 6 had

SPEAKING

10

2 I reckon you're about

3 If I had to make a guess, I'd say that

4 It makes me think that maybe

5 I'd hazard a guess that

6 I'd say she doesn't look

11

2 objective 3 plan 4 feasible 5 instance
6 long-term

12

2 e 3 a 4 f 5 d 6 c

READING

13

2 d 3 b 4 e 5 f 6 c

WRITING

14

2 as a result 3 however 4 In fact
5 conversely 6 accordingly

15

2 ever since 3 after 4 subsequently
5 immediately 6 meanwhile

16

(*See sample answer in Test A.*)

End of Course Test A

LISTENING

1

Audioscript

A: My job is very pressurised and I work very long hours. Most of the time I'm either in meetings or travelling, so I don't get much in the way of exercise. I always pack a pair of trainers and jogging pants in my case so I can get out for a while to clear my head. I really need to be able to do that regularly otherwise I end up feeling really stressed.

B: I don't really have time to myself during the week as I have a pretty busy job and two small children who want my attention when I get home in the evening, but Saturdays are mine. I usually meet up with a group of friends and we have a game of football and then go for a good meal. It's a chance for all of us to relax and get rid of the worries of the week.

C: To be honest, I'm pretty tired at the moment. I've just started a new job so there's a lot to take in. I'm having to stay late most evenings but there's a good group of people in the office so we tend to go out after work. I don't think I've been to bed earlier than midnight for the last few weeks. I'm not sure how much longer I can carry on but hopefully I'll get an early night tonight.

D: There's nothing I enjoy more than reading. It's the best way to relax but I just don't have enough time these days. Whenever I go on holiday I make sure I take a good stash of books so I can curl up and read. I used to be able to find time on Sundays but these days there always seems to be something going on.

E: I seem to be governed by unrealistic deadlines at the moment. Everyone wants everything done immediately and because I'm self-employed I'm aware that my position is precarious. There will always be someone willing to give one hundred and fifty percent. I've been staying up until the small hours but am determined to get a better work life balance.

F: Being outdoors is the best antidote to the stresses of the office. In the summer I can spend all evening pottering. This year I decided to grow vegetables for the first time and really, there's nothing more satisfying than picking your own lettuce and tomatoes for supper. Noticing the daily changes makes you realise just how amazing nature is.

2 C   3 F   4 E   5 B   6 D

PRONUNCIATION

2

2 Out of <u>sight</u>, out of <u>mind</u>.
3 <u>Home</u> is where the <u>heart</u> is.
4 <u>Practise</u> what you <u>preach</u>.
5 <u>Rome</u> wasn't <u>built</u> in a <u>day</u>.
6 A <u>picture</u> is <u>worth</u> a <u>thousand</u> <u>words</u>.

VOCABULARY AND GRAMMAR

3

2 appeal   3 thing   4 trend   5 imagination
6 risen

4

2 embarrassment   3 expertise
4 exemplifies   5 rebellious   6 sarcastic
7 applicants   8 censorship   9 Financially
10 privatised   11 brighten

5

2 beggars   3 wicked   4 forward   5 worm
6 count

6

2 be going   3 due to   4 have heard   5 will
6 starts

7

2 Having spent   3 Not knowing
4 manufactured   5 Considered
6 Having been abandoned

8

2 It's high time we went home.
3 I'd rather you didn't call me at work.
4 Wouldn't you sooner go for a pizza?
5 It's about time you knew this grammar.
6 Mark looks as though he's been working too hard.

9

2 nothing like   3 the more   4 miles
5 marginally   6 barely

SPEAKING

10

2 more   3 point   4 logic   5 joking   6 think

11

2 f   3 c   4 b   5 d   6 a

12

2 out   3 in   4 in   5 By   6 into

READING

13

2 f   3 d   4 b   5 e   6 c

WRITING

14

2 The number of people learning English has grown over the last few years.
3 There has been a gradual decline in the quality of language teaching.
4 The number of teenagers leaving school without qualifications has risen sharply.
5 There has been a steady increase in the level of unemployment.
6 The value of property in the UK has fallen steadily.

15

2 really fascinating   3 pleasantly surprised
4 entertaining   5 highly intelligent
6 eccentric

16

(sample answer)

So many of my most vivid memories are connected with travelling. I think it must have something to do with the fact that all your senses are heightened when you're in an unknown environment. Colours are brighter, sounds are clearer, even the most mundane can appear exotic. One of my most precious memories is of a sleepy little bay in South Africa.

Picture in your mind's eye bright blue summer skies, golden sands and gentle waves rippling backwards and forwards. Look more closely and you will see a colony of small penguins splashing around in the water. No-one knows where they have come from, but they have taken up residence and have been living in harmony with the locals for many years now.

Ever since I was a child, penguins have been my favourite animals so to be able to be so close to them was a dream come true. Like little old men in tuxedos, many of them just stood motionless, staring into the sun, while others ducked and dived into the foaming waves. A simple story of a simple experience, but one which has stayed with me for over twenty years.

(193 words)

End of Course Test B

LISTENING

1
Audioscript
(See test A.)
2 D   3 B   4 C   5 E   6 F

PRONUNCIATION

2
2 Out of <u>sight</u>, out of <u>mind</u>.
3 <u>Home</u> is where the <u>heart</u> is.
4 <u>Prac</u>tise what you <u>preach</u>.
5 <u>Rome</u> wasn't <u>built</u> in a <u>day</u>.
6 A <u>picture</u> is <u>worth</u> a <u>thousand</u> <u>words</u>.

VOCABULARY AND GRAMMAR

3
2 lose   3 trend   4 passing   5 captured
6 risen

4
2 musician   3 dramatically   4 exemplifies
5 loneliness   6 sarcastic   7 exhaustion
8 censorship   9 Financially   10 elusive
11 tendency

5
2 choosers   3 iron   4 foot   5 late
6 chickens

6
2 be enjoying   3 will   4 have left   5 due to
6 starts

7
2 Having studied   3 Not recognising
4 made   5 Considered
6 Having been rejected

8
2 It's high time you went to bed.
3 I'd rather you didn't leave your clothes all over the floor.
4 Wouldn't you sooner have a pizza this evening?
5 It's about time you knew the rules.
6 Stephen looks as though he's been working too hard.

9
2 nothing like   3 barely   4 the more
5 miles   6 marginally

SPEAKING

10
2 joking   3 think   4 more   5 point   6 logic

11
2 f   3 c   4 b   5 d   6 a

12
2 into   3 in   4 in   5 out   6 By

READING

13
2 c   3 f   4 b   5 d   6 e

WRITING

14
2 The value of property in the UK has fallen steadily in the last couple of years.
3 The number of teenagers leaving school without qualifications has risen sharply.
4 There has been a steady increase in the level of unemployment among young people.
5 The number of people learning Chinese has grown over the last few years.
6 Some people believe there has been a gradual decline in the quality of language teaching.

15
2 extremely interesting   3 pleasantly surprised
4 funny and enjoyable   5 highly intelligent
6 peculiar

16
(See sample answer in Test A.)

Pearson Education Limited
Edinburgh Gate
Harlow
Essex CM20 2JE
England
and Associated Companies throughout the world.

www.pearsonelt.com
© Pearson Education Limited 2012

First published 2012

Third impression 2013

ISBN: 978-1-4082-1642-2

Set in Gill Sans Book 9.75/11.5

Printed in Slovakia by Neografia

Illustrated by Sean@kja-artists